One
Little Snake River
Odyssey

Kenneth O. St. Louis

with contributions from

Rita G. St. Louis & David G. St. Louis

Populore®

Morgantown, West Virginia

Populore Publishing Company
PO Box 4382
Morgantown, WV 26504
www.populore.com
stories@populore.com

kenstlouisbook@gmail.com [author correspondence]

One Little Snake River Odyssey is available through Amazon: www.amazon.com.

ISBN: 978-0-9652699-5-7 [black and white paperback]
ISBN: 978-0-9652699-6-4 [color paperback]

Library of Congress Catalog Card Number: 2020923241

About the cover: The wrap-around background photograph shows Sheep Mountain and the smaller Mule Mountain from the southeast, leveling into the mesa overlooking the Little Snake River Valley in northwestern Colorado and southeastern Wyoming. On the front cover are Kenneth, Rita, and David on their horses, Ace, Gypsy, and June, respectively. The Willow Creek School is in the background of the photo. The back cover includes a photograph of the three siblings taken in 2015 near the Elk River, seven miles upriver from Clark, Colorado.

In gratitude for
all the guardian angels who,
knowingly or unknowingly,
taught, directed, and loved me.

Return often
to your rightful place
at the family table.

Settle in and wait
to be filled
in time-honored
and surprisingly new ways.

Contents

Foreword

The times are ending when children in a family can remember a homesteading grandmother, "Dressed with an apron and flesh-colored stockings all of the time, and she pretty much wore her clothes until they were gone," and a grandfather, "driving four horses pulling the binder in the wheat, oat, and barley fields."

Ken St. Louis, author, has woven the story of his grandparents, parents, siblings, and cousins all together in a fine tapestry that glows with the sense of place that formed Ken and his siblings' family. Ken and his siblings' earliest life was in a modest home, where they neighbored next to their grandparents, attended a one-room school, were 4-H club members, and rode horses all day. The family moved from one place to another for short periods of time as his father and mother worked to provide for the family.

The parental side of the family, came to very remote Little Snake River Valley on the Colorado-Wyoming border as homesteaders in the late 1800s. Ken's father was born in 1906, third in the family of six boys who were also raised with four of their boy cousins. Like many frontier communities, many women came to the Little Snake River Valley in the 1930s and 1940s, either as rural one-room school teachers or as guests or staff for the local dude ranches. Ken's mother worked for Lucy Temple at the Focus Dude Ranch, near the St. Louis homestead. Ken's mother and his aunts shared their "wisdom" and introduced the children to art, classical music, and the fascination of world-wide travel. They emphasized the need for post high school education, "There was never a doubt but what we would go to college."

The readers are able to follow the three St. Louis siblings as they recall with vigor and authenticity their family's journey through the 1950s and into the 21st century. Their weavings do not shy away from the twists and turns the generations encountered and acknowledges that the author and his two siblings often viewed and told the same experience in different ways. The siblings reflect on how the deeply engrained sense of place served them well as adults while serving others in international careers. "No one told them they couldn't do it."

— Rev. Linda Fleming
Priest at St. Paul's Episcopal Church
Board Member, Little Snake River Museum

Preface

One Little Snake River Odyssey follows the lives of my two siblings, David and Rita St. Louis, and me from our common beginnings on a ranch in northwestern Colorado to our highly divergent paths as we created our own places in the world. I take it as a given that, for most people, their early years are central in defining who they eventually become. And the families in which they live have been indelibly influenced by the key relatives who came before or other relatives who impacted them. For that reason, this *Odyssey* starts not with the three of us, but with our grandparents and great-grandparents. Generational listings even identify their ancestors. The book introduces us by setting the stage for our entry into the world in terms of place, family, and environment.

After an introductory chapter summarizing our families, a detailed account of a week-long trail ride six years ago involving all three of us ensues. The book then describes our extended families and how they came to reside in the Little Snake River Valley. Chapters then focus on our uncles, aunts, and first cousins. From there, the focus shifts to our parents and then to our childhood, school, and other youthful experiences. The events of our lives and memories from those events are chronicled in great detail for the early years, from each of our individual perspectives. Both chapter narratives and memories are richly illustrated with photographs and also with relevant quotes from letters, newspaper clippings, and various other documents. Finally, stepping back with a "big picture" perspective, the next three chapters summarize the rest of our lives, with focus on careers, travel, families, and achievements, disappointments, and turning points. The book ends with my own attempt to make sense of our life journeys.

One Little Snake River Odyssey seeks to explain how the defining moments of our lives, coupled with our individual personalities, shaped, reshaped, or entirely replaced a common family narrative into three unique individual narratives. Whenever possible, after the stage is set, most chapters tell stories that contributed to those converging and diverging influences. The book is not intended to be a joint biography or even a systematic account of the events of our lives. Instead, much of it might better be viewed as an extremely long but thoughtful obituary for each of us, compiled and written during our retirement years. It seeks to provide one more example of how siblings can celebrate their deep and indelible connections and—if not to celebrate—at least to appreciate the sheer impossibility of truly understanding one another. Equally important, our *Odyssey* intends to provide a lasting legacy for our children, grandchildren, and great-grandchildren after we have departed from this world. In the process, it hopefully will give insight and wisdom as well as to provide chuckles, belly laughs, frowns, or tears to anyone—relatives, friends, acquaintances, or strangers—who might be interested in our stories or pictorial records from a unique corner of the world in a bygone era.

Having been a social scientist for most of my career, in the descriptions and histories of our family and others, I strived for accuracy. No doubt, I was not entirely successful, but *One Little Snake River Odyssey* will have value for historians or journalists who seek to document the past and emerging history of the Little Snake River communities in Colorado and Wyoming. A detailed index is provided for quick identification of names and important topics.

Relatedly, to the extent that anyone might feel the urge to preserve their own story, this book could provide inspiration to do so. It clearly benefited from the advice of my wife, Rae Jean Sielen, based on her quarter-century of experience at Populore Publishing Company assisting more than a hundred others to preserve their stories and memoirs.

Appendices are included to provide relevant background information on our parents and others. Obituaries and written narratives, mainly from our mother, shed further light on the unique circumstances of our parents' lives. Two exceedingly detailed generational listings of relatives, from distant ancestors to the newly born children, are provided for both sides of our own family. Finally, the appendices includes maps, from states, to region, to our own little segment of the Little Snake River, that show where most of the events described in the book took place.

A Word from the Next Generation

I am an Eastern city dweller, but I know all the verses of a bunch of cowboy songs.

I grew up in the mid-Atlantic—between the rural and small-town life of Morgantown, West Virginia, and the suburbs of Pittsburgh, Pennsylvania—and settled in the heart of Washington, DC, in my adulthood. And yet I feel like I have roots in a place I've never lived, but one that shaped who I am in important ways.

We visited my dad's ancestral home in the Little Snake River Valley in northern Colorado nearly every year when I was growing up.

I was largely a cautious, studious, and non-athletic kid. But during our visits to Colorado with my extended St. Louis family, I found myself pushing my own physical and emotional limits to embrace adventure in ways I didn't know possible.

I marveled at the stories about my dad and his siblings and cousins attending a one-room schoolhouse with only members of their own family, about the hard work on the ranch with few of the modern comforts we take for granted, and about the dangerous mishaps involving dynamite or farm machinery or livestock that were (surprisingly for me) retold with hilarity.

With Grandpa George, I waded up to my thighs in rushing, chilly mountain water with a fly fishing rod as he confidently claimed "Now, there's definitely some fish in *that* hole over there!" and rode in the back of his pickup with a huge recently shot rattlesnake that continued to slither around my feet for 45 minutes.

With Aunt Rita and Uncle Hugh, I free climbed rock walls at Fish Creek Falls and hiked across the Devil's Causeway in an electrical storm, pushing through my terror and physical exhaustion. And Uncle David patiently taught me to skip rocks all the way across the river and chuckled as I gulped down a shot of whiskey he served me at the age of five when I asked for a drink.

Those experiences in rural Colorado—far outside the norm of my day-to-day life—made me more courageous, more appreciative of nature, more whimsical, and more self-confident.

It's always been clear to me that my dad's upbringing and the place itself was fundamental to who he was, even though he had moved far away from the Little Snake River. I always noticed that even though he was a renowned academic in his field of speech-language pathology, if you asked him what he was up to on any given day, he was just as likely to talk about a fence he really needed to fix or the firewood he needed to haul on our 20-acre hobby farm than about his academic pursuits. And he always seemed at his happiest when he would return to the northwestern Colorado mountains.

One Little Snake River Odyssey fills in the details of so many stories I grew up hearing about my cowboy grandfather and his five brothers (the infamous "St. Louis Boys") and about the tremendous bond my dad and his cousins shared, growing up in rural isolation but surrounded by deeply connected family.

The lessons resonate particularly in this moment as a deadly pandemic disrupts all our lives, and I struggle with feelings of isolation and fear. I consider the resilience of Grandma Grace, who lost two of her siblings to scarlet fever, and who raised three small children, at first without electricity, running water, and hardly any money. I marvel at how she and Grandpa George were forced to start over multiple times, after losing nearly everything due to the gamble of ranching, real estate, and business decisions.

And the refrain of music-making—of my grandpa's acapella performances of *Punchin' the Dough* and *Sierry Peaks* whenever given the opportunity, of my grandma's singing while doing chores, of my dad's guitar accompaniment for all his cousins singing *Tom Dooley* and *Ghost Riders* around campfires— helped everyone persevere through the times of hard work and hardship. That legacy of music-making has blessed my life and now my 13-year-old daughter's as well.

This book itself is also a reflection of who my dad is: ambitious, curious, determined, introspective, methodical, thorough, honest, earnest.

Once he decided to write it after his retirement, he threw himself into it completely with singular focus. He turned his social scientist curiosity toward his own life and his researcher thoroughness to filling out the family tree in minute detail, pouring over news clippings and oral and written histories by family and members of the community, and painstakingly selecting just the right photos among probably thousands. It turned into a mammoth project, but he was determined to finish on an ambitious, self-imposed timeline. And, most importantly, he told the stories of his ancestors and family and of the Little Snake River, and he documented those stories as truthfully and thoroughly as he could.

To have these stories—and these life reflections from my dad, and my dear aunt and uncle—curated for our family is an immense gift to me, to our daughter, and to future generations. Thank you, Dad.

— Melinda J. St. Louis
Author's daughter

Notes to Readers

The narrative sections of most chapters are written from my perspective. I refer to myself in the first person and to my brother and sister in the third person. Exceptions are the "Memories" after most of the chapters; they are all written in the first person and denoted by "David," "Kenneth," or "Rita" as the paragraph header. Two other exceptions are the final chapters by David and Rita, who wrote their own "Where Did I End Up and How Did I Get There?" chapters in the first person.

Stylistic differences characterize each of our different "voices." Some paragraphs, in the "Memories" especially, are written as each of us might tell the anecdote or story verbally, whereas most prose follows a more formal written style. As a result, grammatical conventions, although mostly consistent, are not entirely uniform. One example is the use of possessives before gerunds, as in the informal "Dad came to watch Kenneth wrestling on the weekend" versus the technically correct, "Dad came to watch Kenneth's wrestling on the weekend." Punctuation, especially in the use of commas, also varied somewhat in the different written styles.

The St. Louis and Ireland generational listings in Appendices H and I require more detailed explanation. Individuals listed are referenced according to the perspective of our own generation (my brother, sister, and me) and are identified as grandparents, uncles or aunts, cousins, and so on. The names and associated information extend back as far as records were located and as far ahead as living relatives were able to identify their siblings, children, grandchildren, and great-grandchildren.

Each family's listing is divided into two main sections. The first provides ancestors who preceded our St. Louis and Ireland grandfathers. Whereas four ancestral lines for grandparents could be included, only for one paternal and one maternal line for each set of grandparents was sufficient information available for both the St. Louis and the Ireland listings. These are separated by generations from the most distant to our grandparents' generations.

The second section begins with our grandparents and proceeds next to the generation of our parents, aunts, and uncles, then to our own or our first cousins' generation, then to our children's generation, then to our grandchildren's generation, and finally, in some cases, to our great-grandchildren's generation. Each generation is separated by indentations, identifiable according to a series of vertical lines on the page.

Not surprisingly, the ancestors' sections are incomplete. I included only the information I was able to locate. Beginning, however, in the second section, I spared no effort in order to obtain accurate and complete information about everyone's full name, birthdate, birthplace as well as spouse's or partner's birthdates and birthplaces. Stepchildren are listed if their parents or other relatives considered them integral parts of the relatives' families. I sought marriage dates, but not divorce dates; yet, the location of marriages was not included. If a person was deceased, the date and location of the death as well as the name and location of the burial place were included.

The reader will immediately notice gaps in the information for many of the individuals listed. Information gaps are identified with brackets. For example, [date/location] indicates that neither the date nor the location of a birth, death, or marriage was available to me. As relatives digest the information, it will also become apparent that there are errors and omissions in my listings. As diligently as I repeatedly tried to contact relatives, and relatives of relatives, the vagaries of communications by email, texting, social media, telephone, and even regular mail resulted in far too many of my queries receiving no replies. My hope is that the listings will be a starting point for relatives who are so inclined to locate and fill in the missing information and correct the errors for themselves. And for anyone who is serious about keeping up their own listing, they will soon discover that it is a continuing process. One's list will change constantly with births, deaths, burials, marriages, divorces, partnerships, stepchildren, and blended families.

Finally, it is important to assert that the St. Louis and Ireland generational listings should not be regarded as *bona fide* genealogy. When available, I used documents such as gravestone records to confirm names and dates. However, unlike serious genealogists who seek to verify every entry, most of the information in these appendices came from previous lists (cross-referenced whenever possible), family and newspaper records, obituaries, and online databases. I rarely consulted such documentary sources, such as census or court house records. For current generations, most of the information came from those few direct relatives or their spouses who have kept their own records. They graciously filled gaps in the skeletons of each family that I sent to them. Without the efforts of these "family historians," a great deal of the information would never have been included.

Chapter 1
Two Brothers and One Sister

The life of every living thing, from a single-celled paramecium to a dandelion to an earthworm to a spider to a bird to an oak tree to a fish to a lion to a human being, is the product of genetics and the environment, or the interplay between the two. And in every microsecond or minute or day or year, past happenings or future possibilities either have made their effects on living things or will do so. It seems pretty easy to figure out why the dandelion did not complete its cycle of making new seeds to fly away and plant more dandelions when it was stepped on during its flowering stage by a large hoof or why the female rainbow trout lived to become one of the biggest of its species by living in a river that was most inaccessible to predators or fishermen. But perhaps it is pure folly to imagine that we might understand the reasons why any person ends up as they do in their twilight years and not an infinite number of other possible places or circumstances.

I have never been one to back away from a challenge, especially when someone tells me it cannot be done. So, here in this book, I have chosen to face my own folly and try to understand where two brothers and a sister ended up in their lives. I am the middle child, second brother, who was followed in birth by a sister. We three, David, Kenneth, and Rita, are at once shining examples of the human potential but also examples of every common family on the globe. We're uniquely remarkable and not special at all. So, if asked the question "Why a book on us three?" my answer would be that by understanding the real reasons for parts of the complexities of our lives, we may strengthen that already-powerful bond that exists among us—and indeed among most siblings—with a deepened understanding of our unique contributions and differences. I hope to have accomplished that by looking at our unique personalities and genetic influences and then how those interacted with or determined the circumstances of our lives, both planned and unplanned.

Introducing the three of us, David, Kenneth, and Rita, at Box Canyon on the Upper Elk River near Clark, Colorado, 2013.

But this is but one of three major purposes of the book. Equally if not more important is to provide a written and pictorial record of our families, with a singular focus on our childhood, to pass on to our children, grand-children, great-grandchildren, and beyond. We lived most of our lives in the middle to the end of the twentieth century, the early years of which were more characteristic in many ways of life for many Americans a gener-ation earlier. The book places our lives in a historical-genealogical context and contains enough amateur genealogy that our relatives can go back two, three, four, or more generations earlier than us, and up to three generations later to see the incredibly wide spectrum of our heritage.

Another related purpose is to simply tell some of our stories, the mun-dane to the outlandish, the comical to the tragic, the joint to the individual. What is recorded is colored by our childhood innocence, by impacts on our individual lives, and by a learned tradition of remembering and retelling our shared memories.

Finally, I hope that we have, perhaps more indirectly than directly, offered some of our wisdom to our offspring and to others, derived from the turning points and lessons of our own lives. Akin to the Jewish tradition of the legacy letter or the ethical will, many of the insights we would like to pass on are contained in this volume.

Do these purposes fold together seamlessly into a coherent narrative? Not likely. Unlike a good novel or even a typical biography, they are not meant to. Instead I intend that they simply put some direction to following us from where we started to where we ended up.

So, following are three obituary-esque summaries of the major landmarks of our lives. Remember that they are incomplete. We are not dead yet.

DAVID

David George St. Louis was born in Hayden, Colorado, on 28 July 1943. He was reared on his parents' cattle and sheep ranch on the Little Snake River (Slater, Colorado) 50 miles north-northwest of Steamboat Springs (Steamboat). He attended Willow Creek School through the eighth grade (1949–1957) except for one year at La Sal, Utah (1955–1956), and five to six months in Salt Lake City (1957). He graduated from Steamboat Springs High School (1957–1961) and then Colorado State University (1961–1965) in animal science.

Immediately after graduation, he joined the International Voluntary Service (IVS) and went to Laos for two years (1965–1967). There, headquartered in Vientiane, he worked at the Teacher Training College, now the National University of Laos, teaching beginning animal science to second-year English students and assisting his Lao counterpart in management of a farm for student training. The farm raised pigs, chickens, and fish. Upon completing this assignment, he was hired as a contract employee by the United States Agency for International Development (USAID/AGR) for two years (1967–1969), to work near the Plain of Jars in refugee resettlement. Focus was to provide pigs, chickens, ducks, and fish to refugee villagers. And subsequent to that, he was employed again by USAID/ADO (Agricultural Development Organization) for two more years (1970–1972).

During his IVS service, David met his future wife, Somchai (Chai) Khamsayin, who was a Thai citizen working in Laos at the time. He adopted her infant son Robert Pyboon St. Louis (born 7 December 1965). Their other children, Benson Petsamone St. Louis (29 July 1968) and Lisa Surilak St. Louis (13 July 1969), were born in Laos. Upon returning to the USA, David entered graduate school in animal science at Cornell University in Ithaca, New York. He completed a master's degree in 1973 and a PhD in 1977. For the last year of his doctoral work, the family moved to San Juan, Puerto Rico, where David carried out his data collection in collaboration with the University of Puerto Rico. After graduation, they moved to Ellicott City, Maryland, where David worked in a pellet mill making animal feed (1977–1978). After one and a half years, he accepted a position as an animal research scientist at Clemson University's Edisto Experiment Station in Blackville, South Carolina, where the family lived for seven years (1978–1985). They moved to Mississippi State

University's South Mississippi Experiment Station in Poplarville, Mississippi, where David worked until he retired (1985–2008).

Before retirement, he accepted two-week consulting assignments with the Winrock Foundation to advise beef and dairy farmers on best management practices in Mali, Bangladesh, Ethiopia, El Salvador, and Nicaragua. After retirement, he had two longer paid temporary employment arrangements in Thailand at Mae Jo University at Chiang Mae (six months in 2009) and in Kasetsart University at Khampangsaen (nine months in 2010).

David currently lives with Chai at their home in Poplarville. Robert and his wife Karen Smallwood Garrett St. Louis live in Seminole, Oklahoma. Robert is employed as a Department of Defense contractor and small business owner. From a previous marriage, Robert has two adult sons, reared in Jacksonville, Florida, Tai Francisco St. Louis (29 July, 1988) and Jourdan Robert St. Louis (14 October 1990). Robert and Karen have custody of Karen's grandson, Kaeden Leland Lucas (23 June 2005). Tai has two daughters, Mia Elizabeth (6 June 2010) and Navy (20 October 2017). Jourdan also has two daughters, Uree (25 May 2010) and Avaleah Enid (16 November 2012). Both Tai's and Jourdan's daughters live in Kissimmee, Florida, with their mothers. Tai lives in Kissimmee, but Jourdan lives in Los Angeles, California. Benson and his wife Karol Scott St. Louis live in Hattiesburg, Mississippi. Benson works for Deep Energy Services in Columbia, Mississippi, as Chief Financial Officer. They have two sons, Griffin Scott St. Louis (23 April 1995) and Spencer Morgan St. Louis (23 May 1998). Griffin currently lives in Aberdeen, Maryland, and Spencer lives in Mississippi. David and Chai's daughter, Lisa, is a high school biology teacher in Philadelphia, Mississippi, who lives with her husband Joseph Odell Knight in Union, Mississippi. They have one son, Jeff David Knight (14 April 1999).

David and Chai at their wedding.

Lisa, Robert, and Benson and their mother, Chai, visiting their great-grandmother Onie at her home on Snake River.

The family posing for a portrait: Benson, David, Robert, Lisa, and Chai.

High schoolers Benson, Robert, and Lisa with Dad (Grandpa).

The family together in Mississippi while working on this book: Benson, Lisa, Robert, Chai, and David, 2019.

KENNETH

Kenneth Oliver St. Louis was born in Steamboat Springs, Colorado, on 9 November 1944. He was reared on his parents' cattle and sheep ranch on the Little Snake River (Slater, Colorado) 50 miles north-northwest of Steamboat. He attended Willow Creek School through the seventh grade (1949–1957) except for one year at La Sal, Utah (1955–1956), and about three months in Maricopa, California (1956). He completed the eighth grade at the Steamboat Springs Junior High School (1957–1958), graduated from Steamboat Springs High School (1958–1962) and then Colorado State University (1962–1966) in hearing and speech sciences (speech therapy).

He then joined the Peace Corps for two years (1966–1968). Upon serving in two different villages as a rural community development worker in Turkey, one in Bolu and the second in Denizli, he was about to be drafted into the Army and very likely to be sent to Vietnam. He was classified by the Selective Service as "1-Y" or eligible to be called up in case of a national emergency. With that reprieve, he was recruited and hired for one year to participate in a government study of the prevalence of speech and hearing problems in the public schools (1968–1969). After that, he completed a master's degree in speech-language pathology from the University of Michigan in Ann Arbor (1969–1970) and a PhD in the same field from the University of Minnesota in Minneapolis (1970–1973).

He met Karen Helen Waterman, also a speech-language pathology student, in Michigan. They married when he was in Minnesota (27 December 1970). They moved to the State University of New York (SUNY) at Plattsburgh, New York (1973–1976), where Kenneth held his first university position for three years, and Karen worked as a speech-language pathologist in a local school district. Near the end of that time, they had their only child, Melinda Joyce St. Louis (14 August 1975). They moved to a small farm south of Morgantown, West Virginia (1976–1978), and Kenneth began working at West Virginia University, where he was employed until he retired (1976–2018).

After two years, they moved to another small farm where they arranged for a contractor to build their log home (1979). Before Melinda started to school, their house was a model home for its parent company, Real Log Homes. They sold log homes for three years in their own company called Natural Shelter (1979–1982). After selling the business, Karen returned to work part-time in the schools, and for nearly three years (1984–1987), they teamed up with another couple to open a private practice for speech,

Kenneth and Karen's wedding, 1970.

Three generations: Melinda, Kenneth, and Dad (Grandpa), where he worked for a few years on Snake River.

Melinda and Peg Wolfe in Fiji, 1990.

Melinda eating a carrot from the garden, age 2 years.

Melinda's graduation from Pennsylvania State University with Karen and Kenneth, 1998.

Kenneth and Rae Jean, 2018.

language, hearing, and academic problems. The buildings and practice were named the Communication Disorders Center.

Kenneth and Karen separated shortly after the business closed and were divorced in 1988. For most of the next five years, Kenneth was in a relationship with Margaret (Peg) Wolfe which ended in 1993. At a national convention, Kenneth met Rae Jean Sielen from Seattle, Washington. They had a short, long-distance relationship, after which she moved to Morgantown. Kenneth and Rae Jean were married 26 February 1994. Together in 1995, they founded a small business, Populore Publishing Company, providing publishing services in Morgantown. Populore is managed almost exclusively by Rae Jean. In 2010, Kenneth and Rae Jean purchased a cabin on the Upper Elk River near Clark, Colorado, which they have typically visited twice each summer.

Kenneth and Rae Jean currently live in their log home in Morgantown as they have for 26 years, with yearly trips to their Colorado cabin in the past ten years. Melinda is employed as an advocacy organizer for the nongovernmental organization Public Citizen in Washington, DC. She has one daughter, Lila Grace Benavente (2 October 2007), who is being raised by Melinda and her ex-husband, Pablo Javier Benavente.

RITA

Rita Grace St. Louis was born in Dixon, Wyoming, on 11 February 1946. She was reared on her parents' cattle and sheep ranch on the Little Snake River (Slater, Colorado) 50 miles north-northwest of Steamboat. She attended Willow Creek School through the fifth grade (1952–1957) except for one year at La Sal, Utah (1955–1956). She completed the sixth grade at the Soda Creek Elementary School in Steamboat Springs followed by the seventh and eighth grades at Steamboat Springs Junior High School (1957–1960). She graduated from Steamboat Springs High School (1960–1964) and then attended Colorado State University for two years (1964–1966) studying English.

Rita married Christopher (Chris) Ottmar Maser on 2 July 1966. In October of that year, Rita joined Chris, who had left a month earlier, in Cairo, Egypt. From there they traveled to Beirut, Lebanon, then on to Nepal where they lived for nine months to carry out research on diseases of mammals.

They then returned to Corvallis, Oregon, to attend school at Oregon State University. Rita got a degree in general science education in 1970. From Corvallis, they moved to Bandon, Oregon, to study land mammals. Their son Erik Maser (later changed to Erik Richards) was born in the coastal town of Coos Bay (22 December 1971). After living on the Oregon coast for a couple of years, they moved to Tacoma, Washington, for about a year, then returned to Corvallis, Oregon. Rita received a master's degree in environmental education in 1974, also from Oregon State University.

Rita and Chris were divorced in 1976, whereupon Rita returned to Steamboat. There, she began dating Hugh Strane Richards III, a former high school friend. They soon moved to Seattle, Washington, and were later married on 18 June 1978. Rita then studied at the University of Washington in wildlife management (1977–1981). She completed a second master's degree but did not complete the PhD degree although she spent several years in the process. Rita, Hugh, and Erik moved to Fairbanks, Alaska, in September 1981 where she was hired by ECS Computer Systems, a computer software company specializing in small business solutions. She worked there for 24 years (1981–2005). Finally, she was employed by the Alaska Department of Fish and Game until her retirement in 2015 and was actively involved in the re-introduction of wood bison into the Alaska wilderness earlier that year. Rita and Hugh divorced in 2001, and Rita married John David Swan on 23 December 2005.

Rita and John live in the home that Rita had built on Ester Dome outside of Fairbanks. Erik married Amy Barnes Stoyles Richards on 2 June 2007. Erik serves as Lead for Human Space Flight Network Integration and Operations in Las Cruces, New Mexico, where he is involved in support for space shuttle launches. They have three sons, Evan McKinley Richards (11 April 2008), Camden Taylor Richards (9 March 2010), and Scott Douglas Richards (7 July 2011).

Rita and Chris's wedding, 1966.

Rita and Hugh's wedding, 1978.

Rita with Erik at age 3.

Erik as a baby at 10 months.

Erik on a backpacking trip in the Brookes Range in Alaska.

Hugh, Rita, and Erik in Alaska with two of their dogs.

Rita and John's wedding, 2005.

COUSINS FOREVER!

New York cousins at the time: Benson, Lisa, and Robert from Ithaca visiting very little Melinda in Morrisonville (missing: Erik).

All five together for the second time in Steamboat: Robert, Benson, Erik, Melinda, and Lisa.

First get together of all five cousins happened in West Virginia: David, Lisa, Mom, Karen & Melinda, Benson, Kenneth, Chai, and Robert (missing Rita, Hugh, and Dad).

Cousins at Mom's burial: Benson, Erik, Robert, Shannon Pike St. Louis, Lisa, and Melinda.

Almost perfect symmetry: Erik, Lisa, Benson, Melinda, and Robert. Quit pushing, Robert!

Two Brothers and One Sister / 11

Chapter 2

The Scenic Route to Whiskey Park Featuring a Retrospective Look at Three Siblings

It was five days near the end of June in 2014 when we tried to relive pieces of our past in the watershed of the Little Snake River. David had arranged the trail ride, and unlike the one he planned six years earlier, we would stay closer to where we grew up. Chai was not well enough to travel long distances at this point, so she stayed home in Poplarville, Mississippi. Rita and John flew in from Alaska. And we staged at our cabin on the Upper Elk River 23 miles from Steamboat Springs, Colorado. Rae Jean and I had purchased the cabin four years earlier and had established a routine of driving out from West Virginia every summer for a month.

The trail ride was a complex mixture of re-connecting, of remembering our roots, of exhilarating scenery, of finding ourselves "old," of overcoming natural and man-made obstacles, and discovering how much we had changed or stayed the same. As in 2008, John joined us, but Rae Jean decided to stay at the cabin. One day was devoted to packing our food, organizing and weighing individual and group camping gear, and making sure that our three saddles that we had kept for more than 50 years were ready to go. David was in charge. His carefully thought-out plan was to leave his pickup at the Three Forks Ranch Resort on the road to the North Fork of the Little Snake River, proceed into Wyoming through the Medicine Bow National Forest to the Huston Wilderness, hit the old Forest Service Sheep Trail (Stock Driveway) to the Continental Divide, and then take the Forest road to Whiskey Park.

On the first day, after finding out that the Three Forks would not let us ride at all on their property, we unloaded our gear on the North Fork road and waited for five horses to arrive, which we had rented from the O'Toole (formerly Salisbury) Ladder Ranch about 11 miles down the Little Snake River. Four would be ridden, and the fifth would be the pack horse for our food and common gear. As we waited for the horses, John and Rita discovered that they had left their tent at our cabin. Instead of driving an hour back to the cabin to get it, John was insistent that he and Rita would make do with a tarp.

After a very late start, we entered the Medicine Bow National Forest, parked David's pickup just inside the Forest boundary, and started toward the Huston Wilderness. The first day went pretty much as planned until we found that the trail narrowed in a large grove of pine trees, most of which were dead from the pine bark beetle kill seven years earlier. The pack horse, which I led, carried panniers that protruded at least a foot on either side, and these often hit the dead trees. A few times I resorted to getting off and turning my horse over to Rita and then walking to maneuver the pack horse around dead trees so as not to hit them and possibly knock them over with the panniers. It became more and more difficult, so we all decided this was not going to work and to proceed back in the open parks. It was late by that time, so we camped close by near a little stream for the first night. It was then that we realized that the O'Tooles had neglected to furnish the long ropes to picket the animals so they could graze. After allowing them to graze for an hour or so by their lead ropes, we tied the horses up the hill at the edge of an aspen grove. After a campfire dinner, David and I slept in our tent while Rita and John bedded down under their tarp over a small log in the center and supported by a post at either end, rather resembling an Army pup tent.

Kenneth with pack horse and David in front, heading for the Huston Wilderness.

The next morning after loading the pack on a big mare, we began to saddle the other horses the same as the day before. Rita, John, and I were to ride three pinto mares, and David would continue on the old sorrel gelding quarter horse, with the swollen knees, the O'Tooles named "George." Rita was saddled up first and on her horse. David had saddled George and was about ready to mount. I was still working on my cinch when George groaned, staggered, and fell onto his right side with his feet up the hill. We were aghast but soon assumed the horse had had a heart attack. However, he was still groaning and rolling his eyes. Working together quickly, with some difficulty, we got the cinch undone and, with all three men pulling, we able to remove the saddle. Rita got her lariat rope out, and we put the loop over the gelding's front legs. Pulling with her horse, Rita was able to roll him over so that his feet were below him. After being rolled over, George got up, stood there for a few seconds and began to graze. We were baffled, but after a time, David put the saddle on him again and cinched him up part way. He staggered again, but after loosening it, he seemed okay for the second time. In small increments, the cinch was tightened, and the horse seemed normal. So, we all mounted up and started on the second day.

Rita and John making a "tent" out of their tarp, having forgotten to bring their tent.

Following David's maps and GPS, we proceeded to another trail that led to the Huston Wilderness. Again, the trail often passed through dead trees, but we managed until we began to encounter large snow drifts in shady areas. Crossing these drifts of 10 to 30 feet in width, the horses could often walk on the "crust," but just as often broke through up to their bellies. Again, I resorted to leading the pack horse around them. As late afternoon approached, David almost casually announced that the GPS on his phone had died because the phone had completely discharged. And with no regret in his voice, he then announced that he left the correct adaptor for his backup charger in his pickup. So, again we back-tracked out of the trees where we had essentially lost the trail. We camped in a clearing near a stream with icy cold water coming down out of the snow melt.

David stirring something for dinner.

The next morning, after the time-consuming task of putting all the gear into the two panniers, being careful to weigh and balance them equally, we decided to pack the gelding and David would

David, John, and Rita with morning coffee.

The horses sometimes stayed on the crust and sometimes broke through.

Kenneth soaking his foot in the icy water from the melting snow to prevent swelling.

ride the large mare that we had used as the packhorse for two days. Everything was about ready, but David needed to tie his saddle packs on the back of his saddle. He could have done it alone, as he always figured out a way to do a two-handed job with only his right hand (as a result of losing most of his left arm in a childhood snow-joring accident), but Rita and I decided to tie it on. She was on the left side of the mare who was tied up to a tree; I was on the right side. For no apparent reason, the mare spun around to the left and kicked Rita with both hind feet. Rita had seen the mare's ears go down and had ducked and rolled but was nevertheless caught on a shin bone with a hoof. She landed about ten feet away. I did not see nor suspect anything but somehow the mare had jumped, come down on top on my right foot, spun around and threw me about the same distance straight back.

I got up stunned and saw Rita lying on the ground. I ran over and asked if she was okay, which she definitely was not. She had come to her senses and virtually snapped at me, "Yes, I'm OK." She wanted no sympathy or attention, and she got up. By then, I was afraid that my right foot had been broken, so John, who had been a medic in Viet Nam, took over. He carefully helped me remove my boot and wiggle my toes to see if bones had been broken. Satisfied that there were no broken bones but knowing that swelling would follow, he instructed me to put my foot into the ice-cold creek for about 15 minutes. Following that, I pulled my boot back on and limped back to my horse.

The mare was fine after that, even though I had been over-ruled while soaking my foot that someone "knock the hell out of her to show her who's boss." The others finished securing the saddle packs with no difficulty. The sorrel gelding withstood the packsaddle with no staggering or falling. After this episode, we departed for the third day.

The next three days were less dramatic but had their memorable moments. The rearrangement of horses worked out satisfactorily except for some concern that my pinto mare had thrown a horse shoe at some point.

We returned to the old Sheep Trail (Stock Driveway) to get to the Forest Service road near Hog Park on the Continental Divide. After losing the trail and crossing a dangerous rock slide (for the horses) to get back to it, we descended into Solomon Creek and camped there for two nights and one full day. The fishing was incredible. I quickly caught enough small trout for John and me for dinner and breakfast. David and Rita never liked fried trout. David had wanted to fish but decided instead to rest. We later concluded that the altitude had caused a worsening of his blood-pressure/heart problems that had plagued him for the previous few years.

Rita, as always, loved to take care of the horses. She would rotate their grazing by tying up three of them with short halter ropes to graze, tying one with a longer rope of pieced-together lariats, and letting the fifth one go free, knowing that one horse would not leave the others. She decided to let one of the mares graze freely that night. At first light upon getting up from our tent or tarp after the second night there, we saw all the horses on the opposite side of the creek. After breakfast and the laborious packing, we noticed that the free-roaming mare and George, who had been tied up, were gone. We found out the hard way that George could not only fake a heart attack, but was also an escape artist at untying knots. I immediately saddled up and went to look for them at the top of the steep hill but to no avail. Somewhat later, Rita decided to go back down the sheep trail to look. David joined me on the search later, and we soon saw in the dust the tracks of the two horses as well as the marks of a rope being drug. We planned to stay in touch with Rita by walkie-talkie, but David apparently forgot to turn his on. Soon, we saw the tracks of Rita's horse going the same way. We decided to spread out to be sure that we would not miss her coming back. About 45 minutes later, I spotted her first as she was returning and leading the horses. She had caught up with them on the North Fork road where we had left the pickup. Had there not been a cattle guard stopping them there, the horses would have continued to the main road back to the Ladder Ranch. As for Rita, she had forgotten the road she had just taken, missed a critical turn, and was starting up the wrong road (the one we abandoned the day before) when I intercepted her.

Rita posing next to the Forest Service sign for the Savery Sheep Trail (officially the Stock Driveway).

Taking a break and letting the horses graze on the Sheep Trail.

Carvings on old aspen trees carry history of sheep herders who camped and recorded their names, dates, and art as they drove their flocks over the Sheep Trails.

Remains of a Sheep Trail bridge to take sheep across the creek, especially in high water.

Dried up pine trees, killed by pine bark beetles seven years earlier had left many roads and trails impassible and required picking more open spaces.

Of course, after finally returning to camp, we got a very late start that day. Immediately from the campsite the Sheep Trail proceeded up a hill, again replete with lots of standing and fallen old and very large beetle-killed pine trees, but mostly passable. We descended into North Fork and started up another very steep hill where the dead trees were closer together. Trying to stay on the Sheep Trail, Rita and David would ride ahead to determine the best path for me to lead the pack horse, and twice, Rita ended up riding in a circle.

We finally stopped to rest the horses and ourselves and to have a brief water and lunch break. John walked up the hill about 20 feet and announced that beyond a few little bushes, we had come to a smooth, wide, graveled road, which incidentally was not on any of David's maps, running perpendicular to the Sheep Trail. We decided this new road must make a shortcut to the Forest Service road going from Columbine to Hog Park. Accordingly, we proceeded south (right) on the road. We were impressed with the excellent water control and culverts for any little creek coming down from the elevation that if followed would lead to the Continental Divide. We followed that road for about two miles when we encountered a pickup with "City of Cheyenne Water Board" emblazoned on the side. We asked where the road led, and the two men there said it ended about a mile ahead. It was getting late so we decided to ride to the end of the road and surely find a trail that would take us to the other Forest Service road. It was not to be. Where the road ended and the forest began, the down timber from beetle kill was completely impassible. Therefore, we rode down the gentle slope, across a meadow, to a creek, and we decided to spend our fourth night. (In retrospect, we learned that had we worked our way through a relatively small grove of trees, we would have been in Whiskey Park.)

Scenic Route to Whiskey Park / 19

On this and facing page: The Little Snake River watershed from the top of the Continental Divide looking west. Peaks that we knew well, from left to right on or below the horizon, are Columbus, East Gibraltar, Piney, Three Forks, West Gibraltar, Beaver, Twin Buttes, Squaw, Mule, Sheep, and Battle Mountains.

I pored over the maps and elevations that David had brought and remembered that the road we had traveled, although curving around every topographical change, had been virtually level. We put two and two together and concluded that this was the road that accompanied the water diversion project carried out many years earlier that our dad had complained about. Cheyenne, Wyoming, had adjudicated all the flood waters on the western slope of the Divide to be collected and tunneled through to the eastern slope.

The next day, we got a reasonably early start and rode back all the three miles we had taken the day before and tried again to continue up the Sheep Trail. Since the water road had been built perhaps 20 years earlier, those who last used the Sheep Trail must have come up out of North Fork as we did but went north on the water road. The telltale reason was that there were many more beetle-killed trees that were six inches in diameter or less above the road than there had been below. If sheep had gone through there, the small trees would have been trampled out. About an hour trying to get

Five bull elk on top of the Continental Divide.

Two of the bulls showing their antlers in summer velvet.

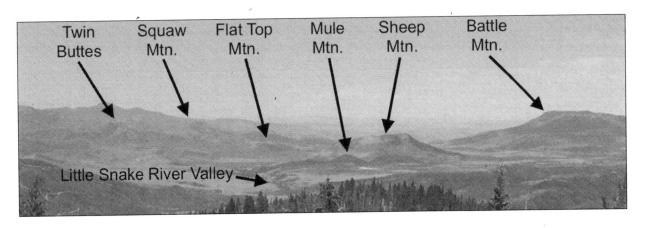

Twin Buttes Squaw Mtn. Flat Top Mtn. Mule Mtn. Sheep Mtn. Battle Mtn.

Little Snake River Valley

through these trees convinced us that we could not go on but would need to continue north on the water road.

That we did for another five miles or so until we came to a road near the top of the Continental Divide. We took the hiking trail rather than the road because of the concern for my horse going lame on the gravel road because by then she had thrown two shoes. It was a climb up to the top to a spectacular view of the entire Little Snake River watershed. We could see the area in the distance where our old ranch and our one-room schoolhouse was located. As we proceeded south, we found ourselves parallel to six big bull elk walking along and angling closer and closer to us as we watched from above. We were able to get wonderful photos and videos of these magnificent animals until they encountered our scent downwind and then retreated into the woods immediately.

The rest of the trip, which was by far the longest segment of the trail ride, took us to the Forest Service road and all the way to Whiskey Park, where we decided to camp next to a creek by the road leading up to Elkhorn Mountain.

We were exhausted. John had dismounted and led his horse for the last two or three miles because the metal in his replaced hip had hurt so badly. My knees had always hurt after about 30 minutes of riding since my early 20s. The pain had progressively become less intense as the trail ride progressed, but the nine miles of the last day left me limping both from a stomped foot and sore knees. Rita and David were tired but feeling better than John or me. And David had more energy than he had since the first day, likely due to the lower altitude.

All that was left was to get the horses to a rendezvous point below the Summit Creek Ranger Station on the main road (Colorado 129) from Steamboat to the Little Snake River Valley. That is where Sharon O'Toole had agreed to meet us and pick up the horses and the gear we rented. The next day, John's

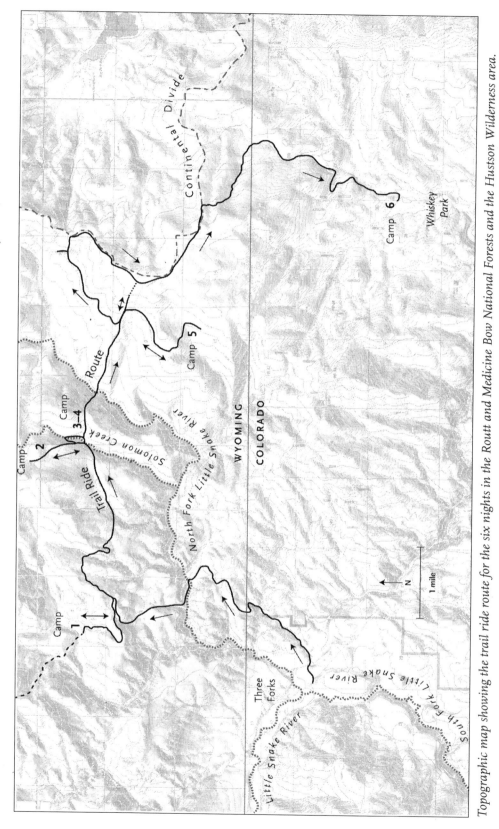

Topographic map showing the trail ride route for the six nights in the Routt and Medicine Bow National Forests and the Hustson Wilderness area.

hip was not doing well, so he stayed in the camp while David, Rita, and I rode from Whiskey Park to the Ranger Station.

It was the only time that just the three of us were together. This several hours together was a time for re-bonding and unspoken understandings among us. We were free of the pack horse and were able to move more quickly. With the potential of my horse still going lame, we stayed off the road through Whiskey Park, took an old wagon road through Crane Park, spurred our sheep herder-spoiled horses across a little creek they did not want to jump, and rode down the dirt road where we as children had helped to trail cattle to "the Forest" each summer for their allotment grazing. It rained and hailed hard for about 30 minutes, and the dirt road got quite muddy and slick. The weather cleared, we joined 129 near Smith Creek, and the remaining few miles up to the Ranger Station were uneventful. During the day's ride, David had discovered that he had left the keys to his pickup at the Whiskey Park camp, so, he would have to go there before retrieving his pickup near Three Forks.

The peacefulness lasted only until we tied up the horses and Sharon arrived a short time later. We unsaddled the three horses and loaded them into the trailer she was pulling. We knew how slick the old road to Whiskey Park was, so the plan was for David to go with Sharon southward on the main Forest Service road (which turned off 129 further up toward Columbine); pick up John, our camping supplies, and the other two horses; come back to pick up Rita and me and our saddles; and drive up the side road past the Three Forks Ranch to get David's pickup. We would then part company with Sharon and drive David's pickup back to our cabin on the Upper Elk River. David climbed into the pickup with Sharon, and inexplicably, with no explanation, instead of turning around to go toward Columbine and the main turnoff to Whiskey Park, they headed towards Three Forks or the Ladder Ranch or both. I was flabbergasted and loudly denounced him for, yet again, ignoring our plans and doing something entirely different. Rita eventually concurred but was not nearly as vocally upset. Given the pickup key situation, we concluded that Sharon had decided to take our three horses back to the Ladder Ranch and then return for the other two horses in Whiskey Park. David apparently would simply ride along.

We did not have cell phone connection. About two hours passed. It was getting late in the afternoon, and we assumed that we would not see David until dark, even assuming that they had not run into trouble on the road. The occasional passing car or pickup had become less frequent, so I flagged down a couple driving towards Columbine and asked them if they would be able to call Rae Jean when they got to Clark. They wrote the number and directions for Rae Jean to come and pick up Rita and me.

About 40 minutes later, Rae Jean arrived. We loaded the saddles into the Prius and drove to the cabin. It was indeed after dark before David and John arrived at the cabin in his pickup. We learned that as soon as David got into Sharon's four-wheel drive pickup with trailer in tow, she assured him that she could make it on the old, shorter route to Whiskey Park that we had just taken, no matter the mud. That is what they did. They picked up John and loaded the other two horses, the saddles, and camping gear and headed to Three Forks. Of course, Rita and I were not privy to those actions because they were on a more northerly portion of 129 that did not go past us, so we were left just wondering what was going on! The reasons for their long delay was that it was slow traveling in the mud of the old road, there was no place to turn the trailer around in Whiskey Park, and Sharon could not back her trailer a quarter mile (David had to do it for her).

On this trail ride, I had promised I would be a good follower. I was successful basically for the first day, but that vow was long forgotten at the end. I did not wait long to express my displeasure at not being apprised of the change in plans with Sharon, as this was not the first time David had acted on a unilateral change of plans with no explanation.

Six years earlier, on the "big" trail ride with David, Rita, John, and I, as well as Rae Jean and Edmund (a friend of David's from Mississippi), David at one point took off ahead to look for Jona Ely, who was to meet us at Diamond Park. There were several trails and roads that could be taken, and aside from some horse footprints from time to time, the rest of us had no idea where he had gone, where we were to meet him, or contingency plans if we did not meet up. Years earlier, while camping with Rae Jean and me at Freeman's Reservoir in Moffatt County, David left the campsite with no forewarning or note and did not return for hours. That time, after searching and yelling for him for two hours, we drove to Craig to consult with Sharon and Steve Andrew about what to do next. When we got back to the campsite, David was there, oblivious to or puzzled by our concern, but eager to tell the story of all the elk he had seen.

The next day was Rita's 50th Steamboat Springs High School reunion to be held at Lexie and Steve's hangar south of town. But Rita woke up with a severe case of vertigo. She could just barely walk, with someone to steady her, so instead of attending her reunion, she and John went to the local health clinic for medication followed by resting in bed. David, Rae Jean, and I did

David, Kenneth, and Rita on top of the Continental Divide.

attend the reunion and explained to everyone why Rita was not there. I wondered how we would have managed had this occurred during the trail ride.

The following morning, Rita and John said, "Goodbye," and got into their rental car to drive back to Denver to catch their plane home to Seattle and then to Fairbanks. David left soon after in his Nissan pickup for home in Mississippi. Rae Jean and I stayed at the cabin for a couple more weeks and then drove our Prius back to West Virginia.

Most of the "debriefing" regarding this second pack trip occurred later in phone calls and later visits. Perhaps more than most of the rare times that the three of us were together long enough to really "be" together, the trail ride experience encapsulated our abiding and deep connections on the one hand and our irreconcilable differences on the other. No matter how far away we had moved from the little valley of our youth, it held a magnetic attraction for all three of us. David was energized by the challenges inherent in finding old routes and discovering new ones in and around our old stomping grounds. Rita loved the adventure, period, and especially the traveling on horseback. I breathed in the familiarity of the flora and fauna of northwest Colorado and constantly hearkened back to childhood memories of riding and fishing.

Our shared connections were evident time and again in an almost invisible, collective "rising to the occasion" during a crisis moment. It was in many ways similar to our actions and reactions when both of our parents were dying years earlier. You do what had to be done. You do it as well as you can. You help out when needed. If four strangers had taken this trip, such easy joining of personalities would not have happened.

We three have been described as "all chiefs and no Indians" where nobody is in charge, but that would not accurately describe our thoughts and actions. Like any siblings who had shared innumerable common childhood experiences, even after long separations and divergent lifestyles, each of us found ourselves drawn or forced into unconscious roles we adopted as children. David believed himself to be the leader and expected Rita and me to believe it as well. He always acts quickly and decisively on logic and senses, but often fails to see all the ramifications of his actions. I generally accepted David's leadership when I agreed with it but was adamant and vocal about plans or decisions that I believed were ill-advised, overly self-centered, or not clearly conceptualized. My personality type also acts on logic and sense, yet always has a Plan A, Plan B, and Plan C in order to have the best outcome. Rita was happy not to be in charge and to "go with the flow," except in isolated situations where she believed both of us were wrong or when somebody had to lead, and somebody had to follow. Her dominant personality type has a drive for adrenalin rushes from excitement and adventure but with a strong secondary penchant for being the loyal caretaker.

As to how each of us described the trail ride in a few words, I called it "a geriatric comedy of errors." At one point, mid-way through the ride, I thought of a song, "Rock of ages, set for me / Let me lead my horse to thee" (in order to get back on the horse). I was glad for the experience but was relieved when it was over and would have to think long and hard before trying another one. David called it a mixture of adventures, either "Oh boy!" or "Oh shit!" Even before the trail ride was over, he was talking about the next one, perhaps in the Bitter Root Mountains of Montana. No doubt he would take a few of the experiences and turn them into part-true-part-exaggeration stories for his Mississippi Storytelling group. Rita loved all of it and would do it again in a heartbeat, but she would want better horses. Perhaps it could be said that we all know that our lives are enriched by the stories we could tell but integrate them into our lives differently. David remembers the stand-out experiences and then embellishes them for an oral audience. Rita remembers the adventures and excitement and simply savors it. I return to all the memories and seek to find meaning in them and to preserve them.

We went home to lives so divergent that most people would never consider us close brothers and sister.

Chapter 3

From Quebec to Colorado: Oliver St. Louis and Leone Morgan

The surname St. Louis refers to the King of France, Louis IX, who ruled in the 1200s. As the name implies, the St-Louis family originated in France. Our first known relative was René Filiatrault dit St-Louis who was born in France in 1646. The date is unclear, but the family immigrated to Quebec, Canada, and lived there for generations. By the time our grandfather Oliver St. Louis was born, the "Filiatrault dit" part of the surname was dropped, but in Canada, St. Louis is still generally written as St-Louis. Presumably, when he became an American citizen, Oliver replaced the dash with the period in our names now.

Our grandmother was a Morgan, and all we know is that her father, William Tecumseh (Billie) Morgan, came from near Tioga, New York, and likely was in the US Army in the Wyoming Territory after the Civil War. Scant records suggest he might have been an orphan as a child. We know much more about the family of her mother, Sarah Mariah McCargar. It goes back to a Thomas McCargar (and very likely his brother, Joseph) who came to this country from Ireland in 1776 via Quebec, Canada, as British soldiers who would fight in our Revolutionary War. As part of Burgoyne's army that surrendered to the Continental soldiers in Saratoga, New York, they were captured but later were released or escaped. Thomas lived in New York, married there, and had children. He could not tolerate the abuse from the family that he allegedly endured as a former enemy. He told his wife he was leaving, but she did not wish to move; thus, he reportedly left his family and went west to Rochester, New York. There, he married again and had more children. Accidentally, he met his son in Rochester and eventually met his former wife again. Details are not clear, but apparently upon telling this to his second wife, she did not wish to remain married to him.

House near Ormstown, Quebec, where Oliver was born and raised, still solid in 2018 and about to be renovated.

We believe Thomas and his first wife rejoined and later moved to Ontario and/or Quebec, Canada. According to one report, unbeknownst to either of them at first, Thomas and his family lived very close to his brother, Joseph. Thomas married yet again after the death of his wife. One son, Robert, who was our great-great-great-grandfather (2nd great-grandfather), married Elizabeth Gibson of North Gore, Quebec. Together, with at least some of their children, the parents eventually moved to Faribault, Minnesota, which is where our great-grandmother Sarah Mariah McCargar was born. She was brought to Colorado by her father, Alfred Henry (our 1st great-grandfather), and introduced to Billie Morgan.

Our grandfather Oliver St. Louis was born in Ormstown, Quebec, near Montreal in 1875, the fifth of ten brothers and sisters. His parents were Oliver (or Olivier) St-Louis and Sophia Sinclair, also born nearby. In order, the siblings were: Alfred, Francis, David, Elizabeth, Lorina Sophia (Laura) Rember, Oliver, William Alfred, John, George, and Annie Louise Alexander. Oliver entered the US and arrived by train and stage on his 21st birthday to a new community at the intersection of Slater Creek and the Little Snake River along the Colorado and Wyoming line. He came to work for Robert McIntosh, who was an uncle to the family who lived on a McIntosh farm near Ormstown that was in line of sight from the St-Louis farm.

It is not well known among most current residents of the Little Snake River Valley that McIntosh had a rich and fascinating entrepreneurial past prior to taking up residence there. Upon emigrating from Canada to the United States, he was a successful builder and contractor in Chicago for eight years before the great Chicago fire of 1871. After that calamity, he accepted a job to work at the gold mines at Hahns Peak for J. V. Farwell. His skills were used to build a 17-mile ditch used to bring water from the North Fork of the Elk River to the mines. After Farwell's operation collapsed in 1879, beginning in the next year, with two partners, Ed Cody and Frank Hinman, McIntosh began the only real profitable placer gold mining operation in the area. They extended and rebuilt the ditch, some of which had been destroyed in a forest fire. After two years, he managed the operation at nearby Poverty Bar himself. He also became the growing town of Hahns Peak's second postmaster. When the placer mining was no longer profitable, McIntosh joined with Billie Morgan to purchase the homestead of Bill Slater at the confluence of the Little Snake River and Slater Creek (which bore Slater's name). McIntosh built a general store that later housed the Slater, Colorado, Post Office. He also raised horses for a lucrative freighting operation and for the US Army. He married Nellie Draper from Illinois and had two daughters, but the marriage did not last. After a divorce, Nellie moved to Rawlins.

All of McIntosh's endeavors and successes could not have gone unnoticed by his family and close neighbors in Quebec, including the St-Louis family. Current details of Oliver's move to the Little Snake River are inconsistent. One version, written for *The Snake River Press* in 1966 by Sylvia Beeler (aunt of my first-grade and David's second-grade teacher) reports that Oliver and a Canadian friend, Jim Kiever, had moved to somewhere in New York state. McIntosh had gone east to purchase better horses to improve his herd and met them by chance and then hired them to help him bring the horses to Slater. They stayed and watched over the herd for a year, whence Oliver returned to Quebec for a year. One year later, he returned, and shortly after that married Onie in 1900 [sic: 1901]. Beeler also related the following incorrect narrative that our St. Louis cousins had also reconstructed. Oliver's mother had immigrated to Canada from Scotland and his father had come from France via Scotland (hence, Oliver's French name but Scottish heritage).

Beeler's version may be partly correct, but an oral history that Sharon Andrew recorded from Oliver's first son, Sinclair (Sinc), makes clear that

Robert McIntosh. (Courtesy of the Little Snake River Museum.)

The Slater Store and Post Office: later years. (Courtesy of the Little Snake River Museum.)

The Slater Store and Post Office: early years. (Courtesy of the Little Snake River Museum.)

Mildred McIntosh inside the Slater Store. (Courtesy of the Little Snake River Museum.)

the meeting between McIntosh and our grandfather was not at all by accident. As noted, McIntosh had nieces and nephews on a farm only about a quarter-mile from the St-Louis farm near Ormstown, Quebec. Most likely, correspondence between the two of them preceded the meeting in New York, if in fact, such a meeting occurred at all. Another version reports that in 1896 Oliver and another brother (no mention of Kiever) may have left Canada so as not to be conscripted into British Commonwealth service to fight in the Boer War in South Africa from 1899–1902. If that was the case, and if Beeler's version of Oliver going back to Canada and then returning is correct, then the dates are plausible. However, recent connections with the St-Louis family in Ormstown revealed that Oliver's father or even his grandfather did not come from France or Scotland. The *Filiatrault dit St-Louis* family had lived in Quebec for generations. Oliver's mother, Sophia Sinclair St-Louis, was Scottish and a Protestant, which reportedly resulted in the family being excommunicated by the Catholic Church, and thereby no doubt influenced more by the Scottish mother than the French Canadian father.

Regardless of Oliver's heritage or the details of his coming to Slater, his first job was to manage McIntosh's herd of horses, the size of which is reported to be about 1000 mares. McIntosh's was allegedly one of three local ranches raising horses for the US Army. In these early years, Oliver and others camped in the open range south of Slater to watch and keep track of the herd. Our father, George St. Louis (Dad), tells the story of how the men were advised to roll up their canvas-covered bedroll each morning. One hired hand did not see the need for that, and one night crawled into it only to discover a rattlesnake had preceded him. He apparently grabbed the snake behind the head and was thus not bitten. As the story was related, he was so traumatized that the other men had to kill the snake and pry his hand open to release his grip on it.

It is interesting that, later, Oliver was allegedly suspected of possible horse thievery because his registered brand, "Quarter-Circle US," was an arc over the letters "US," which was the brand for the US Army. It would have been very easy to add the arc and thereby change the brands.

Robert McIntosh took the eastern part of the extended ranch at Slater while Billie Morgan took the western part. Leone (Onie) Morgan was born in 1879 one to two miles west of Slater in a house near the Little Snake in a home built by her father. It was apparently just barely north of the Colorado-Wyoming line. Billie had met and married her mother, Sarah McCargar, three years earlier in Hahns Peak while working in the gold mines. Onie was the second born of ten Morgan siblings, following Elizabeth (who died between her first and second year of age) and then followed by Oliver Perry (Perry), Jessie, Edwin, Edna, Lotta Josephine (Lottie) Tamney, Chester Arthur, Georgia Izola (Georgie) Rea, and Lewis William Raymond. It has been widely reported that Onie was the first white woman born within the Little Snake River area, but that ignores her deceased older sister.

Onie at 8 months.

Onie at 21 years.

Onie and five of her siblings: Lewis, Georgie Morgan Rea, Chester, Edwin, Perry, and Onie.

Routt Collection/**Tread of Pioneers Museum**
Mrs. Oliver St. Louis, in black, with Mrs. George Fleming.

Oliver and Onie at the time of their wedding, 1901.

Newspaper clipping of Onie and neighbor, Mrs. George Fleming. Eventually, Oliver owned the Fleming Place, which became our primary ranch property.

Oliver and Onie with their five oldest grandchildren. In their arms, David and Kenneth, and in front, Shirley, Sharon, and Jean.

Oliver and his brother, "Uncle George."   *"Uncle George"; his wife, Maud; and Oliver.*

Oliver and Onie met, fell in love, and married on February 20, 1901. Oliver had the intention of moving back to Quebec, and according to Sinc's oral history, Onie traveled with Oliver's father (who must have come to visit) back to spend time with the Ormstown relatives before Sinc was born. She did not like her prospects of living there, got homesick, and came back. At some point, Oliver purchased a threshing machine and, hiring his brother-in-law Perry Morgan as a helper, harvested grain for various neighbors. According to Sinc's history, Oliver and Onie lived initially in her childhood home for about one year. Next, they moved to a house near the Battle Creek

---

Were our St. Louis and McCargar relatives related?

This book is not intended to be a thoroughly documented history, but Mildred McIntosh, Robert McIntosh's daughter who had attended Wellesley College in Massachusetts and who later lived most of her life in Slater, wrote the story of the McCargars. It should be noted that other versions of their coming to the Little Snake River exist, but her carefully written account very likely renders hers the most accurate.

Like Robert McIntosh, the McCargars also originated in Quebec but at least one of them, Alfred Henry McCargar, born in 1831, criss-crossed the United States. He and his wife, who was born in the same town in Quebec, lived variously in Minnesota then Illinois as a wheelwright, and then Minnesota again. In April 1961, the family traveled for five months in a wagon train to California to work in the new quartz mining town of Silica (also known as Round Valley). These were close to the nearby community, later named Greenville, where in 1862, McCargar built the first house. McIntosh indicated that he was interested in quartz mining, but it is more likely that his interest was gold.

He built a stamp mill, a device that would drop a heavy weight on gold ore rocks to crush them. The gold mines were abandoned by 1864, and McCargar and his family moved to Silver Bow, Montana, for more gold mining, and then in 1868 to Dunlap, Iowa, for farming, where their youngest child, Alfred McClellan McCargar, was born. Three years later, the family moved to Topeka, Kansas, where the senior Alfred engaged in the lumber business. In 1874, he and his family decided to move to California. They traveled by train, recently completed, which stopped in Denver, Colorado. There, he met S. D. N. Bennett who hired him on the spot to supervise placer work in a Hahns Peak gold mine.

While working that mine, William (Billie) T. Morgan from Tioga, New York, came to work with him, and became enamored with his daughter Sarah Mariah. Billie and Sarah were married and were our great-grandparents. Two other daughters married Snake River pioneers as well, Caroline Jane to Frank Hinman and Margaret Elizabeth to William Humphreys.

—continues on page 35

The Home Place from the west.

Painting of the Home Place in the fall by Elizabeth St. Louis.

The Home Place from the hill above in the summer.

The big white house and Bunkhouse at the Home Place where Oliver and Onie raised their family and lived most of their lives.

The connections with the St-Louis family and the maternal side of the Morgans may be more than we had imagined. For example, Mildred wrote that the senior Alfred McCargar and his wife, Elizabeth Gibson, were born and reared near North Gore, Quebec, which is only about 85 miles from Ormstown, Quebec, where Oliver St. Louis was born a generation later. The elder McCargar was Scottish, and his Scottish heritage was the primary nationality claimed by Oliver, even though he was a descendant of a long line of French Canadians with the surname Filiatrault dit St-Louis later reduced to St-Louis. According to St-Louis relatives near Ormstown, Oliver's father, also Oliver (or Olivier) St-Louis, was born Catholic but married Sophia Sinclair, who had a Scottish background. Apparently, he was excommunicated from the Catholic Church for marrying a Presbyterian Protestant. It would not be surprising that members of both families knew each other in Canada and were perhaps even related in past generations.

This is all the less coincidental because Robert McIntosh, also of Scottish ancestry, who supervised the mining of gold at Hahns Peak, who owned the horse operation where Oliver first worked, and who established the Slater store and Post Office, was an uncle to the McIntoshes reared about 300 yards from the home where Oliver was born. It would have been after Oliver moved to Colorado, but his niece (daughter of his younger brother, John St-Louis) married a McIntosh descendant (Edgar Outterson, born in 1897). Also, his older sister, Lorina Sophia, married Alexander Pringle Pember, who also had married two women, one of whom was Elizabeth H. McIntosh.

There is little doubt that it was Robert McIntosh who recruited Oliver St. Louis, or Oliver who sought employment from Robert, that was the genesis of our grandfather ending up in Slater, Colorado.

There is another potential connection. Oliver St. Louis's cousin, Thomas (Tom) St. Louis, moved to Arcata, California, likely around the turn of the twentieth century and started a dairy farm. One report indicates that Thomas, whom our uncles erroneously called "Uncle Tommie," was the person who arranged for Sinc, Francis, and Perry to travel to California to work as lumbermen in the redwood forests. And, in the town of Arcata, California, there is a street allegedly named after Thomas St. Louis, that is, St. Louis Road. More likely, however, Oliver's brother, Alfred, who also moved to California, and who was buried in the town of Willits, was the source of work in the redwoods. Arcata and Willits are 225-250 miles northwest and west of Greenville, but it is possible that the senior Alfred McCargar, who had been in California a generation earlier, may have influenced some of the Quebec St-Louis relatives to move there.

Another interesting fact is that a "Sevigny St. Louis" is listed in the McCargar Genealogy (www.mccargar.com). All of this is to suggest that the McCargar and St. Louis families may have been connected well before our grandparents, Billie and Sarah, met in Colorado.

School (the future site of buildings at the late Earl Salisbury ranch), which was across the road from the Old Battle Creek Store and Post Office. Oliver had leased the Wiff Wilson Place there.

The location of the Colorado-Wyoming line was not always clear in some early records. Therefore, the locations may have been recorded in either state. Sinc's birth was recorded in Wyoming since he was born at the original Morgan home, which apparently by the time of his birth in 1903 was judged to be barely north of the line in Wyoming. All his brothers were born "up the River" in Colorado. Onie regarded her pre-marriage home address as "Slater, Colorado," because she clearly and repeatedly wrote it as such in her schoolbook notations in the mid-1890s; yet, her death certificate presumably more accurately indicated that she was born in Wyoming. Onie

Oliver and Onie at Fish Creek Falls, a popular outing spot.

Oliver and Onie dancing at their 50th wedding anniversary.

Celebrating their 50th Anniversary at the dance hall in Dixon.

recorded the births of all her sons in the family Bible, Sinc's as "Slater, Wyoming," and all the others—Alfred, George, Francis, Perry, and Leonard—as "Battle Creek, Colorado." Most of the sons were named after Oliver's own brothers. Thereafter, according to Sylvia Beeler, Oliver and Onie purchased the Frank Potts Place, originally homesteaded in 1887, about 12 miles east of Slater and five miles east of Battle Creek. This became their "Home Place." And it was here that the remainder of their children, all boys, were born. At the time of their birth, Battle Creek, Colorado, was the closest post office.

In early 1910, Oliver, Onie, Sinc, Alfred, George, and Francis traveled by train back to Quebec and stayed at the St-Louis farm for about three months that winter. Some reports indicate that this is when Onie decided not to stay in Canada, announcing at the end of the sojourn that she was going back to Colorado and that Oliver could stay there if he wanted. No doubt, the post-marriage trip from Sinc's interview is likely the accurate account. In any case, there was no more serious talk of relocating to Quebec or anywhere else.

Regarding the Potts Place and other homesteads, most of the early settlers in the Little Snake River Valley had taken advantage of the 1862 Homestead Act. This law allowed any adult head of a family who was a citizen of the US, or intended to become one, to acquire 160 acres of land after paying a small registration fee and living continuously on the land for at least five years. A six-month period was available to anyone who could pay $200 (or $1.25 per acre). Often, a husband and wife would homestead together and "prove up" on their property by building a house on the border of two adjacent 160-acre parcels. Moreover, the government recognized that, compared to the East and Midwest, even 320 acres was likely insufficient to make a living in the more arid West. Thus, many homesteads were for a full "section" or 640 acres. Also, and not well known now, through such laws as the Taylor Grazing Act and Bureau of Land Management (BLM) law, federal land adjacent to many homesteads in the Colorado and Wyoming area was set aside for the homesteaders' use through a "property right" provision. In any case, Oliver and Onie acquired 320 acres and made their home on the hill overlooking the Little Snake River and the one-fourth- to half-mile wide valley where a little creek flowed in from the north and the larger, decidedly murkier Willow Creek flowed from the south.

Because much of the Little Snake River Valley and surrounding range land was homesteaded, each parcel was accorded the owner's last name followed by "Place." Many of these early homesteaders were unable to make a

Onie in her 90s.

Onie at her 100th birthday with her four surviving sons. Back: Leonard and Alfred; front: George, Onie, and Sinc.

living on the 160 or 320 acres in the West, so many homesteads were sold to speculators or neighbors; yet, most of them retained their names for at least two generations. The details are sketchy at this point, but Oliver and Onie gradually acquired a number of these homesteads, either from their owners, later purchasers, or the county through failure of the owners to pay their property taxes Though not verifiable, Dad had commented that some of the land was acquired for two cents an acre. The Great Depression began in 1929, and many of the homesteaders, with insufficient land to generate a living from ranching in the first place, simply walked away from their places. According to our dad, a banker in Rawlins who held title to a number of the defaulted properties, because the homesteaders had borrowed against them, contacted Oliver to buy them. Reportedly, he was only willing to pay cash for more land. Had he taken a loan, he could have easily doubled the amount of land he purchased. Thus, the St. Louis ranch became a combination of the Bryson Place, the John X Turner Place, the Fleming Place, the Hartman Place, and the Hackmaster Place. Most were 320 acres; some were 640. At about this same time other viable ranchers, such as the Salisburys or the Boyers, also acquired numerous bankrupted homesteads and consolidated the ranches we knew as children.

Oliver and Onie's original house was replaced in 1927 by a three-story white house with an unfinished basement. They later built "the Bunkhouse" for hired hands, but it was used as well for guests and their sons' new families. Immediately after several of the sons were married, they lived initially either in Oliver and Onie's house or in the Bunkhouse but later moved to new houses on "places" Oliver sold or gave to each one. The exception was Alfred, who lived almost all of his life at home and did not acquire his own land, but shared Oliver and Onie's land.

The families raised cattle, mostly Herefords, for their livelihood. The long winters from the end of November through April or May required them to raise a great deal of hay to feed the cattle and the horses required to manage the ranches. This necessitated the maintenance of hay meadows in the river bottom that were irrigated by water rights adjudicated to each for purpose of flood irrigation. Ditches diverted water from the river or its tributaries far upstream of the meadows from which water flowed at a minimum drop, less than the river or creeks themselves, so that it could be released onto the meadows above the natural flows. As open range was no longer available, they had to build and maintain fences for the livestock. Fencing was also required for BLM land leased inexpensively for grazing and Forest Service allotments for supervised summer grazing of specified numbers of cattle.

The essential yearly routines involved fixing fences and harrowing meadows in the spring and early summer; supervising calving, branding/dehorning/castrating calves, and moving herds to summer pastures on the Forest in the early summer; irrigating the fields until

Oliver singing or telling a story no doubt at a picnic at the Forest.

Sinc pulling the binder, not with horses, but with his Ford Golden Jubilee tractor.

Perry pitching shocks of grain from one hayrack to another.

From Quebec to Colorado / 39

early July; repairing or readying machinery for haying; cutting, raking, collecting and stacking the hay; building fences or "stack yards" around each stack to keep the cattle away; rounding up cattle in the fall and selling calves and culled cows; and then feeding the cows all winter from workhorse-drawn hayracks on sled runners. Of course, myriad other expected and unexpected duties or crises occurred all the time related to families, schooling, transportation, visitors, sickness or injury of people or animals, 4-H, and many, many other issues.

After their sons, except Alfred, had moved out, Oliver and Onie stayed in their house for many years, indeed through most of our childhood and early adulthood, until they no longer were able to manage the work involved. Sinc had been given the Home Place and land. He sold it to former guests at the nearby Focus Ranch, the Lidstones, who made it part of a new incorporated business named L-O-N Ranches. The house and outbuildings, along with approximately three acres, were reserved for Oliver and Onie's use for as long as they wanted to live there. In 1964, Oliver suffered a stroke, was hospitalized, and eventually was moved to a nursing home in Meeker where he died in 1965. Onie and Alfred lived at the house for several years and then moved to a rented house in Baggs for about one year. Thereafter, Onie moved to Craig and lived with Sinc and his new wife, Deloris, until Onie was moved to a nursing home in Craig. She lived

Visitors were always welcome at the Home Place. Grandpa always invited them for dinner or supper, whether he knew them or not. This appears to be a special occasion that deteriorated into a water fight.

there until her death in 1979 at 100 years of age.

The story of the white house at the Home Place did not end there. It was to be moved to a new location a few miles west as a new home for Jona Kohpay, daughter of our cousin Jean Ely-Landini. One or two days before the upcoming moving was to occur, the house burned to the ground. The fire was variously blamed on lightning from a thunderstorm or arson, but no definitive answer ever emerged.

MEMORIES

Our memories of Oliver and Onie, whom we uniformly called "Grandpa" and "Grandma" are many, but the following stand out.

OLIVER (GRANDPA)

David: The first image that comes to mind of Grandpa is of him driving four horses pulling the binder in the wheat, oat, and barley fields. He'd have two lines in each hand, somewhat of a trick because he only had part of his left index finger. (The first two joints had been surgically removed after blood poisoning set in after he jabbed it with a burlap bag [gunny sack] needle while sewing up filled grain sacks years before.) The slats of the binder would pull the grain into the long sickle at the bottom as the binder moved through the field and the grain would come out the back in twine-tied bundles about one foot in diameter. Those were later stacked, teepee style, into shocks of about five or six bundles each. Later, the bundles are pitched onto a hayrack, hauled to the thresher, and pitched into the thresher.

David: Grandpa used to sing at most social events. With his "bum" leg, he would lean up against a pillar, a doorway, or a wall and sing songs from his youth, a cappella. The song I remember most is his rendering of "Duck Foot Sue." He would also recite poems with a perfect French Canadian accent, "De Skunk and Lac St. Pierre," for example.

Kenneth: I remember Grandpa driving the old team of mostly Percheron mares he called Maude and Dolly who pulled a dump rake in the hayfield. He would sometimes rake the mowed hay into windrows that eventually resembled spokes of a large wheel emanating from the center of the field. Mostly, though, I remember him cleaning up the fields after the buck rakes gathered the windrows of loose hay and took them to the stacks or, years later, after the baler passed over windrows that more resembled concentric circles around the field. Grandpa seemingly never stopped talking to the horses, saying "Giddah, Giddah boys, Hyah," etc. He also had a long willow switch that he would tap the rear of the two mares at least every minute or so.

Oliver getting ready to serve campfire coffee.

Kenneth: I have an image of Grandpa sitting on the low-cut wooden chair next to the kitchen door at the Home Place putting on his shoes, one of which had a wooden extension that went up to a buckled brace on his bad leg, broken years before when he was kicked by a workhorse. (Tex McDowell was reportedly partly responsible.) I would walk in, and he would say jovially, "Hello...Kenneth," the pause probably because he had to think of my name.

Kenneth: Among the other images I have of Grandpa is making pancakes every morning at the wood and coal stove in a cast iron frying pan, three at a time, and turning them perfectly with only a fork and a kitchen knife. I never could figure out how he could to that. At our house, I often was allowed to make the pancakes on our long griddle, six or eight at a time, and turn them with a metal spatula.

Kenneth: A fact about Grandpa that I owe to my nephew Robert St. Louis is a comment he heard from Dad when he worked one summer for him on Snake River at age 14. Dad told him that Grandpa was the strongest man in the Valley. Apparently, a competition involved lifting a very large boulder and Grandpa was the one who either lifted it or did something with it. Dad reportedly told Rita that he was one of the few men who were strong enough to help a mare deliver a foal.

Rita: Grandpa was one of the most satisfied, content people I have ever known.

Oliver and Onie all gussied up, probably either in Denver or California.

Alfred's partly grown-out red hair, dyed several times by Jean. He's standing next to Onie, with the enclosed front porch behind them.

He was at home in his world; he was content with his family; and his life was what it was supposed to be for him. The rest of the world did not seem to really bother him much, because he knew it was either the Catholics or the Communists who caused all of the problems in the world.

Rita: Even in his daily puttering, he was content. Several things he did would annoy Grandma, but even her reproaches did not bother him. He would just tell her, "Oh putt putt tutt tutt, Onie" and continue doing exactly what she did not want him to do.

Rita: One time, Grandpa was bemoaning to Mom how much the price of groceries had gone up by declaring how much more a bottle of whiskey cost than it used to. As a child, I did not know how much nor how often Grandpa and the men drank on a daily basis. I suspect not a whole lot. But I do remember seeing everyone in a circle passing the bottle, and each person taking a swig. On more "formal" occasions such as Christmas and Thanksgiving holidays or when Leonard and family were visiting and there was a big meal at Grandpa and Grandma's house, he would lift from the cupboard a little jelly jar glass with birds painted on it and pour some whiskey into the glass and cut it with about an equal amount of water. If there was a "guest of honor" such as Leonard, he would hand the glass to that person first. Then he would stand and wait. That person had to toss down the whiskey, then hand the glass back to Grandpa which he would fill again the same way for the next person. There was no such thing as each person's having his own cocktail glass; each person had to swig down so the next got a chance at the glass. Once a round of booze had been served, the glass was rinsed and put away into the cupboard.

Rita: My memory of Grandpa's making breakfast pancakes began with his going to the milk house and fetching his crock of sourdough. He would add more flour and other ingredients, and then start cooking pancakes on his griddle on the hot stove. With his bum leg, he would hobble to the stove, pour three pancakes, hobble back to the counter and put the dough down, then hobble back to the stove to turn the pancakes. I worried that he would not get back and forth fast enough not to burn them, but he managed.

Rita: I also remember Grandpa's campfire coffee at brandings or the yearly cattle drive. He had about a two-gallon black metal coffee pot with a swinging metal bucket-style handle at the top and a stationary hand-sized handle at the back. He would build a wood fire and place the pot squarely in the middle of it or on the side of a large branding fire. He would spoon coffee grounds directly into the water and let it boil up two or three times before it was ready, each time using a cut willow with one protruding branch for a hook to raise it before it boiled over. He would use the same stick on the handle and another one or a glove on the side handle to pour coffee into tin cups.

Rita: A really strong memory for me was Grandpa's taking us little kids in the horse-drawn, high spoke-wheeled wagon to the branding. Another is his letting us—as little kids again—ride Maude and Dolly, the gentle old black and grey mares, as he drove the dump rake in the hay field.

Rita: Jean had dyed Alfred's hair red several times, but one time also dyed Grandpa's hair red. As the story goes, he went to the bathroom to look at himself in the mirror and then said, "Well, Mr. Oliver, I can see you're not going anyplace this winter."

ONIE (GRANDMA)

David: My strongest memory of Grandma was getting angry when she played Rummy in the evening, almost always with Grandpa, but often with Alfred. She hated to lose, and even after years of this routine, she loudly complained if she lost more than she thought was fair.

David: Grandma made home-made cake donuts. They were smaller than typical donuts today and were deep fried and covered with powdered sugar. I remember

Onie parading in her side saddle, which of course is obscured by her long skirt.

Closeup of Onie on her side saddle.

going to their house and eating the donuts she had made especially for us kids (her grandchildren).

David: If Grandma did not know where somebody had been for a long time she just figured they were in Denver.

Kenneth: I had little one-on-one time with Grandma, if I remember correctly. I do remember her writing every night (when I was present) in her diary.

Kenneth: Like my siblings, I remember her playing Rummy, and being a sore loser. It was at their large kitchen table next to the stove with cards that were almost completely worn out on an equally worn out oilcloth flower-patterned tablecloth. She kept the sugar bowl and a bowl for teaspoons (but not forks or knives inexplicably) in the middle of that table all the time. The Depression-era, glass bowls were shiny and copper-colored but often reflected multi-colors in the sunlight. Those had to be set aside for the card games. I don't recall, but I suspect I was included in some of the games I remember.

Kenneth: I remember Grandma running—not walking—up the stairs to the second floor where most of the bedrooms were. I also remember her "worrying" about her sons (who were middle-aged men at the time and all married except for Alfred)

From Quebec to Colorado / 45

every time they would go to a dance or go to "have a drink with the Boys down the river" at Dixon or Baggs.

Kenneth: Grandma was famous for riding side-saddle in parades. I always wondered why anyone would do that. I guess it was to be more lady-like on the horse.

Rita: It seemed that personal grooming was not really high on Grandma's list. As a young woman, she wore her hair long, but when we knew her, she had it lopped off into a rather nondescript hairdo. Probably Grandpa or Sinc cut her hair with the clippers and scissors. I never knew her to have worn lipstick, let alone rouge or makeup. Unless she was dressed up to go to town, Grandma wore quite plain clothes, and never very fashionable. I suspect her wardrobe was a product of her entire life in that new clothes were considered a real luxury, and something that people just did not or could not afford. She wore a dress with an apron and flesh-colored stockings all of the time, and she pretty much wore her clothes until they were gone. While they were often faded and old, she did not wear holes. In fact, none of her family wore clothes with holes in them because Grandma mended all holes.

Her denim patches on jeans or jackets were legendary. She would take a piece of denim saved from a leg of pants that were no longer wearable and carefully cut a piece so that it would have a diameter an inch or so greater than the diameter of the hole. She would then, hand sew that patch to the underside of the garment. Then from the right side, she would carefully cut away the frayed edges of the hole and tuck all of the clean-cut edges under and again hand sew that tucked under edge to the patch. Her patches were neat and they really lasted. Occasionally she would add a patch to a patch to make an article of clothing last even longer. In addition to the endless patching that Grandma did, she also made pretty "crazy" quilts out of tiny pieces of cloth cut from dresses or shirts that could no longer be worn. Later in life she made several quilts from discarded neckties of Grandpa and the Boys. At the time I thought those necktie quilts were gaudy and ugly. I now really like the ones that Kenneth, David, and others ended up with. She also did "fancy work" which included embroidery or crocheting doilies or edges onto pillow cases.

Grandma grew up living a hard life, and I suspect she did not feel that she should indulge in wearing pretty clothes or using pretty linens. Occasionally her daughters-in-law would give her something new and pretty for Christmas, but normally she would not use it. She would say that it was just too nice to use; thus, she had several drawers filled with lovely things "too nice to use." There were times that some of us took advantage of that mantra. If Grandma gave us something we really did not like, we would tell her that it was "just too nice to use," and she took it as a great compliment to her gift.

Rita: Grandma would fry really delicious donuts then coat them with sugar. Several could be eaten fresh, but several more had to be saved for a later time in an air-tight can.

1½ cups sugar
1 teaspoon full of each salt, nutmeg, soda and lemon
3 eggs well beaten
2 cups sour milk, butter milk is the best
flour enough to make it just so you can handle
it.
This makes 45 good size doughnuts

Onie's recipe for her famous donuts written in her own handwriting.

Steve Andrew always chuckled about not knowing the "magic number" of fresh ones that one could eat. If the person ate too many, they were just not being careful about leaving enough for a later date, but if the person ate too few, she would declare, "I guess they don't like my donuts."

Rita: Grandma was really efficient and always "on the run." My memory is flavored by the hurt that our mom felt because Grandma seemed to criticize her a lot. I also remember her having been at our house to snoop while we were gone, and her taking the old neck ties from the playhouse down by the river that Betty and Mom had given us. She retrieved them for Grandpa to wear to town.

Rita: I remember feeling pretty "unloved" by Grandma because she made doll clothes for Lilly (Lillyan) and Lexie, but not for me. Eventually she did make some for me, but not for some time. In retrospect, I think I just did not know how to ask her to make me doll clothes.

Rita: I, too, have memories of the evening Rummy games after supper. One night she was having an unusual losing streak. She gathered up the deck of cards and tossed them all into the wood stove.

Rita: No doubt, aside from Oliver's connection to Canada, Elizabeth was the first "foreigner" in Grandma's life. After Elizabeth took the girls to Italy, anytime anyone went overseas, Grandma said they went to "Itly."

Rita: Grandma had a predisposition to "worry" a lot. She worried about her "boys" when they would go to town. In fact, she declared that she could not sleep a

Oliver is dealing the cards for another hand of Rummy. This time happened to be in our living room.

wink while they were gone. However, one could not raise her with the telephone right next to her bedroom with the three-longs-three-shorts ring.

Rita: Grandma also was worried that she could not eat. My ex-husband, Chris Maser, told the story that she declared that she felt so bad that she could not eat a piece of pie. The hay men had left the dinner (noon meal) table for the field; they had forgotten something and sent Chris back to the house. He walked into the kitchen and Grandma was eating a piece of blueberry pie. When she realized that she had been caught, she tried to stuff the whole piece into her mouth at once. Chris said that blueberries were dripping down the sides of her mouth and her chin.

Chapter 4

The St. Louis "Boys," the Aunts, and the Cousins

All born at home, the St. Louis "Boys" became well known in the Little Snake River Valley. Some might even say they were infamous—not in the lawless sense as the famous outlaw Butch Cassidy, whose presence was felt in the Valley, but from reputations of casting large shadows. (See Appendix G.) The Boys were certainly not regarded as quiet introverts. Instead, they were known for working hard, playing hard, entertaining, speaking the unvarnished truth, prize fighting (boxing), never backing away from a fight, and, on occasion, serious drinking or carousing. Although this may have been true of many of the residents of the Little Snake River Valley in the first and middle parts of the twentieth century, the St. Louis Boys were known to all the game wardens in the region for harvesting elk, deer, or fish out of season or beyond the legal limits, at least until they began to guide deer and elk hunters for a fee.

All of them attended the one-room school through the eighth grade across the river and up Willow Creek, hence the name, Willow Creek School. Oliver was instrumental in starting the school, so it is no surprise that some of the teachers stayed at the St. Louis house. The school was about a half-mile south of the Home Place, and the Boys walked there across the river on a foot log. About April, the school year ended before high water occurred, but when the water was too high, Oliver drove them across the river in a high-wheeled wagon. In addition, several of them attended the Piney School, which was at the Luddy Place east of a familiar rock outcrop landmark known as Pine Scope. This was a summer school that functioned to complete years or get pupils ready for the next grade, determined entirely by the teacher's subjective judgment. Dad repeated the first grade twice. All of the Boys but Alfred further attended high school, typically by "boarding" with a relative in a

All six brothers: Perry, Sinc, George, Alfred, Francis, and Leonard.

Alfred, Albert Salisbury, Ted Tamney, Francis, Perry, and George.

Alfred, Leonard, Perry, George, Francis, and Ted Tamney.

Leonard, Perry, George, and Francis.

Sinc and George (probably) crossing the Little Snake River in quite high water. An unfed stack of loose hay is in the field.

George, Leonard, and Sinc in serious conversation.

town or city with a high school. None of the Boys attended college. Except for a few jobs outside for no more than a few months to a few years, all of them except Leonard stayed in the Valley during their early and middle adult years. Five of them (excepting Alfred) married. Aside from Sinc's first short marriage and Leonard's lifelong marriage to a local woman, they married women who came into the Valley for work or tourism. All the Boys loved the place they were reared, and all their lives, even if no longer living there, maintained an almost spiritual connection with their extended family and neighbors in the Valley. Truly, they could be regarded as among the real cowboys of their era.

Oliver and Onie also helped raise four of the Boys' cousins. Ben and Ted Tamney were the sons of Lottie Morgan Tamney. Her husband, Vick Tamney, spent many years in Nevada and California prospecting for gold. Less commonly at the Home Place were Jack and Bill Rea, sons of Georgie who lived in Cheyenne. Onie's father, Billie Morgan, died in 1912, so our grandparents also helped raise Onie's youngest two brothers, Chester and Lewis Morgan. Oliver also helped Onie's mother, Sarah, to care for her cattle.

Leonard, George, Alfred, and Sinc going from hats on to hats off. Well... except for Alfred.

Stories the Boys told of their youth might well have qualified them for a reputation of "juvenile delinquents" in their time, but none of their escapades

The "Boys," the Aunts, and the Cousins / 51

or pranks could be described as having any nefarious purpose—only the "No fool. No fun" intent.

As children and teenagers, the foolishness was evident. Sinc, for example, when his mother was away on horseback, once shaved the tops of the heads of all of his younger brothers such that they all resembled little bald-headed men. At another time, Grandma was not happy with Sinc when she noticed out the window that he had tied a rope to the end of a quilt (quite likely one she had made), encouraged all his younger brothers to get on the quilt, and then pulled them around and around the house on his horse.

As the Boys got older, they became more and more proficient at making and using slingshots with rubber bands to the point that they set a forked cedar post in the ground up on the hill, used an old rubber inner tube for the elastic, and fired a six-inch rock through the roof of the horse barn.

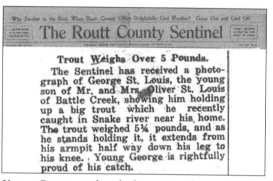

The Routt County Sentinel

Trout Weighs Over 5 Pounds.
The Sentinel has received a photograph of George St. Louis, the young son of Mr. and Mrs. Oliver St. Louis of Battle Creek, showing him holding up a big trout which he recently caught in Snake river near his home. The trout weighed 5¼ pounds, and as he stands holding it, it extends from his armpit half way down his leg to his knee. Young George is rightfully proud of his catch.

Young George catches the largest Cutthroat Native Trout anyone remembers with a grasshopper.

Dad remembered that he and a brother, wanting to fire a large gauge shotgun that apparently had a strong kick, decided to pile weights on it. It is not clear from the story how it happened, but they apparently blew the gun apart when they pulled the trigger with a string. Little explosions were commonplace, as when firecrackers were set off in the excrement below one of the outhouses when a brother was using it.

Farm animals were involved in their shenanigans as well. For example, the rooster at the top of the pecking order would be caught, doused in the river to change its appearance, and then turned loose with the backyard flock to watch the other roosters fight the "newcomer."

As they matured and had more social interactions, stories emerged of being discovered rolling in the hay (literally) and sliding off the Lemmon's grade and nearly into the river while driving home drunk from a New Year's dance in Dixon. As children and teenagers, we witnessed them demonstrating semi-gymnastic maneuvers on the steel support bars that crossed the local Pep Hall (most likely to show off for the Focus Ranch dudes) and getting into whiskey-motivated scuffles or fights outside the dance hall, or even a post wedding "Shiveree."

As noted, the St. Louis brothers were known for fighting. Whether entirely true or not, they claimed that they never started a fight. However, they were proud that they never walked away from a fight. A more accurate interpretation might be that the Boys were often spoiling for a fight, and stories abound about these occasions. One of them took place after the yearly trailing of their cattle to Steamboat in the fall to load them on the train for shipment to the stockyards in Denver. Dad confided that they made their presence known in Steamboat by lowering their spurs so that the rowels at the back would click or ring on the sidewalk as they strode down the street. On one such occasion, someone reacted to their presence (perhaps to say something negative about Alfred, who appeared stunted compared to his brothers and also not as sharp mentally). After a few words, Dad hit the "big son-of-a-bitch" with a right cross so hard that his feet came up and the first thing to hit the sidewalk was the back of his head. The man was unconscious long enough that Dad thought he might have killed the man. On another occasion, details of which are unknown, the Encampment, Wyoming, summer rodeo was paused while Francis single-handedly "whipped" several brothers

Not the expected way to ride a bucking cow. Maybe she got up too fast.

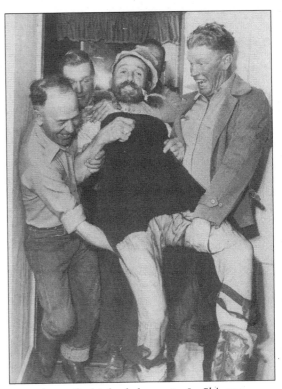

No strippers for his bachelor party. In Shiveree tradition, this new groom is about to be thrown into the river.

from another family in front of the bucking chutes. Once, at a dance in Hahns Peak, most likely when Dad and Mom were courting, Dad was singing a solo while Mom chorded on the piano. Some rowdies from Steamboat who had come to the dance decided to howl during the singing, which reportedly Dad ignored. After the song, he was angry and walked toward them. They started to leave but Francis and possibly another brother blocked the door. After all

Oliver sparring with Francis using the Queensbury rules of boxing.

Flyer for a fight involving Perry followed by a dance in Craig.

of them received a serious St. Louis brother whipping, Dad reportedly stood one of them up to his feet and told him, "Now, if you ever hear me sing again, you just stand quiet and listen." Another version of the story resulted in their subsequently being thrown out of the dance hall.

They also like practical jokes. Dad was the butt of a series of them one night after he had taken his horse to court Mary Hartman. Upon returning, he first put his hand into a rat trap near the lantern in the horse barn. Next, he tripped over a wire strung low across the yard gate. Then, when he opened the door to the house, a box of tin cans fell all over the kitchen floor. And finally, he found a dressed up female mannequin in his bed.

And other infrequent occurrences, sure to happen on a working ranch, also were the subjects of "war" stories told and retold. Many involved horses. Dad tells of the time his horse was trotting up through the field when it stubbed its front hoof on a rock no larger than six inches high, then turned a complete somersault and landed on its back, balanced on the horn and cantle of the saddle. Dad crawled out one side, and the horse fell to the other.

He told of another time he mounted a skittish horse in the middle of the road behind the horse barn on a cold, wintery morning. Like some other horses, this one was most likely to buck early in the morning. He lit into bucking, but Dad got him turned straight up the steep bank such that he couldn't buck up the hill. Once up the bank the horse spun back around and bolted down the bank. When he hit the icy road, all four feet went out from under him, and the horse turned a 360. Dad ducked his head and inexplicably was not touched while he was still in the saddle when horse regained his feet.

George courting a young woman at the famous Fish Creek Falls bridge. We rarely saw him in dress slacks and never saw him wearing white shoes.

Perhaps the zaniest story involved a big red horse named Hornet that was prone to stampeding (running away). Dad had been delivering mail up to the Three Forks Ranch in the winter on this horse. As he was coming back, he tossed a packet of mail off at the Hartman Place, which spooked the horse. Hornet took off, and as Dad tried to stop him, the curb strap of the bridle broke. Wide open, the horse tore down around the icy Temple grade, sliding and slipping as he went around the curve. He raced down the straight grade, across the bridge over the Little Snake River, and around the sharp left at the Focus Ranch. Just as Hornet and Dad sped around the corner, workhorses, which Shorty Temple had moments before unharnessed and turned loose after feeding cattle, were crossing the road to an opening in the river ice for a drink. One of the workhorses kicked up with both hind feet at stampeding Hornet as they met in the middle of the road. Hornet ran his head between the workhorse's hind legs and came to a stop with the tail and rear end of the workhorse basically on the saddle horn right in Dad's face.

In spite of their tomfoolery, the St. Louis brothers were known to be loyal, helpful neighbors who would sacrifice their own comfort or safety to help out someone in need. Strong values that they lived and instilled in all those who came in contact with them were telling the truth, doing what is "right," and respecting women. They welcomed strangers to their homes, they returned strays to their rightful owners, they carried out search and rescue operations for lost or injured persons, and they participated in community efforts.

The "Boys," the Aunts, and the Cousins / 55

There were tragedies and unfortunate accidents as well. As noted, Oliver lost a finger to an infection resulting from sewing up a gunny (burlap) sack full of grain during threshing (we said "thrashing") of oats, wheat, or barley. He also sustained a serious broken left leg, which never healed properly, reportedly after being kicked by a horse. Several nonfatal automobile accidents occurred; one especially bad one happened to Francis, in which he broke his jaw and lost several teeth.

Perry at the age of 26, lost his left eye, which was replaced with a glass eye. There are several versions of what actually happened, so we cannot know for sure, but his daughter, Beverly, likely had the most accurate account. While the Boys were stacking loose hay, Perry was bucking hay from windrows with the two-horse buck rake. Unbeknownst to him, he also had scooped up a large rattlesnake with the hay. When he brought the load of hay to the overshot stacker, a hired worker, Beanie Jones, apparently saw the snake first. This would make sense because his job was to "drive the stacker" (with a team of horses, pull a cable laterally away from the stacker as it lifted the load of hay from the ground to be dumped on top of the stack). Upon seeing the rattler, he threw a pitchfork at the snake to kill it but missed. The fork bounced and pierced Perry squarely in the eye. Some verification of this account follows events at the Carbon County Fair many years later where Beverly had showed and was then selling a 4-H lamb in a sale ring auction. Perry apparently repeatedly tapped the knee of Beanie Jones, who sat close to him, indicating that he should raise the bid. Reportedly, the lamb sold at a surprisingly high price, and Perry confided to Beverly that this was "pay back" for losing his eye.

The hay rack on runners used every day in the winter for feeding the cattle. This time, with Perry, George, and Alfred (maybe), along with three young guests, they may be just going for a ride.

SINCLAIR (SINC) ST. LOUIS AND ELIZABETH (BETTY) ST. LOUIS

Sinc was the oldest of the Boys. Unlike most of his brothers, he played baseball with a team in Baggs, and he also played football and basketball in high school while in Steamboat. There, he boarded with Mr. and Mrs. Dan Fletcher. Sinc sang songs, but not nearly as often at public gatherings as his father, Oliver, and our dad. He did sometimes chord along with songs on the piano.

Sinc worked a time for a neighbor, George Salisbury Sr., and also worked for the railroad, most likely the Union Pacific in Wyoming. This might explain the epitaph on his gravestone, "Head for the roundhouse, Nellie. They can't corner you there." He homesteaded north of the Home Place for 160 acres. He also traveled to California and spent months harvesting giant redwood trees. Also, he learned to shear sheep, and as part of a shearing crew, spent numerous spring seasons in Wyoming shearing sheep with the scissor-like hand shears.

Sinc, Perry, and Francis logging redwoods in California.

He was the first to be married, but his marriage in 1938 to Lila Heikkila of Savery, Wyoming, lasted but a short time. After his divorce, he moved back to the Home Place.

He later met Elizabeth Miozzi when she was a summer guest at the Focus Ranch. She returned a year later as an employee, and their courtship continued. Sinc and Elizabeth, whom we always called Betty, married in June 1944 at an outdoor wedding in the sagebrush near a house, reportedly with a tree growing up through it, located between Slater and Encampment.

Sinc entertaining. Rita, Brett, Lexie, Sinc, and Lillyan.

Elizabeth was born in New York but had grown up in Italy. Her father, Mario Miozzi, was an Italian military attaché. He had come to New York for business but decided to improve his English by enlisting the help of Theresa Young, director of admissions at a law school. Theresa was later to become Elizabeth's grandmother. She was so impressed with this young man that she played the role of matchmaker between him and her daughter, Lillian, who was a journalist, author, and artist. After a very short courtship, Mario and Lillian were married and had Elizabeth. When Elizabeth was a year old, they traveled by steamship back to Italy, allegedly along with numerous horses and with many other Italians living in the US. The three lived in the city of Asalo in the province of Venice during Elizabeth's childhood. Although details are sketchy, they also spent some time in Genoa when Mario carried out some political/military service in Mussolini's fascist state. Lillian died when Elizabeth was 12. Her grandmother, Theresa, along with her aunt Dorothea (Dotty) Young came to Italy at that time, and Dotty took over as primary "mother" to Elizabeth. They moved to Florence and lived there until Theresa died. Elizabeth entered the Florence Academy of Fine Arts to study architecture.

During this period, Mario remarried with a relatively wealthy woman, Angela, who owned a Pensione (Pension) in Rome and little hotel on the Tyrrhenian Sea west of Rome in Fregene (Fregenae). Elizabeth lived in these two places during her teenage years. She continued her higher education in Rome in architecture where she reportedly earned a doctoral degree. She also studied painting. It was at this time in her life when she learned Equestrian style horseback riding and became an accomplished fencer. She mentioned that she would have competed for Italy in the 1940 Olympics had World War II not started with Mussolini's Italy as part of the Axis powers.

Elizabeth returned to the US as the War started and American citizens were recalled from Italy. At the same time, she had decided to move away from her stepmother and join her aunt Dotty in New York. It was there she saw a Gene Autry film and became enamored with the romance of the American West and ranch life, hence her vacations at dude ranches, first in Wyoming and then Colorado (namely, the Focus Ranch).

Elizabeth spoke Italian and English perfectly, was reasonably proficient in Spanish and French, and could get along in German. She loved languages, and later in life learned that she was quite proficient in Portuguese. She also studied and learned some Greek, Turkish, and Arabic.

It is not well known that Sinc originally sought to get to know Elizabeth to discover if she might be an Italian Nazi spy and perhaps be rewarded

Elizabeth feeding a foal from a bottle on the ranch.   *Elizabeth helping to move cattle on horseback.*

A column in the Yampa Valley College newspaper about Elizabeth's summer trip to Italy, Greece, and Crete.

monetarily for such knowledge. (Elizabeth later confided that she knew about this and found it quite amusing.)

After she and Sinc were married, they had two daughters, Lillyan Shirley St. Louis Walter and Alexandra (Lexie) St. Louis Siegal, almost two years different in age. Initially, they lived in the Bunkhouse at the Home Place, whereupon they moved to Craig for a number of years. During that time, Sinc worked at his local bar and club on the west side of town known as Signal Hill (co-owned by his uncle of the same age, Lewis Morgan, and Bruce Castine). Sinc spent a short time in jail, followed by a period of probation, after having been convicted of driving under the influence of liquor in an

The "Boys," the Aunts, and the Cousins / 59

Sinc and Elizabeth with their two daughters, Lillyan and Lexie.

Lillyan, Elizabeth, and Lexie.

Sinc and Elizabeth's house from the road cleared of snow.

automobile accident in which a person died. Later, they moved back to the Home Place. They started building the house at the Bryson Place, eventually finished by Perry and Grace, but several years later, they built a new red frame house next to the river below and to the east of the outbuildings and corrals of the Home Place. Sinc was the only son not to be given a later parcel acquired by their father; instead, he inherited the Home Place of about 3000 acres. Sinc registered "US Two Bar" as the brand for his cattle and "Reverse L S L" for Lillyan's and Lexie's livestock. Later, this brand was acquired by Leonard, and subsequently transferred to his daughter, Kathy.

Rita played with Lillyan and Lexie most of several summers. Mom and Elizabeth became close friends. And, as with the other Boys, David and I had frequent interactions with Sinc doing ranch work.

For one year, Elizabeth moved with the children to Silt, Colorado, to teach fifth grade. Elizabeth, Lillyan, and Lexie then spent one year in Eureka, California, followed by two years in Craig. Elizabeth then purchased a house in Steamboat Springs. She helped start the first college in Steamboat, Yampa Valley College, where she worked full time and taught courses in art history, Italian, Spanish and French. For many of these later years, Sinc and Elizabeth were separated. They divorced in 1969. After retiring from work due primarily to serious rheumatoid arthritis, Elizabeth lived mostly in her house in Steamboat until her death in 1999.

After selling the ranch in 1963, Sinc worked variously in Arizona and Craig. He continued to raise some cattle. Very shortly after his divorce from Elizabeth, he married Deloris Marie Adamek from Craig and then moved to her home to help manage her floral business. He lived there until his death.

ALFRED ST. LOUIS

Second born, Alfred was the only St. Louis brother to remain a bachelor throughout his life. He was much shorter than the others, about five feet two inches in height, with small feet and hands. Additionally, he was not as smart as his brothers, struggling more in elementary school and not attending high school. No doubt part of the reason was that

Sinc with Deloris.

he had very poor eyesight, and before getting glasses, he could barely make out what was written on the blackboard in school. This arguably was a main reason he was regarded as a slow learner. The family did care for and protect Alfred, as in standing up to anyone who might bully him and always including him in family activities. In actuality, however, they were likely overprotective, believing that there were many things he could not do, such as learning to drive a car or a tractor. It was for that reason that Alfred always waited for someone to take him to town, to one of the bars "down the River" in Dixon or Baggs, to visit various people who lived further than the few miles he could reach on his horse, or on long trips. It is interesting that after his father died and his mother was unable to advise him, he learned to drive a tractor in just a few days.

Alfred did have his own cattle, run with his father's herd, with the brand "Slash AL." He participated in all the cattle roundups and drives, although in our memory, his role in branding calves was usually relegated to helping Sinc "mother up" calves before roping them and dragging them to be branded, dehorned, castrated, and vaccinated, although he sometimes assisted in the more strenuous "flanking" of calves and holding them down.

Riding to check cattle in the summer often required all-day rides. Alfred knew most of the Mexican sheep herders in the area and which sheep wagons he could stop by for a free noon dinner.

Alfred became famous in our family for the dead serious—yet humorous—things he said. Some of them were off-the-cuff comments; others were

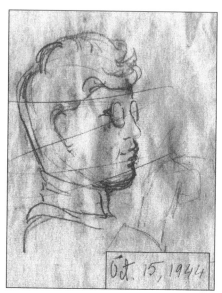

Oct. 15, 1944

Sketch of Alfred by Elizabeth St. Louis in 1944.

Alfred at home with Grandma after Grandpa died.

pontifications he was prone to make in a deep and authoritative voice while intoxicated. Perhaps the most widely quoted of the latter litany of "Alfred sayings" was "I've been more places than you've ever been. I've seen things you've never seen. No matter how drunk you get, that Los Angeles (or that Pacific Ocean) will sober you up." Or, of the casual comments, when asked by Sinc which cow was the mother of a calf he had roped for branding, Alfred pointed with a curved index finger in the general direction of perhaps 50 Hereford cows and said, "No by God, the one with the white face." (Of course, they all had white faces.) Or the time he told Elizabeth that he knew Latin, and when she asked him to say something, he said, "Washa disha Iya willa." Another story that she laughed about was a time when several of the Boys and she were sitting on their horses in a circle and talking about where they would go next. At least one of the men had a leg slung over the saddle horn to the same side as the other leg in the stirrup. It was a hot day, and deer flies and horse flies were everywhere. During a long, quiet pause, Alfred suddenly pointed to one horse fly and blurted out, "Look at that fly!"

Perhaps also because he was overprotected, Alfred did not learn to control his drinking. All six Boys were known to drink to excess; yet, more than once, when driven to the Dixon Club or the Bank Club Bar in Baggs, he would sit on the bar stool and drink until he fell off onto the floor.

Alfred had a soft spot for his nieces and nephews. We all received a card and a dollar on our birthdays. He also pored over the Montgomery Ward catalog each December to pick out clothes for nieces and told Grandma what to buy them for Christmas. Nevertheless, he was sometimes quite cross with us. We often played in the haylofts of the horse barn and cow barn, much to his chagrin. He did not like us making tunnels in the loose hay or making forts or houses out of the bales, and if he caught us (which I don't recall that he ever did), he warned that he would "tan our hides."

When Onie became unable to manage at the Home Place, she and Alfred spent one year in Baggs. After that, they both moved to Craig, Onie to live with Sinc and Deloris, and Alfred to the Baker House (hotel). Alfred lived there for three years, spending winters at Sharon and Steve Andrew's ranch in Maybell, Colorado. Later, he rented a new senior apartment (Sunset Meadows) affiliated with the Senior Citizen Center. He died in 1982.

GEORGE ST. LOUIS AND DOROTHY GRACE (DOT) ST. LOUIS

Dad was third born. He had long wavy blond hair and was the most popular entertainer of the clan. Like his father, he sang songs a cappella at family gatherings, dances, and any other occasion someone might want him to sing. He was famous for his vocal renditions of "She Never Came Back," "Punchin' the Dough," "Sirry (Sierra) Peaks," and "Ain't We Crazy." He also picked up his father's spoken renditions of "Persian Kitty" and "Skunk Polecat." He often "called" square dances (or gave the instructions for the complex movements of the four couples). Unlike those who sang their "calls," Dad would shout his instructions over the music. He also played the harmonica on occasion.

Dad learned to box with his brothers and was typically in the middle of most Saturday night fist fights. He mostly lived at home until he was 37 years old. He acquired the George Fleming Place next to Beaver Mountain

Our "Slash Diamond Slash" brand carved into a quaker below David's brand, "VD Bar."

Looks like George is showing off a beautiful work horse named Rex.

The "Boys," the Aunts, and the Cousins / 63

south of the Home Place as his ranch to operate, either by paying his father a low purchase price or as a gift. His brand was "Slash Diamond Slash."

Dad's future wife, Dorothy Grace Ireland (Mom), was born in Sedgwick and had attended school in numerous places on the prairie in northeastern Colorado. She completed high school in Steamboat Springs while boarding with the Hubbard family in exchange for housekeeping. After graduating, she worked two summers for Lucy and Shorty Temple at the Focus Ranch as the cook and housekeeper for the paying guests or dudes. It was there that she met George. After a half-year courtship, they were married in 1941. We were their three children, David, Rita, and I. Chapter 7, "Dad and Mom" provides a great deal more detail.

Francis St. Louis and Agnes St. Louis Russell

Francis was one year younger than Dad, and they were very close as children and youth. They attended high school together in Cheyenne, Wyoming, boarding with their aunt Georgie Rea. As noted, Dad had repeated the first grade twice at the Willow Creek School near the Home Place. This and other "adjustments" we cannot know resulted in Francis and Dad finishing elementary school in the same year.

Francis was no doubt the physically strongest of the brothers, being able to chin himself with either hand at least ten times. He was also reportedly the toughest in the boxing ring, being able to take a punch without faltering. Had he not been in a serious automobile accident that knocked out teeth and broke his jaw, his brothers speculated that he might have become a professional prizefighter.

Francis learned to play the piano by ear and also played the violin. He would often fiddle to square dancing tunes played by Gretchen Hancock or another local pianist while George did the "calling."

Like Sinc, Francis worked for several months in the redwoods of California. He also worked briefly in Cheyenne for the Union Pacific Railroad at the roundhouse and in Denver at a business that made fishhooks. Upon returning to the Home Place, his brand was "F Slash L."

His future wife, Agnes Caswell, was born in Upton, Wyoming, and was reared in Spearfish, South Dakota. She attended the Black Hills Normal School and Teacher's College as well as the University of Wyoming, earning a degree in education. Agnes first taught school in South Dakota for two years, then in Florence, Colorado, for one year, and then did not work for a year. Thereafter, in 1938, she successfully followed up on an advertisement to come to the Little Snake River and teach at the Battle Creek School, where she taught for two years. It was there that she met Francis. They were married in 1940 and had three children, Sharon Lou St. Louis Andrew, a son who died shortly after birth, and Joyce Ellen St. Louis Miranda. The daughters were six and a half years apart.

Regardless of Francis's earlier automobile accident, Agnes reportedly had no interest in his pursuing a boxing career. After they married, Francis worked the Hartman Place and, later, bought the Hackmaster Place from his father, which was up the river from the Home Place just west of the Honnold Place. They moved the original Hackmaster house from the mesa down to a

Francis and Agnes at the time of their wedding, 1940.

location next to Cottonwood Creek in 1947. After a renovation, the family moved into the new house in 1950. Francis added a barn, and corral. Tragically, one night in May 1951, as Francis was driving home on his Ford tractor, with no lights, the tractor went off the narrow road cut into the hillside and upset directly on top of him in a ditch below. His untimely death at the age of 43 meant that the family could not continue to work the ranch. Dad helped maintain the Hackmaster Place for Agnes during the irrigating and haying seasons for about six years while Bruce McAllister lived in the house and fed the cattle in the winters. As I got older, I was heavily involved with the irrigating and haying.

Agnes, Sharon, and Joyce moved to Craig for the winter of 1951–1952, where the girls attended school. At the end of December, on Christmas Day when David's accident occurred (explained in Chapter 12), they returned to the River to stay with Rita and me while Dad and Mom were in Denver at the hospital with David. This lasted three to four weeks.

In the fall of 1952, Agnes was hired to teach school in Wamsutter, Wyoming, for three years and then in Craig for one year. While they were in Wamsutter, we had considerable interaction with Sharon and Joyce partly because Dad had arranged to winter our band of sheep nearby in Red

Desert. Additionally, he and his uncle Lewis Morgan hired a local pilot, Carl Baker, to "run" wild horses into a trap in a dry gully in that area. After trapping a number of horses, they would haul them in a flatbed truck to a corral in Wamsutter. As explained in Chapter 9, most were sold for slaughter, but the best ones were kept or sold for ranch horses.

Later, Agnes married Forrest (Mike) Russell and moved onto his ranch on the north side of the river west of Dixon, Wyoming. After many years, they moved to a new house in Dixon.

Agnes was always a warm, helpful person for us. She had many interests, including sewing and other crafts. She became an accomplished quilter. Yet, because Francis died when we were so young, we did not have the benefit of years of experience with him as we did with his brothers as we grew up. On the other hand, we came to know the Russell brothers well, especially Mike and Harry. Mike worked extremely hard, milking at least five cows by hand twice a day in his ranching years. In partial retirement in Dixon he maintained a marvelous vegetable garden and was known for custom, inlaid woodwork.

After Mike became so frail that he lived, and in 2001 died, in a nursing home in Meeker, Agnes moved to an apartment in Craig and lived there until her death in 2007.

PERRY ST. LOUIS AND GRACE ST. LOUIS

Perry was the fifth brother. He, like Sinc, Dad, and Francis, completed high school, boarding in Cheyenne with Aunt Georgie. And like Francis, Perry was an accomplished boxer in the ring. Perry was not a singer, but he was the family percussionist. He set up his drum set and added to the music the bass and snare drums along with cymbals. He also accompanied dance

Mike and Agnes in Dixon.

Agnes feeding her chickens.

Perry at the time of his high school graduation in Cheyenne.

Wedding portrait of Perry and Grace.

tunes with his "bones," or beef ribs cut about six inches in length such that a pair in hands could generate complex rhythms with deft rotations of each wrist, accentuating the clicking and clacking with wild upper body and arm gesticulations. Later, these were replaced by wooden "bones" made of ebony. Or he did the same things with spoons. He was also known for his seemingly endless supply of funny stories and jokes. And, like Sinc and Francis, he worked for several months in the redwoods of California.

Shortly after Grace Burkardt was born in Illinois in 1909, the family moved to Odebolt, Iowa, near her maternal Auchstetter grandparents. There, she attended elementary school. Later, the family moved to a farm near Parkston, South Dakota, where Grace finished elementary school and graduated from high school. At the age of 17, against her father's wishes but with the financial help of two unmarried aunts who were nurses, Grace enrolled at Iowa State Teachers' College (now the University of Northern Iowa) in Cedar Rapids. In three years without going home, she received a bachelor's degree in English with a teaching credential. After graduation, she returned to live at the Parkston family farm for two years while teaching elementary school at a nearby one-room school. Grace's parents divorced, and, with the help of Auchstetter sisters, her mother bought a farm near

Perry holding baby Jean at the Home Place.

Perry and Grace's ranch in winter.

Holstein, Iowa, about 50 miles east of Sioux City and moved there with her other four children. For her part, Grace was intrigued with going further west and, thus, responded to an ad for a teacher in Savery, Wyoming. With her brother, Paul, and a boyfriend named Frank, she drove to Savery, Wyoming, for the school year that began in 1931. The men returned to Iowa, and Frank was no longer in her life. Initially, Grace lived with the Logans, who lived across the road from the Savery School where her husband, Johnnie, was employed as custodian. Later she moved down the street to rent a room at the home of Nell Gooldy.

At one point during her eight years in Savery, Grace drove to see a fire that had erupted on Battle Mountain. This is where she met Perry, who had come to check on her landlady. After a courtship, they married in 1939. Immediately after their wedding, Perry worked for United Airlines for about one year, first in Cheyenne, Wyoming, and then by transfer to Oakland, California. They returned to live with Oliver and Onie in the Home Place for two years. In 1940, Grace traveled back to Iowa to stay temporarily with her nurse-trained aunts in order to deliver her first daughter, Jean Alberta, in Sioux City. Shirley Marie was born 14 months later in Craig, Colorado. Thereafter, Perry then took a one-and-a-half-year job working for Harry Laramore south of Rawlins on a ranch called LaMarsh. Following that, they again moved back to Snake River, to the Grieves Place about three miles east of Slater. During their three years there, Beverly Ann was born in Hayden, Colorado. Jean rode horseback to attend Battle Creek School for her first grade.

The family then moved back in with Oliver and Onie for the second time while waiting for their house, earlier started by Sinc and Elizabeth, to be finished about a half-mile west. Perry and Grace had acquired the adjacent Bryson and John X. Turner Places. Perry finished the two-story log house, barn, outbuildings, and corrals. At their ranch there, the family raised cattle and some 4-H sheep under the brand "J Slash Horseshoe."

Perry's life too was cut short in 1962 by a tragic head-on collision with an eighteen-wheeler near Baggs. Jean and her first husband, Don Ely, continued the ranching operation there and, currently, their son, Grady Ely, owns and manages the now-expanded ranch.

After an eight-year break from teaching, Grace taught at the one-room Willow Creek School, about one mile east of their ranch, for five years, beginning in 1951. She then taught one year in Craig and then three years at the one-room Battle Creek School until it closed in 1962. Next, she taught full-time for seven years at Savery and then four years in Baggs, where she had bought a house and moved. After mandatory retirement at the age of 65, she proceeded to substitute teach in Baggs for another ten years, followed by eight years more of tutoring students in her home. In her late 80s and early 90s she spent several winters in California with Shirley and intermittent time with Beverly. At age 94, she moved to a private assisted living home in Craig until her death in 2007.

LEONARD ST. LOUIS AND DORIS ST. LOUIS

Youngest of the six Boys, Leonard also boarded with with Aunt Georgie, for high school. By this time, she and her family had moved to, Nebraska. He married a local girl, Doris Honnold, who was actually his third cousin. She had attended Colorado Teachers College in Greeley, Colorado, and returned to Craig to teach elementary school. They did not live with Oliver and Onie but moved to Bakersfield, California, and had one daughter, Kathy Ann St. Louis Russell Ward, after losing a daughter, Kay Lynn, shortly after birth. The family first moved to Oakland, California, where Ted Tamney lived, so that Leonard could train in the tool and die trade. They had hoped to return to Laramie for work there, but that option did not work out. Instead, Leonard accepted a position with Lockheed Aircraft in the Los Angeles area during World War II. Following that job, he worked for Coca Cola Bottling Company and then for Frito-Lay. Subsequently, they moved to Bakersfield from Burbank in 1951. Leonard spent the rest of his employment years with the Sperry-Hutchinson Company (S & H Green

Doris, Kathy, and Leonard getting ready for a ride at a yearly visit to the Home Place.

Stamps) until retirement in 1975. Although Doris was trained as a teacher, she remained a homemaker.

Even though they lived far away, Leonard, Doris, and Kathy drove the thousand miles back to the Home Place nearly every year during our childhood. Every visit involved at least one big family dinner together at Oliver and Onie's house. In later years, it always involved horseback riding for fun or for work. Otherwise, we had little contact with the Leonard St. Louis part of the family and were therefore minimally influenced by them as children.

Leonard, too, liked to sing, especially a harmony line to George's lead. He was known to have strong opinions and shared his "outside" perspectives on the news with the St. Louis clan every year. From his contacts in Bakersfield, various businessmen and professional persons came to the Little Snake River for fishing in the summer and deer and/or elk hunting in the fall. They were variously guided by Sinc and Dad. In fact, it was through one of these contacts, that I received my first speech therapy experience (See Chapter 12).

Upon Leonard's retirement, he and Doris moved back to the River and built a new log home at the site of the old house at the Hartman Place. They lived there until they moved to Grand Junction for their final years. Leonard passed away in 2004, and Doris, in 2005.

MEMORIES

SINC

David: I drove the side delivery rake most of the summer while haying and Sinc pulled the baler. Many of the hay fields had small tributaries or watersheds coming

St. Louis Cousins

All St. Louis cousins at the Home Place. Back: Sharon, Jean, Shirley, Kenneth, and David; middle: Joyce, Kathy, and Lexie; front: Beverly, Rita, and Lillyan.

Singing "Put on your old grey bonnet..." at Grandpa and Grandma's 50th wedding anniversary. Rita, David, Shirley, Jean, Sharon, Kenneth, and Beverly.

McCargar Reunion, 1976. Back: Kenneth St. Louis, Don Ely, Jean Ely, Fred Runnion, George St. Louis, Grace St. Louis, Leonard St. Louis, Doris, and Steve Andrew; middle: Karen St. Louis holding Melinda St. Louis, Shirley Ely, Beverly Runnion Rave, Alfred St. Louis, Shirley Schultz, Carrie Andrew, Kirsten Andrew, and Sharon Andrew; front: Shana Ely, Vickie Runnion, Jona Ely, Grady Ely, and Julie Andrew.

Cousins at Steamboat in early 1980s. Back: Sharon, Jean, Kenneth, and David; front: Joyce, Rita, Lexie, Lillyan, and Kathy.

Cousins celebrating George St. Louis's 80th birthday in Savery. Back: Jean, Shirley, Sharon, David, and Kenneth; front: Lexie, Beverly, Rita, and Lillyan.

Cousins at Grand Junction, Colorado, 1994. Back: Lillyan, Joyce, Sharon, Beverly, and Lexie; front: David, Rita, Kathy, Jean, and Kenneth.

Cousins at Mack, Colorado, 2012. Back: Sharon, Beverly, Kenneth, Lexie, and Jean; front: Rita, Joyce, Kathy, and David.

We often sing when we get together and with our cousins.

Cousins at the reunion in Quebec, 2018. Back: Beverly, David, Kenneth, and Dwight St-Louis; second: Lexie, and Maria Ann St-Louis Templeton; third: Shirley, Rita, and Anita St-Louis Miller; front: Julie Andrew, Sharon, Jean, and Joyce.

in from the side, and the rake typically worked clockwise around the field progressing from the periphery to the middle. The first two rounds with the side delivery rake had to be made counterclockwise to pull the hay in from the field edges; then the third round was clockwise to make a triple windrow and to make space for the next windrow. Ordinarily, the baler would need to go counterclockwise around the field. The first round was always the hardest to bale because it contained a triple row of hay, and the tractor had to be run clockwise to stay out of the rest of the hay. So, when Sinc came to the small tributaries, he sometimes had to make a sharp left turn. Often the spots were in low, wet places with heavier hay that could clog the baler. These places could easily cause the "power take off" (PTO) shaft giving the baler power to break. One day, he blew up at me for the way I had raked the hay on the first round. I was afraid, but didn't know what to do to fix the problem. I later figured out how to make the windrows swing out wide at these corners, even though four to five rows were combined. After that, Sinc later said I was the best raker he had. I wished he hadn't mentioned that because I got very tired of raking.

David: One time we were gathering cattle and one old cow wouldn't come out of the willows in Willow Creek. Sinc called me to help him because he had been going around and around, back and forth, and the cow kept going back into the willows. He probably had the hottest temper of all the Boys and was hollering and cussing a blue streak. The only way he could get the cow out of the willows was to go in after her on his horse. Sinc charged into the willows, and I heard the cussing even louder than before. Directly on the other side of the willows that the horse had run through was a five-foot bank drop off into Willow Creek. When I went to see what was wrong, there stood Sinc, soaking wet, standing in the water, with his hat and glasses missing. His horse was standing down the stream a ways. Still cussing a blue streak, he ran for his hat floating away and then went back to look for his glasses in the bottom of the creek. I knew I could not say a word. He later told the story of what happened, but it was not nearly as funny as what I saw.

Kenneth: Sinc was always "there" with the Boys in my memory. I knew he was a good rider, a good roper, and good with about any piece of machinery used on the ranch. I was impressed with his ability to sharpen sheep shears and all his knives (no doubt learned from his years of shearing).

Kenneth: I remember Sinc as a no-nonsense man, but, in retrospect, I think he wanted and expected to be in charge. I liked him, but I don't think we talked much. He always appreciated the fact that I could work hard in the hayfield. Elizabeth told me once that he very rarely complimented anyone but had mentioned to her that

"Kenneth is a 'live hand' in the hayfield." I remember about that time that he was appalled and furious that a hired hay hand, Owen Fett, who was about six feet six inches tall, muscular, and about 220 pounds, was driving the slip to pick up bales and I, five feet eight inches and 120 pounds, was loading the slip with 80-pound bales and then stacking them while he loaded the elevator.

Rita: I remember Sinc as a hard worker, but he lacked the patience that Daddy had with us kids. Whether we were riding or doing other things, he would yell at us a lot if we did not do things as he thought we should. Because he was probably the best roper, he was the person who roped the calves during branding.

Sinc was famous for his Dutch-oven biscuits.

Rita: I, too, remember that Sinc was a master at sharpening sheep shears, so we always had him sharpen ours. He also kept all of his knives really sharp, a skill that my genes don't seem to have.

Rita: One winter, Sinc and some others had gone to get an elk for meat near Three Forks. They had killed an elk and then dragged him with a horse through the snow across the road to the barn leaving a clear trail. Dallas Morgan, the game warden, came by, saw the bloody trail in the snow, and easily followed it to the barn to confront the culprits. Sinc apparently told him, "The only good game warden is a dead game warden." This and the poached elk cost him a thousand-dollar fine.

ELIZABETH

David: After their trip to Italy, Lillyan and Lexie were always telling how good pizza was. I had never had pizza, and one day while I was at their house, Elizabeth's made it. Everyone raved about how good it was, but I didn't like it. It was something new and had lots of oil on it. I'm sure I would like it now.

Kenneth: I always felt a special bond with Elizabeth. She apparently cared for me in ways that were not the same for all my cousins. She was the one who told me some of the few things I know about my first few years of life, more so than Mom in many ways. She said she thought I was a beautiful baby. (I was told that I looked like the Gerber baby on the baby food jars.) But when I got older, she said she really did not like me so much until I was perhaps in high school because I had somehow "hardened" in the elementary and junior high years. Later in life, although we did not spend much time together, we had a very special bond.

Kenneth: Elizabeth affected the trajectory of my life in so many ways. She regaled us with stories from Rome, and I remember looking at photographs of the Coliseum, fountains, and buildings with marble edifices. "Italy" was my fairytale place of splendor. I believe it was from her that we heard about Yma Sumac, a famous Peruvian soprano whose vocal range was four and a half octaves, and for whom we bought 33 rpm records for hours of listening and memorizing. With absolute certainty, I can trace my interest in learning another language, wanting to experience another culture, and becoming a global citizen to Elizabeth.

Kenneth: I remember that she always spoke perfect English. She would not tolerate swearing in her presence, even though I had acquired a bad habit of swearing frequently (and the habit has persisted, unfortunately).

Kenneth: Although I never said anything to her during my "hardened" years, I regret that I took the sides of my dad and uncles in at least feeling critical of Elizabeth for her "different" ways. Some of these were her abhorrence of unnecessary killing of animals (even mice), her summer sun bathing (which would make your skin "leathery"), and even occasional skinny dipping in the river.

Kenneth: I have held Elizabeth up as a role model for how I would like to deal with a serious illness. Her rheumatoid arthritis became severe and debilitating. She seemed to me to handle it with more grace than I could (and still can) imagine. I feel especially blessed that I shared her last good day (confirmed by Lexie) one day in Steamboat shortly before she had to go to Arizona, where she eventually died.

Rita: Elizabeth was my "second mother." I spent many hours at her house because I played a lot with Lillyan and Lexie. We called her Betty then. She was always quietly amused as she listened to our childhood games; she offered wisdom that I did not even realize was "wisdom" at the time; she introduced us to art, classical music, and good books. I remember she had a complete set of Encyclopaedia Britannica, which was pretty unheard of in those days.

Rita: Elizabeth taught at the Willow Creek School when I was in fifth grade. What a great teacher she was! We, of course, followed the curriculum, but on nice days during recess when we were playing in the willows or on the rocks, she would let us continue and not call us in to lessons for an hour or more. At Christmastime we made a crèche of construction paper, clay, and cotton balls (sheep). We invited Lucy Temple to see it, and I remember Elizabeth served pecan sandy cookies and a beverage. We felt so special to have a guest come see our creation. Interestingly, the day of the show, we had to hustle and make more cotton sheep because the mice had carried away the original ones during the night.

The "Boys," the Aunts, and the Cousins / 75

Rita: In later years, I loved Elizabeth even more. She was always loving and caring, and she really seemed to understand teenage girls. I was always comfortable around her. In later years she was even a more important confidant to me. In retrospect, I hold her in even higher esteem because she suffered tremendously from arthritis. Unfortunately, some of the St. Louis relatives thought she just needed to gut it out and not be such a "woosy." But truly, she suffered a lot, and I do not remember her complaining.

LILLYAN

David: Lillyan was the easiest of the cousins to con into anything. One day, I dug a hole in the dirt about the size of a teacup in the darkest area just inside our wood-shed. I put some fresh cow manure in the hole, and I told Lillyan, "Whatever you do, don't go in the woodshed. Don't go over to that hole and put your finger in there." That's exactly what she did, and then she was mad as hell because I had tricked her.

David: Another time, when Rita reminded me that we were playing bride and groom, I fed Lillyan some little pellets of sheep manure.

Kenneth: I was closest in age to Lillyan than to all the other St. Louis first cousins. Nevertheless, she was much closer to Rita than to me. Since they played together so much, with our houses only a half mile apart, and since Mom became close friends with Elizabeth, I spent a lot of time with Lillyan as a kid. She enjoyed teasing me, by doing or saying anything that might get a protest from me. As a result, we fought a lot. I suspect our mothers would not leave us alone together very much for that reason.

Kenneth: I did not accept the fact that Lillyan, like her mother, did not accept "normal" killing of pests, such as ground squirrels, skunks, or mice. Nor did I accept Rita, Lillyan, and Lexie dressing up their horses or bum lambs with makeup and rib-bons. So, of course, these were opportunities for more disagreements or fights. One fight I remember, but not the reason for it, was while ice skating near their house in the river. She hit me with the blade of her skate.

Kenneth: Even so, I was always interested in the stories Lillyan brought back from their trips to Oregon or to Italy. In high school, we "made up" and became good friends. I always enjoyed visiting Lillyan and Lexie at their home in Steamboat when I came back from college.

Kenneth: And as adults, we shared many good times together at Lillyan and Stan's home in Denver, while Melinda got to know Sara and Cameron. After that, we drifted apart and were somewhat estranged. But working together on this book has rekindled our friendship.

Rita: Lillyan was my very best friend as we grew up. We played endlessly and spent every day together that we could muster. Lillyan read a lot so she had the "knowledge" about princes, princesses, Robin Hood, and many of the medieval people we pretended to be. I have a special picture in my mind when Lillyan was about 15 years old. She had her hair cut into a butch haircut, and it seems that she laughed most of the summer.

Kenneth and Lillyan. At least we got along for this pose.

Rita: The Little Snake River was shallow in the summertime, and perfectly safe to play in. In fact, there were only two or three real swimming holes that we knew of. Between my seventh and eighth grades in school, we would ride our horses bareback about four miles to the swimming hole near the Hackmaster Place. We would shed our clothes, take the horses in to wash them off, then as they were drying, we would swim ourselves. We always took swimming suits "in case" someone else was there.

One day we were on our way to the swimming hole we saw someone walking in the meadow beyond the irrigation ditch. Of course, we could not ride up like civilized people, so we went tearing across the meadow as fast as our horses could run to see the person. I was in the lead on our horse named June; she raced toward him, jumped the ditch, and stopped. I went sailing over her head and landed right at his feet. I was so embarrassed. It turned out to be John Chandler whom we had all met at a dance the night before. We invited him to swim with us, so he rode double with one of us to the swimming hole. I remember Lillyan's doing a summersault under the water and coming up to do a giant belch about six inches from John's face. I also remember on our way home, I decided to go up onto the mesa to collect our milk cow that we had taken to a bull to be bred. Lillyan and Lexie went home, but John asked whether he could ride double and go with me. I said he could, and I remember it took longer than I had anticipated, and it was getting pretty dark by the time I found the cow and drove her home. Daddy was all in a tizzy, and he had Sinc and Shorty all worked up because the honor of his daughter was at stake with this dude guy.

Rita: I was around 14 or 15 when Lillyan, Lexie and I were discovering boys, but we still spent a lot of time pretending that we were Indians as we rode our horses.

The "Boys," the Aunts, and the Cousins / 77

We were riding bareback as usual—I remember I was on our big buckskin mare, Queen—and we had ourselves and our horses all decorated with cattails. We pretended to be the "Calattiyat" Indians. We were across the river from our house headed upriver toward the Focus, when we encountered three of the young dudes, Bob Chandler and two cute little red headed girls taking an afternoon ride. Again, we could never let an opportunity go by to impress the dudes with our riding prowess, so we told them that we were from the Calattiyat Indians and would like to take the three of them to our tribe who especially liked red heads. We asked them to come with us. Most of the details are murky, but I do remember Bob's being a bit apprehensive, and he would not ride into the willows with us because he said his horse was scared of the willows. In truth, he just did not trust what we would do to him. At one point, Queen was galloping along, and some willows got caught between my legs and her, and she just ran right out from under me. The game wore on, and at one point we ended up inside the Hartman Barn where we either tied Bob to a post or locked him in (most likely the latter because I don't know how we would have had a rope) and left him and took the girls back to the Focus before we returned to release him.

LEXIE

David: Lexie had a little black garter snake that was not wild and she could pick up. She called it her pet. She would go get it from time-to-time out by their porch and show it to us. She would pick it up and play with it and even kiss it.

Kenneth: Lexie was about three years younger than I, and that, in childhood, is a big difference. For that reason, I don't think I had much of any interaction with Lexie alone during our youth at the ranch. Most of our interactions occurred with Lillyan, Lexie, and Rita or at school (See Chapter 10).

Kenneth: As with Lillyan, I became much closer to Lexie when they lived in Steamboat, after I had graduated from high school. We enjoyed a number of afternoons at Elizabeth's house or evenings at bars during college vacations.

Kenneth: As adults, we have continued numerous positive interactions at family reunions, funerals, and visits to Lexie's condo, Steve's hangar, or our cabin near Steamboat. I really like Lexie's energy. We disagree politically, but it never seems to get in the way of good times. Lexie has also been especially supportive of my professional work.

Rita: I was close to Lexie growing up mostly because she was Lillyan's sister. Nevertheless, we had countless good times together. During high school we did more together because she and I both sang in trio and triple trio.

Rita: When we would ice skate on the river close to Lillyan and Lexie's, we would play "Crack the whip" on the ice. Whoever was the biggest was at the head of the chain; Lexie was the smallest, so she was at the end. One time she was going so fast that she let loose, fell, and hit her head on the ice. She was dizzy and sick because she probably had a concussion, but we were not concerned because we thought she was just being dramatic.

Rita: I remember when Lexie was little and riding the grey mare, Flossie. Flossie was running to the barn, and Lexie couldn't stop her. The reins had lots of slack, so she was trying to pull back on them without moving her hands up. So, there she was, with her hands over her head and leaning back almost all the way back to Flossie's rump trying, unsuccessfully, to stop her.

Rita: Lillyan, Lexie and I went camping on our horses in the weaning corral, which was about a quarter mile down the river from the Home Place. We released our horses into the same corral where we were camping so we could catch them. We made several trips back to Grandpa's wood pile to get loads of wood to replenish our firewood. We got in our minds that the big and muscular hired hand, Owen, who was staying in the Bunkhouse, was out there watching us. We yelled and yelled into the dark for him to go away. During all of that yelling, we were further humiliated because Daddy drove down the road and called to us across the river asking if we were okay. (We were in the "wilderness" camping, so we certainly did not need a parent to check up on us.)

Rita: At one of Harry Russell's barn dances, where the dance took place in the open loft, the men or older kids often had their bottles of booze downstairs. Lexie, Charlotte Salisbury (I think), and I watched where they hid their bottles, and when they were not looking, we poured the booze into a jar and replaced it with turpentine. We were delighted to see a few of them swig the turpentine and gag and spit. Luckily we did not kill someone.

Rita: During high school, Lexie and I went camping a couple of times. Once we went to the forest allotment where the old cow camp had been. We each had a riding horse and we had our big pack mare, Agate. Agate was fairly heavily packed because we took a heavy tent, two really bulky sleeping bags, and lots of food. In fact, Daddy sent an enormous supply of potatoes with us so we would not be hungry. We cooked only two of the potatoes in the coals, and they were so overcooked that we could not eat them.

Rita: I took another four- to five-day trip in the Zirkel Wilderness area with Lexie. That time, we wanted to take minimal gear because all of our provisions were tied

Rita tying close the boots she slit because she could not get them off when wet. Gypsy is the packed horse.

behind our saddles. We did not have a tent, but Delby Hyde had convinced us to take a big piece of black plastic. It was a good thing because it rained the entire time. My boots got soaked and then shrank. Lexie told me that cowboys cut their boots to get them on, so I took a pocket knife and slit mine from the top clear to the instep. For the rest of the trip, I had to hold them shut with a string.

ALFRED

David: Alfred loved to tease people, maybe because he was teased while he was growing up. I really hated when he called me "Davy" or "Davy Crockett." No matter how mad I got, he wouldn't quit.

David: Before we baled our hay and stacked it loose, Alfred and Grandpa did the raking until we kids grew up enough to take over. Alfred would run the dump rake and scattering rake. The windrows would be made like spokes of wheel from the outside to the center of the field. You had to drive around the field and dump the hay at exactly the right time to line up with the previous rounds. I was awed at how Alfred could make the windrows so straight.

David: Around the Fourth of July, Alfred always had firecrackers, and he thought it funny to throw one under someone's horse when they weren't expecting it.

David: The next day after a Pep Hall dance, we often would have to go back up and look for Alfred's false teeth and his glasses. It was not uncommon to find them near the fence a short distance from where a car had been parked and next to a pile of vomit.

Kenneth: Alfred scared me a bit when we were little because he seemed gruff. But I always liked his birthday card with a dollar in it.

Kenneth: Alfred always got up very early in the morning. I remember numerous times he would say that he got up to build the fire in the wood and coal stove at four o'clock in the morning. I could never understand what he did for the next two hours before chores.

Kenneth: I remember Alfred riding his black mare with no name and part of one ear clipped off at the top. During the summer, Alfred would often be seen on the horse carrying a shovel over his shoulder to go and "change the water" (flood irrigate the hay meadow) across the river. He would often sit sideways in the saddle, and I did not understand that either. Later, I learned that his chronic bad back made him very uncomfortable riding, although I never heard him complain.

Kenneth: Alfred liked to show us his elk tooth Elk's Lodge pin. I never got to pull an elk "tusk" like that.

Kenneth: I wondered why Alfred typically wore bib overalls rather than the waist-length Levis like his brothers or David and I wore. I thought bib overalls were ugly and were for farmers, like our Granddad Ireland—not ranchers. But when he went "down the River" to a bar or to the Pep Hall for a dance, he would dress up in new Levis. When they had not yet been washed, or even when they had, the pant legs might be folded up into a cuff sometimes six inches high.

Kenneth: At least once, I was involved with rescuing Alfred from a vehicle accident on the gravel road passing our places. Inevitably, he would come out bloodied a bit but having lost or broken his glasses. This particular time was with Harold Rice, who, according to legend, ran off every grade on Snake River. In fact, one of Alfred's famous sayings was from Dad when, as mentioned earlier, Dad, Leonard, and Alfred were coming home from a New Year's dance in Dixon, quite drunk, during a snowstorm. They ran off the Lemmon's grade and nearly went into the river, but for a tree that stopped the car. Alfred lost his glasses but stepped out of the car which was several feet from the ground. His famous saying from that episode was, "Watch that first step, George. She's a son of a bitch."

Rita: Alfred was a real tease. I did not like it very much when I was little, but in retrospect, I know that he really was fond of all of us nieces and nephews. Alfred liked going to town and to the bars, so when there was an opportunity, he took it. He did not drive, but he seemed to have a predisposition for riding with someone who should not have been driving. More than once he would be in a car accident, and inevitably he would lose his glasses and his teeth, and someone would have to help him find them the next day.

Rita: We also liked to tease Alfred. One time we cinched his saddle to the saddle stand. His response when he tried to get the saddle for his black mare, "Goddam little farts."

Rita: Alfred would drink a lot when he got the chance but would often blame the next day hangover on "them corn fleks I et."

Rita: For some reason, Jean dyed Alfred's white hair red, and did it several times. He must have liked it.

Rita: Alfred was really kind, though. He always gave us a dollar for Christmas and for our birthdays. He always gave his brothers a carton of Lucky Strike cigarettes for Christmas.

FRANCIS

David: I remember that Francis played violin at some early dances at the Pep Hall.

David: Francis drove his 8N Ford tractor from home to work during haying season and other times. As described above on the night of his death, he was on his way home one evening on his tractor and stopped in the road in front of our house to talk and visit with Dad and some other men, probably uncles. Francis said he had to get going before it got dark, but they kept lingering and talking, and, as I remember, they had a bottle of whiskey they were passing around. It was almost dark when he left our place. The fault, if any, in my opinion, was on everyone who did as they always did—lingering and talking. We live our lives peacefully in this way, lingering and talking, and sometimes we die an untimely death because of it.

Kenneth: Francis's tractor accident occurred when I was only six and a half years old. I remember being in our bunk bed at home and Dad waking us up in the morning after the accident and telling us Francis had been killed. That was the first time I had dealt with death and did not really know what to make of it except that it was very bad.

Kenneth: Most of what I remember about Francis was from Dad. The two of them were no doubt the closest to each other in terms of spending time together, so there were many stories. Dad talked about how strong Francis was and how tough he was in terms of taking a punch.

Kenneth: For me, the most memorable thing about Francis was the often repeated second-hand knowledge from most of my uncles that Francis stuttered. It was never particularly emphasized or regretted; it was simply that. He stuttered. And, of course, I was reminded of that because I stuttered.

Rita: I was so young when he died, that I have very little memory of Francis.

AGNES

David: Of all the wood-fired kitchen stoves in the family, Agnes's was the most ornate. I remember once when I was staying with Sharon at the Hackmaster Place. We had cornmeal mush for supper. The next morning, for the first time in my life, Agnes fried the cornmeal mush for breakfast. I was a picky eater, so something new was suspect. To my surprise, though, I liked fried cornmeal mush with butter and syrup almost as well as I liked pancakes.

David: Agnes liked to fish, and, with her family, we caught lots of trout in Roaring Fork.

Kenneth: As explained earlier, Agnes, Sharon, and Joyce came to stay with Rita and me while Mom, Dad, and David drove to Denver and stayed there for some weeks following David's sledding accident. (See Chapter 12.) It was Christmas Day in 1952 or shortly after my eighth birthday. I remember the accident clearly and Agnes being there in our driveway while everyone was running around frantically. But I have absolutely no memory after that. Clearly, I repressed it all, and even after working to recover the memory, which clearly traumatized me, I remember nothing.

Kenneth: I always liked Agnes and had numerous short interactions with her later on. These occurred at their house at the Hackmaster Place, where I spent many summers cleaning ditches, irrigating, and haying. I also remember clearly our much anticipated visits to Wamsutter, where Dad would stay for much of the winters to help herd our band of sheep. We would stay with Agnes and play with Sharon and Joyce. Mostly, we were amazed at the long Union Pacific trains that would go right by the house several times a day. We would sit at the window and count the train cars.

Rita: Agnes was a really kind person. She always seemed to have a positive outlook on life as well. I remember she was a really wonderful seamstress, and in later years she made many beautiful quilts. She was a fantastic cook, and her holiday meals were legendary and beautifully presented.

MIKE RUSSELL

David: Most of what I remember about Mike was during the summer I worked for Harry Russell. Mike ran the baler while Harry did the mowing. He was a very hard worker.

David: Later, when Mike and Agnes were living in Dixon, I was amazed at all of the intricate tiny woodworking pieces he put together in the cribbage boards, the little tables, and the little boxes, all inlaid with different colored pieces of woods.

Kenneth: A few times, I visited and stayed a day or two with Mike and Agnes at their ranch near Dixon. Mike was always jovial and friendly, so he was fun to be around. He was also a very hard worker. He milked more cows in the morning, all by hand of course, than anyone I knew at the time. I always wondered, though, that as hard as he worked and as thin as his brother, Harry, was, why he always had a big belly.

Kenneth: I, too, enjoyed visiting Mike in his later years, when he and Agnes lived in their new house in Dixon, and surveying his incredible vegetable garden, chicken house, and shop where he cut many kinds of wood and inlaid them on custom furniture and boxes in intricate patterns, one of which we have at our Colorado cabin.

Rita: Mike was always fun to be around. When I would go spend the night with Joyce, Mike would always joke and play games with us. He let me come "help" him milk his many cows, but I'm sure I was in the way more than I helped.

SHARON

David: Sharon was the first one to teach me how to smoke cigarettes. When they lived at the Hartman Place, she had swiped some cigarettes and matches from her parents. We went up behind the house and ducked down behind some tall sagebrush near the fence line and lit up.

Kenneth: Sharon was three years older than I, so I did not spend much time with her as a child, except at family gatherings, 4-H, and other social events. I have positive memories of Sharon during those childhood years, but they are fuzzy regarding the details.

Kenneth: I learned in high school that Sharon decided to major in speech pathology at CSU, but she and Steve Andrew got married in 1960, and their first child came along. Thus, she did not continue her degree. Steve was still in school, and I remember riding with them from Steamboat to Fort Collins and having nice conversations about the department after I started there as a freshman. Mom mentioned numerous times how impressed she was with Steve, whom she regarded as a perfect gentleman.

Kenneth: After middle age, I always sought out Sharon and Steve at family reunions or visits to Colorado. We always seemed to click and shared an interest in the family's history. She, though, was the family genealogist, and I was just interested in what she found. It was not until working on this book, did I really appreciate her efforts.

Kenneth: Sharon was hired by the US Postal Service to serve the mail route from Maybell, Colorado, through Brown's Park, into Wyoming and even into Utah. Steve was her substitute driver, so either one or the other delivered the mail, and sometimes with help from two daughters. Each trip involved 180 miles round trip on gravel roads containing only about 20 stops from Maybell, with another 60 miles to drive round trip from Craig. They delivered mail there for 36 years. It is one of the longest mail routes in the US and the only one that crossed three state lines. A highlight of relatively recent memory was when Steve took David, Rae Jean, and me on this route where we saw the high desert, the few ranches, and amazing wildlife, including elk.

Rita: Both Sharon and Joyce seem to have acquired their mother's genes for absolute kindness. Sharon embodies the qualities of hard, honest work, kindness, absolute loyalty, an inquiring mind, and always available if someone needs something. She also seemed to have acquired Agnes's gift for quilting, sewing, and crafting of all sorts because she continues to have ongoing lovely crafting projects. Her knowledge of our ancestors has been a boon for all of us.

JOYCE

David: My specific memories of Joyce are hazy, but I do remember that she had a unique and pleasant tone to her voice.

Kenneth: My memories of Joyce, who was the youngest St. Louis living in Colorado, are dim. She did come to stay at our house at least twice when she was very young. She had her own unique way of talking that contained more than the usual amount of hesitations and sound substitutions.

Kenneth: I remember Joyce would ride the big white gelding named Steel. She was very small, but she could get her left leg up almost head high to the stirrup and then use the saddle strings to pull her way up onto the horse.

Kenneth: I had returned from working a year on a National Speech and Hearing Survey for CSU in 1969 and was taking a few courses there before heading to Michigan to work on my master's degree. At that time, Joyce was deciding whether and where to go back to school. We spent a few days together, which was a special time for both of us to get acquainted as young adults. She ended up attending CSU, where she met her husband, Jimmy Miranda.

Kenneth: Joyce and Jimmy moved to his native Hawaii. They eventually started a business of taking tourists for rides on the beach in Kauai from their stable there. Joyce hosted Rae Jean and me for our 25th anniversary in Kauai and showed us a marvelous time, including watching their periodic private rodeo and whales in the Pacific Ocean a short distance beyond the fences.

Rita: Joyce lived with us one summer, and I am ashamed to say that I was pretty mean to her. We shared a bed, and I would kick her if she came too far onto my side.

Rita: Joyce was a really loving little girl with beautiful blue eyes. When she lived with us that summer, she called our daddy, "Daddy." At our meals she would say, "I get to sit by Daddy," which she would do as often as she could. Once, when our uncle Gus was visiting, she said, "I get to sit by Daddy" whereupon she sat next to Gus.

Rita: That same summer we went to Encampment to a Rodeo. In those days, it was safe to let kids wander, but Joyce wandered away and when she returned, she had five dollars. Mom inquired about the money, and Joyce told her that a man told her she was pretty so gave her five dollars. That really upset Mom.

Rita: As little kids, when Joyce was around, Lillyan, Lexie, and I would play "Hawaiian" in the river. Joyce apparently thought, and we agreed, that to play "Hawaiian," you had to be naked. So, we always took off all our clothes. (It's kind of ironic that Joyce ended up in Hawaii as an adult. In fact, someone joked wondering when Joyce realized that Hawaiians wore clothes.)

Rita: Joyce went to 4-H camp when she was nine years old. You had to be ten to be a full 4-H member, but you could go to 4-H camp as an associate at nine years. I remember that Joyce went with all of us, and Mom was a chaperone that year. Joyce had a big suitcase full of clothes. She changed her clothes several times and ran out of things to wear the first day. After camp, Joyce was recounting the trip by telling, "Him was nickin (necking) with her and her was nickin with him."

Rita: I was once really incensed when I came home to Elizabeth's house, where I was living between freshman and sophomore years in college. Joyce met me at the door and was not going to let me enter because she did not recognize me. (People were having quite a party there that night.)

PERRY

David: I remember at some of the first dances at the Pep Hall, Glen and Fern Johnson from Glen Eden came over from Elk River to play the guitar and piano. Perry played the drums and he let me "help."

David: It was no secret that Perry had an alcohol problem. One time when he was mowing hay, he did not stop and come to dinner (midday meal). Later, there he was by his two-cylinder John Deere tractor, still running, asleep on the ground. He was obviously dealing with a hangover.

Kenneth: I remember Perry as the uncle I felt most comfortable to be around. He was always laughing and telling jokes, many of them X-rated. The few times I "stayed overnight" with Jean, Shirley, and Beverly, Perry went out of his way during supper to say that he wished he had a son like me.

Kenneth: I mostly remember Perry during riding. He rode a sorrel horse named Red, who was exceedingly fast. At one point, we were going full gallop after some cattle behind Sheep Mountain, and his horse simply fell over and died. Perry was not hurt as I recall, but the consensus was that the horse had suffered a heart attack.

Kenneth: When the Boys put up loose hay, I first began to help out in the hayfield driving the stacker, Perry drove a buck rake. Prior to that, I liked to ride behind the teeth in front of him and watch the hay pile up higher and higher in front of me. It sometimes came over the two- or three-foot high wooden barrier at the back and forced me to stoop down below that level. Later, when we switched to baled hay, Perry did most of the mowing for the hay crew on his John Deere tractor. Given that I either raked hay, loaded the slip, or stacked, I did not have contact with him except at the noon "dinner" meal.

Kenneth making sure Perry's haircut is even all over, perhaps the first practice for cutting his own hair after losing most of it.

Kenneth: Perry was an entertainer like his brothers, but he was most animated playing the bones, where he would gyrate his entire body as his wrist rotations would generate the complex rhythms. I learned to play the bones myself from him.

Kenneth: I was always sad in Perry's later years before his untimely death that he was unable to manage his liquor. I never talked to him about it, but I suspect that his alcoholism was one reason I did not drink much at all until I finished college, fearing that I might too become an alcoholic.

Rita: I did not know Perry very well. I do know that he liked to tell jokes, and he never seemed to tell the same one twice. Like my brothers, I recognized his accomplished playing of the bones. However, because of his drinking I remember a few times when, to me, he was cruel to animals. Unfortunately, I held a negative reaction to him for that.

Rita: A story that I remember about Perry was a time they were poaching elk in the winter. Perry apparently got so excited when a good shot at an elk presented itself that he completely emptied his rifle by repeatedly ejecting shells without firing at all.

Rita: I know that Perry eventually tried very hard to stop drinking and did so very successfully for a good bit of time. This really positive time was cut short by the head-on vehicle accident that ended his life.

GRACE

David: Jean and Shirley said that their mother had a "teacher face" and "mother face." When I stayed overnight and with Jean and Shirley, I could never feel comfortable around Grace when she put on her housewife "mother face" because, to me, she was still the teacher.

Kenneth: Whereas Elizabeth had a profound effect on my desire to travel and dream beyond Little Snake River, Grace had an equally profound effect on my education. After a wonderful first grade with Laura Lee Beeler as my teacher who seemingly adored me, Grace was my only teacher until I reached the sixth grade. Unlike most people I have known since, I have no special memories of any particular grade (except the first grade). They simply all blended together. I did not know if I was smart or average because I was always the only one in my grade, but I did know I was not slow. I remember worrying every week about a test I had to take, possibly on Mondays in the mid to later elementary years. Grace was very organized and absolutely unapologetic for any rules that any of us might not have liked. I did not like the charts for health every day and worried I might not get my star at the end of the week. But in her matter-of-fact way, Grace simply taught us. Chapter 10 describes the school.

Kenneth: I remember Grace always being on time. Picking up her four-inch brass bell with protruding handle, she would step out of the school and ring for several seconds when school was about to begin and when our morning and afternoon recesses would end.

Kenneth: In her later years, Grace seemed to be a happier person. At family reunions, she became more and more animated and sometimes downright funny. I did not experience her that way at Willow Creek School or even at their house. Instead, then, she came across as efficient, organized, practical, and stoic, as the stereotype of her German cultural background might suggest.

Kenneth: I regard Grace as one of my few real educational mentors.

Rita: Grace was a really good teacher, and I am fortunate to have had her for my early school years. I felt she was a little too "proper" all of the time and I did not see any sense of humor in her. At that time, I did not appreciate her dedication to all of the cousins' learning, and I thought she was too strict. I felt she was too mean at times when she would not let Beverly come play with Lillyan, Lexie, and me. In later years, Grace showed a happier, warmer side that was fun to be around.

JEAN

David: Jean being the oldest was the smartest in grade school. I thought someday, when I was in the first, second, or whatever grade, I would be able to read, spell, and do arithmetic as well as Jean could. That was my goal.

David: When I was in Salt Lake City at Shriners Hospital for Crippled Children Hospital, Jean was the only one that I can remember who came to visit me besides

Mom and Dad. She visited right after my arm was amputated. I was really self-conscious, whereas before with my arm paralyzed, I never thought about it. She was going to high school at the time at a Catholic boarding school, St. Mary's of the Wasatch, and I was in the eighth grade.

Kenneth: The oldest of the St. Louis cousins, Jean ruled the roost. In most school and even many 4-H activities, she was in charge, if she chose to exercise her authority. Being four years older than I, it is no surprise that I did not play with her or follow her around. I did admire her horsemanship skills.

Beverly, Perry, and Grace enjoying a holiday meal.

Kenneth: We got along, but I knew I could not push Jean. I especially learned that lesson in the back of Harry Russell's truck driving to 4-H camp, probably about the time I was 11, and Jean, 15. She and others (no doubt including Linda Sheehan) were sleeping or resting near the front of the truck. With some younger kids (I don't remember who), we were fooling around throwing sleeping bags at each other. I decided to throw one at Jean. She jumped up without saying a word, came back and began hitting me in the face with her fists.

Kenneth: In our later years, Jean and I became very close, perhaps because of the mellowing effect of age. This started when she and I organized the first official St. Louis reunion in Grand Junction where we all recorded stories from our youth. It deepened when Mom was in the hospital in Grand Junction before her death. And our simpatico deepened further after Carl's death in 2018 and later when we traveled to Canada together to meet our St. Louis cousins there.

Rita: Jean was "too old" while I was growing up. Mostly I remember various young men courting her, and we would make up songs about them. Jean was always the "boss" at school, and I believed that she wanted to be "the boss" most of the time I was around her.

SHIRLEY

David: If there was a fight at school, Shirley was the one to break it up and decide who was right and who was wrong. No one questioned her authority in these matters because she was strong enough to back it up.

Kenneth: If Jean was the General in charge when we were children, Shirley was her Colonel (which, in fact, she became in the Air Force). She did not take charge unless it was needed. I don't remember it specifically, but Grace said that Shirley would tolerate the younger kids' antics just so long and then step in and quickly get everyone back in line. Like Sharon, Shirley was three years older than I, so I did not play with her or spend much one-on-one time with her as a youngster.

Kenneth: Shirley had (has!) an infectious laugh. She always was able to see the light side of about anything. And like her father, she told lots of jokes. She loved to tell stories as well, as when she threw a shovelful of fresh green cow manure out the barn door and hit her dad squarely on the side of the head.

Kenneth: It was in high school that I really began to have an occasional serious conversation with Shirley. I remember that she was studying to become a nun but was home for a break during the summer haying season. I had begun to learn something of Christianity from MYF (Methodist Youth Fellowship). We had at least a couple of memorable conversations about what was calling us to take religion seriously.

Kenneth: I really enjoyed my interactions with Shirley at the several family reunions she organized after the first one that Jean and I did jointly. Her knowledge of medicine (as a certified Nurse Practitioner) was impressive as well when we needed it at the high altitude setting near Paonia. Since then, while we enjoy our company together as much as ever, our differing political beliefs seemingly have made that relationship more tentative.

Rita: Shirley was also "too old" for me, but she had a wonderful inclusive sense of humor that caused everyone to enjoy her. To this day, her infective laugh and light-heartedness make her fun to be around.

BEVERLY

David: For a number of years when we were younger, we only had one horse to ride. And taking turns didn't give everybody a chance to ride as much as they wanted. So, we began pulling a wagon behind the horse with a lariat rope with someone riding in the wagon. Not surprisingly, we pulled the wagon faster and faster. The road from the house to the barn had a curve in it where it went over a culvert in the slough. At the lower end of the culvert was "the stinks," so-called because this is where the septic tank drained directly, with no leach field. It was Beverly's turn in the wagon. I was pulling her on the horse, but in rounding that curve at full gallop, the wagon rolled over and dumped her into "the stinks." She came out bawling, covered head to foot with black sewage waste. And she smelled just like the sewer.

Fortunately, Mom was doing laundry that day. She undressed Beverly, put her in the bathtub, and washed her clothes. It took quite a while for her to get rid of the sewer smell.

David: Kenneth took Beverly up the hillside between our sandstone cliff and the one above the school to an old abandoned coal mine. Dad had told us to stay out of there because it might cave in. But they went in there anyway. I saw them and told Dad about it, and he spanked Kenneth. He also called Perry to see if he knew where Beverly was. She remembers Dad turning to her and saying, "Your dad would like you to come home." She also remembers the horse hair whip that Perry used on her.

Kenneth: Beverly was about the same age as Rita, so they were the only two in the same grade most of my years at Willow Creek School, two years behind me. We all played together most recesses in the "willows" next to the school or on the playground swings and bars.

Kenneth: Grace organized us as a square dance set (four couples). I was paired with Beverly, David with Lillyan, Rita (as the "boy") with Lexie, and Shirley (as the "boy") with Jean. Beverly and I were not especially graceful in our moves, but we knew them perfectly and executed them with gusto. We could "balance and swing" like no one else in the set. I'm not sure if she was my regular partner for the Schottische or "Put Your Little Foot," but no doubt we stomped our way through those dances like little pros as well.

Kenneth: Whether or not it is true, Beverly always seemed to me to be quietly mischievous. She was the one who fed stilbestrol to the chickens and stopped them from laying. Even after she reached high school age and had spent at least most of her high school years at St. Mary's of the Wasatch Catholic high school, she could tell X-rated jokes that would make a sailor blush.

Kenneth: In the past decade, I have had more political discussions through social media and email with Beverly than with all the other St. Louis cousins. We could not be more opposite in our political views, but, thanks to our willingness to put that aside, we have maintained a close relationship.

Rita: Beverly and I were in the same grade in school, so we were highly competitive. I remember in first or second grade we were writing spelling words on the blackboard, ten times each. Beverly learned that if you write all of the first letters ten times, then the second letters ten times, it would go faster, and she could beat me. One time we were neck and neck in the contest to see who could finish first, and I dared not quit, because I had a chance of winning. Well, I couldn't wait, and I peed my pants and there was a huge puddle on the floor under my feet.

The "Boys," the Aunts, and the Cousins / 91

Rita: I remember that Lillyan and Lexie had a cat that they named "Pussy Pants Ruffles." Beverly thought that was a terrible name for a cat. When I asked her why, she said, "When you get to be as old as Shirley, you'll understand."

Rita: My horse, Gypsy, could run really fast. She was never outrun by any horse I pitted her against. However, one race might not have been a fair contest. Beverly had a big pinto gelding named Tabor that was really fast too. We decided to have a race in the meadow across the river from Beverly's house to see which was faster. Both horses were flying full out when Gypsy hit some boggy ground and did a somersault. I was tossed off to the side. Luckily neither of us was hurt. I guess one could say that Tabor won that race. Beverly reminded me also of a different time that Gypsy had gotten loose, and Beverly and I went to catch her on Tabor. The problem was that we had on ice skates, so every time I would touch Tabor with my skates, he would buck a little. She also reminded me of my ride on her horse, Casey. He ran off with me because his bridle had a flawed bit or curb strap, so could not be stopped. He ran all the way from Pine Scope to our house, between two to three miles, jumping at least two cattleguards.

Rita: Beverly and I were 15 or 16 at a dance at the Pep Hall, where a young dandy guy was asking all of the girls to dance. I do not know who he was: George Salisbury called him "the hand in the hat." He wore a big new hat, some new jeans hiked up really high on his waist, and a fancy belt buckle. No one wanted to dance with him, but he persisted. Beverly and I became annoyed and decided that we would "take the dance right out of him," so we accepted his invitation to dance. First one of us, then the other, took turns on the dance floor with him, and around and around we went. We were strong, and we could really man-handle him. One of us would bulldoze him around for a while; then, the other one would take over. We whirled him and twirled him through at least two or three entire songs. Finally, he extracted himself and made a bee line for the door. He did not come into the dance hall the rest of the evening, and we never saw him again.

LEONARD

David: After Leonard and Doris built their new cabin at the Hartman Place, he was unhappy at how things had changed on the River. He really liked that Dad and Sinc were still there, but he was not happy when they sold their ranches.

Kenneth: As noted in this chapter, we only had contact with Leonard and his family during their yearly summer visit to the Home Place. I remember those visits, mostly at Grandpa and Grandma's house, very well, but I mostly listened. Leonard liked to interact with his older brothers and often took the lead in whatever conversation might be going on. Although I thought nothing of it at the time, he appeared to be the self-appointed bringer of important news to the Valley from the outside world.

Kenneth: Indirectly, I owe my first speech therapy experience to Leonard. He had referred Gordon Holmes to Dad for deer hunting (as explained in Chapter 12). On my way with Perry, Grace, and Beverly to California to work on my stuttering, we spent one night with Leonard before he drove me to Maricopa. I remember his showing me a big crack in his stone or block fence that had been caused by a sonic boom.

Kenneth: I only had one-on-one conversations with Leonard after he and Doris moved back to Colorado and built their log cabin at the Hartman Place. I had several nice visits with them, and with the Weges (former guests at the Focus Ranch) who lived up the River at the time. I was always struck with how every single thing, even the kindling he used to start a fire, was perfectly uniform and placed.

Rita: I have very few memories of Leonard; yet, to me, he seemed more opinionated than the other St. Louis uncles. I might be wrong, but I felt that after I married Chris, he distanced himself from me because he did not care for Chris.

Doris

David: Of course, I knew Doris, but nothing stands out as a specific memory of her.

Kenneth: I have very few significant childhood memories of Doris. I don't think she singled me out much during their yearly visits. Nevertheless, I felt very comfortable around her.

Rita: Doris was an easy person to be around, and after I was an adult, I enjoyed visiting her and Leonard. However, I have very few childhood memories of her. I do remember how dedicated she was to her mother, Hattie Honnold, after Hattie had a stroke and needed care.

Kathy

David: I have few specific memories of Kathy although I did get to know Tom on an elk hunting trip several years ago.

Kenneth: Kathy was the "baby" of the family. We always remembered to include Kathy as one of the cousins, even though she was mostly not with us. Leonard, especially, would show her off when she was a baby or toddler, so we got to know her as well as one could under the circumstances.

Kenneth: When Kathy was a teenager, she sometimes brought a California friend with her to the ranch. One year when I was 19 and Kathy was 13, she and her friend rode their horses to "visit" me irrigating at the Focus Ranch. There appeared to be some youthful crush going on with one of them, but I could well be mistaken.

Kenneth: In the writing of this book and some earlier interactions, I have also grown much closer to Kathy. We share common views about a number of topics that neither of us expected of the other.

Rita: I did not know Kathy because she only came once a year with her parents to visit. I remember her parents' being really protective of her. One time she was at our house and she fell off of the horse. Kathy was not hurt, but Mom was really worried about having to break the news to Leonard.

Rita: Of all of the cousins, I feel I know Kathy the least. That makes me a bit sad because I really admire the woman she has shown me, and I know I would enjoy getting to know her better.

Chapter 5

From Illinois to Colorado: Joseph and Fanny Ireland

The Ireland family is reported in most genealogical records as coming from Ireland. Our family has been traced back to a Thomas Ireland who immigrated to America in the late 1700s or very early 1800s. His son, and our third great-grandfather (great-great-great-great-grandfather), Noble Ireland (reportedly born in Ireland), fought in the War of 1812. The family eventually ended up in Louden Township, Fayette County, Illinois, near the town of St. Elmo. It was there that our 2nd great-grandfather, William Ireland Sr was born, lived, and died. One of his sons, William Ireland Jr, and his wife, Elizabeth Jane Ritchie, were our great-grandparents. They, too, stayed on the family farm, and their first child, Joseph (Joe) Otto Ireland was our grandfather.

Our grandmother's family, the Galvins, also emigrated from Ireland in 1883. Second and third great-grandparents were born in Ireland, but settled in Kentucky and then Missouri, south of Kansas City. Fannie Galvin was born in Missouri and, with our grandfather, moved west to Colorado.

Joe, whom we called Granddad, born October 14, 1883, on the farm near St. Elmo, was the oldest of six brothers and sisters. In order, they were: Joe, Emma Lodema (Dema), Fred Eugene, Robert Lee, Lula, and Nancy. His future wife, Laura Francis (Fannie) Galvin, was born in Vernon, Missouri, near the town of Nevada on April 3, 1888. Her parents were Thomas Henry and Elizabeth Galvin. Fannie was the fourth of eight siblings: Addie Mae, Sarah Margaret, Minnie L., Fannie, Harrison Thomas, Robert J., Lizzie M., and George D.

Joe and Fannie were married in Moundville, Missouri, near Fannie's home on September 17, 1905. Their first two children were born in St. Elmo, Illinois, Elmer Thomas and Ruby Mabel. The third child, Clarence Joseph, was

William and Jane Ireland family in Illinois. Back: *Bob, Fred, Dema, Joe, and Lula;* front: *William and Jane.*

born in Kenesaw, Nebraska. In 1910, Joe and Fannie had filed for a 160-acre homestead in eastern Colorado about two miles west and four miles north of Sedgwick, Colorado, not far from the South Platte River. They arrived at the property in 1911. Six more children were born there: Gladys Jane, Velma Rose, Nora Violet, Doris Evelyn, Dorothy Grace (Mom), and Mary Lois.

Members of both sides of the family moved from the greener and treed lands of Illinois or Missouri to the much drier and barren plains of eastern Colorado, at least partly from being enamored with the prospect of coming to own 160 acres via the Homestead Act. Joe's younger brother Fred, who farmed near St. Elmo, Illinois, decided in 1909 to homestead seven miles from Sedgwick. He built a tar paper covered shack, built some fence, and tilled a few acres. The next year, Joe filed for his homestead, quite likely adjacent to his brother's place. In 1911, another brother, Robert (Bob) Ireland bought the Fred Ireland homestead and moved there as well. Fannie's sister, Addie, and her husband, Orren Chezem, also moved to Sedgwick, as did another sister, Minnie, and her husband, Elmer Williams. In 1927, Joe's brother, Bob, sold his farm and opened a creamery in nearby Julesburg, Colorado. Remembered stories include visits to and from Ireland or Galvin

Joe and Fannie's wedding portrait, 1905.

Joe as a young man.

Clarence and Bertha Cowgill, Belle Hodges, and Joe Ireland.

The original Joe Ireland homestead near Sedgwick, Colorado, 1912 or 1913.

The Ireland homestead in the 1920s.

Remains of Joe's concrete milk house.

aunts, uncles, and grandparents. We never learned how Joe and Fannie met and remember no stories about that. It might well have had something to do with at least five of the Ireland and Galvin families, with basically the entire state of Missouri between them, making joint decisions to relocate near one another to Colorado.

The family engaged in dairy farming and dryland farming using horse-drawn machinery. They raised corn, beans, and other vegetables as well as pigs, mules, and horses. They milked about 30 milk cows by hand every day, separated the cream, and sent it in ten-gallon cans to Denver by rail to be sold. Joe was innovative at preserving the milk and cream by building a concrete building with two rooms. Water pumped from a nearby windmill flowed into and out of a depot in one of the enclosed rooms and the milk cans were placed down into the cool water. Given that no one had electricity, this kept the milk and cream fresh for several days. Cans of cream were taken to the train depot en route to Denver, and a check arrived back on a regular basis based on the butterfat content of the cream. Usually a man was hired to help on the farm, and Joe, an accomplished carpenter, supplemented the farm by hiring himself out to assist with building projects.

Tragedy visited the Joe and Fanny Ireland family several times. In 1918, three of the children became gravely ill after everyone had reportedly attended a traveling musical show known then as a "chautauqua." Those not sick and Fannie were moved to the schoolhouse across the road while Joe and the three very sick children stayed at the house. The house was completely disinfected, and everything that could not be boiled was burned. Nevertheless, Clarence and Gladys died four days apart, and it was only after the first death that scarlet fever was diagnosed as the cause. No one attended the second burial. Velma, also extremely ill, survived, allegedly due to the care given by a trained nurse who had been brought in to help. Somewhat surprisingly, according to family stories, no one suspected it might have been the "Spanish Flu" that began as a worldwide epidemic in 1918. Nine years later, the youngest daughter, Mary Lois, died three days after birth, and then in 1933, Fannie passed away.

All the children walked or rode a horse to a one-room school first about three miles away and then later walked to a new school built close by for their elementary school. For high school, Elmer and Ruby drove a mule-drawn buggy for the six miles to Sedgwick. Ruby eventually began dating and then married a hired man from Paxton, Nebraska, Louis Lawler. They moved to a farm near his childhood home.

From all accounts, Joe demanded that everyone work; yet, he often exempted himself from the daily chores himself. He was not by nature a nurturing individual. Fannie, by contrast, was reported by several of her daughters as constantly gentle, warm, and kind. She apparently tolerated Joe's sternness and self-absorption with the absence of complaints. She was an exceptional cook, and always was able to have simple but satisfying food for everyone at the table, and sometimes had a sweet treat afterwards. Her fresh biscuits were eagerly anticipated in the mornings after the chores. Fannie was also a talented musician in the sense that she sang hymns as she played the family pump organ. Reportedly, she had never had music lessons; she played by ear, being able to play a song only after hearing it. Fannie whistled and hummed much of the time she worked around the house. For a short time she played at the Sunday School meetings at the new schoolhouse built across the road from their Sedgwick homestead.

Children playing on swings and a bar. Second from the left on the bar is Elmer and standing at the left of the right swing is Ruby.

Violet and Velma at the Sedgwick home.

Doris, Violet, Grace, and Velma at Sedgwick.

Children at Pleasant View School and schoolchildren near Sedgwick. Violet is standing left. Mom is sitting left, and Doris is sitting right.

The four oldest Ireland children: Clarence, Ruby, Gladys, and Elmer. Both Clarence and Gladys died in 1918 in a scarlet fever epidemic.

Of their mother, in 1979, Ruby wrote, "I don't believe that her singing was because she was happy. I believe that it was because she was an extremely brave and patient person and was determined to make the best of a not-so-good situation. Life was difficult. There was so much work to do. There must have been very little diversion or recreation of any kind. I firmly believe that our mother is one of the saints in heaven."

In 1930, no doubt influenced by the Great Depression, Joe sold the Sedgwick farm and moved to a farm 13 miles south of Akron, Colorado. Shortly thereafter, Elmer married Lillian Chabot. The first year, in order for Velma and Violet to attend high school, these two sisters along with Doris and Mom, attended

Fannie and two of her sisters with Sedgwick neighbors: Fannie, a neighbor, Addie Chezum, a neighbor, Minnie Williams, and a neighbor.

schools in Akron after Joe had rented part of a mice-infested house in town. The four children lived there together for the year. Velma decided to quit school, and Joe would not permit Violet to live alone; therefore, neither graduated from high school. Doris and Grace then attended another one-room school four miles from their farm. They rode a black horse with a star on her forehead named "Nell" to and from school. On extra cold and snowy days, they sometimes rode backwards to keep the wind from their faces.

It was a year and a half later when Fannie suffered a massive brain hemorrhage and died ten days later in a Denver hospital. This tragedy was followed by the recruitment of a series of housekeepers. Joe would place a want ad in a Denver newspaper asking for a "housekeeper for a motherless home" and then drive to meet the woman answering the ad and bring her back to the farm. Details are sketchy regarding the number of housekeepers and the durations of their stays, some for only a few days or weeks, but it was very hard on the children. In fact, Velma and Violet apparently did what they could to discourage these outsiders to stay. One housekeeper, whose first name was Becky, came several times. The first time, she brought her son who was about a year older than Doris, but after that, he lived with someone else in Denver. Becky and Joe were married and divorced and then married and divorced again.

Windmill near Akron and similar to windmills all over the prairie.

Joe Ireland riding "side saddle.

Becky and Joe at one of their marriages.

About 1935, 25-year old Sylvia Sanford was hired. She also later became Joe's wife in 1937. The house-keepers were directed not to work outside as not to spoil the children. The girls were expected to build the fire in the morning, do all the outside chores including the milking and separating cream, and then cook breakfast and get themselves ready for school. They also did many of the household duties. Reportedly, Joe did not do much of the physical work on the farm himself during these and subsequent years. Instead, he busied himself with exploring new options for making money, such as securing mineral and oil rights from his home place in Illinois or buying and selling land in eastern Colorado, always retaining the mineral and oil rights.

During their early years near Akron, Velma and Violet began dating two Gebauer brothers, Louis (Louie) and Joe, whom they later married and joined them in local farming operations nearby. Also, Ruby and Louis Lawler moved to a farm south of the Ireland farm for several years before eventually relocating to Scottsbluff, Nebraska. At the same time, Elmer and his wife, Lillian, also lived in and near Akron. The younger girls intermittently spent summers living with and helping their elder sisters or brother.

Joe's sister, Dema, lived near Evans, a small town just south of Greeley, Colorado. Shortly after Fannie died in 1933, he took Doris and Mom with him to live with Dema, but the brother and sister could not get along. As a result, they moved into one side of a house, infested with bedbugs, that was owned by a smelly man. After that, for about a year and a half, they moved to a farm again, with cows to milk, near the Lower Latham Reservoir. Doris and Mom attended the one-room Auburn country school. Thereafter, Joe purchased a liquor store with adjacent gas station in Evans wherein he managed the

Remains of the Ireland ranch at Hahns Peak.   *Remains of the outhouse.*

liquor store and rented the filling station. The two sisters then returned to school in town. During all of this time, the coming and going of housekeepers continued. Both Doris and Mom finished junior high school in Evans. During summers, they lived with and worked, alternately, for Velma and Louie or Violet and Joe on their farms near Akron.

During this period, Joe went back to Illinois for about two years, no doubt to engage in legal maneuverings that resulted in his acquiring a significant share in proceeds of oil that had been discovered on the original Ireland farm in Illinois. In 1937, upon receiving a sizable oil settlement, partnering with his son, Elmer, Joe bought the Omar and Katie Folden "Elkhorn Ranch" of about 500 acres next to the once thriving gold mining community of Hahns Peak. It is almost certain that he considered Hahns Peak because his first cousin, Rose Wheeler, born in Kenesaw, Nebraska, had previously moved to Hahns Peak with her husband, James, from Sterling, which is near Sedgwick. Three of Elmer and Lillian's daughters, Hazel, Norma, and Darlene, came with them, and their youngest daughter, Donna, was born in nearby Steamboat Springs. For two years, Hazel walked or skied through the deep snow to the one-room schoolhouse in Hahns Peak.

Before and after their father left Evans, Doris, and then one year later, Mom, attended high school in nearby Greeley. Doris stayed with one family; Mom, another. While Elmer's family lived at Hahns Peak, Joe and Sylvia lived in a house near the train depot in Steamboat and apparently spent some time in Evans, coming to the ranch only in the summers. Both Doris and Mom spent two summers at the little house there between later years of high school. Mom finished her last year of high school in Steamboat

Joe's lake property southeast of Steamboat Springs, now the site of Casey's Pond, a planned community for seniors.

Joe and another carpenter building one of three cabins on the south side of the lake.

while staying with and keeping house for the Hubbard family. After selling the ranch in Hahns Peak and leaving Routt County in 1941, Joe and Sylvia bought a house in Fort Morgan, Colorado, where they lived until 1957. They frequently visited our ranch when we were children. Joe and Elmer were instrumental in building a considerable number of log homes west of Fort Morgan in a new community later known as Log Lane in the mid 1950s.

Sylvia left Joe, eventually remarried, and moved to Idaho where she died in 1975. After she left, Joe sold his house in Fort Morgan and moved back to Steamboat. He bought a small farm about three miles southeast of town on US Route 40 featuring 20 acres of meadow, a farmhouse, outbuildings and sizeable pond and three smaller ponds feeding into it. He built three

Joe, obviously pleased with himself about something.

Joe and a housekeeper, Mrs. Bitabeer, at his Aspen home in Steamboat.

two-bedroom cabins next to the large pond that would become rentals. Joe lived in the farmhouse until 1959 but then moved into town. Joe first rented a second-story unit in the Rustic Lodge on Oak and 7th Street, across the hall from a larger rental unit where Mom and all three of us lived during our second year in Steamboat. After that, he bought a small house on Aspen Street and lived there until he died on April 26, 1963. During that period, he had another housekeeper, Mrs. Bittabeer. She was a nice lady, but Granddad was ornery to her as well.

> **Missed opportunity.**
> It is notable that our parents had the opportunity to buy Granddad's 20-acre lake property plus the adjacent 20 acres for forty dollars per acre at that time, Dad was concerned about the water rights for the property but wanted to go ahead with the purchase. Mom, however, declared she would "not live out in that snowbank." The entire property now houses a high-end senior assisted living/ nursing home facility adjacent to numerous condominiums associated with the later-developed Mount Werner ski resort.

Joe was an entrepreneur. Although never dramatically successful, he was a visionary in his time. He predicted future developments, saw opportunities when others did not, and thrived on lawsuits that eventually allowed him to reap benefits from investments that others had not recognized. Perhaps one of the main reasons for his not becoming wealthy was his unkempt personal appearance and hygiene. For example, he chewed tobacco and spit the juice virtually anywhere he happened to be in his own domain. The cans that he had placed about to catch the spittle were missed as often as hit, so his car, his floor, and even his new constructions were marked everywhere with the dark brown stains of tobacco. He drank too much in later years and did not shave until his white whiskers were a quarter-inch long. Dad was able to cut his hair, shave him, and clean him up better than about anyone. In spite of declining health, Joe's mind was sharp until he became ill for the final time.

Fannie's influence on our family was only through what Mom told us and through the patterns of behavior her mother had unconsciously passed on to her. Joe's influence was felt by us more strongly. Unfortunately, it was often experienced in negative ways, but also, positively, in giving us models for overcoming obstacles. It is clear, however, that Joe loved his family and wanted the best for them. His failing may have been that he had not learned himself how to demonstrate love personally and emotionally.

MEMORIES

GRANDDAD

David: Granddad used to open his fifth or quart of whiskey and fill the little metal lid and give it to us to drink. Usually, we would come back begging for more.

David: When we would come around and aggravate Granddad, he would threaten to "box our ears."

David: Mom didn't particularly appreciate it when Granddad showed up unannounced, especially when we had other company. One time when we had hunters whom Mom had to take care of, he came to the ranch. He said he was going to sleep in his "camper," which in my memory was nothing but a bunch of boards cobbled together on the bed of his Studebaker pickup. And all he had brought for food was some cans of sardines. Granddad basically acted like he planned to take care of himself, but I don't think he slept one night in his camper. Bottom line: Mom took care of him.

David: Granddad spit tobacco in every vehicle he had. He had one coffee can inside the vehicle to spit in, but sometimes he would spit out the window. Half the time, he missed the can and hit the floor, and half the time, he missed spitting out the window resulting in tobacco juice running down inside the driver's side window. We acquired his boxy, brown and tan Plymouth station wagon after he no longer could drive. The mechanism was so clogged with dried tobacco juice that the window would hardly roll up and down until I cleaned it out.

David: We got along pretty well. When I worked for Granddad for one or two winters fixing his fire, taking out the ashes and clinkers, and shoveling his sidewalk, he always wanted me to stay and visit. I stayed to visit with him as long as I could stand.

David: Granddad had a strategy of selling a piece of real estate to someone with a quit claim deed with a contract to pay him back over time. His plan was to reclaim the property when they could not make the payments. I don't know the details, but on one occasion when he "shafted" someone like this, the buyer came to his house and confronted him. During the argument, Granddad stuck the man with his pocket knife. It was probably legal, but the other guy was not careful in dealing with Granddad. In a later instance, Granddad sold his interest in the lake property in Steamboat to Casey (now called Casey's Pond). In that instance, the payments were made, and this deal, to Granddad, went sour.

Joe did most of his scheming and thinking while sitting quietly smoking his pipe.

David: Granddad would sit for days in his rocking chair, smoke his pipe, chew tobacco, make all kinds of smells, and so on while "figuring." Then, all of a sudden, he would jump up and go to work, having "figured" whatever he had in mind. No doubt, he had worked over in his mind all of the pros and cons of his plan beforehand.

Kenneth: I have a number of images of Granddad as a child, but regrettably, most of them are not positive. I remember first being intrigued and, later, somewhat disgusted by all the tobacco juice liquid and stains on the floor and all along the outside of the driver's side of his car or pickup when he and Sylvia would come to visit us at the ranch. I remember Dad's stories of his spitting tobacco juice on the new wood floors in the houses they built in Log Lane and at the lake property in Steamboat.

Kenneth: I remember vividly that we had driven to Fort Morgan to Granddad's house. He had a television, which I had never seen. I was captivated as I watched the black and white screen (full of the "snowy" distortions) for hours. (We did not get our first TV until we lived in the house on Oak Street in Steamboat.)

Kenneth: I have an image of Granddad sitting in his rocking chair in Steamboat, smoking his pipe, often listening to—but not watching—the television far off to one side. He was often not feeling well, and I remember several times him blaming it on what he ate for breakfast rather than the fifth of whiskey or the six-pack of malt liquor he had consumed the day before.

Kenneth: When Granddad lived across from us at the Rustic Lodge, he would sometimes eat dinner with us. I have foggy memories of that, but again, most of them were not positive. I do remember that he once told a dirty joke when a girl had joined us for the evening, and I was ashamed.

Kenneth: In the process of researching for this book, I have come to appreciate Granddad far more than I did when he was alive. The fact that I did or could not look beyond his careless appearance and habits as a child and teenager was my great loss. He was clearly the kind of visionary I could have appreciated.

Kenneth: Granddad had worked hard to get his share of the revenue that came from a large oil discovery on the Ireland family farm in Illinois. That was divided to his children, and, although modest, Mom's monthly oil check during our childhood was often the difference between buying only the basic necessities and purchasing these along with an occasional luxury.

Rita: I must admit that as a child, I did not like Granddad. He just seemed like a dirty old man who was mean to Mom. He seemed to take great delight in making other people uncomfortable. He stank, and his house stank. I remember an old crony of his, Ben Savage, would come to his house on Aspen street and they would drink malt liquor. Ben allegedly had quite a bit of money, and I remember some lady's marrying him (for his money as the gossip went). She put up with him for a few years, and instead of inheriting his money, she died first.

Rita: I also remember the tobacco juice cans. He would "by accident" tip a can over in houses or in cars, or he would legitimately spit out the window, and as David remembers, there was tobacco juice down the inside of the door and down into the window well.

Rita: A story that I remember involved Gus and Granddad. They had been doing something illegal such as fishing and getting too many fish, taking sage chickens, or killing a deer out of season. They were stopped on the road, and just then, the game warden came by. To divert him, Granddad hustled away from the vehicle, pretending to have diarrhea, and dropped his drawers right at the edge of the road. That action distracted the game warden enough that the others had time to hide or get rid of the evidence.

Rita: Mom said that after a few months during our first year in Steamboat, we moved from the cabin on the lake into a rented house in town because Granddad was ordering her around like he used to. She decided that she would never tolerate that behavior again.

Rita: One time when we lived in the Rustic Lodge, someone had to bring sandwiches to school for an event. Mom had them all done and put them on a chair. Granddad came into our side and sat on the sandwiches.

Rita: Granddad did give Mom ten dollars for Christmas every year. I still have the lamp that Mom bought with the money he gave her for Christmas one year in Steamboat.

SYLVIA

David: I have no specific memories of Sylvia.

Kenneth: At this point in my life, I have virtually no clear memories of Sylvia. I know I was always comfortable around her and enjoyed her company when she and Granddad would come for a visit to the ranch.

Rita: I barely remember Sylvia.

Chapter 6

Our Ireland Uncles, Aunts, and Cousins

As important to our heritage as our mother's extended family is, it had far less influence on our childhood than that of our father's clan, except for the Ranch family, as explained below. Consequently, this chapter is much shorter than that devoted to the St. Louis family. Even so, it is important to note that most of our Ireland cousins remembered much more of our family than we did of theirs, mostly because all but a few of them were older than we were. For example, after Mom's death, Patricia Lawler Ham wrote in a letter, "...I want you to know that Aunt Grace was a very special person to me. Whenever I think of her

Ireland sisters and husbands at a reunion. Back: Louie Gebauer, Joe Gebauer, George St. Louis, Louis Lawler, Gus Ranch, and Frank Jenik; front: Velma Gebauer, Violet Gebauer, Dorothy Grace (Grace) St. Louis, Ruby Lawler, Doris Ranch, and Lillian Ireland Jenik.

Five sisters. Back: *Violet, Ruby, and Dorothy Grace;* front: *Doris and Velma.*

it is with her half turned away, but then with a look back and devilish grin. She always made me laugh. My earliest memories of her were when we made the trip to your home out of Slater when I was quite young. We had such a great time, seeing your log house, the cave blasted out of the hillside, riding the horse (Sally?). We also went to a branding and I got the autographs of Rod Cameron and Forest Tucker."

ELMER AND LILLIAN IRELAND

In 1932, Elmer Ireland married Lillian Chabot, and they moved to Fort Morgan, Colorado. Our first cousins from his family included: Hazel Mae, Norma Francis (deceased), Darlene Louise, and Donna Lee (deceased). After working on various farms or other jobs near Akron for about five years, the family moved to Hahns Peak, Colorado, in 1937. They had partnered with his father, Joe, to purchase a ranch. Hazel and Norma began their schooling at the one-room school in Hahns Peak. Janice Kay Juel, whose family owned the store in Columbine, came to live with the Irelands during the school term. The family went to Steamboat for supplies only twice a year. The ranch was sold in 1941. From there, Elmer's family moved to Pueblo, Colorado, where he worked at the Pueblo Steel & Iron Works steel mill. Next, they spent a year in Leadville, Colorado, where Elmer helped to build Camp Hale. His father, Joe, had bought a farm in Fort Morgan, and in 1944, Elmer, Lillian, and the girls moved to join him. They first lived with Joe and Sylvia, and then moved to a farm about five miles southeast of Fort Morgan. Their income was largely from dairy cows, which the girls milked every morning and evening. After their daughters graduated from high school, Elmer and Lillian moved two miles west of town, but Elmer's health declined. He died in 1958. Six years later, Lillian married Frank Jenik of Sedgwick.

RUBY AND LOUIS LAWLER

Ruby Ireland married Louis Edward Lawler from Paxton, Nebraska, in 1928. They met when he had been hired by Joe to help shuck corn in Sedgwick.

Elmer and Lillian Ireland at their wedding, 1932

Elmer taking a break.

The Elmer and Lillian Ireland family and children. Back: Ron Parachini, Edwin Jess, Darlene Hellmuth, and Jerry Hellmuth; middle: Norma Parachini, Frank Jenik, Lillian Ireland Jenik, and Hazel Jess; front: Debra Parachini Jones, Terri Parachini Ireland, Lyle Jess, Randy Jess, Irwin Jess, Ricky Hellmuth, and Christopher Hellmuth.

Our Ireland Uncles, Aunts, and Cousins / 113

Elmer and Lillian at their 25th wedding anniversary, 1957.

Edwin and Hazel Jess at their farm.

Hazel, Norma, Darlene, and Donna about 1943.

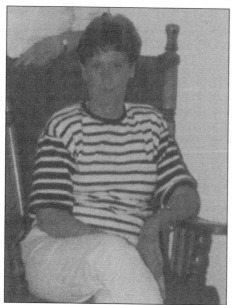

Darlene relaxing in her rocker.

Donna on her couch in North Carolina.

Initially, they farmed close to Louis's family farm near Paxton but later moved to a farm south of Akron, Colorado.

In 1932, the family moved to Scottsbluff, Nebraska. Louis owned a local pub featuring beer only, pool tables, and a small hunting goods counter. He also had an outboard motor and gun repair business for some time. They had seven children: Mildred Maxine (Maxine) (deceased), Lawrence Edward (Larry) (deceased), Frances Fae, John Leroy (Jack), Dorothy Luann (deceased), Patricia Rae, and William Lynn (Bill). A few years after Louis's death in 1980, Ruby moved to Texas to be near several of their children. She died in 1996.

Louis Lawler and his roadster, 1919.

VELMA AND LOUIE GEBAUER / VIOLET AND JOE GEBAUER

Velma and Violet Ireland met and married two brothers, Louis (Louie) and Joseph (Joe) Gebauer, who were dryland farmers near Akron, Colorado. Louie and Joe were among the oldest of ten children who were offspring of one family of Catholic immigrants who had immigrated in 1884 from

Ruby and Louis at their wedding, 1928.

The seven Lawler offspring as children in the 1940s. Back: Jack, Francis; front: Larry, Patricia, Dorothy, Bill, and Maxine.

The Lawler siblings in the 1970s. Back: Jack, Francis, and Bill; front: Larry, Patricia, Dorothy, and Maxine.

Ruby and Louis at their 50th wedding anniversary, 1978.

the Schoenwalde region of Germany and settled around Akron in Washington County. These Gebauer children initially only spoke German and had been sent home from the one-room school because they did not know English. The family then spoke only English at home and taught one another.

Cream separator mailbox.

In any case, the two Ireland/Gebauer couples lived on farms only about two miles apart for most of their married lives. After their wedding in April 1934, Louie and Velma moved to the farm, the Boyer Place, that Joe had purchased and where he and Fannie had lived until Fannie died. For a short time, previous to Louie and Velma's arriving, Elmer and Lillyan had lived there. Not long after Fannie died, Joe moved with the two youngest daughters, Doris and Grace, to Evans. Violet spent a period of time in Greeley during her courtship with Joe. After Violet and Joe were married in December of 1934, they lived on at least two different rented farms nearby before settling at the farm where they raised their family, which was two miles east and one mile south of Louie and Velma's farm. In that their parents were siblings, the two Gebauer families' children were "double cousins" to one another and first cousins to us. Louie and Velma's four children were David Louis, Charlotte Lorrainne, Mary Lavonne (deceased), and Jeannette Lois (deceased). Joe and Violet's seven children were: Joseph Jr. (Joey) (deceased), Richard Eugene, Agnes Marie, Thomas Edward () (deceased), William John (deceased shortly after birth), Rosa Irene (Rose) (deceased), and Patrick James. Violet passed away in 1986 and Velma in 2001.

The Gebauers' lives revolved around planting, cultivating, and harvesting. Over the years, Louie expanded his original farm of about 320 acres with rented and later purchased land as it came up for sale. The farm was later managed by David, and now by his sons. On both farms, the Gebauers raised wheat, oats, corn, and cane. They also had Hereford cattle, hogs, draft horses (plus a few riding horses), and chickens. A few dairy cows were milked during the early years. Louie and Velma later joined with other Gebauers and neighbors to develop a large feedlot for fattening cattle for slaughter. Joe was well known for his ability to break horses.

Velma and Louie Gebauer's family. Back: Beverly Gebauer, David Gebauer, Louie Gebauer holding Dianna Gebauer, Velma Gebauer, Mary Sybrandt holding Larry Walton, and Jeannette Walton holding Mary Lee Walton; front: Kevin Gebauer, Tony Gebauer, Danny Gebauer, and Vickie Walton.

Velma and Louie Gebauer posing outside.

Mary Sybrandt, Charlotte Kumor, and Jeannette Walton.

Charlotte and Leon Kumor at home in Grant, Nebraska.

Mary and Van Sybrandt on the ranch on Elk River.

Michael Sybrandt riding.

Violet and Joe Gebauer in their house.

The Joe Gebauer family. Back: Agnes, Tom, Rose, and Patrick; front: Joey, Joe, and Richard.

Joey, Richard, and Agnes Gebauer, 1943.

Women in the families. Back: Beverly Gebauer and Dolly Gebauer; front: Agnes Friedly, Linda Gebauer, Rose Hazlett, and Charlotte Kumor.

Richard and Linda Gebauer.

David and Joey Gebauer, 2005.

DORIS AND GUS RANCH

Doris Ireland met Augustus (Gus) Ranch during a summer stay in Hahns Peak. Gus was born in Ogden, Utah. His father, Augustus B. Ranch, later owned a ranch near Clark, Colorado. After failing health, Gus senior sold the ranch and moved back to Ogden, Utah, where he died in 1919. His wife, Minnie, stayed in Routt County and later married Evart McFadden, another Elk River rancher, and she had one more child, Jack McFadden.

Gus and Doris were married in 1941 and had three children, Darrell Dafford (deceased), Larry Augustus, and Clifford Eugene (deceased). Over the years, the Ranch family moved often. They lived in Craig, Idaho Springs, and Montezuma in Colorado; at the Honnold Place on the Little Snake River in Colorado; in Lander, Wyoming; at Great Divide (an area south-west of Baggs, Wyoming, and northwest of Craig; see Appendix F); in Craig again; at La Sal, and then, finally, Moab, both in Utah. Darrell married and moved to Williston, North Dakota, and then to Sidney, Montana. Larry married twice; he and his second wife spent most of their lives in Eaton, Colorado. Clifford married and stayed in Moab, Utah.

Gus and his Moffatt County truck at Great Divide.

Mom was closest in age and experience to Doris, and they remained very close until Mom's death. Dad and Gus became good friends as well, but it is likely that they were acquaintances before they married two Ireland sisters. The closeness of the two families was responsible for a number of major or minor projects and undertakings in our lives. These included dynamiting our garage out of the sandstone cliff across the road from our house and prospecting trips looking for minerals. They carefully inspected the abandoned Ferris-Haggarty copper mine near Battle Lake and actually reopened a mine on Beaver Creek east of Hahns Peak and northwest of Pearl Lake in search of molybdenum. Other connections included our family's moving to La Sal, Utah, for a year so that Dad could work in the Homestake uranium

The Doris and Gus Ranch family in
the early 1950s. Back: Darrell, Doris,
and Gus; front: Clifford and Larry.

Anne and Darrell Ranch along with brothers Larry and
Clifford, 1963.

Clifford, Darrell, and Larry Ranch in middle age.

Gus and Doris Ranch at their 40th
anniversary.

mine along with Gus and, later, Mom's purchasing a building lot in Moab, Utah. For David, Rita, and me, the two most important influences and memories came from the school year living at or near the mining camp near La Sal and the numerous summers when, sequentially, Darrell, Larry, and Clifford came to live and work with us at the ranch. All three Ranch boys claimed with pride that it was Dad who taught them how to work. Gus and Doris lived in Moab until they died in 1983 and 2006, respectively.

MEMORIES

THE IRELANDS, GEBAUERS, AND LAWLERS

David: One summer on their visit, Dad took Louie, Velma, and probably some of their kids fishing on King Solomon Creek. Dad always drove like a "bat out of hell" on those narrow Forest Service roads. Often, the trees would be hanging out on both sides, so it was almost like driving through a tunnel. On this particular fishing trip, Velma was sitting in the front seat. She was scared to death of driving in the mountains anyway, but on the way back there was a big switchback before the road came to a bridge. Dad was going fast, and instead of taking the switchback, he drove off the road and onto the Sheep Trail that came out down to the bridge as well. This really scared Velma. We thought it was funny, but Mom was really mad about it because Velma had wet her pants.

David: I worked for the Gebauers in the summer of 1964 before my last year of college. I lived with Velma and Louie in Akron and drove out to their farm every day. David Gebauer was more or less the boss; he told me what to do, and I did it. Mostly, I drove a tractor. For their summer fallow, I drove around and around the field to kill the weeds. Once, I drove the combine in the wheat harvest while, at other times, I drove a truck to haul the grain. It was David who taught me how to drive a tractor straight. He and Louie couldn't stand crooked rows. I learned that on flat land, you can make straight rows on the first round if every time you make a turn, you line up with something in the distance like a windmill. You drive as straight as you can to that windmill until you get to the end of the field. Then, you make your turn and line up on something else in the distance. Sometimes in the summer fallow, they would run the machinery back and forth in one operation, and then the next time, run them on the diagonal.

David: My working at the Gebauers was the summer I turned 21, and they did a good job of breaking me in for that event. Richard and some of Beverly Daniels's family took me up to Sterling to a bar and introduced me to margaritas. They were good! I later learned that with margaritas, you don't know how much alcohol you drank until you try to stand up. I got sick in the car coming home.

Kenneth: My memories of these families are mostly of their coming to the ranch to see us in the summer. Typically, without notice beforehand, an entire family of Irelands or Gebauers, or several of the Lawlers, would appear during the summer, typically in July during haying season. It was almost always immediately after their wheat harvest at the end of June. Since Mom was the youngest of

A visit by the Lawlers as our garage was being dynamited from the cliff. Bill, David, Rita, Patricia, Kenneth, and Dad.

her family, all but two of the cousins were older than we were. Therefore, my memories are vague regarding details; they were mostly influenced by listening to stories about their families as we sat around the kitchen or dining room table.

Kenneth: I do have one clear, but unfortunate, memory when one or more of our cousins were at the ranch. (I believe Jeannette was there, but I am not sure. It was a teenage female cousin.) With our Ranch cousins, we used to climb up on the yard fence near the woodshed, and then up on the board and slab roof, stand on the edge, and pee as far out from the shed as possible. At least two of us were peeing that way while the older cousin(s) stood watching us with much amusement. In the middle of this, I suddenly realized that what I was doing was "bad." I hurriedly climbed down, ran to the house and to my bed and cried inconsolably for a long time. Even when everyone came to tell me it was fine, I remember not feeling any better at all. I can remember this humiliation experience more vividly than any other such experience as a child.

Kenneth: I have a memory of Mom driving David, Rita, and me to Scottsbluff to visit Ruby and Louis and their family, but mostly to attend Francis's wedding. I remember being impressed with the neat rectangular city blocks where all the houses were located and the wonderful concrete sidewalks that would be so wonderful for roller skating. At home, we had the clamp-on metal roller skates that we affixed to our shoes with the little keys included. The only place we could really skate was between our living room, halls, and kitchen at home. There was no flat concrete outside. I vividly remember a hike on the real Scotts Bluffs, the 800-foot high rocky outcrops for which the town was named. Mom also told the story that I

Our Ireland Uncles, Aunts, and Cousins / 123

The first Ireland Reunion at Estes Park, Colorado. Back: *Joe Gebauer, Lillian Jenik, Gus Ranch, Ruby Lawler, and George St. Louis;* front: *Violet Gebauer, Doris Ranch, Dorothy Grace St. Louis, and Velma Gebauer.*

came in from the cold and rubbed my hands in front of the electric cooking range as I would do at home with the wood and coal range. Ruby was apparently very amused.

Kenneth: I remember at least one trip to Akron as a child to visit both Velma and Louie and later, Violet and Joe. I don't remember if Dad was there or not, but I do remember that the three of us kids had to sleep in the same bed. I was impressed with how flat the land was and how far I could see on the prairie. Louie, especially, was always jovial and wanted to show us around the farm. He took us for rides on his big tractor. Velma was a take-charge person and seemed to me to have an unusual accent.

Kenneth: I remember Joe was also genuinely very friendly to us, but not as out-going as Louis. Violet, too, seemed softer and more sensitive than Velma, although I have no specific memory that supports the impression. David and I did play with Tommie, both at their farm and at the ranch more than any other Gebauers because he was, at that time, the youngest in both families. (Rose and Patrick either had not yet been born or were babies at the time.)

Kenneth: Joey and David Gebauer were so much older than we were that they seemed almost as the adults when they came to the ranch. We did hear lots of

Charlotte Kumor at their farm in Grant, Nebraska, 2018.

Ron Kumor who does most of the farming at Grant. He flies from his home in Casper, Wyoming, in his airplane.

stories about them as "hellions" as teenagers in Akron. The only older Gebauer cousin whom I recall spending any time talking to me was Agnes, but the specifics fail me.

Kenneth: I remember, when I was ten, going to Log Lane where Elmer and Grand-dad were building houses for sale. Dad had been there for a time helping out. At one point, Elmer spent at least an hour listening to, arguing with, and eventually resolving a very serious conflict with a home buyer who was absolutely enraged about something.

Kenneth: I really began to know some of my cousins through the Ireland Reunions. The first one at Estes Park was especially memorable when all the aunts and Mom dressed up and presented a silly skit. I attended the reunion in Moab, two in Ridgway, one in Steamboat (which I organized), and the last one at Yellow-stone. I became impressed with David Gebauer, who, sounding very much like his mother with her robust Colorado accent, could recount story after story about not only his family but our St. Louis family as well, along with details about escapades in Steamboat, Dixon, Baggs, and our old stomping grounds. I have also become well acquainted again with Charlotte and have really enjoyed visits to the Kumor farm in Grant, Nebraska, as we have driven cross-country from West Virginia to our cabin near Steamboat.

Kenneth: More than anything else, it has been in the research for this book that has brought me closer to my Ireland relatives. Through the innumerable emails, phone calls, texts, and letters to complete the Ireland generation listing, I have dis-covered that I am related to several hundred people, the majority living in Colorado or adjoining states. I fully expect that the remainder of my life will be enriched by the contacts I have made with my Ireland kinfolk in this process.

Rita: Rarely did we go visit the Gebauers, but I remember spending one Christmas season with them. I was fascinated by having to use an outhouse at Joe and Violet's. I also remember having some delicious canned tomatoes at their table. The tomatoes were gone, and I said I wanted more. Mom objected, but I persisted, and Violet sent one of her kids to fetch another quart. Well, they opened the tomatoes, and I was served another portion. However, one of the tomatoes had a tiny yellow spot on it, and I refused to eat any of them. (No spoiled brat here!)

Rita: At times, our eastern Colorado uncles, aunts and cousins would come to visit. I remember returning from the fair in Rawlins, and there were 21 unannounced guests waiting for us. Daddy and Mom slept in the hayloft at the barn. After that, they declared that they would never give up their bed again.

Rita: Some of our cousins wanted to have horseback rides. As I got older, I was the designated guide. I usually took them too far, and by the time we finally got back home, they were really sore and did not want to ride again the rest of the visit. Another time, I remember taking someone to the top of Sheep Mountain. I only remember how absolutely terrified my guests were as we made the ascent and descent. I just did not realize that they were not accustomed to mountain terrain.

THE RANCH FAMILY

David: When Darrell and Larry came to work for the summer, behind the house near the trees, we built a two-foot wooden base for our wall tent from rough-cut boards for an extra "room" with two single cots. I wanted to sleep there and was afraid somebody else would get to instead. Darrel and I did get to sleep there, using electric blankets. I remember sleeping really well.

Kenneth: My first memories of the Ranch family was when they lived at the Honnold Place. One of those was riding from our ranch up the road for the five miles on a horse-drawn sleigh of some sort (not a hay rack), on a very cold night and covered with warm quilts. Another, in the summer, was the three of us and the three Ranch cousins playing in the field near the log outbuildings. We boys wore long underwear with a button-up flap to cover our backsides. I can visualize Clifford, probably two or three years old, always following us with his flap hanging down unbuttoned leaving his bare bottom showing.

Kenneth: When I was in the sixth grade (as was Darrell), I remember Mom driving us to the Homestake mining camp. Dad needed to finish haying before he could join us. For a few weeks, Mom, David, Rita, and I stayed with Gus, Doris, and three cousins in their 35-foot mobile home (trailer with a shed roof). I recall not being concerned about how crowded it was. We moved to an abandoned house in the tiny town of La Sal until about Christmas and then, "halleluyah," finally to our own shiny silver trailer back in the mining camp (see Chapter 12).

Kenneth: I remember walking to and riding the school bus that Gus drove to and from La Sal every school day. On nice weekends, we took several Saturday hikes to some undercut rock ledges on a hill two or three ridges distant, built a fire on the rock ledge, and roasted wieners for lunch.

Kenneth: Most of my memories of the Ranch cousins were at our ranch in the summer. I recall Darrell being so strong that he was able to throw 70- to 80-pound hay bales up to four high on the hayrack so hard that, standing on top, I had to catch them. When Larry came the next year or two, I recall that he and I did not always get along so well. He did not appreciate my "necessary supervision" (most likely excessive bossiness), and we would end up in loud arguments.

Rita: When I was very young, Mom told of Clifford's and my sleeping in the large drawers built into the bottom of my closet when the Ranch family came to visit at the ranch.

Rita: I remember a game that the boys played to see who could pee farthest off of the back porch. Since I was not able to participate in that part of the contest, I would run under the five arcs of pee and try not to get wet.

Rita: I played with Clifford more than with the other two. He and I were pretty good buddies, and we remained friends through most of our lives. We used to Indian wrestle. (Two people would lie side by side with legs pointing in opposite directions. Each person lifted a leg and hooked it around the other person's leg and then, on signal, pull.) I could usually beat him, but I remember after he got older, we tried it and he nearly tossed me across the room.

The St. Louis and Ranch kids in winter. Back: *Kenneth, David, Darrell, and Larry;* front: *Rita.*

Larry and Darrell as preschoolers.

Darrell getting ready to pile on Dad with the rest of us in some horseplay in the yard.

Our Ireland Uncles, Aunts, and Cousins / 127

Chapter 7

Dad and Mom

George Edwin St. Louis (Dad) met Dorothy Grace Ireland (Mom) in the summer of 1941 when she worked at the Focus Ranch. Most likely it was at a dance at the Pep Hall, but it would not be surprising if Dad saw a young woman scurrying between cabins or in the kitchen when he happened to drive or ride by the dude ranch. Whatever the circumstances, he was drawn to her, and she to him. It could be said that he swept her off her feet as she described the first summer when they courted. Dad was an outgoing entertainer, his few flings with other women had not worked out, and he likely realized he was not getting any younger at the age of 35. If he was to marry, time was of the essence. After all, even his brother of ten years younger had been married for two years. He had always taken it for granted that he would marry, move onto his own ranch, have kids, and raise cattle for the rest of his life. He had been told in high school that if he were to go to college, he would be a happier man, but it is likely that this was as far as he got toward thinking about any future education for himself.

For her part, Mom, at age 18 but going on 19, was young, attractive, and no doubt impressionable. She had lost some weight, partly and by design from becoming a cigarette smoker. She was a good dancer, and she could hold her own in a conversation. She no doubt saw marriage at her first available age to be a potential blessing. Her father, Joe Ireland, was a hard man. She told us that he worked his women to death, and maybe she thought he was responsible for her own mother's premature demise. Whether or not that was the case, Joe rarely did outside chores if any woman was available to do them, and he certainly did not do any indoor chores. Having just graduated with mostly excellent grades from high school, we might suspect that she had thought seriously about going to college, but likely rejected the idea. She had grown up poor and clawed her way to a good high school education but would not have had any money to pay the tuition, room, and board. In

Dad at the time of his graduation from high school in Cheyenne.

Dad at the Home Place dressed for a dance or something special.

Dad at the Bunkhouse in 1941, the year of his marriage to Mom.

Dad sitting tall in the saddle.

Dad leaving someone's barn on horseback.

Dad at the Johnson ranch near Columbine, 1976.

Dad celebrating Christmas with Ken-
neth and family in West Virginia.

Dad getting ready to fly fish in the Little Snake River at the Hon-
nold Place.

Dad at one of his several trailers in the 1980s.

Dad at Trail Ridge Road about 1980.

Mom's Steamboat Springs High
School graduation portrait, 1940.

Mom's portrait in Greeley, 1941.

Mom posing for a photo, 1941.

Mom at a house in Steamboat,
1963.

Mom at her 7th Street house in
Steamboat, 1972.

A portrait of Mom in Steamboat.

Mom at her home in Grand Junction.

Mom in front of a castle she visited with Kenneth in her only trip overseas to The Netherlands, 1991.

Mom posing for a church portrait in her later years in Grand Junction.

fact, she finished high school by doing all the housework as a boarder at the Hubbard home in Steamboat Springs. Among her old mementos and records, in a memories booklet from her senior year she wrote that she wanted to become a nurse, a goal or dream she never mentioned to us. In any case, Mom spent the preceding and following summer at her father's and brother Elmer Ireland's ranch in Hahns Peak, and then, with her sister, Doris, she worked one month for Lucy Temple at the Focus Ranch in the fall of 1940. Later that fall, winter, and spring, she lived with another sister, Ruby Lawler, and her family in Scottsbluff, Nebraska. From there, she applied—and was hired—to work full time for Lucy Temple the next summer. In the interim, Doris had just married Gus Ranch from Hahns Peak.

On November 9, 1941, in the First Christian Church in Greeley, Colorado, Dad and Mom were married. The pastor, whom Mom greatly respected, was Rev. Clifford Cecil. He had baptized her almost three years earlier. Dad, in three hurried letters, wrote of nearly having to postpone the wedding. Alfred had just been hospitalized for appendicitis that had been rendered near fatal by Oliver's cure for about anything, namely, a dose of Epsom salts. Furthermore, a frightful snowstorm had hit the mountains, and the travel on the roads was dangerous and slow. In one line, Dad commented that if things got worse, he would resort to calling Mom long distance.

Our parents entered the marriage with different expectations. We do not know the reason why, but Mom thought that they would live in Denver, where Dad would seek work. Dad expected that he would return to his ranching duties with no interruptions. He had written to her about the fact that he had hoped to build themselves a house on the ranch before they were married but had not been able to do so allegedly because of a very stormy year that delayed the grain harvest. Therefore, after their wedding, they immediately moved into the Home Place with Oliver, Onie, Alfred, Perry, Grace, and babies Jean and Shirley. One month later, Dad was called to report for military duty in World War II, but Grandpa arranged for him to receive an agricultural deferment, obviating the need to leave the ranch. Mom intensely disliked the living arrangement, so she set about to "redecorate" the adjacent log bunkhouse with wallpaper to cover the magazines on the wall and make other changes, all to the chagrin of Onie. They moved into the building after six months, using the closest outhouse and carrying water from the main house. This arrangement went on for two years, including David's first year. Mom wanted her own home. She had endured a series of housekeepers after her own mother had died at her age of ten

Mom and Dad shortly after their wedding in Greeley, Colorado.

Mom and Dad, 1952.

Mom and Dad dressed up at the ranch.

Dad and Mom in the Oak Street house in Steamboat.

years, the family had moved numerous times, she had attended a number of one-room or few-room schools throughout northeast Colorado, she had lived with sisters or other relatives, and she had lived with strangers. She also found Onie to be snoopy and overbearing. She wanted, expected, and no doubt demanded that they have their own home.

Accordingly, although we do not know the details, Dad acquired or purchased, perhaps with the help of Gus Ranch or Joe (Granddad) and Elmer Ireland, a log building in Hahns Peak. It had been a saloon that possibly had been converted from a church meeting house. As explained in Chapter 8, in the early spring of 1944, he dismantled the logs of the saloon, marked each log, and hauled them down to our ranch on a horse-drawn sleigh. It was re-erected immediately on seven acres purchased from Shorty and Lucy Temple that was then between the St. Louis and Temple meadows, adjacent to the Focus Ranch. Without plumbing, an even completely enclosed outhouse, cupboards, and many other "necessities," Mom, Dad, and David moved in before I was born. Mostly finished the next year in 1945, the house was where we grew up.

Dad and Mom with baby David in front of the Bunkhouse.

Our Snake River log house dismantled in Hahns Peak and re-assembled at the ranch.

Mom wanted us to know about her childhood and early years with Dad, so she recorded her memories in two essays. Appendix C provides a detailed account in one combined narrative.

We all lived together on the ranch throughout our childhood and teenage years. One notable exception occurred in about 1950. Our parents had decided to "sell out" and move to Montana. We don't know for sure, but it is likely that this occurred after Dad had a highly stressful and unprofitable experience with his 50 cows and calves that were summered at the Frye Place near Hahns Peak (now underwater in Steamboat Lake). An outbreak of "foot rot" occurred in the herd, requiring repeated "doctoring" that involved roping an animal, tying it down, and applying medicine and bandages. Aside from the time and

Ewes and lambs grazing.

A sheep wagon in the forest or on the Sheep Trail.

stress of doctoring, no doubt the calves did not gain the weight they would have otherwise. In any case, near Bozeman, Montana, they located a ranch that they wanted to buy and had settled on the price and all the arrangements. When they came back to Snake River to sell everything and prepare for the long move, the elderly couple who owned the Montana ranch had a change of heart and backed out of their verbal agreement. With nothing in writing, Dad and Mom determined that they could do nothing, so the whole idea of moving was abandoned, and as we remember, was never considered again until after we children had moved away from home.

The years were punctuated by far more failed business deals than successes or even break-evens. Mom and Dad struggled to make ends meet for most of our childhood and beyond. After the "foot rot" epidemic, in the early 1950s, they abandoned the familiar cow-calf operation as their main ranching endeavors in favor of a "band" of sheep (typically regarded as 1000 ewes with lambs). Of course, the necessary routines were changed accordingly. These included "docking" the lambs or cutting off their long tails as well as castrating the rams, and branding with paint or tar on the wool rather than burning the hide. It also involved "trailing" (driving) the sheep on Forest Service Stock Driveways (Sheep Trails) to the Wyoming high desert for the winters where far less hay was required. In these winters, Dad had to leave us for weeks at a time to live with a hired Mexican sheep herder where they had to sleep together in one sheep wagon. One summer, the sheep business led to the only complete family "vacation" we ever had, when all five of us rode horseback (with Rita and I riding double) over the Continental Divide from Whiskey Park and over to the Damfino Creek Forest allotment. We camped there in an old logging or mining shack, caught hundreds of fish to eat, and loved the time together.

The sheep business was risky as well. One year, a staggering percentage of ewes and lambs were frozen to death in a spring blizzard on the Sheep Trail.

An Austin-Western grader similar to the one Dad operated.

A similar grader with V-plow and side wing for breaking through heavy snow and pushing graded snow off into a snow bank.

And our last flock of 500 ewes was descimated by coyotes, especially one particularly wily male that killed one or two ewes or lambs every night during an entire summer without eating any of them.

Intermittently, during these years, Dad bought yearling steers, summered them on grass, and sold them in the fall. At least one of these enterprises, involving a motley collection of cattle from Mississippi, turned out to be surprisingly successful.

Beginning in 1958 and continuing until the ranch was sold, Dad was employed by the Routt County Bridge and Highway Department to maintain the gravel road on the Little Snake River. His charge was the segment from the Wyoming line in Slater to the Three Forks Ranch in the winters as the road (Colorado 129) between Three Forks and Clark was closed due to the heavy snow. In summers and fall he maintained the road to Columbine. Dad operated a red Austin-Western grader several times in the summer to smooth and distribute the gravel and, in winter, to clear the snow whenever necessary. For snow, he mounted a large V-plow in front to break through heavy snow and a "wing" blade on the right side to push the snow further laterally after the standard blade cleared the roadway beneath the grader. In winters, too, although not legally authorized to do so, Dad often opened individual driveways and, occasionally, haystacks in neighbors' fields. Once, he cleaned all the ditches at the Fleming Place. We called the machine, which was typically parked at the left side of our driveway, "the *road*-mun-*ta*-ner."

In these years on the ranch, our parents provided transportation for most of our early social outlets. These included family dinners with the aunts, uncles, and cousins at the Home Place, overnight stays with another St. Louis family, dances at the Pep Hall or Dixon, and occasional movies ("picture shows") in Baggs. Others were trips to Craig ("town") to buy groceries or to shop for Christmas or to attend joint Christmas programs at either the Willow Creek or Battle Creek schools. Transportation for 4-H activities included meetings at the Savery Schoolhouse, 4-H Camp for four days in the summer, County Fair in Rawlins, Wyoming, and later, some livestock judging trips. Dad organized much anticipated all-day fishing trips in the summer and sledding parties on the Temple grade or ice-skating parties on the river at night in the winter. Later, we drove ourselves to many places that were not in town, well before we were old enough to have driver's licenses.

In 1957, Mom moved with the three of us to Steamboat Springs so that first David, and later, Rita and I could attend high school. A routine evolved wherein Mom would live in Steamboat for each nine-month school year while Dad remained on the ranch. We lived first for several months in one of the cabins built by Granddad about three miles southeast of Steamboat on US Route 40. We then lived the rest of the first school year in a little yellow rented house on Park Street close to the hospital. Then, we lived for the 1958–1959 school year in a three-story motel, the Rustic Lodge. In the summer of 1959, Mom and Dad bought a house on

Newspaper advertisement featuring Mom at IntraWest Bank in Steamboat.

Oak Street, where we lived until 1963, when the house was sold. For Rita's senior year of high school, after our ranch was sold (see below), Mom, Dad, and Rita rented a little house on 3rd Street and then moved back to Granddad's place east of town. Mom worked at several jobs during these years. She started as a clerk at the Kinney Drug Store. Thereafter, she applied for and was given positions at the Routt County National Bank, Northwest Colorado Finance, and finally to the new IntraWest Bank transitioning from bank employee to loan officer. Until the sale of the Oak Street house, on weekends, Mom and the three of us would drive back to the ranch, especially in the early years. Later, and when the roads were bad or weekend high school activities intervened, Dad either came to Steamboat or everyone stayed where they were.

After Rita graduated from high school in 1964, Mom was increasingly ambivalent about going back to live on the River. As noted, the experience a few years earlier wherein coyotes had practically wiped out our flock of 500 ewes left Dad discouraged and ready to try something new. This was after he and I had fenced the entire Fleming Place and the adjacent BLM ground on Piney Mountain with woven wire, precluding the need for a herder. Thus the cost of having 1000 ewes would have been reduced by half with the same expected income.

All of this led to the beginning of what might be the biggest upheaval of their lives. In late 1962 and early 1963, Dad and Mom decided to sell our ranch to Kenley (Herrick) and Marcia Lidstone, a couple from New York who had been dudes at the Focus Ranch for several years and wanted to own a ranch on the Little Snake River. At fire sale prices, they acquired our land, houses, barns, machinery, and livestock. Our entire ranch was sold for

Mom and Dad's house in Boulder while they managed the Glacier Laundromat.

$52,000. Sinc and Elizabeth, who then owned the Home Place, decided to sell it to the Lidsones as well. An arrangement was made for Oliver and Onie to have a life legacy, that is, to live in their house and about three acres until they died. Otherwise, everything was owned by a new company, named the L-O-N Corporation. Dad was hired on as foreman to manage the ranch, and Mom was to be a cook. They could live in our childhood-log house.

Knowledgeable ranch hands as well as several high school boys from New York City were recruited to come and work on the ranch in the summer. Rita was hired to manage 700 yearling steers and 72 cow-calf pairs, and I was hired to be a "straw boss" to supervise the city boys. Even with all the new vehicles and machinery, Dad and Mom could not take it. Dad lamented that the appointed manager "would lie when the truth would fit better." Worse, he found it almost intolerable to be managed by a person who knew next to nothing about cattle.

At about the same time as the ranch sold, so did the Steamboat house in early 1963. After one year with the L-O-N Corporation, Dad quit. Both he and Mom ended up again in Steamboat in a rented house on 3rd Street in the late fall of 1963. During the winter, they moved to Granddad's place with the ponds southeast of town. Dad searched for and wanted to buy a large sheep ranch near Steamboat, but Mom was not interested. It is said that timing is everything. Jim Temple, Shorty and Lucy Temple's son, appeared in a time of great weakness for both of them and offered to sell them the Glacier Laundromat he owned in Boulder, Colorado. He told them that it was very profitable but that he needed to sell it. So, they bought the laundromat and moved to Boulder to run it in September of 1964. Not too surprisingly, it was not a financial bonanza. While Rita and I were at Colorado State University in Fort Collins, 50 miles away, both Dad and Mom worked extremely long hours trying to learn a new business and to keep old customers while getting new ones. They absolutely hated it. After one year of this, they managed to sell the business, and Dad said it was like "getting out of jail."

The next chapter in their lives was not unlike the attempt about 16 years earlier to move to Montana. They traveled all over the Northwest and eventually found a ranch, complete with cattle, near Cusick, Washington, that they purchased. Pulling up stakes again and moving nearly 1000 miles away from their "home," they worked very hard to work the ranch and keep it going. In addition to numerous other problems, many of the newborn calves contracted "white muscle disease" and died.

All of this was simply too much for Mom, who experienced a "mental breakdown" with serious thoughts of suicide. She could not adjust to being so far away from anyone she knew, and her children were gone. She was extremely fearful of about everything, but especially about running out of money. She experienced agony going to the store to buy anything. Meantime, Dad was trying to run the new ranch, while Mom was sure he was doing everything wrong. As a result, they decided to sell the ranch. Of course, there was hay to bring in, cattle to gather and sell, and all the other ranch chores.

Rita and her fiancé, Chris Maser, came to the ranch that first summer and got married; yet, Mom confided later that she remembered nothing of it. It was clear this would not work, so they immediately put the Washington ranch up for sale. Chris needed to go to Egypt to start on a grant-funded project while Rita stayed for the rest of the summer to help. Rita helped with gathering cattle, with haying, and with selling the cattle. A nearby family, Bob and Claudette Heitman, and their young teenage children, were a real Godsend. They helped Dad a lot, they believed in him, and they generally offered the only support he had.

In late September, Rita loaded the horse trailer with household goods and, with Mom, drove it to Steamboat. Dad stayed in Cusick until the sale of the ranch was finalized. Mom and Rita initially stayed at Elizabeth's house, but Rita soon departed to join Chris overseas.

After the ranch sold, Dad came back to Colorado, but sadly, at that point Mom initiated a separation. She bought and moved into a cozy red house in Steamboat on 7th Street in October 1967. Their divorce was finalized in 1971.

Mom's lovely red house on 7th Street.

Mom and Nick after their wedding.

Mom enjoying her backyard and flower garden in her house in Grand Junction where, after her death, some of her ashes were scattered.

After a few years, Mom reconnected with a high school friend and local attorney, Nick Magill, who had represented her in the divorce proceedings with Dad. Nick's wife had recently died. After a short courtship, Mom remarried in 1978. She moved into Nick's house but kept hers as a rental. This, too, did not work out. The marriage lasted only two and a half years. Mom moved back into her house in November 1980, and they divorced officially four months later. Mom legally changed her name back to Dorothy Grace St. Louis, and she stayed in Steamboat and worked at the bank until her retirement. She developed emphysema and learned to manage the tubes of oxygen in the house and portable unit for traveling about. But managing Steamboat's deep snow every winter became too much for her.

Accordingly, she sold her house and moved to one she purchased in Grand Junction. She lived there, volunteered at the Chamber of Commerce, reconnected with the First Christian Church, developed a few good friendships, the closest of which was her niece Maxine Forrest, and took care of her beloved flower garden until her death. Mom's obituary, which I wrote, is provided in Appendix B.

After their separation, which Dad decidedly did not want and which hurt him badly, he first worked for various ranchers in the Steamboat area. Then between 1969 and 1975, he moved back to Little Snake River, intermittently working for the Focus Ranch wrangling dudes in the summer and guiding hunters in the fall, but often staying at the Home Place with Grandma and Alfred. Within the first year of this period on the River, he had three angina heart episodes. An X-ray after the third heart attack revealed that he had lung cancer as well. He was hospitalized in Denver and a lobe of his lung was surgically removed. He quit smoking cold turkey then and there and, beating the odds of surviving lung cancer, completely recovered. In fact, only a few weeks after his surgery, he headed up an elk hunting camp, which was several hours horseback ride from the road. In 1976, in addition to working at the Focus Ranch, Dad bought and summered 50 to 100 yearling cattle near Steamboat. The fences in the leased property were bad, so Rita, who lived that summer with Mom, helped with the riding to return the strays back into the property.

A large bull elk bagged during hunting season. Ed Buchanan, Sinc, Dad, Bob Bogle.

Dad married Vivian Hunt, whose husband, Harry Hunt, had previously divorced her. A marriage actually occurred twice. After allegedly "tying the knot" the first time, they decided they would not be married. A few months later, not long after Mom had married Nick Magill, Dad and Vivian made it permanent. Beginning in 1977, for the next five years, they lived at the Lazy C–2 Bar ranch at the old Luchsinger Place then owned by Roger Stull, where Dad managed the ranch. One summer, Rob-

Dad and Vivian having a good time.

Dad and Vivian's camper and main mobile home at the Gilbert Williams Place near Slater.

ert (David's eldest son) came and lived with Dad and Vivian to help out and learn ranch work. In 1982 while chasing a cow, Dad was thrown from his horse because the saddle cinch broke. This seriously injured his shoulder. He continued to work for some time but in a reduced capacity. Thereafter,

Dad and Vivian's modular home just west of Dixon.

he and Vivian lived in at least two mobile homes and a series of smaller camper trailers at the Gilbert Williams Place in Slater and in Craig. Eventually, they bought a modular home and placed it on a lot purchased just west of Dixon. Winters were variously spent in Grand Junction in a motel or in St. George, Utah, in their camper.

Vivian suffered a series of progressively more serious health problems until she died at their home in Dixon on April 4, 1989. Dad continued to live there for the rest of his life. He kept lots of old friends and made new ones, and continued to be the entertainer he always had been, especially at the Dixon Senior Center. Sadly, while accompanying David and Chai to Thailand on his first trip abroad in the fall of 1990, he had a serious episode that resembled a stroke, but which turned out to be a seizure. He improved after a few days but never recovered. Upon returning to the US, he sat in uncharacteristic silence as David drove him from Colorado to Mississippi (for the purpose of spending the winter there). About two days later, David took him to the hospital in Hattiesburg. During his first night there, Dad suffered massive seizures again and became mostly comatose. He died in the hospital on New Year's Day in 1991. His obituary, written by his then son-in-law, Hugh Richards, is in Appendix A.

Throughout their post-divorce lives, Mom and Dad stayed in touch. It was never an issue for us to visit one and then the other on our trips back to Colorado or Wyoming. On numerous occasions, Mom would have him stop by her house in Grand Junction while dealing with Vivian's health issues. She even helped care for him for the few days between his episode in Thailand and his trip to Mississippi. She had mentioned many times that she always loved him but simply could not live with him. The years of failed business deals had taken their toll.

Mom lived in her house in Grand Junction until her health mandated that she move into an assisted living facility, which she arranged almost entirely on her own. In 1997, after one year there, her worsening emphysema and associated problems began to affect her overall heath and memory. With declining pulmonary function and aspiration pneumonia, her last few months were in St. Mary's Hospital, where she died on June 8, 1998.

Dad and Mom's burial site at the Reader Cemetery in Savery, Wyoming, with Kenneth.

The cremated remains of both Dad and Mom are buried at the Reader Cemetery west of Savery, Wyoming. Because Dad knew that Vivian still loved her ex-husband Harry Hunt (who had previously died in an automobile accident), he arranged to bury Vivian next to Harry in that cemetery. And, Mom, in her last few weeks, confided that she would like to be buried next to Dad. Knowing that he would have liked that as well, we replaced his headstone with one showing both of them.

What did this couple bring to their marriage and to their children from their own personalities, upbringing, and experiences? Both had come from large families and were comfortable with the hustle and bustle of familiar people coming in and out of the house. But Dad's siblings were all boys, and all but one of Mom's siblings were girls. Neither was accustomed to having or spending lots of money, although it is likely that Dad felt more secure in his cattle business financially than Mom had felt most of her life. This was in spite of the fact that he tried and failed in many more endeavors than she did. Dad was an extroverted person, quick to make friends, and trusting of everyone. Mom, however, was more introverted— at least with strangers—and learned that she needed to be a very careful accountant to make sure that income could meet expenses. She also "sized people up" quickly and was almost always right about the extent to which they could be trusted. Mom took charge of the household completely and of the family finances. She did not have the knowledge or even the desire to acquire the knowledge of how to handle cattle—or later sheep—so she left the day-to-day ranching to Dad. Surprisingly, even with emphysema and its terrible toll on her, Mom said she did not regret smoking and did not blame anyone else for it.

Dad was generally a patient, accepting person; Mom was too, but, when things were not going well or as planned, she could be quite impatient or even downright demanding. Dad might be regarded as a reactive person, dealing with whatever came up, sometimes with surprising insight and innovation. On the other hand, Mom was more proactive in her approach, planning carefully and then following the plan as best she could. Both of them valued hard work, honesty, and straight talk.

Our parents also gave us music. Both sang all their lives and could hit the notes perfectly on key. Dad, like his father, entertained (although his penchant for jumping at any chance to do so embarrassed Mom a little). He also went about much of his work with a sort of tuneless whistle of one song or another. Mom clearly hummed or sang various songs while she worked, no doubt a carryover from her experience with her mother before her untimely death. We all three liked to sing and did so through our adult lives. And our children and grandchildren were blessed with pleasing voices that they share with others.

The misfortunes both Dad and Mom experienced were serious and lasting. Yet, neither one ever gave up. They had remarkable resilience to rise again from misfortune or try again after failure. Except perhaps for Mom's emotional breakdown, they always seemed to be able to see better possibilities for the future.

We as their children have been indelibly affected by our dad and Mom. Both wanted the absolute best for us and were willing to sacrifice whatever was necessary to accomplish that. As children we never heard that we might not go to college; instead, we were encouraged to do well in school so that we could go to college. At the same time, we were minimally guarded from our childhood curiosity, which led to some potentially dangerous consequences, such as riding alone by ourselves at a young age, playing with fire (or firecrackers), using knives and guns, riding our bikes freely on the main county road, and driving tractors or pickups as pre-teenagers.

Memories

Dad

David: As kids, we learned to figure things out by watching Dad. For instance, Dad maintained the Hackmaster ditch, which for the most part was cut into the side of a very high and steep hill directly above Roaring Fork. One very steep portion washed out every year. He figured the solution to the problem was to put a section of pipe across that place. It was a lot of work but easier than digging a new ditch further and further back into the bank every year. One year, a huge boulder had rolled down off the hill and into the middle of the ditch. It was too big to move by hand, so Dad taught us how to use dynamite to break the rock. Most people unknowingly would have placed the dynamite beneath the rock. That would have blown a big crater in the ditch. At the same time, the rock would have gone up into the air and likely back into the crater, thus making the problem worse than before. It didn't make sense to me at the time, but Dad put two sticks of dynamite on top of the boulder and packed it down tight with mud. When the dynamite went off, the boulder was broken into small pieces that we could lift out of the ditch. Dad explained, "Dynamite blows down—not up."

David: Because Dad maintained the roads, he convinced the County that he needed dynamite to blow out beaver dams and to unplug the culverts. A beaver dam had been built in a creek next to the road, and he showed me how to blow it out. He explained that you don't place the dynamite into the back of the dam; instead, you place it in the water in front of the dam down about midway where the water presses

Kenneth trying to feed Bonnie some watermelon.

A later puppy trying to wake up its master.

Dad and Mom / 147

against it. He set the charge, and the blast blew the dam out perfectly without leaving a crater. He came by his knowledge of dynamite at a young age by blowing out big cottonwood tree stumps to clear land for hayfields. He told a funny story about a prize Hereford bull wanting to challenge the smoking fuse coming from a stump that was about to blow up. The blast blew the bull back about 12 feet.

David: Kenneth and I bought our new spurs at the same time from the Montgomery Ward catalogue. I first used mine on my horse, June. Dad said, "Be careful and keep the spurs out of her, or she'll jump out from under you." I didn't know what he meant until I thrust June's belly a little too hard with the spurs. She made a heck of a jump. She didn't lose me, but I learned a valuable lesson.

David: Until I was older, I could never figure out why Dad would get so mad at "those damn beavers" and "those damn gophers." When we were old enough to irrigate ourselves, and had to tear out beaver dams by hand almost daily, or when the water would first leak and then basically run out of the ditch because of gopher holes, then I understood.

David: Dad was my idol and everything he did was right until one time he did something that really confused me. We were taught not to steal, but one day we loaded up several pickup loads of cedar fence posts that belonged to the Three Forks Ranch and took them home. They were in a big pile by the gate between the Hackmaster Place and the Honnold Place. They had laid there for several years for the purpose of building a new fence between the two places, but the new fence was never built. Dad justified the theft by saying they had forgotten about the posts, didn't need them, or something like that. It was a hard pill to swallow that Dad was not perfect. The disappointment seemed to ease when we built a tepee tent with the posts and covered them with blankets.

David: I only saw Dad cry one time. I was walking with him to the barn on the morning after he had found the tractor turned over on top of Francis. I suppose this is why I used to believe the truth in the words of the old Sons of the Pioneers song, "Teardrops in My Heart": "A cowboy can't reveal a broken heart until he's all alone, someplace to play the part."

David: Dad was always looking for a way to make extra money along with ranching. During the uranium boom, he and Lewis Morgan went prospecting in Powder Basin below Baggs. They noticed that everyone was staking claims down on the flat, so he said to Lewis, "I believe there's more uranium up here on this ridge." They staked some claims there, but then they got busy with haying and ranching and never filed the claims. Someone "jumped" the claims and filed them. Not long thereafter, uranium mining began by simply by scooping up sand into dump trucks and hauling the ore to the mill. And, it turned out that richer ore was taken from the ridge. That was one time Dad said we could have been rich. Another lost opportunity was his failure to buy Granddad's lake property in Steamboat.

David: Growing up, we never allowed cats or dogs in the house. However, when we were going to high school in Steamboat and Dad was alone at the ranch, he would let our border collie, Bonnie, stay in the house. He said, "She keeps me company."

David: One of Dad's sayings was, "There's nothing wrong with that man a good whipping wouldn't cure." And, if need be, he was ready, willing, and able to do the job. I believe that saying is true of many people I know.

David: Dad thought he could fix almost anything. All you had to do was take it apart, blow or clean it out, and then put it back together again. Once, he was waiting for me in our GMC pickup, and I heard the horn honking as when a car alarm goes off. When I got there, the hazard lights were flashing, the horn was honking, and Dad had the horn and all the mechanisms inside of the steering wheel torn apart. We soon figured out all that was needed was to pull out the button that he had pushed to honk the horn.

David: I won't forget the time our septic system backed up. Dad dug down and took the top off the septic tank so he could figure out what was wrong. After poking around with rods and wires, he decided the pipe from the septic tank going out to the slough ("the stinks") was plugged. Try as he might, he couldn't get it unplugged. He said, "I believe a small stick of dynamite will blow it out." So, he lit a small dynamite charge in the septic tank. It may have unplugged the pipe when a whole section of the pipe and the top of the septic tank were blown off and black shit was everywhere, including the side of the house, the windows, and the roof. The whole septic tank had to be replaced with new pipe into and out of it.

Kenneth: I spent most of my time with Dad as a child. I remember when he took me up the Hackmaster ditch to clean it out in the early summer when I was ten. I remember working with a shovel all day and have an indelible memory of eating our lunch on the ditch bank at a sharp corner in front of a large pine tree. As noted, much of the ditch was built on a very steep hill or even a cliff. It took a great deal of digging to move the ditch back into the hill where it had washed out on one of the steepest parts. I still dream about walking that ditch and cleaning it out and wish I could revisit the place now.

Kenneth: As a child, I was not aware of how patient Dad was with me, showing me how to do hundreds of jobs. Not being a patient person myself, I am forever thankful that he was able to maintain that encouragement when I certainly must have been difficult to deal with. On the other hand, I believe he was proud of how hard I tried, how quickly I learned, and then how hard I worked. I never regretted staying at home in the summers, all the way through high school, earning the very limited wage that Dad and Mom were able to pay me.

Kenneth: Dad was so comfortable in the saddle. He always sat up straight and moved with his horse.

Kenneth: Dad would let us try about anything, even though he was concerned about our safety. So long as we were learning and progressing in getting our many, many jobs done, he let us experiment. For example, after one or two demonstrations, we learned on our own how best to corner and catch our horses, and then to properly adjust the cinches of our saddles. Dad showed us how to drive a tractor to pull a side-delivery rake, or how to pull the slip to pick up bales, but then he just turned us loose to figure out the details. We figured out how to get close to but not into deep ditches on a tractor. We learned how to use the hydraulic lift of our little Ford 9N to pull a heavy load of hay on the slip, balancing between rearing the tractor over backwards or simply spinning the back wheels. We learned to be independent thinkers and doers.

Kenneth: Dad was always proud of my school and adult accomplishments. He did not say a lot about them, but there was no doubt in my mind that he was proud.

Kenneth: Occasionally, Dad would lose his patience, and I was surprised and a little scared when he did. Sometimes, he would start to run from one place to another when otherwise he always walked. He would yell "Whoa" to a piece of machinery. He would cuss even more than usual.

Kenneth: I really liked to take days off with Dad, for all-day fishing trips to North Fork, for hunting deer, or for driving up in the forest for various reasons. He knew where to go for the fish or game; he exuded excitement himself; he told stories about nearly every place we went.

Kenneth: I was always surprised at how ticklish Dad was with his feet. He literally could not stand any tickling there.

Kenneth: Dad had a simple way of looking at things, and these were often not particularly informed by knowledge outside of his realm. Once, when a former hunter from California, Fran Krugh, who had become a family friend, drove out one summer to visit us in a new Porsche. Dad looked at the little car and asked, "How fast will that go, 40 or 50 miles an hour?"

Kenneth: I was not a witness to any of Dad's many fist fights, but I recall a few times where he was ready to fight. Once, when he and I were riding to the Damfino sheep allotment on the Forest, we came upon another sheep man who was not going to let us take our sheep across another park beyond Hog Park. They talked awhile, and the man would not budge. Just like that, Dad stepped off his horse and told the guy to "Get off!" and they would settle this. The man backed down and that was the end of it.

Kenneth: A rather long story involved Dad getting tar that would be used to brand the sheep at docking time. Someone from the Wyoming Highway Department had given him permission to get a few five-gallon buckets of road tar from a large storage tank in Baggs. Dad drove our Jeep pickup under the large spigot, the end of which was an elbow of a large pipe that had been rotated to a vertical position. It would ordinarily be rotated 180 degrees downward into an opening on top of a tanker truck. Then a large wheel closer to the tank would be turned to open a valve that would start the flow of road tar. Once a truck was filled, the wheel would be turned the other way to shut off the tar, and then the elbow would be returned to its elevated position to prevent any remaining overflow.

Of course, the apparatus was much higher than our pickup, so Dad climbed up on the stock rack to rotate the spigot, which was about six inches in diameter, down toward a bucket in the pickup bed. He then climbed up again and opened the valve. Nothing happened, so Dad opened the valve more. Eventually, about two minutes later, a six-inch uninterrupted flow of tar began to ooze out and slowly continued for about six feet until it went into the first bucket. Of course, it filled the bucket in about two seconds and Dad moved another bucket under it, with lots of spillage into the pickup and onto himself. This happened for about four buckets, and Dad realized it was completely out of control. He yelled at David to turn off the valve, but when David climbed up to try, the big wheel was too stiff for him to turn. At the same time, Dad had turned the spigot vertically, but the tar simply came down over the sides in a much wider flow, all down his arms, his chest and stomach, his legs, and his shoes. With tar by then covering the entire bed of the pickup, Dad abandoned trying to catch any of the tar in the buckets and climbed up to close the valve. Of course, after doing so, it took a seeming eternity for the flow to stop, just as there was a delay in getting it started. By the time it did stop, everything in the back of the pickup, as well as Dad was covered with black, sticky tar.

I don't remember much of the conversation for the 30-mile drive home except that he once remarked that all he needed was to be rolled in feathers to be "tarred and feathered." It took a great deal of gasoline and scrubbing to clean the pickup seat and floor, the steering wheel, the pickup bed, his shoes, and even his body. I don't remember, but I suspect his clothes were discarded and burned.

Dad listening to a song about him written and sung by his kids at his 80th birthday party.

Kenneth (with contributions from David and Rita): As with Dad's fights when I was very young, I was not an actual witness at the time, but I woke up one summer on the ranch in my early college years to find a bloody guy sleeping in the bed next to mine. I got up to find Dad in the kitchen, probably having not gone to bed. The escapade he described involved himself (about the age of 55), Grandpa, Steve Andrew (cousin Sharon's husband), and Walt Stokes (a young boyfriend of Rita who apparently knew judo). Walt was the chap in bed next to me.

They had all met at the Bank Club Bar in Baggs, because Dad was taking Grandpa home from the County Fair in Rawlins. Dad had arranged to pick up Walt to work for us, as he had finished working for Steve. The fiasco apparently started after a few drinks in Baggs when Steve was being teased after Grandpa, an 80-year old man, beat him at arm wrestling. On the way up the River, they stopped at Dixon for more drinks before proceeding to take Grandpa home. They were nearly to Grandpa's house when one of them realized that Walt had left his saddle and belongings next to the Bank Club Bar in Baggs. At that point, they dropped Grandpa at the Home Place and drove 30 miles back to Baggs to retrieve them. The Bank Club Bar was closed, but Walt's belongings were still there in the street. Of course, they had to stop by Dixon again for more drinks. There, as Dad explained, Walt was bragging that he could "press" Dad, or lift him over his head. He tried to do so but dropped Dad headfirst onto the floor. Dad got mad and threatened to fight Walt. Steve stepped in to stop a fight, so Dad took a swing and hit Steve. Then, he got into a real fight with Walt, who had warned Dad that he was an expert in judo, such that his hands were registered as dangerous weapons. Undaunted, Dad challenged Walt, "Well then, just bring on your judo." Regarding Walt, Dad remarked to me the next morning, "He's tough. Every time I knocked him down, he got up." The night ended up with Dad deciding that he should take care of Walt, so he drove him home and put him in bed in my bedroom (without waking me up).

With the sketchy details it is hard to explain why, as Steve recalled, they ran out of gas after midnight and had to wake up "old Roubideau" to pump gas from a 55-gallon drum, unless Dad made not two but three trips to Baggs. It was also not clear why Steve was there and not at home. Steve never wanted to talk much about the incident, possibly because Sharon was less than happy about it.

Dad and Bob Bogle after bringing down a big (mule deer) buck.

Rita: Writing a few paragraphs about one of the most important persons in one's life is in truth impossible. Nevertheless, the man and father, George St. Louis needs to be recorded somewhere besides in my memory. Daddy was a complex enigma of simplicity, strength, humor, honor, and naivete.

Rita: Daddy never knew a stranger. He liked people, and people liked him. While a man of strength, he was pretty wishy-washy when it came to some of his opinions. I always stated that his opinion was that of the last person he talked to. I think he "wanted to get along and be likable," so he often agreed with whomever he was talking to. He could also easily be influenced by other people's persuasion. That got him into trouble because he was also a man of honor. He believed that a man was as good as his word; and if he gave his word, it was binding. Documents and signatures were not important to Daddy. As a result, he was often hornswoggled into deals that were not in his best interest. Specifically, I remember some sheep deal with Lewis Morgan. "Here's the deal..." Lewis talked Daddy into jointly having a band of sheep, and while I was too little to know the specifics, I know that Daddy spent the winter on the desert with that band of sheep, and Lewis ended up with most of the profit.

Rita: For several years Daddy guided hunters. A few were not a good fit, but there was a core group from California who came for several years. They would bring all kinds of fruit, and candy to us kids; they would bring cases of liquor, and their main mission was to enjoy the beautiful Rocky Mountains and get some deer while they were at it. Their names have mostly slipped into oblivion, but I remember Pappy Gray and his son as well as Bob Bogle. They were all not only clients, but they

Dad, no doubt giving his rendition of "The Persian Kitty."

Dad singing a cappella one of his Western songs, quite likely, "Punchin' the Dough."

became good friends to our family.

Times were so very different then too: I remember that Bob either got bucked off or kicked by our horse Rondo. Bob picked himself up; he was sore; but no big deal. (Imagine the law suits these days if something like that should happen.) One time the game warden, Dallas Morgan, came by to inspect the deer that the hunters had bagged. That very day Daddy and the hunters had poached a bunch of ducks, which Mom had cooked for dinner. Daddy invited Dallas to dinner, then he took him out to view the deer carcasses and, on the way, they passed a pile of fresh duck feathers. Meantime, Mom was scrambling to hide the cooked ducks and come up with something to feed Dallas. Luckily Dallas did not see, or pretended not to see, the feathers and luckily further, he said he could not stay to eat.

Rita: My earliest memory of Daddy was my sitting on his lap and counting matches from his pocket. I do remember his helping us onto our horses and including us in his daily life as much as he could. One time I had just gotten an orphan lamb that I carried to the barn. I put the lamb down just as Daddy turned the milk cows out. One of the cows stepped right on the little lamb's neck and it lay there lifeless. Daddy told me, "You just got your lamb killed." Mortified, I ran crying to the house squalling "The lamb's dead, the lamb's dead..." Mom came out because of my screaming, and instead of any sympathy, she started to laugh—because the lamb was running as fast as it could to catch up with me.

Rita: Daddy taught me to ride and to handle cattle and sheep. He taught me how to drive the wild horses so they would not panic. With utmost patience (I do not remember him ever losing patience as he taught us stuff) he taught me how to run a dump rake in the hay field, and how to harness a horse. He taught me about lambing and how to get the ewes to "mother up" with their lambs. He ran the road grader and would make the Temple grade extra slick so we could have sledding parties in the winter.

Rita: My sense is that Daddy never seemed to totally catch up with the times. He remained the person he learned to be as a young man. Daddy was a gentleman. He took off his hat when he entered a house; he did not tell shady jokes around ladies; and he would always be a protector of women. In fact, he did not want me to witness my mare, Gypsy's being bred by a stallion because that is something that ladies were not supposed to witness.

Rita: But Daddy always had a delightfully "sideways" way of looking at things. For example, one summer after we were fully grown and out on our own, Kenneth and I thought it would be fun to herd sheep. We were having dinner at the Dixon Club, and Kenneth asked Daddy whether anyone hired sheep herders any more. His answer was, "Stratton hired a sheep herder, and he got bucked off his horse and hit his head on a rock, and it damned near killed him." Was that an answer? I'm not sure. Another example was when he and Vivian came to Alaska in the 1980s. We drove them around in the state, and after it was over, I asked Daddy what his favorite part was. He answered, "I liked that town, Elmer." "Do you mean Homer?" I asked. He said, "Yes, Homer. I knew it was one of the Beeler brothers, there was a Homer and an Elmer."

Rita: Daddy was also the quintessential entertainer. Give him an audience, and he would give them a song. Of all of the brothers, Daddy seemed to have "inherited" Grandpa's love of singing and entertaining. Sinc's version of "When the Work's All Done this Fall" stays with me, but Daddy had "She Never Came Back," "Siree Peaks," "Ain't We Crazy," and "She's a Pretty Little Dear." He had a few poems too, and the one I remember most was about a stray tom cat courting a spoiled rich female kitten.

Rita: I believe the end of Daddy and Mom's marriage was the hardest thing for Daddy. He was really sad, lost, and lonesome. But somehow, he gathered himself together, returned to Snake River, his home, and started a new life working at the

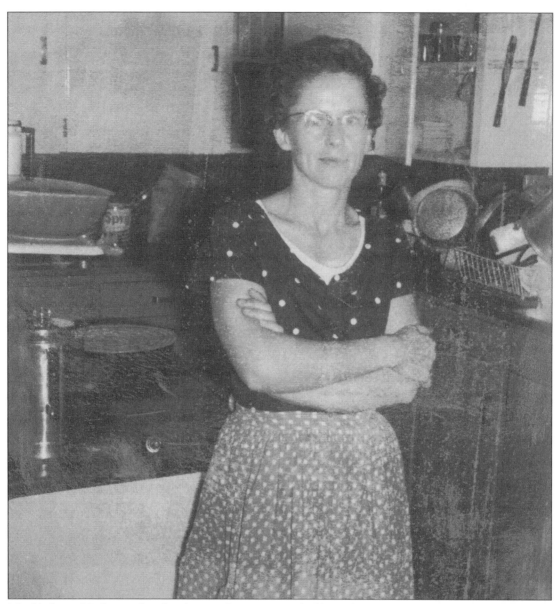

The kitchen with the wood and coal stove where Mom worked her culinary magic three times every day.

Focus Ranch irrigating, frying fish, and entertaining the dudes, and at the Lazy C–2 Bar Ranch. I believe "returning home" to Snake River is the best thing he could have done. He was always a bit of a fish out of water anywhere else. Sometime during those years, he hurt his shoulder because a cinch broke and he got tossed from a horse. In subsequent years—he was in his 80s—he told me that from that accident he got workers' compensation. He was a bit embarrassed about it because I suppose in his mind that was some sort of welfare. But he justified it to me because he told me he could not throw a rope anymore.

Mom

David: My early memories of Mom were mostly in the kitchen. She was always busy, and I was just hanging around. When I was old enough, she put me to work helping. One job was to help churn butter. I would turn the crank on the churn until it got hard to turn, and Mom would finish up.

David: As the cake, cookies, or bread came out of the oven, Mom would always let us have a small taste. That fresh-baked bread was so good; I couldn't get enough of it. For me, the soft bread inside the crust was the best part. Once, when loaves of bread were cooling on the cabinet, I pinched a small hole in the back of one of them so that I could reach through and get the soft bread in the middle. I kept taking pinches of bread until most of the loaf was hollow inside. Mom did not realize what happened until she started to slice it.

On one of the many trips Mom and Dad took David to best treat his paralyzed arm.

David: Early on, when Mom made cookies or cake, she would let me lick the bowl and spatula. I remember feeling so accomplished when she showed me how to follow a recipe and make cookies and cake on my own. I'm sure I made a big mess that she cleaned up after me.

David: It seemed I was always getting a spanking, no doubt for something I did wrong. I would guess that the spankings were usually due to my teasing or bullying Kenneth and Rita. But within these discipline lessons, there was always a test of wills. Sometimes after a good spanking, I would hit Mom only to get a harder spanking. Other times, I was determined not to cry, no matter how hard the spanking.

David: Mom was always supportive of me, and I know she always wanted the best for me. She was the first person I saw on the train between Craig and Denver when I briefly regained consciousness after my accident. Again, when I regained consciousness in the Shriners Hospital after they amputated my arm, she was there. Mom and I rode thousands of miles together back and forth to doctors, such as a train trip to the Mayo Clinic in Rochester, Minnesota. We talked a lot on all these trips, I suppose about everything, but I remember a number of discussions about the philosophy of life.

David: I knew at a young age that Mom and Dad had some problems getting along together. I overheard her once saying to Doris, "I grew up, but he never did!" I worried about having to choose sides, but fortunately that never materialized.

An example of Mom's careful calculations to ensure that each of us was treated with perfect fairness in terms of expenses and receipts for our sheep.

David: In high school, even though she was good with numbers, Mom was truly sorry that she could not help me with algebra. I would just have to figure it out on my own. I did figure it out, thanks to Mrs. Campbell who was probably the best teacher anywhere for algebra and geometry. The next year, Kenneth got so frustrated with algebra homework that Mom finally said, "David figured it out on his own. You can too." I do remember helping Kenneth a time or two.

David: I had a rock collection that started when I was young and continued through high school. The collection filled two old suitcases, which were very heavy. When I left home for college, for Laos, for New York, for Puerto Rico, for Maryland, and for South Carolina, Mom kept that rock collection for me, even though she moved several times herself. Finally, she sent some smaller rocks to me in South Carolina, which I still have today. The big rocks that she threw away are lost, but C'ést la vie!

Kenneth: Both Mom and Dad expected us to work, but it was Mom who enforced that at an early age. My "chores" at a very early age were to help bring in wood for the wood box on the porch. David and I had to go to the woodshed for wood, probably twice a day. We carried four sticks at a time, each one no more than three or four inches in diameter. It seemed impossible to fill the wood box; thus, we typically brought in only two or three loads or just enough until the next morning or evening. We loved it in the rare times the wood box was full because we did not have to bring in so much.

Kenneth: I have no stand-out memories of coming home for lunch from the Willow Creek School except that we walked the 150 yards or so every day. I also have no memories of the typical menu, but Mom clearly had to have lunch ready for us a few minutes after noon when we arrived.

Kenneth: Mom was big on lists. In high school, when she worked at the drug store or bank, we'd come home to find a written list of what we were expected to accomplish. Even when she was in the assisted living facility and hospital shortly before her death, she had pages and pages written on small yellow legal pads on her adjustable bed table. I always joked that we should have put on the back of her tombstone, "Be sure to weed around the stone. Clean it once a year...."

Kenneth: I know that Mom thought Grace was too strict on us for the "Health" classes. I would complain when I did not get a particular colored star for brushing my teeth, combing my hair, and whatever else was on the chart. Still, I'm quite sure she never said anything to Grace about it.

Kenneth: When things got bad financially or when there was a crisis, Mom always took charge and did what needed to be done. She also was the one who made sure that we were paid our allowance, our share of sheep sales, and, in high school or college, our living allowances. Everything was calculated to the penny.

Kenneth: Mom always sang as she worked. She did not complain at the time but told us later that she was so sad that we learned to sing off-key at school, as several other cousins did, assuming that we could not carry a tune. Maybe that is why she bought an upright piano at home and arranged for a few months or years for us to take piano lessons. She was thrilled that about the time we turned 11 or 12, we all three discovered that we were good singers and that we could easily sing on key.

Kenneth: Beginning in high school and continuing into college and beyond, I occasionally had very long talks with Mom that would run well into the middle of the night. They would be about what makes us tick, about psychology, or about the family. I learned a great deal about how she thought, and I believe I adopted many of her views. Yet, she had no interest in politics and always believed she did not know enough to vote intelligently.

Rita: Since relaxing was hard for Mom, and since her own growing up included having to be tough, I do not remember Mom showing much affection by holding me in her lap, or hugging me, or telling me that she loved me.

Rita: I can't help wondering whether I was a bit of a disappointment to Mom. She already had two boys, and finally got a little girl. What mama does not love dressing a little girl and making her pretty? Unfortunately, I was not interested. I hated her "fixing" my pretty blond curls, I hated dresses, and I hated "girly" clothes. My favorite outfits were hand-me-down shirts and pants from my brothers. Mom wanted a little girl who played with dolls. I did not really like dolls. In fact, Mom told me that one Christmas season I came to her and said, "I sure hope I get a double holster gun set instead of a doll for Christmas." I loved horses and riding, and Mom didn't. I enjoyed our animals, and Mom didn't seem to very much. To her credit, even though she was never comfortable around horses, she never kept us from being around them. Furthermore, I now wonder whether all of the other animals—lambs, kittens, puppies—just represented more work for her, and she was already very busy. So, instead of having a little girl, she had a tomboy.

Rita: For Mom, there was always a list of more tasks to complete than there was time to complete them. Part of that had to do with her very high standards of cleanliness. Sheets were changed once a week, whether the bed was slept in or not; clothes were changed daily and washed once a week in the old wringer washer. While our clothes were not always new, she made sure that the holes were patched and mended. A metal "scratcher" was used daily to scrub out the cast iron skillets, and the top of the cook stove was shined at least once a week; linens were folded into the closet in an exact way; walls, ceilings, cupboards, and floors were scrubbed regularly. (Much later in her life, I remember her being bored with nothing left to clean, so she decided to paint the insides of her closets.) It was important for her to have a nice house, so she sewed pretty slip covers for the furniture, and the surfaces of things were dusted daily. In addition to all the cleaning, Mom cooked substantial meals daily. She canned fruit and vegetables; she raised and slaughtered 50–100 chickens every year and froze those that were not cooked for the hay crews; and she helped Daddy cut up and wrap the beef, pork, and game for our freezer. She churned butter from the cream, and she baked wonderful breads and cakes.

Rita: While most of us liked camping, Mom really did not. She told me that she spent too many years sleeping in drafty places and using the bushes and outhouses, so that none of that was a treat to her.

Rita: At brandings, and events where the wives brought lunch to the men, Mom and Elizabeth agreed that Grace and Grandma, who could slice one cake to feed 15–20 people, were way too stingy with the desserts. To needle them, Mom and Betty would bake several huge cakes and put about an inch of frosting on each. Instead of slicing the pieces, they would hand the men the whole pan with a spatula and encourage them to "help yourself."

Rita: Mom was not a good driver, so she gladly turned the wheel over to the three of us as soon as we could drive. When she was a passenger, she regularly gasped and "braked" from her passenger side of the car, with a clearly audible intake of air on the "s" sound. In her later years, she would plan her driving trips to the store so that it was in midday without much traffic, and she would plan her routes so that she did only right-hand turns. Occasionally she would sojourn to Moab where Doris lived, but that was the extent of any "long haul" trips. In Grand Junction in her retirement years, she told Kenneth that she was going to buy a new car and that she preferred a Dodge because to get into the Dodge dealership, you did not have to make a left turn.

Rita: When we moved to go to school in Steamboat, Mom worked even harder keeping two households going. On weekends, she would clean the house at the ranch, do laundry, and cook meals to leave for Daddy. Then in Steamboat, she kept our house and took care of us. In addition, she worked full time at a paying job. It was difficult for her to join the work force after having been away all those years. I remember she went to the beauty parlor and got her hair all fixed nicely, and she bought a few outfits of nice clothes then went job hunting. Her first job was at Kinney Drug Store where prescriptions were filled and normal "drug store" items were sold. There was also a soda fountain where people sat to visit and to eat ice cream products. At first, she was a clerk doing everything at the store except fill prescriptions, but Don Kinney realized that she was really good with numbers. She became the person who balanced the book and paid the bills.

She had made friends with Kathy Smith who worked at the Routt County National Bank, next to the drug store, and after a year or so, Kathy invited Mom to come work with her at the bank, which Mom did. From then on, while in Steamboat, Mom worked at some capacity at that bank, at a credit union, or at subsequent banks that had taken over the one at which she worked. There was one short spell in which she worked at Safeway for a few months.

Rita: Mom did not have a lot of friends, but there were a few really close ones. Among them were women who worked at the bank with her, including her niece, Mary Sybrandt. Mom and Mary would complain that they would train various men for jobs, and then those same men would become their superiors or bosses. Gender discrimination was alive and well during those years, so she never really advanced very far in title, but she researched and became the main expert at that bank on retirement plans when 401(K)s and others came into being. Even the bank officers would come to her for advice.

Rita: After she bought her little red house on 7th Street in Steamboat, Mom realized that she would probably live the rest of her life alone, which turned out to be true except for a short unsuccessful marriage to Nick Magill. She seemed comfortable with being alone. Unlike many women of her era, she knew that she had only herself to truly count on, and not depend on having a man to look after her. Even when she was married to Nick, she insisted on continuing to work because she was not going to be in the position to ask a man for money.

Rita: While I was in high school, Mom and I went through the normal mother-daughter squabbles. Some were serious because of my sneaking around with Chris when I was forbidden to. Others were for reasons I do not even remember. We were not really very close. While I surely did not admit it at the time, I knew that my self-esteem and welfare were important to her. She bought me new furniture for my bedroom in Steamboat, and I always had nice clothes. For proms and dress-up occasions, she always seemed to turn up with a really pretty new dress. (This was important to her because as a child she did not have nice clothes, and she did not want her daughter to suffer the embarrassment she had suffered.) While we had our many differences, she always encouraged and believed in my academic ability. She truly believed, and she told me, that I could do anything I wanted to do.

Rita: In later years, I feel that Mom and I really "made up for lost time." As years went by, we became really close and were good friends. At that point, we really did hug and tell one another, "I love you." We would call one another every week and chat for at least an hour. Visits were always fun, and we had lots to talk about. When Chris left Erik and me, Mom invited me to bring Erik and live at her house in the basement. She spent a lot of time with Erik and offered him stability that I was not offering during those months. When Hugh and I started dating, Mom welcomed him into her life. They became really good friends. In fact, she would make a case of peach jam for him every year. (I would tease her and ask her whether she did that for anyone else in her family.) She came to visit us in Seattle and Alaska about every year.

Rita: We confided more and more, and became closer, as the years went by. One wonderful memory was my taking her to eastern Colorado to visit her sisters in 1996 or 1997. Her health was already pretty bad, and I remember her having difficulty breathing as we drove over one of the highway mountain passes to get there. But the visit was wonderful, and one of the last ones she had with her kin folks. We visited as many relatives as we could, she and Velma sang old songs together, she visited Joe Gebauer and his family, and we went to her old home near Sedgwick. She could not walk very far, so I carried her piggy-back across a sagebrush field to get to her childhood house. Part of the foundation was still standing, as was the old "spring house" where they ran cold water across the milk containers to keep the milk fresh. That trip was probably the last time I was with her while she was still able to do much for herself.

Mom visiting her childhood homestead for the last time. She is standing beside the concrete milk house her father had built.

Rita: The time frame during her last few years for me is hazy, but Mom began failing quite fast. Being her typical "take charge" self, she did all the research into assisted living quarters, she researched the cost of everything and what her insurance would pay. I cannot imagine how hard that must have been! But she was a person who just "did what needed to be done." Then the day came when she had to move out of her beloved little house in Grand Junction and go to the assisted living place. She had a single room there, and she brought only a few of her precious items to have with her. Everything else she left at her home for David, Kenneth, and me to sort through, divide up, or sell. Even in her home, she had her affairs in order, so ours was not a difficult job in that regard, but it was difficult knowing that we were telling our mother good-bye.

Rita: After a year in assisted living, Mom took some pretty severe turns for the worst, and was soon in and out of the hospital. Each of us would visit as much as we could and she would rally, but inevitably had to get back to our homes and jobs. The last time I saw her was in the hospital. We both knew she was dying but did not know when it would be, and I had to leave. As I walked away, the last words from her were, "I love you my darling." I took that gift of those words, and I shall keep them as long as I am drawing breath on this earth. I feel like the most fortunate daughter in the whole world to have had that.

Rita: None of us was there when she died, but she—and we—knew she was ready to go. Agnes Gebauer Friedly and Agnes's sister-in-law Dollie were with Mom. They were all being quiet, and one of them was rubbing her feet, when they realized that she was gone. I am eternally grateful to them for being with their aunt Grace.

Chapter 8

Our Early Childhood on the Ranch

George Edwin St. Louis (Dad), born January 26, 1906, and Dorothy Grace Ireland (Mom), born December 7, 1922, were married on November 9, 1941. Maybe because they knew that their difference in ages (just shy of 36 versus 18 years old), might have meant that time was of the essence. Or maybe it was just the thing that happened to newlyweds back in the early 1940s or the same urge that generated the surge of Baby Boomers during and after World War II. In any case, David was born on July 28, 1943, and 15 months and 12 days later, I, their anniversary baby, was born on November 9, 1944. Rita came along 15 months and two days later on February 11, 1946. We learned later that a vasectomy ended this fertile progression.

After they were married, Dad and Mom lived first in the Home Place and then in the Bunkhouse. That was apparently expected, because Perry and Grace as well as Sinc and Elizabeth had lived there before their houses were built. Mom was not happy with this arrangement and pushed Dad to build their house. They bought seven acres from Shorty Temple a half-mile up the Little Snake River from the Home Place. In late winter or early spring of 1944, Dad purchased and dismantled a log saloon in Hahns Peak, marked each log, and hauled them 20 miles to our new property on a horse-drawn hay rack on sled runners pulled through the snow by two mostly Percheron horses. With help from Sam Bell, a local carpenter who allegedly could pound nails equally well with either hand, Dad built the log house that was our childhood home.

> **Where did my name come from?**
>
> In the course of writing this book, Rita recalled Mom telling her that my name was to be "Morris," although I had no memory of ever hearing that. In fact, Mom clearly did tell at least a few people that Morris was to be my name because in the "Upper Snake River" news section of the November 16, 1944, edition of the *Steamboat Pilot*, the following paragraph was published: "A son, Morris Oliver, was born to Mr. and Mrs. George St. Louis on November 9 at Steamboat Springs. By a happy coincidence, this was also Dot and George's wedding anniversary. Dot and the baby are both fine." When and why "Morris" was chosen and then changed to "Kenneth" is a mystery.

David at 9 months holding himself up with a stick horse in front of the Bunkhouse.

David at 21 months visiting Francis and Agnes at the Hartman Place.

Portrait of David at 2 years.

Kenneth at about 5 months.

Kenneth at our log home at one year.

Portrait of Kenneth at one year.

Rita at one year with the Bunkhouse in the background.

Lexie, Rita (with hat), and Beverly as kindergarteners and first graders.

David about 2 years and Kenneth about 6 months.

Rita, David, and Kenneth in the summer of 1946.

David, Kenneth, and Rita on the back porch of our house, David sporting his cowboy wrist covers. Apparently, those fly buttons on our pants were too hard to manage.

David, Rita, and Kenneth in front of the Bunkhouse, 1947.

The same day as in the photo to the left but in front of a car at the Home Place.

Our first professional studio photograph together, about 1949.

A whole family studio photograph about 1952.

Our Early Childhood on the Ranch / 167

Our house in the 1950s during winter.

The house in the late 1980s after being sold with an added building between the main house and the woodshed.

The house had a front (living/dining) room, two bedrooms, a bathroom, a kitchen, and large open back porch with a large unheated room off it for fruit storage and the milking supplies. The kitchen had a wood and coal cook stove with an attached hot water tank. A well dug in the yard supplied water, which originally was pumped by hand. David and I first slept in bunkbeds in one bedroom while Rita slept in a crib in Mom and Dad's bedroom. She later moved to a bed in the boys' room. At first, since the house did not have indoor plumbing, the privy was first "the willows" and later, an outhouse.

A year or two later, with the help of uncles, Dad piped gravity-fed water from a spring across the river to the bathroom, kitchen, and porch. We kept the well and hand pump because twice, the pipe froze for several weeks during the winter and, in the spring of the year, the floodwaters were likely to break the pipe that crossed the river. Also, the spring flow was sometimes not enough for our needs. When electricity came to the Valley in 1949, Dad installed a pump and pressure tank in the cabinet next to the kitchen sink. The intake pipe went down into the old well. We learned later that the well water was high in minerals and iron. We had few, if any, dental cavities as children, and I had teeth stained with brownish stripes, presumably due to excessive fluoride in the water. This condition, known as "Colorado brown stain," was a type of fluorosis discovered in native-born children from Colorado Springs who had unusually high resistance to dental cavities. Aside from the fluoride, the water did not always agree with guests, however, as we found out during our high school years.

Lights in the evening were from hanging white-gas lanterns. Like Coleman lanterns, they had mantels, but near the top of a long rod was a ring that was inserted through a hook in the ceiling. We cannot remember how many were used but know that one was in the kitchen, and another hung over the dining room table. The lanterns took about a minute to go out after being turned off; thus, we could turn off the lanterns and get into bed before it got dark. The Rural Electric Association (REA) brought us electricity in 1949, as noted.

Dad with our first horse named Queen, showing the open back porch.

Later, an enclosed front porch was added, and the back porch was closed in, featuring built-in benches doubling as storage units at the far end on three sides that surrounded a large table. The original milk separation and canning room was divided with about two-thirds of the space being remodeled as a bedroom for David and me.

About 1950, with the help of our uncle Gus Ranch, Dad dynamited a garage (which we called the "tunnel") out of the sandstone cliff across the road. They rented a jackhammer, and Gus directed the drilling and setting the charges. The house was directly across the road from the "tunnel," so before each blast, Mom would gather all "us kids" inside the house because of flying rocks. Some

Our aunt Velma Gebauer visiting. Behind her in the oak-floored living room is the fuel oil drip heater for the entire house in the winter and Mom's desk.

front room windows were broken by the rocks that were blown out. Once the dynamiting was finished, Dad had to replace the windows and patch holes in the roof of the house.

The garage was actually quite amazing. It had a long entry for one vehicle with ample space to walk and open doors. Side rooms opened off both the right and left sides in the back. The left one was turned into a root cellar and storage space for canning jars. The other side room was to be a walk-in freezer that was never built. Once the new doors on the front were shut, our "tunnel" never froze in the winter. It should be noted that it caved in many years after the ranch was sold.

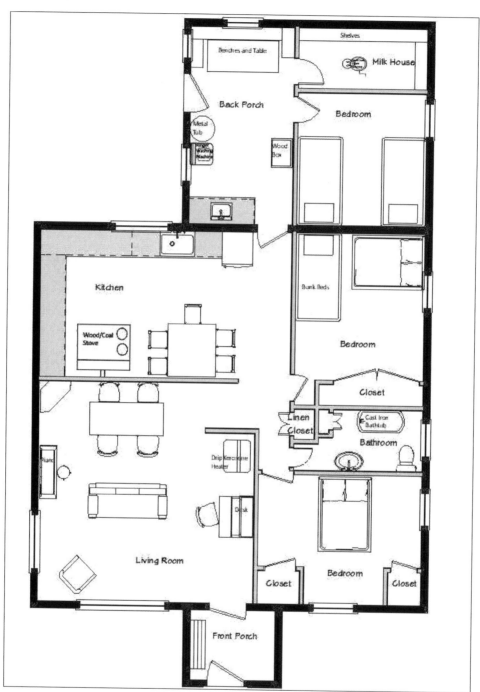

Floor plan of the log house we lived in as children.

The following labels appear within the floor plan:

Shelves

Benches and Table

Milk House

Back Porch

Bedroom

Metal Tub

Wringer Washing Machine

Wood Box

Kitchen

Bunk Beds

Wood/Coal Stove

Bedroom

Closet

Linen Closet

Cast Iron Bathtub

Bathroom

Piano

Drip Kerosene Heater

Desk

Living Room

Closet

Bedroom

Closet

Front Porch

Above: *Our house and driveway across the road from the inside of our garage that we called the "tunnel. It was blasted with dynamite into the sandstone cliff across the road.*

Left: *The "tunnel" photographed from our house. Our first mailbox is at the foreground.*

Dad closing the left door after taking out the John Deere tractor.

A photo taken from an airplane about 1950 shows a birds-eye view of our ranch: buildings, irrigation ditches, sloughs, river, and other landmarks. A subsequent closeup labels the structures and places that became important landmarks of our childhood. Another photo from high on the hill to the north of our ranch shows many of these same landmarks as well as the river.

We had a flat driveway north of the house large enough to park several vehicles. The fenced-in yard was mostly gravel and was not topped with topsoil and planted to a lawn until we were in elementary school. The large weathered logs in the house remained unpainted for the entire time we lived there, and between them was chinking consisting of barbed wire covered with cement.

> **Orientations and directions.**
> It is worth mentioning that most of the houses on Little Snake River were built so that each side faced more or less north, east, south, or west. David and I at least learned to navigate according to the compass points, rather than using "right" and "left." In fact, Mom could never keep straight her right or left; she had to remember her right hand to orient herself. Instead, having grown up on the prairie in eastern Colorado where everything was laid out in square mile grids, she was known to identify the location of a piece of clothing on the "north side" of the second drawer.

Beyond the south side of the back porch was a log woodshed and ice house. When we were very young, blocks of ice cut from the frozen river were buried in sawdust in the ice house to be dug out and used in the summer for making home-made ice cream, lemonade, and so on. Later, after REA came with electric refrigeration, the interior was changed to a shop. The woodshed had a divider for wood on the left and coal on the right. We cut fallen aspens (quakers) for wood, and bought our coal from a mine near Dixon. The roof of the woodshed was made of long boards running down each side and with rounded slabs over the gaps between the boards. The roof was not steep allowing for easy climbing and running on the roof. Sometime during this era, Dad bolted up a very large pair of elk antlers on the front facing the shed.

The wood box was on the back porch and was filled every day with pieces of split wood for the kitchen stove. Additionally, a coal bucket (scuttle) with an elongated top and handle to "pour" coal into the stove was filled each morning. The large blocks of coal from the mine, sometimes up to 18 inches in diameter had to be sledge hammered into pieces small enough to fit into the fire box of the kitchen stove. Clean smacks on flat surfaces could shatter a large block of coal in two or three blows.

Next to the ice house/shop and an irrigation ditch was the outhouse, which was little used during most of the years of our childhood. Just beyond that was the fenced-in rectangular garden with its rows of onions, radishes, carrots, lettuce, and potatoes. Lots and lots of rows of potatoes!

Behind the shop, at the end of a slough was our "ash pile," an area of greyish dirt filled with burned paper, cans, bottles, and miscellaneous trash that could not be burned and topped daily with ashes from the wood stove. (Carrying out the ashes was part of Dad's early morning ritual along with starting the wood stove fire.) This site also was the location for scalding and picking (removing) the feathers from the literally thousands of chickens that Mom killed then cut up for immediate frying or freezing.

Another slough, usually full of water, separated the house and woodshed from the barn, corral, and other outbuildings. A culvert and fill was put across it to get to the barn. Near the crossing, our sewer, aptly labeled "the stinks," emptied into the slough. In later years, Dad added a square concrete septic tank next to the house, but a leech field was never built. Effluents from the septic tank still had a sewage odor and still emptied directly into "the stinks."

Our two-story barn did not have the gambrel-roof look of a traditional barn, but inside, it had all the important elements. There was a small room with bins of wheat (for chickens) and oats (for horses) replete with space for "gunny sacks" (burlap bags) of various kinds of feed, depending on the animals at the time. Spikes with hanging harnesses for two workhorses were in the main throughway followed by an open area with stanchions for three milk cows. On the other side were two stalls that could accommodate four horses, each with a manger for hay. Later, one stall was cut in half to become an area for storing saddles. A lowered groove in the floor and out the opposite door into the corral, the width of a flat scoop shovel, was where the cow and horse manure was shoveled and then pushed into a growing pile in the corral. Cut-out holes into the hayloft were above the stalls and stanchions so that hay stacked in the loft during the summer could be dropped down into the mangers to feed to the animals in the winter.

A rectangular corral was adjacent to the far side of the barn. It was not a typical pole corral seen at most ranches, except for the gate, but was made of slabs nailed vertically onto two poles. Years later, during our elementary and high school years, one side of the corral was replaced by another log building taken apart log-by-log from the Honnold Place (now part of the Three Forks Ranch spectacular resort). This became our sheep and lambing shed and adjoined another added building next to the barn used for 4-H animals.

The only other building in our early years was the chicken house, which had a very shallow-pitched shed roof (perfect for walking on) and a fenced-in area to keep chickens safe at night from skunks. Inside the chicken house

Aerial photo of our ranch about 1950. Shown are the meadows, sloughs, sandstone cliffs, alfalfa fields, and haystacks on the mesa above, and Mule Mountain.

was a roost made of three or four 4-foot poles nailed to two other poles which slanted from one wall to the floor rather resembling a wide ladder slanting against the wall. The other wall had waist-high boxes in which the hens would lay their eggs. We gathered the eggs from those boxes every evening. To the right of the chicken house was the attached pig pen, which was later to give way to the bum (orphan) lamb pen. Several years later, we added a brooder house where Mom would raise chicks, purchased via mail order, for meat during the summer and also frozen for winter.

Machinery parked around the barn usually included a hay rack used for feeding in the winter and hauling hay in the summer; a massive old threshing machine with intricate belts, knives, and pulleys; and later, a horse trailer and a sheep wagon.

Our original seven acres was rectangular and bordered the county road on the north, with the hill and sandstone cliff across the road. On the east was the border with the Focus Ranch, a dude ranch for paying guests, owned by our neighbors, Shorty and Lucy Temple,. The south border crossed a larger

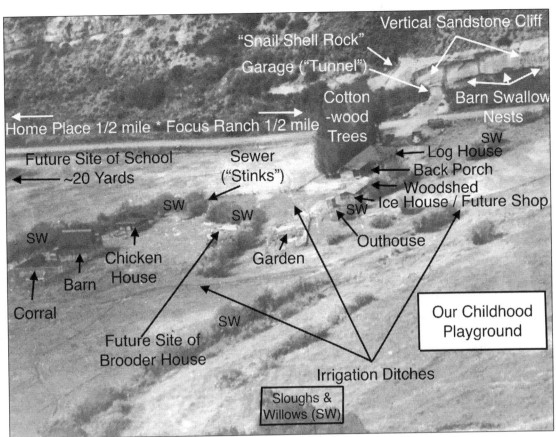

Our childhood playground: house, outbuildings, garage, irrigation ditches, willows, and sloughs about 1950. The later site of the Willow Creek School is shown with an arrow.

slough and was close to the Little Snake River, and the west side bordered Grandpa's ranch. We later acquired five more acres of Grandpa's property, and that ran all the way to the river and bordered the donated land to where our one-room Willow Creek School was moved after the end of my first grade and David's second grade.

Other elements rounded out our childhood "playground." The sloughs were surrounded by "pussy" willows that were useful in all kinds of activities such as making stick horses, building forts, playing Indians and outlaws, cutting switches for riding, and making bows and arrows. The sloughs and irrigation ditches provided endless opportunities for catching little fish (suckers) by hand, aquatic exploring, engineering feats, and playing practical jokes. The sandstone cliff across the road had a sliding area, which we called the "Snail Shell Rock," and unlimited potential for road building, stone throwing, climbing, and exploring. The large cottonwood trees in our yard and just beyond it had limbs just waiting for someone to climb up into them. And we had the river for fishing, swimming, and ice skating. We

View of our house, outbuildings, sloughs with willows, irrigation ditches, cottonwood trees, and Little Snake River from the hillside to the north.

had tame cows and calves, chickens that would follow a person anywhere, horses, dogs, cats, and later, a small flock of bum lambs.

Most of what we remember from our common upbringing was after our early preschool years; yet, those years set the stage for our lives in ways we may either clearly or only dimly understand. Because we three siblings were so close in age, we have no memory of our first couple of years. We have little information at all on our toilet—or outhouse—training in the early years, but it was probable that we learned to control our bladders and bowels no later than our second birthdays due to the work involved in keeping us in clean diapers.

In one of her short essays in *Stories Across America*, "Country Life in the Forties," reprinted in Appendix D, Mom described the weekly arduous process of Monday wash day, which took all day. She wrote:

"While the children were little, wash day was repeated on a lesser scale on Thursday. On the other non-wash days, I pre-rinsed the diapers, boiled them in a large kettle with soap, rinsed them twice, and hung them out to dry. I used the soapy water from the boiling for cleaning and set aside the rinse water for soaking and pre-rinsing more diapers."

Mom recalled her relief when this extra burden was no longer needed, that is, when Rita toilet trained herself at about a year old. That she was overwhelmed was likely the reason that our parents placed the following ad in the *Steamboat Pilot* on January 17, 1946, not quite a month before Rita was born: "WANTED—Girl or woman for general housework in country. Write George St. Louis, Slater, Colo." Apparently, no one answered the ad or anyone who did was not deemed satisfactory.

The brooder house and chicken pen to the left of the horse and our open double horse trailer on the right.

MEMORIES

HAZY MEMORIES AND STORIES WE LATER HEARD

David: I don't have many memories before the age of three, but Mom told us that I was an "easy" baby. She thought she was an expert in infant care because I slept through the night early, didn't cry a lot, and learned fast.

Cousin Clifford Ranch doing something we all did, that is, licking salt from a 50-pound block put out for the cattle and horses. It was much smoother when the animals had hollowed out an area with their tongues.

When we lived in the Bunkhouse, she tells of the story of me climbing up into the attic and falling through the ceiling onto the wood stove. Thank goodness, the stove was not hot, and I was not hurt.

David: One story that Mom remembered about me was the time I got into the flour and lard. In the kitchen, we had a large bin for flour and another for sugar, which we filled from 50- or 100-pound bags. In the lower cupboard beside the flour bin was a cupboard with a five-gallon can of lard. One day I opened the flour bin and the lard can and mixed them together by hand in the bin, the can, and on the floor.

David: As I got older, I suspect Mom may have changed her mind a bit on how "easy" I was. As a toddler and preschooler she admitting giving up having the last word, because, no matter how severe the discipline (translation: spanking), she knew I was always going to have the last word. Every day I knew I was going to get a spanking. Mom hid spanking sticks handily all around the house. So, one day I found all of the spanking sticks and hid them. When she couldn't find a stick, she used a piece of firewood.

David: Every Christmas, we hung stockings so Santa Claus would fill them. I became suspicious that Santa was real, so that one year, I counted all the oranges on Christmas Eve. Three were missing the next morning and three were in our stockings

David: I always wanted to be with Dad. Several times he told the story of his building the corral at the back of the barn. He was nearly finished drilling and bolting all the poles in the gate. At the age of 2, I picked up the hand saw and started in on one of the poles. Dad did not think I could do any damage except to put some scratches on the pole, but when he looked a few minutes later I had nearly sawed through a three-inch pole. He had to take the gate apart and replace that pole.

Kenneth: Mom told me later in life, that I was not such an "easy" baby as David. My "Baby Book" indicates that she breast fed me briefly but soon supplemented with cow's milk. What was significant is that although I always had a big appetite, cow's milk did not agree with me. Apparently, I was starving to death at some point at about two months of age because I would spit up all the milk that I drank from the bottle. An urgent, long trip to Denver to see a specialist (pediatrician likely) revealed that I was allergic to cow's milk. After some time in the hospital, I thrived after having my formula changed to a baby soy milk.

Kenneth: I was reportedly very close to our aunt Elizabeth (Betty) as a baby. I surmise one of the reasons was, as the middle child with siblings just a little more than a year older or younger, there was not much time left for me beyond tending to my basic needs. After I grew up, Elizabeth shared with me a few memories of those early years. She said I was a beautiful baby and that I looked like the "Gerber baby" on the baby food jars with my long blond curls. At one point probably before my second birthday, apparently, I was not completely toilet trained because as she once was cleaning the floor all around my soiled diaper, I sat there and said, "Me have fun too." The point of that story is not the lack of bowel control, but that I was quite verbal and intelligible at an early age. On the other hand, I was the slowest of the three of us to walk, at 14 months.

Rita: I entered the family a few hours sooner than expected. Daddy was driving to Craig but made it only to Dixon, Wyoming, where Dr. Noyse delivered me. (This is the same Dr. Noyse whose "hospital" bed collapsed as Elizabeth was delivering our cousin Lillyan!) Mom said that she had to tell the doctor how to do certain things because he had not dealt with a new baby in a long time. I was a very difficult baby. After caring for me, Mom shared that she really was not an expert in caring for babies. She said I would cry all day and then cry all night. Like Kenneth, I also had serious problems thriving. I was very skinny, and they had to take me to Denver to the doctor as well. And, as with Kenneth, baby formula did not agree with me. Furthermore, I surmise from what I was told that I also had colic. Unlike Kenneth who spoke early and walked a little later, I walked before I was a year old, but spoke late, and only my family could understand my speech until well after my third birthday.

CLEARER MEMORIES

David: I remember that we were continually fighting over one tricycle until we each got our own. After each getting our own but before the back porch was enclosed, Rita rode her tricycle straight off the end and fell headfirst into the slop bucket. This was the slop for one to two pigs consisting of skim milk—often sour—that we did not need after separating the cream from it, leftovers from meals, and virtually any organic material, such as potato peelings. Sometimes we would pretend our tricycles were horses. At other times we pretended they were cows, and we would jump off and pretend to milk them.

David: Mom eventually got a wringer washing machine and placed rinse tubs around it. I remember that she would get mad because she couldn't start the gasoline engine that powered it. When we got electricity, the gasoline engine was simply replaced by an electric motor that always ran.

> **What were George and Grace to us?**
> We all called our parents "Mommy" and "Daddy" when we were young. Sometime in the later elementary and high school years, "Mommy" gave way to "Mom" for all of us. For a time in college, I called her "Mother," as Dad had referred to Grandma, but later I changed back to "Mom." "Daddy" gave way to "Dad" for David and me, but never for Rita.

Kenneth: We always had a fairly large garden. During most of our preschool years, we also had a very tame, but hard to milk, Guernsey milk cow that we called the "Old Yellow Cow." She managed to get into the garden about once a year, and Dad would "raise hell." I never understood what was so bad about that. I liked to grab her tail as she slowly walked along and let her pull me.

Kenneth: I don't recall disobeying Mom (the family disciplinarian) as a young child; I believe I might have been the most compliant of the three of us. Still, she tells of some preschool "orneriness" when she could not find her shiny, wooden, heart-shaped brooch. She asked David if he had seen it, and he denied that he had. She then asked me, and I reportedly said, "Yeah. I took it out by the old dead tree [beyond the "ash pile"] and the pigs ote [ate] it." I do not remember saying that, but I do remember following David up past the "Snail Shell Rock" and watching him hide it in the trail. Later, he went and retrieved it for Mom.

Kenneth: I remember our bedroom as a four- or five-year-old. David, had the top bunk and I, the bottom bunk. But the top bunk was much more fun for playing. We often would climb the ladder to the top and then jump to Rita's bed below which was only about two feet away. Until this writing, I had forgotten that Mom would get mad at us for jumping on the bed, although I knew that she tried her best, but often unsuccessfully, to prevent us from such "romping" in the house.

David and cousin Bill Lawler in the top bunk. The back of the metal bed to which we jumped is shown at the bottom.

Kenneth: Also, very likely when I was four or five, it was a treat to be able to go with Dad to the Fleming Place to "change the water" (flood irrigate). David and I would follow him in his thigh-high "gum" boots folded down below the knee while carrying a shovel over his shoulder. It was hard for us to walk through the tall grass (destined to be winter hay), and he could not carry us. (Once or twice I recall he was carrying Rita.) Therefore, we each would grasp one back pocket in his Levis and let him pull us up the hill to the pickup parked on the road near the fence adjoining Babe McCargar's Place on Gold Blossom Creek or across Willow Creek and up to the old log cabin.

Kenneth: I stuttered ever since I can remember, although I don't know what that first memory was. This means that I probably stuttered for some time without being particularly aware of it. David also stuttered apparently. I talked to Mom a lot about my early stuttering, and she was convinced that since I copied what David did, as do most younger siblings, I copied his stuttering. But he stopped stuttering, and I did not. Probably about the age of three, Dad and Mom took me to Denver to see a speech therapist at the University of Denver. I have a very vague memory of talking to a lady, but that is all. Mom and Dad were told to ignore the stuttering and not make an issue of it, and that is apparently what they did since I have no memory of anyone telling me how to speak.

Children from the Willow and Battle Creek schools and those who had not yet started to school. Back: Darrell Ranch, Sharon, Connie Salisbury, and Jean; second: Georgie Salisbury, David, and Shirley; third: Deanna Salisbury, Robbie Salisbury, Kenneth, and Larry Ranch; front: Beverly and Rita.

Rita: Mom said I learned from my older brothers. We all liked to count Dad's matches. After supper (our evening meal), I would wait for him to intersect his fork and his knife and place them in an inverted "V" on his plate. This was the signal he was finished eating, whereupon he would push his chair back and reach to his left shirt pocket for a cigarette. I would then climb into his lap and get out the wood matches in his right shirt pocket and count them. I sensed that Mom did not warm up to unnecessary touching as much as Dad did. I remember wanting to climb up into her lap but feeling unwelcomed.

Rita: David and Kenneth started to school in consecutive years, but I had to wait two years to start after Kenneth. For that reason, I must have learned a lot about school from them by simply being around them. Mom was amazed that I had some-how learned to "meld" in the game of Canasta, which meant a melding player had to calculate the sum of various cards worth 5, 10, 20, 50, or 100 points. Every year, our one-room Willow Creek School would share a Christmas program with the similarly sized Battle Creek School about six miles down the river. After one program when I was four or five years old, the younger children were allowed to present something.

Our Early Childhood on the Ranch / 181

David, Kenneth, and Rita riding on Sally. It is said that the middle child is squeezed.

I volunteered, stood up, and said, "Mary had a little horse and he was very human. Every time it raised its tail, you could see Harry Truman." Apparently, this horrified Mrs. Hancock, the Battle Creek School teacher, but otherwise it brought the house down with laughter.

Rita: I remember wanting to "grow up and be a big man like Daddy" undoubtedly because he was so loving and patient in his own way. I remember riding from a very young age. We all rode at a very young age. Our first horse was an old white mare named Sally. Sally was so tame that I remember putting a blanket over her and playing house underneath. We later acquired a pinto mare named Dolly when I was about four years old.

Rita: When we got electricity, one of the first purchases was a Frigidare. We called it the "Frigidare"—not the "fridge" or the "refrigerator." We children were so excited about having ice cubes that we checked every few minutes to see whether the water had frozen yet. Finally, the next morning we had ice cubes.

Rita: I have no clear memory of ours, but I do remember Grandpa's "ice house," which was a little log building up the draw from his house. Our uncles would cut big blocks of ice out of the river and carry them on horse-drawn sleds to the ice house and intersperse them with layers of sawdust. The ice was "harvested" out of the shed and put into boxes called "ice boxes" so that cream, milk, and butter could be kept cool.

Where did my stuttering come from?

From my adult perspective as person who has studied, taught, treated, and researched stuttering for nearly 50 years, I'm quite sure I did not start stuttering by imitating David. Even shortly after it started, I probably was aware of and frustrated by not being able to say words that previously I could say. This would be the typical case for a child who was an early talker and generally quite verbal. It is possible that David simply had more than the usual number of disfluent words or syllables as an early talker, but it is more likely that he really stuttered.

Given that he was probably about three years old when he started to stutter, he would most likely have been speaking in short sentences for about a year before the stuttering began. That is the most typical pattern, and 80% of children who start to stutter simply stop stuttering spontaneously after a few weeks or months. I would have had to be close to two or two and a half years when I started stuttering, earlier than average but not highly unusual.

The fact that I did not quit stuttering after a few months is probably what motivated Mom and Dad to seek help. The advice they received was based on the theory that parents (usually the mother) show or express too much concern about their child's normal disfluencies (such as repetitions or breaks which also peak about the age of three or four years).

The so-called "diagnosogenic" theory held that when parents react to normal disfluencies, the child then reacts to their reactions and becomes even more disfluent. This becomes a vicious cycle and eventually results in stuttering.

We now know that the diagnosogenic theory is not what causes stuttering except maybe in very rare instances. Instead, evidence is clear that a genetic influence is the most powerful—but not the only—cause. Stuttering ran in the St. Louis family. Uncle Francis stuttered, and, when I was older, I heard over and over again that he stuttered. As noted in Chapter 4, he was killed in a tractor accident when I was about five years old, so I never had the chance to talk to him about it. My daughter, Melinda, stuttered between the ages of two and four years, and Rita's son, Erik, also stuttered mildly. Surprisingly, when I was in my 40s, Dad told me that he used to stutter and remembered it well. He apparently recovered on his own, but much later than typical cases. Francis did not. That Dad and Francis stuttered also strongly suggests that they knew stuttering when they heard it, even with David.

Chapter 9
Our Later Childhood on the Ranch

Chapter 8 set the stage for our later childhood experiences that we can more clearly remember. Remembering that this book is focused on three siblings who shared a common environment as children but with different personalities and outlooks, this chapter describes both the commonalities and the differences that affected us as children. It is said that children's work is their play. We certainly played as young children. But rural life on a ranch also had a great deal of real work to be done, and much of our free time that was self-directed play in our early years evolved into productive work in later years.

Beginning at about the age of six or seven and going through our elementary school years, our days were a relatively predictable sequence of play inside and outside interspersed around school, three full sit-down meals, chores, evening games, listening to the radio or records, some homework, and then sleep. School is described in Chapter 10. We read comic books voraciously, but surprisingly, we did not learn to read a newspaper from our parents. Someone who knew us, perhaps a guest at the Focus Ranch, wanted us to have a newspaper and therefore paid for and had sent every week the Sunday edition of the *Miami Herald*. It likely arrived a week or so late, but it was a sad waste of money for the sender and lost opportunity for our family. The newspapers in those hefty three-inch brown rolled packets piled up for years and were used mostly to start fires in the woodstove or outside.

The *Miami Herald*s came with our mail, which was delivered every Monday, Wednesday, and Friday. Our Post Office was Slater, Colorado, approximately 12 miles from our ranch. It had long been moved from McIntosh's store to Beryl Kelley's house about a half-mile east. Beryl was the "mail man." Three days a week, he would deliver a large canvas sack—approximately 18 inches square—with a riveted leather handle and our name painted on it to

The three of us playing on the pipe between the horse trailer and the hayrack. The chicken house is in the background, and the brooder house is on the right.

A studio photograph of Rita, Kenneth, and David, 1952.

Striking poses by David, Kenneth, and Rita.

our "mail box." Over the years, the mail box located next to the road across from our house was either a box resembling an average size dog house mounted onto a wooden stand or a 55-gallon drum mounted on its side. Beryl would drive by and fling the sack with its contents into the mail box. We would empty the sack and add any mail that we wanted to send, and then hang it on a stick that contained a clamp protruding from the mail box. On his return trip he would collect the sack by retrieving it from the stick.

Our telephone system was a 22-member party line. To call someone, you would crank a lever on the right side of the elongated wooden phone mounted on the wall to accommodate a standing adult. This would cause everyone's phone to ring. Every household had a unique ring. Ours was two short rings; the Focus Ranch was two longs and two shorts; Perry's was long, a short, and a long; Grandpa's was three longs and three shorts. The correct protocol was to pick up the receiver hanging on the left side and listen to see whether someone was using the phone line. If so, you should hang up. If not, you would ring the party you wanted to reach and then talk into the microphone projecting from the box with the receiver held by your left hand directly out from your left ear. If you were already talking, and you heard the click of someone trying to access the line, you were supposed to cut your conversation short and relinquish the line to whomever wanted to use it.

That all seems simple enough, but the way it really worked was if you rang someone, you would hear click-click-click of people who wanted to listen to the conversation or as we said, "rubberneck." The more people who listened, the worse the reception was. Occasionally, you would have to ask the rubberneckers to hang up.

To make a long-distance call, you would have to call the long-distance operator, "Mabel," at the Telephone Company in Baggs by ringing one very long ring. You would tell her the name of the person you wanted to call, and she would connect you. Again, as soon as folks heard that one long ring, even more curious click-click-clicks could be heard. Being able to hear long distance was often quite difficult. Or if you needed to have a private conversation, you needed to drive 30 miles to Baggs and go to the Telephone Company office to call. To make a long-distance call "upriver" beyond the Focus Ranch, you would call the Focus, tell Lucy Temple your message, then she would go to a second telephone and call the other person and relay your message. Then she would come back to the first phone and tell you their reply.

Outside play was whatever we could think of to do that was within some rather vague bounds set by Mom, because Dad was almost always working outside somewhere else. Mom reportedly remarked to Elizabeth once, if the children were playing outside, and if they both agreed that no one had come running to the house crying or otherwise in trouble, the kids must be okay. Mom most certainly would not have approved of everything we did at play. It included a lot of climbing: on the cottonwood trees in the yard, into the hayloft to play in the hay, on machinery such as the threshing machine, on the sandstone outcrops or hill across the road, or on the tops of the woodshed

A threshing machine similar to the one parked near our brooder house that we played on. Kenneth fell off one of the side wheels and broke his arm.

David soaking up some sunshine in the summer.

Step away from the clothesline! Kenneth with at least three holstered cap guns and two badges.

"Stick 'em up!" Kenneth and Rita on a warm, early spring day.

or chicken house. And in later years, she would not have approved of our standing back and throwing matches into the lids full of gasoline next to 55-gallon barrels of gasoline or kerosene. Or shooting our BB guns at swallows on the electric lines or on the cliff across the road.

We rarely came back into the house for such necessities as getting a drink or going to the bathroom. The irrigation ditches, creeks, or river were fine for drinking water, so long as it appeared clear. Giardia was not a problem in those days, so no one ever got sick from drinking outside. As boys, we peed wherever we happened to be, and were known to have contests for the length and arc of the stream as we urinated off the back of the chicken house. Rita was not quite so flexible.

Games of "cowboys and Indians" predominated in much of our early organized outdoor play. We asked our parents for and were given two-gun holsters for cap pistols, which we strapped onto our waists for many of these games. Of course, we intermittently had to play "dead" if we were shot.

As we got older, play increasingly involved our horses. As explained in Chapter 8, we had ridden "Old Sally" as preschoolers, often several of us at a time. Dad wanted us to learn to ride, so in 1948, when we ranged in age from 2 to 4, he placed an ad in the *Steamboat Pilot* for "a gentle saddle pony for small children." A horse did not materialize from that ad, but about 1950, he bought the pinto Welsh-mix mare that we called Dolly from Harry Russell. Sometimes, with Mom's help, we would catch and saddle her, get a clock, and then alternate riding her for perhaps ten minutes at a time. This would involve galloping around the field, although in Dolly's case, it did not involve jumping irrigation ditches as she would often simply stop instead of jumping. As we got older, we began pulling our red wagon or a sled with another horse with a lariat rope tied to the saddle horn. David

David riding Pal with his first saddle with the metal horn; Rita and Kenneth are riding double on Dolly bareback. The woodshed with its shallow slab roof is shown behind us.

usually rode the horse, and I usually rode in or on the wagon or sled. Of course, we wanted to go fast, and at least twice we basically ruined the wagon or sled by assuming it too would jump a ditch. The front wheels were either knocked off or seriously bent on the wagon and the front of the sled was bent straight down after slamming into the ditch bank on the other side.

Rita's "horse play" typically involved Lillyan, and sometimes Lexie. They were known to dress up and put makeup on their horses.

Kenneth and Rita (with double holster cap guns) standing in front of Pal and Dolly.

When Dad had sheep on "the Desert," he collaborated with one or both of his uncles Lewis and Chester Morgan (Grandma's brothers) and a local airplane pilot, Carl Baker, to trap and sell wild horses or mustangs. Driving horses into a trap built into a natural gully with a single-engine Piper Cub, they caught about 100 horses one year. Any mare with a foal too young to

Our Later Childhood on the Ranch / 189

wean was released. Aside from a few kept to break, they sold the rest for "fox feed."

Dad picked out two foals (we called them all "colts" regardless of their sex) that were big enough to wean. He branded and castrated one of them, a grey named Ace who was to become my horse and branded a bay filly named Satellite (after the first Sputnik satellite) who was to become David's. He turned them loose with our other horses until they were 3-year-olds. Dad had taught Ace to lead in ten minutes as a colt, and he was very easy to break to ride. Satellite was extremely hard to break to lead even using an electric prod pole ("hot shot"), and she was equally difficult to break to ride.

With these two horses, Dad taught us to break horses in the manner his family had done for years. After breaking a horse to lead with a halter, the horse was then "sacked down" or taught to tolerate and later accept the totally painless process of a burlap bag ("gunny sack") being slapped across its back, belly, rear, neck, head, and feet. Next, the horse was bridled with a snaffle bit and strong reins. It was saddled and then led around the corral for some time. Next, the horse's head was pulled around to one side and tied to the saddle. When the horse stopped struggling and began to walk in a circle in that direction, its head was pulled to the other side to repeat the process. It was important not to let them walk long because, according to Dad, this would make it hard to teach them later to neck rein. After all of this, if the horse was reasonably calm, Dad tied the stirrups together to help prevent being thrown off if the horse bucked, and then mounted the horse.

Neither Ace nor Satellite bucked when he got on them. Thereafter, nearly every day, the horses needed to be ridden, first in the corral and later in the pasture to teach them to start with leaning ahead with a little kick, to stop when the bit was pulled up, and, eventually to turn, not by pulling on one rein or the other but by gently moving the reins sideways so slight pressure on the left side of the neck signaled the horse to turn right, and vice versa.

Our outside play also involved diverting water or catching suckers in the ditches and fishing for trout with worms (first) and flies (later) in the river. We built little rafts out of firewood to float chickens out into a slough. The chickens had been put to sleep by putting their heads under one wing and swinging them from side to side for several minutes. Getting soaking wet in the ditches or sloughs was a frequent consequence. Later, we learned to swim, mostly on our own, in the river down near Sinc and Elizabeth's house where it would be dammed to raise the water to go into their irrigation ditch. Rita, Lillyan, and Lexie went through a phase of "skinny dipping" at the swimming hole.

Kenneth, Rita, and David in the front yard. At the right is the Ford tractor, which the boys had learned to drive by this time, and the family's 1952 Pontiac. The rifle and hat on the fence indicates that deer hunting season had arrived.

Beginning about the age of 10, we got bicycles that we would ride up and down the gravel road. Several times we would be seen "pumping" (or standing as we pedaled) up the hills between Perry and Grace's house and the Focus Ranch. At the latter was the Pop Shop, or the only "store" around where we could buy candy and carbonated drinks ("pop"). Trips to the Pop Shop were special and were either on horseback or on bicycles. With horses, the trips were often opportunities to show off our horsemanship in front of guests ("dudes") who may be watching.

We made arrows out of willows and shot them with bows made of larger willows. We made sling shots (the real sling shots with long rawhide strings with a pocket in the middle, of the sort that Goliath was killed with by David) and rocketed little rocks hundreds of yards up the hill. I threw knives at trees to try to get them to stick.

The Fourth of July was always a treat because we were able to buy lots of firecrackers. We set them off everywhere. We lit and threw them to blow up in the air (and learned that this had to be done quickly lest the firecracker go off in one's hand—which did happen occasionally). We learned to light them under little tin cans from the fuses protruding and see how high we could send the cans into the air. We put them in fresh cow manure piles to see how much manure we could splatter around. We set them to go off near unsuspecting persons to scare them. We probably even threw firecrackers

Kenneth getting ready to go fishing.

David, Kenneth, and Rita playing Sorry *at the dining room table.*

among the 30 to 40 hens to scatter them as well, although I do not believe we ever tried that when someone was riding a horse, even though our dad and uncles were known for doing that.

David and I, but not Rita, were taught by Dad to hunt with a pump action .22 caliber Winchester when we were about 10 and 11 years old. We had to hunt alone for safety. Dad would give us five .22 shorts and let us hunt jack rabbits in the winter. We'd walk down the road in the evening and try to shoot them as they sat at the edge of the willows below the school. On one occasion, to Dad's great dismay, I broke the stock of the gun by using it to club a wounded rabbit after I had run out of "shells."

Later, David acquired a .22 pistol, and I, a .22 rifle. We hunted ground squirrels, which were considered to be pests and a danger to livestock with their many large holes. Hundreds, if not thousands, were killed. Jack rabbits were also hunted, especially after the first snow, from the back of a pickup being driven at night around a field. The family harvested deer for meat, often out of season, and both brothers participated in that. We learned to "gut" a deer in the field and then bring it home for skinning and cutting up.

David and I especially liked going on one of the rare summer fishing trips with Dad, and perhaps a relative who had come in from the Ireland side of the family after their wheat harvest was finished in early July. It would be an all-day affair wherein we would drive the 4-wheel-drive pickup as far as possible and then hike in and out to access a stream that few fishermen knew about. We'd catch "creels-full" of small brook and native trout, clean them all, and bring them home for freezing and later eating. Again, fishing limits had little bearing on our activity, and it did not matter to Dad if the creek was in Colorado or Wyoming.

Inside play during the winter and in the evenings often involved card and board games. Dad and Mom taught us to play *Rummy, Canasta, Casino, Pitch, Cribbage, Poker,* and other card games. We also had board games of *Checkers* or *Chess, Chinese Checkers, Monopoly, Clue,* and *Sorry.* Later we added *Scrabble.* Of course, there was the usual "romping" (wrestling, Indian wrestling, or arm wrestling) until Mom had enough of it in the house. We liked to listen to records and to listen to such radio programs after school as *The Lone Ranger.* We also loved comic "funny" books that we could buy in Craig for ten cents. We read and reread these. Later we read full-length books or looked up things in the set of encyclopedias that filled two corner bookcases.

Our favorite winter activities were the sledding parties at the Temple grade. It was the perfect sledding hill because it was steep, had a sharp curve in it, and was followed by a long flat portion at the bottom. Virtually no traffic was on this part of the road because no one lived beyond Temple ranch in the winter. For these parties, with the grader, Dad would grade the road so that the snow was well packed and there were no rocks to hit the sled runners. Most of our uncles and aunts and others down the River would bring their families, gather at the Pep Hall at the bottom of the grade, build a big bonfire to warm up next to, and have cocoa for the kids.

We would pull our sleds up the grade, or occasionally be pulled up by a lariat rope from a horse, and then slide down, either by lying down on our stomachs alone or sitting up when two or more were on a long sled. Of course, the sled needed to be turnable by pulling on the right lever and pushing its left side to bend the front of the runners to the right enough to make the sharp turn about a third the way down the grade. If not, we would go off the road into the deep snow in the gulch below the turn. When the conditions were perfect, we could start all the way up at the Fleming Place entrance road and be going fast passing the Hartman Place and mild incline before the grade itself. By the time we reached the steep part, we were going so fast that the sharp turn was especially difficult to make. If we could negotiate the turn, which was a trick, we could fly down the rest of the hill, pass the bonfire, cross the bridge, and come to a stop next to Shorty Temple's corral.

From an early age, we all had chores that we were expected to do. It started with picking up our toys to carrying in firewood each day for the wood box

Rita, David, and Kenneth getting ready to take our skis and sled up the Temple grade.

Someone whizzing by on their sled.

and grew from there. Depending on our age or capabilities, we all participated in the "chores" before breakfast, which included scattering wheat and other feeds in front of the barn for the laying hens, feeding grower feed to chicks in the brooder house in the summer, feeding 4-H and other sheep grain in the summer and hay in the winter (see Chapter 11), feeding cows and horses hay in the winter, milking cows and then separating the milk from the cream with the hand separator, feeding milk to our bum (orphan) lambs in the summer, feeding calves milk and/or grain, and giving slop and some grain to the pigs when we had them or the slop alone to the chickens when we did not. There were also ordinarily one or more dogs and several cats to feed. In the house, we sometimes helped Mom make our typical breakfasts of hot oatmeal, fried eggs, fried bacon, pancakes, fruit juice, and milk. Evening chores were often similar but also included gathering eggs and shutting up the chicken house and pen to keep out predators such as skunks or dogs.

In the house, we were expected to make our beds after about the age of eight. Also, Mom gave us weekly chores of dusting and vacuuming. We often were asked to wash and/or dry the evening dishes. Later, we were expected to clean out the bathtub with cleanser after our baths. In these early years, we were paid an allowance of 20 cents a week.

In 1953, we received from Mom, or possibly Grandma, diaries to write our daily memories. Rita and I began ours in March; David is not sure that he had one that year, but he did fill one out for about half of 1955. Featured are excerpts from Rita's recording nearing the end of her first grade at age seven as well as a sample a year and a half later as a third grader. Samples of

David shoveling manure in front of the barn with the chicken house in the background.

my entries are shown for the same period as Rita's first writings, when I was eight and in the third grade. After these are samples from David two years later when he was a sixth grader. They show how intimately connected we were with the other St. Louis relatives and how our lives were full.

We lived in an area of the Valley with big sheep companies all around us. Nearby were fenced areas that served as their lambing grounds. In those days, most sheep companies "trailed" (drove) their sheep on designated "Sheep Trails," the timing of which would be reserved in advance so that bands of sheep would not intersect and become hopelessly mixed up. Herders for the sheep companies drove their bands from the "desert" (semi-arid land north of Baggs with much less snow than at our more mountainous terrain) to the lambing grounds in the early spring. After lambing was completed, many of the bands of sheep were trailed again to individual allotments in the National Forest. Inevitably, a small number of lambs would become orphaned during lambing. It might be from ewes who had little milk, or maybe the mother would not claim a twin or a triplet, or a lamb could not compete in the suckling. It was rare that another ewe would accept a lamb that was not her own. The vast majority of these orphans simply just died in a day or two because in the large bands, it was not possible for the herders to take care of them, and the owners did not want to raise them elsewhere.

In the summers, we raised bum (orphan) lambs from our own band of sheep as well as those we were given from these big sheep outfits. The herders and owners of the large outfits, like Cow Creek, obviously did not prefer

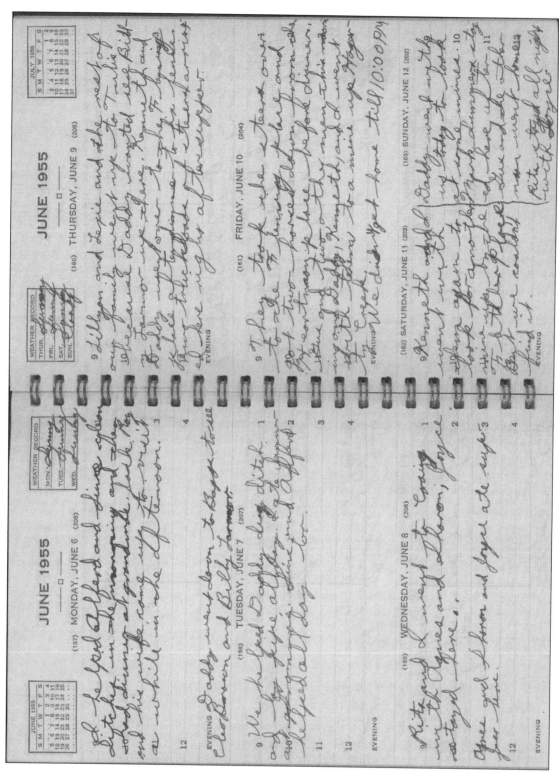

Diary sample from David, Grade 6, June, 1955.

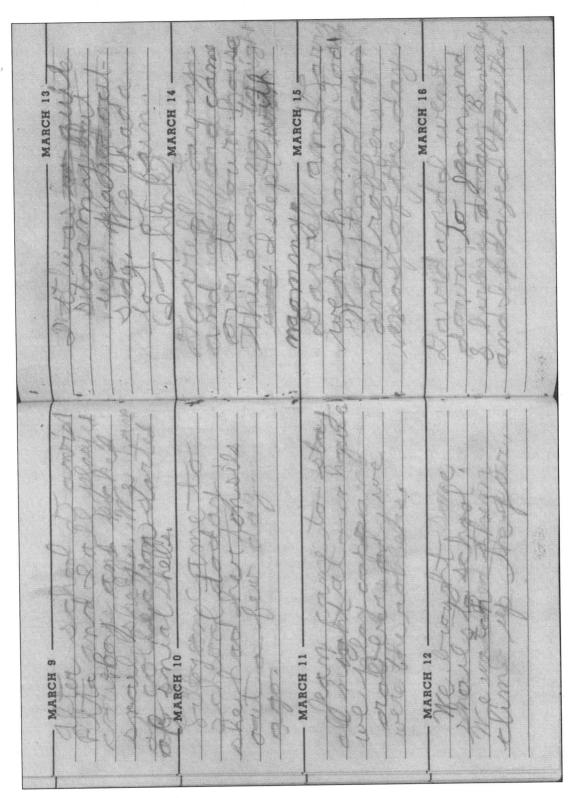

Diary sample from Kenneth, Grade 3, March, 1953.

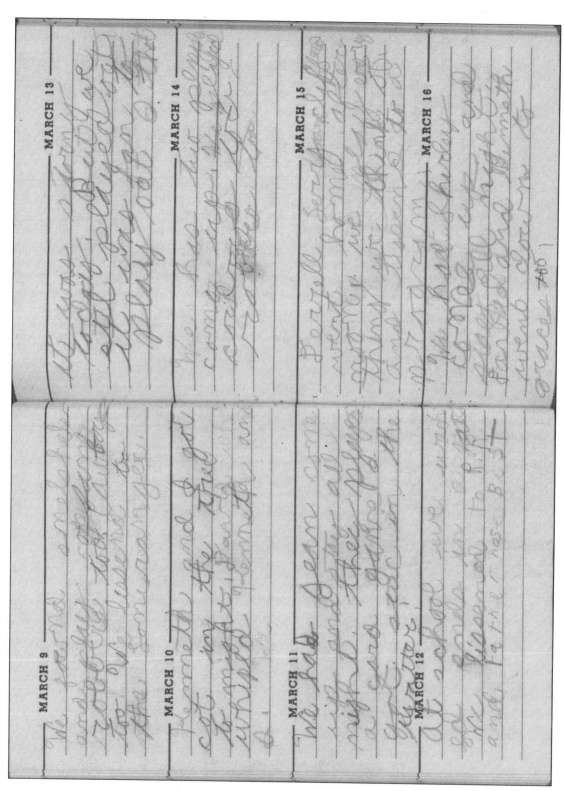

Diary sample from Rita, Grade 1, March, 1953.

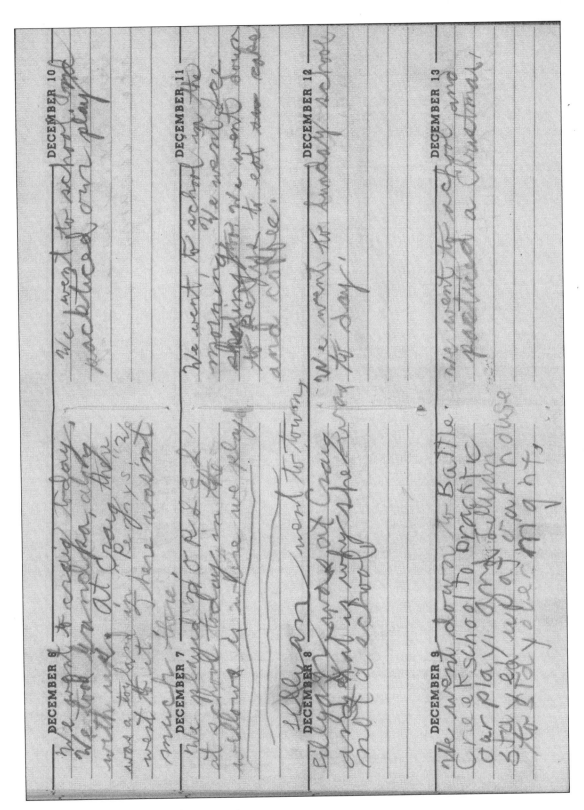

Diary sample from Rita, Grade 3, December, 1954.

One band of sheep in the lambing ground.   *Sheep shading up during the heat of the day.*

to let the orphans simply die and were happy to give them away. Once the word was out, managers would drop off bum lambs at our house as they drove back from checking their herders during lambing. We took as many as we could handle, raising them first on cow's milk and then on the grass on our seven acres.

Several of the orphans died anyway, but in most cases, we could nurse them back to health and raise them until fall when they would be sold with the rest of our sheep. We three started off with a few lambs, but after a few years, we would raise up to about 20 lambs every summer. This became a major part of our chores each morning: taking bottles to the barn, filling them with warm milk from the cows, putting nipples on them, feeding the lambs milk (and later grain), and later washing the bottles. Mom and Dad paid all the expenses, but the money we earned from selling the lambs went into our individual savings accounts at a bank in Craig. And it was with this money that we bought our boots, saddles, bicycles, and other things.

A "band" of sheep was considered to be about 1000 ewes, so with lambs that often involved twins and triplets as well as a few dozen rams, each band might have 2500 sheep in it. And some sheep men had four or five bands. Most sheep were not fenced in consistently, especially those that were grazed on the Forest in the summer. Thus, as might be expected, sheep from one band commonly would get separated from their band and end up in another band. Less common, but possible, especially on the Sheep Trail, one band would get entirely mixed up with another band. In these fiascos, the entire combined flock would have to be driven to the next available corral and resorted; yet almost certainly, a few ewes and lambs would not end up in the right band.

Virtually all of the sheep in Routt County and surrounding areas were raised primarily for meat, so lambs would be sold and shipped to market in

Dad getting ready to take a sheep herder's tent, camp, and supplies to the Damfino Forest allotment with three pack horses.

the fall. At the same time, ewes to be kept would be branded prior to trailing them to various winter ranges. It was exceedingly rare that one band of sheep did not have strays owned by someone else. Unlike cattle, where brands were burned into their hides and changed brands could nearly always be recognized, sheep brands of paint or tar on the wool would wear off or could be changed.

Although not universally accepted, most sheep men knew that they could well be losing strays to others even if they had strays themselves. The only fair thing to do was to authorize a third party—a "stray picker" or stray puller"— to gather all the strays, take them to his own pasture, and then arrange for return to their rightful owners. Chester Morgan had been the stray picker for years, but he decided to give up the job. He encouraged Dad to take the position, and Dad did so for a few years.

The process during these fall seasons, when we were pre or early teenagers, went like this: Dad had to call all the sheep men to find out when and where they were going to ship lambs. No doubt some of them were reluctant to tell him. Thus, he acquired some of his information from the relatively few trucking companies available. Dad had to be at each owner's sheep corral at daybreak before lambs were loaded on the trucks. When owners had not communicated with Dad, a few of them were surprised and

Rita, Lillyan, and Beverly holding down a ewe while Rita is milking it.

unhappy that he had called the truckers and showed up. Others accepted it as a friendly and necessary process. All the sheep, mostly ewes and lambs, were run down a long chute with cutting gates that led into side pens. The first gate was to cut into a pen the strays that were identified by having brands different from the main herd; the second was to separate the owner's ewes and rams into a separate pen. The lambs traveled straight ahead and up a ramp into the trucks. When all of the sorting was done and the trucks loaded, the main herd of ewes was turned out to pasture. Dad then loaded the stray sheep into his pickup and hauled them home. Our pasture next to the school typically held anywhere from a few to about 50 stray ewes and lambs. All strays belonging to an owner could then be picked up for a per-head fee plus a daily boarding fee beyond a minimum time since his strays were picked up. To avoid the boarding fee, it was not uncommon that owners would come more than once to load a few strays into their pickups. Each collection involved rounding up the entire flock of strays and driving them into a small corral we had built. Of course, the more times the same strays were driven into the corral, the more reluctant they were to enter. But, once all were in the corral, we would grab sheep with the owner's brand and wrestle them into a smaller pen, and after paying, he would haul them away. When we were not in school, we helped with the stray picking and, later, often were mainly involved in returning the strays.

As we were able or wanted (which was often the case) we helped with the riding for cattle or sheep, harrowing fields in the spring, repairing or building fence, irrigating, and haying. Rita was always an accomplished rider, and she often did much of that work. David, especially after losing his arm, also rode a great deal. My work usually involved fixing fence and irrigating. David and I both learned to drive a tractor by the age of six or seven, and we worked in the hayfield from about the age of ten on.

We became part of the hay crew of all the St. Louis uncles putting up hay on all their ranches sequentially. We started by driving the overshot stacker, which meant driving a tractor laterally away from the loose haystack that pulled a cable which propelled the loose hay up and dumped it on top of the stack so two men on top of the stack could place it in a squarish manner. Later, after the Boys purchased a baler, David was promoted to driving our 1952 9N Ford tractor and raking hay into windrows with a New Holland side-delivery rake. Sinc, would then pick up and bale the hay with the New Holland baler pulled and powered by his Golden Jubilee Ford Tractor. I began pulling the slip (a plank platform drug on the ground to circulate around the field to pick up bales) with a Ford tractor. Cousin Darrell would often ride and load the slip. Upon filling the load, we would drive to the stack and place the bales, one after another, on a gasoline engine powered elevator that would move them to the top of the stack, where people stacking would grab and arrange the bales so they inter-tied and the stack would stand all winter.

Only when we were quite young did the St. Louis family use horse-drawn mowing machines as this one driven by Dad.

Photo at our Fleming Place showing David driving the dump rake with Maude and Dolly (with burlap nose covers to help them deal with flies), the overshot stacker is at full height, and Dad helping someone top out the stack.

Later, in my high school years, I typically loaded the slip or worked on the stack, usually whichever job lacked the harder worker. For this work, we earned $3 per day at the beginning and, by high school, my pay increased to about $10 per day. Rita was told that Sinc was incensed that he had to pay such high wages to his own nephews who were not even grown men.

The debut of our work in the hayfield occurred when Dad needed to stack the loose alfalfa, either first or second cutting, at the Hackmaster Place. It was not a large field and required only one stack. In this year, Dad had a crew of four young kids to help him. Rita (about age seven) drove the dump rake, pulled by Grandpa's very tame team of mares, Maude and Dolly. Frequently, the team would simply stop, and Dad would have to get a willow switch to get them going again. Dad drove the buck rake with our team of geldings, Chub and Snip, David ran the stacker, and Darrell and I were on the stack. Someone came by and upon seeing this "crew," was completely amazed.

Haying was also a big job for our mother and aunts. While the crew of ten men (or young cousins) would be haying at one of the family's places, they would eat their dinner (noon meal) at that family's house. Cooking for the hay crew often took most of the time of the wife involved and any cousins who were available to help. We loved when the hay crew was at our home, because Mom made the best fried chicken anyone in the family could remember.

Three other work events were eagerly anticipated. First, was the branding of calves in the early summer. As little kids we started by watching our dad and uncles; as we got older we began to help out. Sinc was ordinarily the roper who walked his horse into the herd of cows and calves looking for calves that had "mothered up" or found their mothers. Checking the brand on the cow, Sinc would drop a loop on the calf and drag it to the branding area near a large fire. There, someone would grab the rope as the bellowing calf was dragged toward him. Upon reaching the calf, the man would reach across, grab the calf by the flank, and then "flank" the calf or lift and throw it on its side. Immediately he would jump onto the calf's neck with a knee and then bend and pull up on the upward front leg so the calf could not get to its feet. Another man would grab the upper hind leg, sit down behind the calf, and put one foot against the other hind leg, pushing it forward while stretching the held upper leg straight back.

Immediately, the calf would be set upon by someone burning the correct brand, called out by Sinc, on the calf's left side. Someone else would be boring out any horns that were just starting to grow and shaking "blood stopper" powder on the wounds. Another person would inject into the calf the allotted number of cc's of vaccination for "black leg" with a large syringe under the hide in the pocket created by its upper front leg being held up and away from its brisket. Sometimes a large pill would be placed in the back of the calf's mouth with a long "pill pusher" device (and thereby swallowed by the calf). For bull calves, another person would cut off the bottom of the scrotum, pull out and cut off the testicles, and add more "blood stop" powder. All the while, the calf would be bellowing in pain, but we did not think about that. It was simply the way things were, a matter of branding, castrating, dehorning, and vaccinating the calf as efficiently as possible.

A St. Louis branding with Dad (most likely) branding a calf, Oliver standing near the fire, Sinc on the white horse, and other riders holding the herd.

Dad branding a calf being held at the front and rear while Oliver looks on.

Shirley, Kenneth, and Jean each holding a branding iron, presumably before the fire heated them much.

As children, we were often given the testicles. We would impale them with a piece of baling wire and then roast them on the fire until they popped. Then as they cooled, we would eat them, often again to the horror of any dudes who may have come to watch the proceedings.

As we got older, we assumed various of these duties, but typically did not do the roping or branding, both perfected by Sinc and Dad, respectively. I often flanked or held the back legs of calves. David often vaccinated. Rita

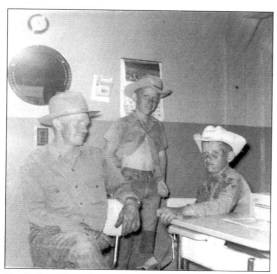

Dad, David, and Kenneth resting in the kitchen after spending the day docking lambs.

also helped hold either the back legs or the front leg of the calves.

Second, though not as dramatic, perhaps, was the "docking" of lambs (cutting off their long tails to a length of about two inches) in the spring. It was different from branding calves, and "docking" really meant more than shortening the tails. There was no "mothering up" involved because lambs were docked one band of sheep at a time, and we only had one band. All the flock would be driven into a large pen with wooden sides about three–four feet high. A smaller pen at one end would then be filled with perhaps 30 ewes and lambs. At the far end would be one or more docking stations, consisting of a horizontal board nailed on top of the wall.

A person would go into the pen, catch a lamb by a hind leg, lift it up and cradle it on its back with the person's left and right hands holding front and hind legs crossed together on each side. He or she would then hold the lamb on the horizontal board while a person on the other side of the fence would first castrate any ram lamb by cutting off the scrotum and then pulling out the testicles while holding tightly on the upper scrotum so as not to herniate the animal. A large pliers-like tool was often used, but some sheep men used sheep shears to cut the scrotum and their teeth to pull out the testicles. This large instrument had scissors-like cutting edges (like shears) used to cut off the tail in one quick closure. "Blood stop" powder was applied, especially to the tail, from which an artery would squirt blood into the faces of both persons there. Next, the lamb would be rolled over onto its stomach held only by the front feet and draped down toward the outside. Someone else would come and brand the lamb by taking a hand-held iron with the brand (in our case & [ampersand]) dipping it into hot paint or tar, and then stamping it painlessly on the wool of the lamb. Thereupon, the lamb would be released outside the pen. After all the lambs in the small pen were docked, the ewes were also released outside, the gate closed, and the pen filled again from the larger corral.

In later years, we used "Elastrators" instead of "surgery" to dock and castrate lambs. This involved placing a thick rubber washer about the size of a nickel over four metal prongs of the hand-held Elastrator. Upon squeezing it, the four prongs would open and stretch the rubber to about a one and a half-inch square opening. One rubber was placed at the top of the scrotum near the body and another was placed on the tail about two inches from the base. Once the Elastrator was pulled away, the lamb was branded and released, with no bleeding at all. While seemingly more humane, the lambs would soon be seen intermittently lying down and groaning in agony. This would subside in several hours and certainly by the next day. The complete cutting off of the blood supply would result in those body parts' dying. Thus, in about three weeks, the scrotum and testicles as well as the tail would simply drop off.

Docking was an especially filthy job. The pens would become very dusty, so one's clothes and entire upper body would become layered with blood, sweat, and paint or tar, all mixed with dirt. Even so, it was exciting and necessary. We eagerly participated in the annual event.

The third event that was always anticipated was driving all the cattle from the uncles' ranches to the Forest in the early summer. After several hundred head of cows, calves, and a few bulls were rounded up from the early spring range close to the ranches, riders from all the St. Louis families would join to drive them to the Forest Service allotment northwest of Columbine near the Middle Fork of the Little Snake River. On the first day of the drive everyone would meet, typically at the Home Place, at 4:00 a.m. on horseback. We would ride to the "gathering pasture" in near darkness, and as soon as we could see, we would gather the cattle and drive them onto the road. We had to be really careful to get the little calves who might be lying down and not seen. We would then drive the cattle up the main road. Grandpa would meet us past the Three Forks ranch for breakfast in a lane that was well fenced on each side so the cattle could not escape to the side. We'd have Dutch oven biscuits, potatoes, and eggs cooked over a campfire as well as coffee from a huge pot that with two willow hooks Grandpa would pour into tin cups.

The drive would continue throughout the day, with lots of bellowing by the cows that were looking for their missing calves and by bulls challenging one another to a fight. In the afternoon, we would arrive near Box Creek and there brand the rest of the calves missed in the earlier branding. We'd also have our noon dinner there from food brought by Grandpa. Thereafter, we would hold the herd at the "Cow Camp" on the opposite side of the hill near Box Creek overnight. To keep them together, riders often had to be posted to hold the herd in a fenced corner all night so that cows could not sneak off. The next morning, early, the herd was driven to the northern and east-ern-most part of the allotment and turned loose. There, they would spread out to graze, held on the north and west by the Middle Fork canyon and on the other sides by a "drift fence" in order not to stray to non-allotted Forest or private land.

A record of our childhood would not be complete without an account of the Focus Ranch and the Pep Hall. James (Shorty) Temple was raised on the next place up the river from our ranch. He married a Southerner from Georgia, Lucy Wood, and they had two children, James Jr. (Jim) and Patricia (Patty Ann) Green. They ran one of the first, if not the first, "dude" (guest) ranch in our region, which they named the Focus Ranch. City folks would pay to take their vacation on a real Western ranch, complete with daily horseback rides, cookouts, brandings, fishing, hunting, and as many other "real" ranch life experiences as could be made available. Of course, it involved lodging in cabins, joint meals, and other local entertainment. And whenever possible or convenient, it included interaction with the "locals" in their own work and play activities.

The Wege family from Chicago at the Focus Ranch. Back: Ralph, Kay, and Janet; front: Charlene and a friend.

Janet, Ralph, and Kay with two of Janet's children attending Dad's 80th birthday celebration.

Our family, being only a half-mile away from the Focus Ranch, had many, many interactions with Shorty and Lucy and the dudes who came once or on a yearly basis. A recount of all the connec-tions would number into the hundreds, if not thousands. These would include interactions between the St. Louis Boys and the Temples before they started their own families, Mom and Doris coming to the Little Snake River for the first time to help cook for Shorty and Lucy's hunters and then Mom returning the next year to cook and clean for the dudes, Elizabeth's introduction to the Valley as a dude at the Focus, and get-togethers with Jim and Patty Ann and their families on the ranch and later in Steamboat.

Later, David and I contracted haying for Shorty, I worked one entire summer at the Focus, former dudes became the family that purchased our ranch as well as Sinc and Elizabeth's, and Dad worked at the ranch after returning from Washington state. For us, however, the contact with the dudes was our main social outlet aside from 4-H and our regular St. Louis cousins and Salisbury neighbors. At least two of us remember our first teenage "loves"

The Focus Ranch staff getting ready to take dudes on a hayride. The Pop Shop is in the background.

with guests at the Focus, one or two of which persisted into family friendships that lasted for years.

Lucy Temple had the acumen to own the only little store between the Savery and Columbine stores, each about 20 miles away. The Pop Shop of course sold pop (soda), but also candy, gum, and a few sundries. For the dudes, it also sold hats, Western clothes, and some fishing supplies. It was the only place that we as children could go to buy pop or candy on our own, a half-mile on foot, bike, or horseback. As we grew older, it was also one place where we could sometimes interact with dudes of about our own ages.

The other place was the Pep Hall. Its name came from an earlier era but denoted vibrant, social, and communal interactions. When it was built originally and who named it is not clear to us, but the first Pep Hall was at Three Forks, and among the first retrievable newspaper accounts of its use was in 1924.

The Pep Hall was a consummate community center. The building was used for dances, school programs—especially in the 1920s and 1930s for the Three Forks, South Fork, and Pine Grove

The Pep Hall in winter after someone needed to shovel a heavy snow from the roof.

(Piney) Schools—community theater, voting, church or Sunday School, luncheons or dinners, community or even legal meetings, and no doubt other purposes. Perhaps because gradually fewer and fewer people lived at or near Three Forks, the Pep Hall was moved to a location on the Focus Ranch property just across the river from their barn and corral. It occupied a level piece of land next to the road, with plenty of parking space, between the Temple grade and the only bridge across the Little Snake upstream from a bridge about ten miles away. The level field across the road was a pasture, but in the 1940s or 1950s, occasional rodeos were held there.

An August 3, 1944, *Steamboat Pilot* article entitled "Large Group at Snake River Service" read: "The Pep hall on Snake river, moved and remodeled last summer thru the efforts of the home demonstration club on the river, is serving the community in many ways. At a recent Episcopal church service conducted there by Father Callahan, who ministers to the Snake river parish, 32 persons were present. Almost all Snake river community activities are conducted at this edifice, which has been so constructed that the church altar can be closed off from the main room when activities other than church services are being conducted there."

It would be easy to speculate that Lucy and Shorty Temple provided access to their land for the Pep Hall because it was the perfect venue for their dudes to join in real Western doin's. Our memories of the Pep Hall were almost all related to the dances held there numerous times each year. Everyone would dress up, drive to the Hall, and park in rows along two or three sides of the building. Prior use typically involved live music, as with Gretchen Hancock playing the upright piano and perhaps Francis playing the fiddle and Perry playing the drums. Dad would often "call" the square dances. Continuing into our memories, Grandpa and Dad would often sing solos a cappella or recite such favorites as "The Persian Kitty," typically to the delight of the children and dudes who were in attendance. Mom would ordinarily sit looking very uncomfortable as Dad would let his extroversion and showmanship shine.

At most community social events, a collection was taken up or a fee was paid by individual families or organizations who organized their own dances or events. The proceeds were given to Grace (Perry's wife), who kept the books that recorded revenue and expenses for years. She also paid the bills, primarily for the monthly electricity expense and various repairs. (Repairs were ongoing; a 1933 newspaper account reported that Dad and Fritz Clover installed rods through the building to strengthen it.) About 1950, "the

A square dance at the Pep Hall with Francis playing the fiddle, Gretchen Hancock playing the piano, and Dad calling. Doris Honnold and a partner are in the front; Shorty Temple and Elizabeth are swinging in the middle.

Shorty and Lucy Temple are meeting in the front; Elizabeth and Sinc are meeting in the middle.

Our Later Childhood on the Ranch / 211

Club" purchased a good record player with public address system, complete with microphone, that thereafter typically replaced the live music. And 78 or 45 rpm records were bought to provide the background music for square dances, waltzes or crooning music for slow dances, and early rock and roll for the younger generation.

Mostly the dances were good, clean fun. We loved them. We had learned to square dance at school and 4-H, so we joined in with the adults in all the dances. We also knew "Put Your Little Foot," the Schottische, and polka steps. In our memory, as most evenings wore on, the women stayed mostly in the hall sitting on benches next to all four walls. A fair number of the men, and later the more adventurous women, would go outside to their vehicles and pass bottles of whiskey around, each person taking a long swig and making the expected pained look on their face before passing the bottle to the next person. Some would get drunk, even to the point of getting sick. Others would re-enter the hall and continue dancing and, between dances show off their gymnastic skills on the three-fourths- to one-inch steel rods, joined in the middle by turnbuckles, that held the two sides of the large room with no partition from moving laterally. Dad was often one of those who showed off this way. Occasionally, a disagreement would occur, and the men would go outside and get into fist fights.

As children, we were too young to get involved in any of the drinking or fighting, but we certainly witnessed it. We also noticed how our mom and aunts either tolerated these wild extracurricular activities or showed visible disdain. As we became teenagers, the dances became wonderful opportunities to dance with dudes of the opposite sex, especially at those dances arranged primarily for the Focus Ranch guests.

In front of the Pep Hall, and no doubt using its toilet facilities, we also enjoyed sledding parties as children. Mentioned earlier, the Temple grade was the perfect sledding hill and the steep hill next to it was a challenging toboggan hill.

MEMORIES

CHRISTMAS

David: I remember one Christmas Eve when Dad said, "I believe Santa has come around already. He might have left something for us on the front porch." We ran to find two new saddles with shiny iron saddle horns for Kenneth and me.

Kenneth: One year at Craig, Mom gave each of us a dollar to buy Christmas presents. I remember going to the dime store and carefully buying four different gifts, one for David, Rita, Dad, and Mom. It took a long time. I do not remember this, but Mom often told the story that David thought that this was too much effort, so he bought himself a cap gun and holster.

Kenneth: I remember loving Christmas because it was the time Mom and Dad splurged for us. One year, I remember David and I both got new red coats. Of course, the Christmas I remember the most is the one in 1950. That is the one in which we got a beautiful new sled. And it was later that day that Jay Green offered to pull us down the road in his Jeep pickup. David and I argued about who got to ride on the sled, and he won out. I rode in the back of the pickup watching Dad on the right side of the road on skis, Patty Ann Green on the left on skis, and David in the middle on our new sled tied to a long rope. We went around a corner between Grandpa's and Perry's places and I only remember a blur. Coming the opposite way, Bruce McAllister had nearly driven off into the river but ended up running over Patty Ann's legs and tearing her skis off (but miraculously not breaking her legs) and running directly over David lying down on the sled. Dad simply fell into the bank. David was lying on the road unconscious. Dad was frantic. I remember being in the driveway at home while hurried plans were being made to drive David to Denver. And there my mind went blank...and still is. This event was a turning point in all of our lives.

Rita: Every year, Daddy would go out and cut a really nice Christmas tree for us. He and Mom really liked a blue spruce, even if the needles were really sharp. When we were little, all the fragile glass ornaments were on the top half and we were forbidden to touch those, but we got to decorate the bottom half. We had little glass birds that we would make nests for out of icicles (tinsel). We basically redecorated the tree daily.

Rita: It must have been the year we went to Akron for Christmas and we had our Christmas at home early that, while Mom kept us in the kitchen, Daddy went out to "do some chores" but circled around the house and came onto the front porch. We didn't hear anything. We later went to the porch and found the presents, a beach towel for each of us with our name on it, saddles for David and Kenneth, and something major for me (I don't remember what). Mostly I remember wondering how Santa Claus could have come in so quietly without our knowing it.

Rita: When I was little, we went Christmas shopping in Craig and brought the presents home. I snooped into all the sacks and found a little clothes line with little clothespins for doll clothes. I knew it was for me, so at supper, I told everyone that what I wanted most for Christmas was a little clothesline and clothes pins. David and Kenneth got mad at me because they knew I peeked. Of course, I denied having done so.

Our Later Childhood on the Ranch / 213

Our hand-cut, perfectly decorated Christmas tree.

Getting ready for Christmas about 1952.

Rita: After David's accident, he slept in the living room. One Christmas, he got up early and opened all of his presents before anyone else got up.

DAILY LIFE

David: With the gas lanterns, we had time to get to bed before the mantles stopped glowing, I recall that when we got electricity, it was hard to find my bed after I turned the switch off.

David: I remember when we used to go to Craig, we would buy comic books at the store that was across the road from Darrell and Larry's house when they lived there. We would take our used comic books to trade, and we would buy other comic books. Mom hated us going there because it took us so long. We would sit there and read a few of them to decide if we wanted them or not. The owner did not like to talk, and she didn't have much patience for kids.

David: Our (Kenneth's and my) room was off the back porch. It had a low window we could climb in and out. In the summer, we slept with the window open. One summer we had two yellow kittens that would jump up and through the windows and climb onto our beds, sometimes waking us up by curling up on our faces.

David: Our swimming hole was down the river from us about half way to Sinc's or the Home Place. They dammed the river there for irrigation. It wasn't very deep and the water was not fast moving. Lillyan and Lexie, Darrell and Larry, and the three of us often swam there.

David: I often filled bottles with milk at the barn for the bum lambs. I got so good at it that I could pour straight from a milk bucket into the large beer or Coke bottles without a funnel. As we acquired more and more bum lambs, it took too long to feed them one or two at a time. Thus, one summer Dad built a special trough to feed them all at once. He drilled holes in both sides of boards nailed together in a long V shape. The holes were arranged alternately and were the right size to hold the bottles tightly enough so that the lambs could not pull the nipples off. But when we opened the gate to the pig pen where we would first feed the lambs some grain, it took at least two of us to get each lamb onto a nipple and then to keep them from butting another lamb away once they finished their milk.

David: Before our purebred sheep business, our main income for the year was selling these bum lambs. We also sold muskrat hides, and a few times we were paid a bounty for dozens of frozen jackrabbit carcasses we delivered to Craig in the winter. When Dad guided deer hunters, they gave us the hides. After the hunters skinned out the deer, we put salt on the hides and laid them out to dry on the top of the woodshed. We sold those in Craig as well, but we didn't get much money, partly because so many of them had holes in them from poor skinning. I couldn't figure out why they were cutting so many holes in the hides until it dawned on me that Dad and hunters were mostly drunk in the afternoons or evenings after a hunt when they dressed their deer. It's a wonder somebody didn't cut a finger off.

David: I remember a spring when all the family but me went to Fort Morgan while I stayed with Sinc and Elizabeth. At that time, we had five old ewes and 11 lambs (four sets of twins and one set of triplets) in Grandpa's shed, which I fed. During that stay, I was to walk the half-mile each day to feed our chickens and cats. I remember feeding eggs to the cats. Another memory of that time was that the well water in Sinc's house became contaminated with cow manure from runoff from the cow barn.

David: Dallas Morgan, who rented the Willow Creek School teacherage for a few summers had some hound dogs that he used to hunt bear and mountain lions. When he had to be gone for several days to a meeting, we would feed his dogs since we lived about 150 yards from the school. With the game warden being gone, this was always an excellent opportunity to fill our freezer with fresh out-of-season venison.

David: I got into a fight with Georgie Salisbury at a Dixon dance after he said something bad about a woman. I was not going to back down and punched him in the belly so hard that he quit the fight.

David: With the stray picking, it was amazing to me how many sheep could be packed into a pickup. Sometimes, Dad had to make two or three trips to haul all the strays from one truck loading. Eventually he raised the stock rack on our GMC pickup so he could haul sheep in a double deck. It's amazing to me now how over-loaded it was at times.

David: During the stray picking years, we would help Dad whenever we were not in school. On weekends, we would often ride three or four in the cab of the pickup leaving home in the dark to arrive somewhere in the mountains by daybreak. We learned all the different sheep brands. A few times, Dad let me run the stray cutting gate, which meant I had to recognize a different brand instantly. Sometimes when the owners came to pick up their strays, Dad was not home. No problem. We could round up the sheep from the pasture and put them into a corral as well as any adults. The owners were sometimes surprised that we told them exactly how much they owed us. Sometimes we saw displeasure on the faces as we collected the cash.

Kenneth: We first practiced our reading by reading cereal boxes in the morning. But we soon loved to read comic books (we called them "funny books"). We could buy them for ten cents at Woolworths or the "Dime Store" in Craig. I would not say that we collected them, but we read and reread every one until it was ragged and torn. We did have a few of the Golden Book series children's books, but it was with the comic books that we practiced our reading outside of school.

Kenneth: I accepted the adult talk that our sliding down a steep incline at the west side of the sandstone cliff was not a good idea, but it did not bother me much and likely did little to stop us. We liked to climb up the side of a steep incline of about 20 feet of sandstone and slide down on our butts. We called this place the "Snail Shell Rock," because it was there that we often found little, pearly white, coiled snail shells. The reason Mom did not want us up there was not because of the danger (It was not dangerous!) but because we would wear through the seats of our Levis after several trips down the sandstone slide.

Sample of the cereal boxes and comic books where we basically practiced our reading.

Kenneth's "The Night Before Christmas" Golden Book.

Kenneth: We could not reach the phone mounted on the wall as children. We would have to drag a chair in front of it, climb up on it, and then stand on it to make a call.

Kenneth: Although David and I remember it a bit differently, the two of us decided we were going to build a raft and float it down to the swimming area. We went out through the trees toward the river from the house and chopped down and cut to length several green cottonwood trees that were about eight to ten inches in diameter. It was a lot of work and took us more than one day. We arranged them into a platform about four by six feet and nailed boards on top of them to hold them in place. It was very heavy, but we dragged it to the river and floated it down to the swimming area. It barely floated out of the water on its own, but when one or two of us got on it, it would float several inches to a foot below the surface. And of course, if you got on one side, it would tilt so much that you'd fall off.

Kenneth: As we got older and more daring, with Mom's ignorance of our activities, David and I would climb higher than the Snail Shell Rock incline, walk over to near the face of the cliff over the garage, and aim rocks at the mailbox below. At one time as well, drawing on the knowledge we had learned about taking water out of the river upstream into ditches to irrigate the adjacent meadows, we took shovels and built a little ditch above the sandstone incline in the little creek that flowed by during wet weather and diverted it above the incline straight to the cliff. As such, we created a waterfall over the cliff that we proudly regarded as an engineering masterpiece. The waterfall was short lived, however, because it tended to fill the irrigation ditch flowing by below with dirt and rocks.

Kenneth: We loved to have cousins come at night and play "kick the can" in our yard. The game could go on for one or two hours. I found one tree that I could climb quickly and hide on a low branch. No one ever found me there. No doubt related, I learned to climb small aspen trees that were about three inches in diameter at the base. When I got near the top, the tree would bend over and lower me to the ground.

Kenneth: Dad showed us how to trap muskrats in the winter. I learned to recognize the trails that the muskrats used to leave the water, set traps in the trails, and wire them to a good-sized tree or bush. I'd need to go there every day to see if I had caught a muskrat. If so, I would first quickly stun it and then kill it with a club, remove it from the trap, reset the trap, and carry the muskrat home by its long tail to skin. Skinning was a delicate job, because any slip of the knife would ruin the pelt (and we ruined some before learning how to skin with the knife directed away from the skin). Once removed, we would then pull the pelt, fur side in, over a flat piece of

Running to hide after someone sneaked by the one who was "it" and kicked the can.

Kenneth climbing a small aspen (quaker) tree that when he reached about two-thirds of its length would bend over and lower him to the ground.

quarter-inch plywood smoothed and tapered to a rounded arrow at one end. After a few months, the pelts would be dry and could be sold in Craig for a few dollars. I remember one cold morning walking through the snow and then falling through the ice up to my waist in the slough just up the road from our house near Temple's fence.

We helped Dad trap beaver sometimes, but the traps were too stiff for us to set. The beavers also might fight back in the trap. But mostly, beaver skinning was extremely difficult because a solid, opaque layer of fat lay between the skin and the muscle. The fat had to be left on the carcass but without nicking or cutting the pelt. I grasped the idea, but I never practiced or perfected the skill.

Kenneth: Before we were old enough to help in the hayfield, we still liked to spend time there, when virtually all the work putting up loose hay was done with work horses. We especially liked to ride on the front of the buck rake, standing on a pole behind the vertical fence between the two horses and in front of the driver. It was fun to watch the hay fold over itself and pile up as the buck rake went down a windrow. When full, the driver (Dad or Perry, typically) would pull back and lock the lever that would raise the sharpened, smooth pole "teeth" about a foot off the ground and go back to the stacker. Upon driving the buck rake to the back of an opposing set of horizontal and vertical poles on the stacker, the lever would be lowered and the horses backed up to leave the hay on the stacker. Then, the driver would raise the teeth and punch the load as far back on the stacker platform as possible. Sometimes, we would ride in front of the buck rake fence and let the hay pile up against us. On a few occasions, a kid was completely covered up and had to be rescued before finishing the load.

Kenneth: Because our bedroom window was open much of the summer, when we had to pee before bed or during the night, we simply peed out the window. At some point, to keep out the mosquitoes, Dad put a screen over the open window. We simply peed through the screen but noticed after a couple of years that holes had rusted through the screen as a result.

Kenneth: One spring, as the snow was beginning to melt, when we were probably about 12 or 13, David and I decided we would drive toward the Fleming Place to hunt rabbits. We took the old red Jeep with no top and no spare tire out of the "tunnel," chained up the front wheels, drove up to the turnoff above the Hartman Place, and started up the road, which had not been cleared at all in the winter. David was driving. With some spinning of the chained front wheels, we dug through about six to eight inches of hard crust (frozen snow) and turned south into the lane that paralleled the Hartman fence. It became easier to drive and we easily drove about 100 yards down that lane. I remember just commenting on how much the snow had smashed down the fences on both sides when, with a "whoomph," the Jeep broke through the crust and went down about four feet.

The old red Jeep readied for an excursion for guests.

We had two scoop shovels with us, so we thought we would shovel ourselves out. After about an hour of shoveling, we had the snow around the Jeep cleared and about six feet back. The only thing that was visible was the top of the windshield sticking out of the snow. We gave up and walked home. The next day, Dad decided to open the road up to the Jeep with the V plow on the grader, but, even with that, he could not break through the frozen crust. It was probably then a day or two later that Dad brought our team of work horses, Chub and Snip, above the road in the Hartman Place where the snow had mostly melted, and with a good bit more shoveling on the upper side, pulled the Jeep up the bank and out of the deep snow.

Kenneth: I remember that we were really good square dancers. Probably not with perfect grace, but we already knew and could execute almost all of the complicated maneuvers that everyone else would have to be taught at a dance.

Rita: Several times, I stayed up all night or got up every hour or so to try to save a bum lamb near death that somebody had dropped off. The trick was to keep them warm and to give them tiny amounts of milk about every 15 minutes. Most of these sick lambs had scours (diarrhea) as well, so some of them didn't make it.

Rita: We fed the bum lambs with milk that we put into large glass pop or beer bottles. The black rubber nipples we would put on the bottles for the bum lambs had just tiny holes in them, so it would take forever to feed a bottle to a lamb. Thus we opened the holes larger—but not too large—by holding a match under a needle to heat it up and then put it in the hole to melt enough rubber to enlarge the hole.

Rita: David convinced me that the bubbles that floated down the river or a ditch were horse slobber, so when I bellied down to drink, I would always be careful not to suck in a bubble.

Rita: At one of the sledding parties, I remember that Shirley and I did not make the turn on the Temple grade and went off into the draw. We no more than got ourselves upright in the deep snow, when Kenneth and Lillyan came over the edge next to us. Then, a few seconds later, David and Jean came flying over. There were six of us in a heap.

Rita: On April first, we would ring our own ring several times on the telephone and as soon as we heard the number of clicks for "rubberneckers" that we had hoped for, we would yell "April Fools" and hang up.

Rita: Some sheep man was calling a message to another on the party line, and it involved their meeting at Damfino (a region east of the Continental Divide). One person could not understand, so Lucy kept shouting "Damfino" into the phone. She had a room full of guests having dinner, and they all started laughing because they thought she was shouting "Damned if I know."

Rita: Mom used to get so disgusted about Alfred's listening to her phone conversations that once when Alfred had heard Daddy tell her that he would be coming home from the desert in a few days, Alfred asked, "When's George coming home?" Mom knew that he knew full well from the conversation that he had "rubbernecked," so she told Alfred that "he won't be home for a week or so." To which Alfred responded, "I thought it would be in just a few days."

DAD

David: Dad tried to teach us to box. Kenneth would quit after being hit in the nose once. If I had both arms, I would probably have been in too many fights.

David: Dad was a hard worker and enjoyed working. He would tackle any job. For example, when we got electricity, Dad decided to wire the house himself. I remember lots of cussing in the attic that had only one small access in the ceiling of our back porch. Some of our switches would not turn the lights on; some would not turn them off. Eventually, Shorty Temple came to help. Dad remarked, "Shorty Temple sure knows a lot about electricity!"

David: I enjoyed riding with Dad in the road grader, especially in the winter. I got to raise and lower the wing (a long angled blade that would raise or lower on the right side of the grader) in order to push the plowed snow back into the existing banks or simply move the banks back to allow for more snow in the days ahead. Later, as a teenager, Dad let me run the grader alone all the way to Columbine.

David: Dad probably did use the grader somewhat beyond the County's work. One year he used it to open ditches at the Fleming Place.

David: Every year in the early summer Dad and Mom would plant the garden at home. Dad gave us each some carrot seeds for "our" gardens. We would watch our carrots and usually pull and eat them before they were ready.

David: For several summers, Dad irrigated the Hackmaster Place. He also planted a large patch of potatoes there, so while he was "changing the water," each of us was assigned a row of potatoes to weed. We started with hoes, but we cut so many potatoes with the hoes that Dad insisted that we pull the weeds by hand. Some of the weeds had stickers. We never finished a row, and Dad would say, "What kind of workers are you guys?"

Kenneth: Mike Thomas was the owner of the coal mine where we bought our coal. He was a nice man and not the least bit unattractive, but we later had a ewe whose face reminded us so much of him that we named her "Mike Thomas."

Kenneth: After we "graduated" from our double holster cap pistols, David and I each got Red Ryder BB guns. I would target practice for hours with mine, shooting at rocks, cans, or whatever I thought I could hit, even though I was not nearly as "good a shot" (accurate) as David. With it, I sometimes aimed at barn swallows, which were everywhere, having nested by the thousands under a long ledge on the sandstone cliff across the road. (I actually hit one very rarely.) It was not powerful enough to stun anything else; at least once, David hit me with a little copper BB from his gun.

Kenneth: Dad taught me to drive the Jeep pickup in the summer when he would drive to the Fleming Place to change the water (irrigate). I'm pretty sure when I was six years old, he let me (and David) sit on his lap and steer while he managed the clutch, brake, and gas pedals. When I was eight, he started letting me drive alone, and I had to look through the steering wheel to see out. We learned to drive a tractor alone even before that. Later, some neighbors were very critical of his letting David

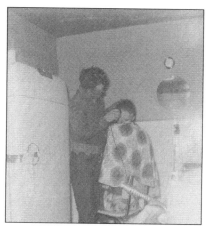

Dad always cut David's and Kenneth's hair first with a comb and scissors along with hand clippers, and then as seen here, with electric clippers after we got electricity.

and me drive so young. He always answered that he preferred it that way because we "paid attention" much more that we would have done as teenagers. I think he was right.

Kenneth: Dad used dynamite a good bit. One use was to open up the Willow Creek ditch going to the Fleming Place in a steep area next to the creek that slid almost every year and would completely obliterate the ditch. Here, the ground was a bluish, sticky clay that, when wet, you almost could not shovel because each shovelful would have to be scraped off the shovel. When hard, it would be like concrete. Thus, when it was wet in the early summer, Dad would put a half-stick of dynamite into holes about a foot deep every few feet across this slide area, which was about 20 or 30 yards long. He would clamp a blasting cap with a fuse onto one of them, and the explosion of that one would detonate all the others. When it worked, the explosion would open a ditch almost perfectly about three feet wide and deep through the sticky clay.

One spring, Darrell and I were helping Dad, and we wanted to watch the explosion. Dad said okay but told us to go way up on the hill so we would not get hurt. We climbed the hill and stood and watched Dad light the fuse and then walk down the ditch about 100 yards to get behind a tree. A little explosion occurred and blew some mud straight up in the air. It turned out that only the lighted half-stick of dynamite had gone off. He set a larger charge for the next try but told us we were too close and needed to go back to another hill further away. We did so, waited, and watched. All I remember about the explosion was that a wall of mud and rocks went up into the air straight toward us. I dived into a bush face down, an extremely dumb thing to do. A rock about ten inches in diameter landed next to me in the bush. Darrell was not hurt either, but we were extremely lucky.

Kenneth: As we got older, probably early teenagers, Dad started a "tradition" of "waking up the Valley on the Fourth of July." He would tie a half stick of dynamite to a willow branch, usually below the school and set it off about 5:00 a.m. Being in the air and not close to anything solid, it would do virtually no damage but would make a thunderous, cannon-like noise and scare people out of bed. One year, when Dallas Morgan was living in the teacherage, the bang brought him out, and he immediately called someone declaring that the Russians had attacked.

Kenneth: I was a little jealous that David got to do more grading with the road grader than I did. I, too, got to run the wing in the winter. I was with Dad and Darrell or Larry at the Fleming Place "changing the water" one day when Dad became concerned about David who had been permitted to level the steep grade on the "Jeep road" just west of the Hackmaster Place. We drove there and found that David had caught the blade on a large rock in the middle of the road causing the entire grader to pivot 90 degrees such that the front wheels were completely up in the air over the steep hill below. It took hauling in a bulldozer from somewhere to pull the grader back onto the road.

Rita: One memory that stands out is me crying to Mommy because I thought Daddy was going to die in the "desert" (near Wamsutter) when he went there to winter the sheep.

Rita: Daddy taught David and Kenneth to drive the Jeep pickup when they were only eight years old. When I turned eight, I wanted to learn too. He let me start on the flat section going toward the Fleming Place, with only sagebrush on either side of the road. I had watched Daddy drive, and he would look out the windows sideways a lot, so I thought that is what you needed to do. I looked out the side window and drove off the road into the sagebrush. I was upset that Daddy did not let me drive after that because he said I didn't "pay attention" like my brothers did.

Rita: Daddy told us about almost wrecking the grader while coming down Butter Hill (near the St. Louis Forest allotment). It had thrown itself out of gear and barreled down the steep hill. Daddy was barely able to keep it on the road because the steering was not by a wheel but with a horizontal lever that hydraulically turned the front wheels by raising or lowering either side. If a car had been coming toward him as he went around the right turn at the bottom, it would have been a disaster.

Mom

David: I remember Mom asking the three of us to paint the picnic table. She gave us a gallon of black paint. We painted the table but began painting each other as well. Black paint was everywhere, even on the front of our "Turn-a-Rocker" earth moving toy. We were all punished for the mess.

David: Mom and Elizabeth were good friends. Mom taught her things about country life.

David: Mom caught her finger in the ringer of the Maytag washing machine that could be spun around to rinse clothes from either the washer or from one of several

tubs placed in a circle around the washer. She always worried that we would get our fingers in the ringer.

David: I knew that Mom was afraid of loud noises like gunfire and firecrackers. When we bought all of our fireworks, I would wait until just the right time when she was doing dishes at the kitchen sink but not looking out the window. I'd light a firecracker on the window ledge to watch her jump. Sometimes I put firecrackers in the coal bucket so they would explode when she added coal to the stove.

Kenneth: It was a real treat when Mom would let us ride our bikes up to the Pop Shop to buy some pop or candy.

Kenneth: I remember Mom showing me and then expecting me to milk the "Old Yellow Cow" twice a day the first year Dad lived on the desert with the sheep. The cow was difficult to milk, and I remember telling her I couldn't do it. She didn't listen to that at all but made me keep it up until I learned.

Kenneth: I always liked to get through with my morning barn chores early so I could come into the house and spoon the pancake batter on the big griddle on the stove and then turn the pancakes.

Kenneth: I remember Mom teaching me how to dance when Dad was at the desert. We learned the Schottische, Put Your Little Foot, and the polka. Mom also taught me to chord to songs on the piano.

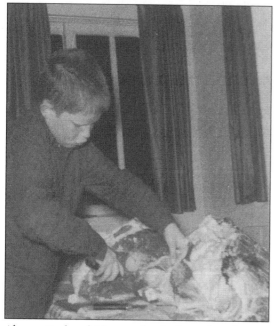

Above: *Dad and Mom posing during a day of cutting up meat.* Below: *Kenneth is cutting steaks from a hind quarter of beef on the back porch table.*

Kenneth: I also liked to help Mom kill chickens and get them ready for cutting up. We would put a half-inch galvanized pipe, about three feet long on the ground and stand on one end of it. We'd lift the

Dad, a neighbor, and Francis getting ready to butcher a pig. The hair, which is removed by scraping, is loosened from the carcass by being scalded in the tank in the background. A fire is built under the tank to heat the water.

other side, place the chicken's head under it, and then step down on the other side and at the same time pull hard. No chicken ever suffered more than a split-second this way. We'd then throw the headless chicken several feet away so it would not splash blood on us as it jumped and flopped around until dead.

Eventually, I learned to pluck all the feathers off at the ash pile, singe the remaining feathers, and then scrape off the pin feathers. Then we would cut them up in the kitchen according to an inflexible pattern. The feet were cut off at the joint first. Thighs were next, and then separated from fleshy lower legs. Wings were then removed and folded into triangles. Next, the wishbone was removed by cutting up from the bottom and breaking the two joints. The back removed above the ribs and then the top separated from the bottom. The front of the chicken was then cut back to front near the top of the ribs, the top side including the neck. The bottom half with the breasts was cut in half back to front. Finally, the part of the gizzard containing stones etc. was peeled back and thrown away. Then, it was cut in the middle and turned inside out to make three side-by-side lumps. The liver and heart were removed from the entrails.

Kenneth: I also liked to help Mom and Dad with butchering beef and deer. My first boyhood ambition was to be a butcher.

Rita: Going to Craig for shopping once every month or two was a big deal. Mom would get dressed up, and Daddy would too. Daddy would wear a neck tie and nice shirt, and Mom would wear a dress with nylon stockings (hose). On one trip she noticed that she had an unmatched set of stockings; one had a stripe up the back (the fashion at the time) and the other did not. She was embarrassed about that all day. The trips to shop took all day, and we'd usually fill the back of the pickup with at least four grocery carts of groceries. This included 50-pound bags of flour and sugar, which would be dumped into the flour and sugar bins in the kitchen. We would always eat dinner (lunch) at the Midwest Café. I remember Mom's being mad at Daddy because he would not pay attention to us but, instead, sit so that he could greet anyone coming or going whom he might know.

HORSES

David: Our first horse was Sally. I usually got to ride in front when all three of us rode her.

David: We had a stud (stallion) named Pal who was to become my horse. Pal had chewed up the back of our "Old Yellow Cow" when she was in the stanchion. Dad came to believe that he was too dangerous for kids, so he castrated him. Mom remembered me saying, "That tud isn't a tud anymore cause Daddy cut him."

David: Our next horse was Dolly, whom we all rode, but who became Rita's horse. Dolly had been bred before we bought her from Harry Russell. Her foal, a filly, was born in June, and that became her name.

David: Dad purchased another large, roan mare, named Queen, and that was a Tennessee walker and had been a barrel racer. Shortly after we got her, Dad was riding Pal, and I was riding Queen near the Focus Ranch. Queen suddenly stampeded, but I just held on. Dad could not catch us on Pal. He sold her after that.

David: Dad then bought another mare that I mostly rode, a buckskin that he also named Queen. When Dad and Gus were opening up an old molybdenum mine on East Beaver Creek near Hahns Peak, we were hauling Queen in a horse trailer to help in the process. The pickup was pulling our trailer, which was wide enough to accommodate two horses. Its sides were about six feet high, and it had no top. Dad went over the little raised bridge at South Fork across from the Three Forks Ranch a bit too fast, causing the hitch of the trailer to bounce off the ball of the hitch. A safety chain on only one side jerked the trailer violently from side to side before Dad could stop. The trailer nearly tipped over backwards and then sideways, but Queen fell down at the bottom keeping the center of gravity of this wide trailer low enough to keep it upright. When we unloaded the horse, she would not then or ever walk into a horse trailer again. On that day, I had to ride her all the way to East Beaver Creek, a distance of about 25 miles.

David: When June was three years old, Dad broke her, but with more than usual difficulty. For example, she would not break to lead. After dragging her around with another horse and pulling on her for two days, one jolt from an electric prod pole ("hot shot") on the nose ended all the balking. June was a very good horse, with an exceptionally smooth walk, that became mostly my horse.

David: As Dad was breaking Satellite, he let me lead her into and out of the corral only; he did not trust her enough to let me ride her yet. The horse had a back as round as a barrel, so the saddle cinch had to be pulled extra tight. She was very rough riding and also had a "cross-country lope" like a dog, which made it feel like one stirrup was longer than the other. It took forever to teach her to neck rein, and Dad had to re-teach her every year after being turned out for the winter. Satellite would shy at anything. She might jump 15 feet sideways if a chipmunk ran across in front of her.

David: Kenneth and I once went camping at the branding corral over by Beaver Mountain. We had two horses, Ace had the saddle and Pal had the packsaddle, so we had to take turns on who would ride on top of the pack and who would ride in the saddle. We rode the three miles or so over there and put the horses in the corral so they would not run off. We set up the tepee tent next to it and built a fire there. We had brought along what we needed and had supper. When we went to bed that night, we darn near froze to death because we did not have sleeping bags but just blankets. Also, during the night, the horses were stomping and raising hell because they wanted to join some other horses that came around on the other side of the corral. It made all kinds of racket so, of course, we were kind of scared. We didn't sleep much but the next morning for breakfast we were going to have cereal with cream on it. We put the cereal in the bowls and took the cream out to pour on the cereal. We poured buttermilk because the shaking of the cream on the way up the day before had turned the cream into butter. Even the butter didn't taste right because it was unsalted.

David: I remember Kenneth and I were riding Ace and Satellite across the river near our spring. As we started loping, Satellite took off and ran away with me. I pulled her head around so far that her mouth was next to my foot. Even so, she

Ken about to get on Ace.

Posing on Ace in mid-spring with the school in the background.

continued running straight ahead so fast that I couldn't jump off. She ran completely through a big bunch of willows and into the river. She finally stopped on the slippery rocks.

David: Satellite never did buck with me, but I knew she could buck, partly because she could jump so high. Dad eventually sold her to a rodeo contractor. Apparently, as her debut, at a rodeo in Dixon, they announced a "new bucking horse." In showy, Old West fashion, they blindfolded her, and a good bronc rider mounted her. When they removed the blindfold and pulled up the flank strap, which she had never experienced before, Satellite immediately bucked him off.

Kenneth: I always was proud that Ace was "my horse." He was a grey gelding as a yearling but changed more and more each year to an off-white color. He was short and stocky like many mustangs, but he had the perfect qualities and disposition for an all-around ranch horse. His only undesirable trait was that he often did not want to be caught. But, once haltered or bridled, he was perfectly obedient. On any ride he was sure-footed, had an easy gait, would not "shy" dramatically (startle and jump sideways) when something unexpected happened, would ease himself out of a bog, and would cross deep water with ease. Ace was amazingly fast for his size, easily outrunning a yearling steer or heifer in the open sagebrush. In addition to that, he was tough! He never seemed to tire and never balked at galloping up a steep hill or at responding willingly after even 24 hours in the saddle.

As I got older, Ace learned to protect my legs as we rode through aspen and pine timber or through heavy willows, serviceberry, choke cherry, or oak brush. Ordinarily, the rider has to push the horse left or right with his hand on a tree as his knees would pass. Unlike most horses, and more like cattle, Ace would lower his head and move slowly through a brushy obstacle—not reluctantly put his head in and then lurch ahead. He would even walk steadily right through the middle of a barrier presented by a 10-foot high and wide bunch of willows if lightly spurred to do so. I discovered all of this as I became the rider who could most easily get cattle out of some down timber (timber with lots of fallen trees piled up) or could most effectively "dog" (chase) wary bucks out in the open so that our paid hunters could get a shot at them. In the few times I hunted from him, I could see a deer, pull the rifle from the scabbard under the left stirrup, jump off, and shoot from the ground. Ace would run back about 50 feet so the gunshot would not hurt his ears and then just wait for me. He did all of this without ever being specifically trained to do so. Ace never fell with me and never bucked. How lucky I was to have him.

Rita: Horses were a major influence in my life. As little kids we shared Sally, an old white mare that was perfect for little children because she was so patient, and actually "looked after us." Our next horse, Dolly, had learned before we got her that if someone did not know how to ride, she could get away with all kinds of annoying behaviors such as rearing if she did not want to go, rubbing her passenger's leg against a building, going under low branches of trees to knock her passenger off, lying down in water, or just plain balking and doing nothing no matter how much kicking, screaming, crying, or cajoling one did—and I did all of those. Annoying as Dolly was, if someone fell off, she would instantly stop. In spite of it all, I really liked Dolly, and thought she was beautiful. I would fantasize about tearing around the countryside with Roy Rogers (his horse Trigger reared too!) and catching bandits.

Rita: Eventually I got Gypsy in junior high or early high school. Daddy had bought some heifers, and the seller said that he could have that two-year-old palomino filly for 40 dollars. Daddy bought her and gave her to me. Daddy mostly broke her, but I helped too. In retrospect, I know that I let her get away with all kinds of things I should not have, so she was pretty spoiled in lots of ways. At one point, she got her hind legs tangled in some barbed wire. She cut one of them really badly, thus had a huge scar right at her knee joint the rest of her life. After that, she was terrified about getting anything wrapped around her legs and feet, so tying her with a long rope while camping so she could graze usually ended in her getting tangled, terrified, thrown down by her own jumping and bucking, or simply breaking her halter or lead rope. But she did turn out to be a pretty good cow horse, and I used her to help my friends, the Elkins, run their cattle while I was in college. She also got really good at galloping in unison with fifteen other horses in a quadrille team at Colorado State University.

Our Later Childhood on the Ranch / 229

I had her bred to a palomino stallion of Stratton's, and in 1963 she had a pretty little filly I named Mischief. Mischief caught a rare blood fluke, and, even with several months of free veterinary advice from Dr. Earl (Pinky) Smith, died before she was eight months old.

Kenneth and I trailered Gypsy to Cusick, Washington, after our parents moved there when he graduated from CSU and I was about to get married. I then left her with Daddy's neighbors, the Heitmans, while I went to Nepal with Chris. After returning from Nepal, I went back to Cusick, collected Gypsy, and kept her with some horses of friends where we lived near Corvallis, Oregon. The problem was that she was an alpha horse, so she bossed and chased all other horses around—this has been true since I owned her. Thus, this arrangement with our friends and their horses did not work out, and I really did not have a good place to keep her or to ride her. I ended up giving her to a man I knew who was working on a ranch in Montana. That was really heart-breaking for me, and occasionally to this day I still dream about Gypsy.

Rita: I also had a really nice sorrel gelding I named Cimarron that I had acquired somehow from Sinc. He was a good, solid, sure-footed horse willing to do anything. What little roping I ever did, I did from Cimarron. But in addition to my limited roping skills, he usually could not run fast enough to keep up with the steers. When I worked for the L-O-N Corporation in 1963 and did so much riding, I used Cimarron and a little black mare named Carol. (I did not ride Gypsy much that summer because she had the foal.) Carol was a short, broad-rumped little mare that was really spirited. If I let a day go by without riding her, she would try to buck. I really appreciated her because I always had to pay attention while riding or she would try to unload me. She was one of the toughest horses I have ever ridden. Specifically, I remember going to the top of Beaver Mountain with several other riders. Their horses had to stop several times along the way to rest. Carol would stop, take a breath or two and just keep going. I could ride her hard all day long and she never seemed to get tired.

Chapter 10

Willow Creek School

The Willow Creek School in Routt County was built from rectangularly sawed pine logs near the Ledger Place on the Willow Creek tributary to the Little Snake River most likely between 1910 and 1920. Aside from Sinc's starting school in Slater in a stone schoolhouse built by McIntosh, all the St. Louis brothers attended the Willow Creek School. Some of the teachers roomed at the Home Place and some at the Focus Ranch. In 1946, the school was moved to Shorty and Lucy Temple's mesa at the top of the Temple grade, in direct sight of the Hartman Place house. Entry to the main log schoolroom was through a teacherage that consisted of a small mud room and then one larger room with a curtain divider. Only one teacher, Miss (or Mrs.) Frederick, ever lived in it. Each day, water was carried by students from a spring box in the draw (little valley) below the road. About 25 feet away was a building that had a coal bin in the middle and separate outhouses for boys and girls on either side. This relatively low and long rectangular building was perfect for playing "Antie-Antie-I-Over" or throwing a ball over the building from a team on one side and the team on the other side needing to see and catch the ball before it hit the ground. Also, a two-horse stable was built for the days when some students rode horses to school.

David and I attended kindergarten for at least a few months at the Temple grade location, as well the first and second grade for David and first grade for me. Vesta Martin was David's kindergarten teacher, and Paul Polk, who roomed at the Home Place, was his first-grade teacher as well as my kindergarten teacher. Laura Lee Beeler was David's second-grade teacher and my first-grade teacher. Thereafter, in the summer of 1951, the main log building was again moved to a location about 150 yards west of our house on property donated by Oliver St. Louis. The outhouses on the hill were replaced by indoor plumbing with separate boys' and girls' bathrooms, but the outhouse/coal building was moved and used for storage. The wood- and

David standing beside the Willow Creek Schoolhouse when it was located at the top of the Temple grade.

coal-fired brown rectangular heating stove was replaced by a drip oil stove. Finally, a new teacherage was built as a hallway with the two bathrooms followed by a separate kitchen and living room. At that point, our aunt Grace (Perry's wife) returned to teaching and was our teacher most of the years we attended Willow Creek School. As a result, the teacherage was never needed for a teacher. Both school locations had outdoor swings. The new one featured a slide, two swings, a set of rings, and a four-foot high swinging bar that was about three feet wide.

The teacherage was rented for a few summers to Dallas Morgan, a local game warden. Later, after the school was closed, and after the George and Sinclair St. Louis ranches were sold, the building was also used as a bunkhouse. Finally, it was moved to the lower end of the Bryson Place and became Don Ely's home after he was divorced and the ranch was being taken over by his son, Grady. The building still stands there as of this writing.

Over the years when we or our cousins attended Willow Creek School, teachers typically picked up schoolchildren in their cars on their way to school and drove them back home at the end of the day. Children carried their lunches. After the move, transportation was unnecessary for the three of us because we lived only about 150 yards from the school and were able to walk home every day for lunch.

Each day began with the Pledge of Allegiance and various checklists that teachers acquired to assure that children had brushed their teeth in the morning, combed their hair, and so on. The room was typical of one-room

Willow Creek School during our elementary years.

Battle Creek School about 7 miles west that is still standing. At the left is the building with a separate boys and girls outhouse and a stable for horses in between.

Kenneth posing in front of his long-closed elementary school.

The main school building moved to the Bryson Place where Don Ely converted it to his home.

schoolhouses. There were two sizes of desks to accommodate younger or older students, each having a seat as well as a slanted fold-down writing surface over a metal bin for books, papers, pencils, and personal items. (These replaced the intersecting desks at the previous school location where each had an inkwell-endowed writing surface and underlying shelf for the student behind and a fold-down seat for the student in front.)

A small mud room at the entrance (north side) had benches and hooks where children could leave coats, hats, mittens, and boots. From there, one entered the main room. Near the top of the wall to the left was the familiar cursive writing guide for capital and small letters exactly framed at the top and bottom with large lines and in the middle with a dotted line. These were above a large blackboard with chalk and erasers. Straight ahead in the front of the room was a wooden teacher's desk as well as a pull-down map of the United States. The right wall was lined with windows below which was a long linoleum-covered shelf about two and half feet wide where we would grade-by-grade "come to class" to have our work checked by the teacher and to get new assignments for the various subjects: arithmetic, English, penmanship, social studies, spelling, and so on.

For several years, there were only St. Louis first cousins at the school. Jean, Shirley, David, Lillyan, Lexie, and I were the only ones in our grades. The exception was one year when a young boy named Jackie came from Three Forks. Only Rita and Beverly were in the same grade. Everyone started school and returned from lunch or recess when a hand bell was rung by Grace. Recesses, one in the morning and one in the afternoon, were 15 minutes, and typically involved our playing in the willows next to the school, on the swing set, or in the high snow banks at the edge of the road in the middle of winter. We did not play the usual children's games of softball, kickball, or other team sports. Instead, in the willows we used our imaginations to create houses or corrals, to arrange fights between cowboys and Indians, to create our own herds of stick horses, and so on.

Each spring, before school ended for the year, the Routt County Superintendent of Schools would come to the school to administer the standard County-wide achievement tests. We always scored amazingly high. One year, several of us achieved the highest scores in the County, each in a different grade.

Of course, through the years, the schooling of the St. Louis cousins happened in other towns, but most of us owe our strong foundation to our years at Willow Creek School. The St. Louis cousins have made significant educational achievements. These include at least two years of university training for all eleven cousins, nine baccalaureate degrees, seven master's degrees, one advanced physician's assistant degree, and two PhDs.

About the Willow Creek School, teacher Grace wrote the following essay:

"...The little log school house in northern Colorado furnished part of the inherited country background for these boys and girls. When I was their teacher, we definitely had a St. Louis institution because everybody there had the St. Louis name. Three of the students were my youngsters and the rest were nieces and nephews. They mostly represented different ages, so they were scattered throughout the grades one to eight.

It was a studious bunch who had already known the reason to be in school. Hard to believe, discipline was no problem. The children settled their own disputes at recess time, and I can't remember ever seeing any fights. Their games at recess were a continuation of the previous weekend as they often assembled to play. All rode horses and became expert help in gathering cattle with their fathers.

My brag and blow sheet contains the names of this group. One year the County Superintendent of Schools from Steamboat Springs came to give the achievement test at the end of the school year. Our school rated the highest of rural schools in the county. All pupils had placed first or second place in their grade. I am proud to say these people went through high school and I believe all have college degrees. Today, we find the eleven living in different parts of the nation, including Alaska and Hawaii. Hopefully they are successful in their chosen undertakings.

As for myself, I've spent many years connected with school. After teaching thirty-three years in a classroom, I retired, then substituted for fourteen years. Following that I did volunteer work for eight years spending part of each morning in one grade conducting a remedial group..."

> **Other schools attended by our St. Louis cousins.**
> Of course, Kathy went to school entirely in California. Sharon and Joyce received part or most of their schooling in Wamsutter, Wyoming, and Craig, Colorado. Lillyan and Lexie were schooled for two years in Silt, Colorado; Eureka, California; and Corvallis, Oregon. David, Rita, and I attended school for most of one year in La Sal, Utah. Except Jean's first grade at Battle Creek School, all of Jean's and Shirley's elementary and junior high schooling occurred at Willow Creek School. Beverly attended Willow Creek through the third grade but finished her elementary and junior high years in Craig and the Battle Creek School.

MEMORIES

David: Even though our cousin Darrell Ranch was a year older, we both started kindergarten at the same time when the school was up above the Temple grade.

Miss Martin was our teacher, whom I remember as being mean. She would make us sing, "Lavenders Blue Dilly Dilly; Lavenders Green," which, to me, was a dumb song. Kindergarten was only in the morning, so after lunch, we would walk home, about three-fourth of mile. We played a lot and took our time getting home so that some days the rest of the school was out before we got home.

David: Mr. Paul Polk was my first-grade teacher at the school on the hill. I remember an art class, where he gave each of us a bar of Ivory soap to carve. Mr. Polk had a soap sculpture of a naked woman that he kept hidden in his desk. Jean saw it, so word got out.

David: It was during that first grade that Freda and Bobby Armbruster came to the Willow Creek School. They may have lived at the Honnold Place.

David: I don't remember this, but Mom said that Mr. Polk had to pin a note to my hat if she was going to read it. Otherwise, I would forget to give it to her.

David: With Mr. Polk, recesses lasted longer in the winter, sometimes at least an hour, because we went sledding, not on the road but on the steep hill beside the road down to Temples. We slid down that hill with toboggans, scoop shovels, and even the hood of a car one time.

David: One thing we learned to do very well was to play marbles. We dug five two- to three-inch holes in the ground, four arranged in a square and one in the middle. We took turns shooting our marble from hole to hole, first around the four corners, and then to the middle. If you missed the next hole, you had to wait for your turn again. The first one to get to the middle hole won, and the prize was that you got more marbles. Another marble game was set up with a ring drawn in the dirt. We all had to put so many marbles in the middle. In turn, we had to shoot from the ring and eventually shoot marbles out of the ring without our "shooter" going out. We got to keep the marbles we knocked out and could keep playing our turn until we didn't do so. We sometimes used ball bearing "steelies" for "shooters," but they could break the other glass marbles.

David: The alphabet poster that ran all the way across the top of the blackboard sticks in my mind. It showed all the letters in both printed and cursive form. We learned that were two ways to write an "r" and a "t" in cursive.

David: Dad always played Santa at our school Christmas programs. Before anyone else, I knew he was not the real Santa because I noticed that Santa was wearing Dad's overshoes.

David: When they moved the school about a mile from the hill to beyond our house, they jacked it up, put wheels under it, and pulled it with a Ford 8N tractor.

Left: *Laura Lee Beeler Dodd and her brood—David, Shirley, Kenneth, Jean, and Sharon.*

Above: *Valentine card received by Kenneth (aka "Cookie") from Miss Beeler the next year.*

"Us kids" were allowed to ride inside the building while they were moving it. What a treat! We were disappointed that we had to get out when crossing the river. The bridge on the road was too narrow, so they had to pull it through the water. They were afraid they might have trouble pulling it up the bank on the other side, but that did not happen. Back on the road, we continued our ride in the school watching out the window as we traveled.

David: When Grace was our teacher, she would start each lesson, say Arithmetic, with the youngest person, like the second grade, and then progress up to the third grade, fourth grade, and so on. She often told the older kids, like Jean, to help a younger kid.

David: From Grace, we learned how to sew. This included darning socks, sewing on patches, and doing embroidery.

David: During recesses, we mostly played in the willows. We all had our stick horses stashed somewhere. We did try to learn to pitch or bat a ball, but we quit because nobody was any good at it. At some point, I hit Lexie next to her eyebrow with a baseball bat, and she still has a scar to prove it.

Kenneth: I went to school when it was above the Temple grade for a few months in kindergarten with Paul Polk as the teacher and for the first grade with Laura Lee Beeler. I must have been the "teacher's pet" because she gave me lots of extra time and called me "Cookie." I have vague but wonderful memories of the first grade. I remember learning to read the "Dick, Jane, Sally, and Spot (the dog)" beginning reader. I can almost recall being pleased when it all "clicked," and I really could "read" rather than recognize a few words.

Kenneth: My memories of the school after being moved just down the road from our house are much more vivid but still not what I would expect them to be. I can picture the places more than the activities. One thing I don't remember is reciting the Pledge of Allegiance (which, I am told we did every morning), even though I remember learning at some point the "under God" needed to be added. I don't remember Jean or Shirley helping me with my work, although that probably happened as well. I do remember Grace calling me, "Kenneth, come to class," over to the corner to sit at the long ledge. I know I would bring the correct book (arithmetic or social studies or whatever) and whatever written work I had been assigned, although I don't have clear memories of those either. As an adult, Mom told me that I would come home from school and tell her things I had learned, such as parts of the body, science facts, and so on, even though I have no memory of that either.

Kenneth: I do remember doing art work, which involved coloring with my box of crayons, finger painting, cutting and pasting (especially with rubber cement), and drawing. I remember learning on my own to draw the profile of a horse that was pretty good.

Kenneth: I liked learning and practicing a variety of climbing, swinging, hanging, and little gymnastic moves on the swing set outside.

Kenneth: At recess and noon hour (after coming back from lunch at home), I mostly remember playing in the willows below the school next to a slough. We knew the willows like the backs of our hands, and this is where we played horse, cowboys and Indians, and various other games. We knew which bunches made the straightest stick horses, of which we all made many, including carved brands for each. We knew which ones had lots of little straight shoots that were perfect for weaving panels for our houses or corrals. We even identified some bunches that were more or less willow-free in the middle where we could hide from the other kids or turn into private dwellings. Of course, I always had a pocket knife to cut them. In the later grades, I learned how to pick out a stout willow to make a bow and then to carve smaller willow shoots for arrows. The arrows would have an intact one- to two-inch tip next to its sharpened point while the rest of it would be whittled down to about half of its original diameter so that when released from the bow, the heavier front would keep it going in the right direction.

Rita: Being a student at our one-room country schoolhouse holds lots of wonderful memories. I started first grade at the Willow Creek School that had been moved from above the Temple grade one summer before I started school.

Teacher Grace and her students, all her own children, nieces, and nephews: Rita, Lillyan, Jean, Kenneth, Lexie, David, Shirley, and Beverly.

The St. Louis kids, some serious and some silly. Back: Jean, David, and Shirley; front: Kenneth, Rita, Lillyan, Lexie, and Beverly.

Rita: My memory sees a typical school day in which we would get up, eat breakfast, do our morning chores, then strap on our toy pistols, put on our outdoor gear, and walk to school. School was close to our house, so we usually went home for lunch. Jean, Shirley, Beverly, and Grace would drive to school, and I think Lillyan and Lexie walked approximately three-eighths of a mile to school.

Rita: We had a pretty standard, strict school day. At exactly 8:00 or 8:30, Grace would call school to order. That meant that coats were hung up, boots and mittens were put away, our fannies were in our seats, and it was time to learn. We all had tasks and assignments that we were to do. At distinct intervals, Grace, sitting at the end of a long shelf, would say, "Third grade come to class," or "Eighth grade come to class." Each grade, except Beverly's and mine, had only one student. Students would sit next to Grace, and she would go over their lessons and make new assignments. Meantime everybody else better be studying at his or her desk! She did not put up with any horseplay or nonsense during school hours. During each day, Grace would read aloud to all of us. I remember not liking most of those books because I was pretty young, and the books appealed more to the older kids.

Rita: Each year saw a different dynamic. Jean, then the next year, Shirley, graduated and went to high school in Salt Lake City. When David was in eighth grade, he left for a while to go to Shriner's Hospital in Salt Lake City to have his arm amputated. Kenneth went to California for a while to live with a family where he could get speech therapy in school. In fourth grade a really nice young teacher, Joan, who was somehow related to Marie Salisbury, taught us until about Thanksgiving when we moved to La Sal to go to school. (La Sal was so different from Willow Creek; my memories are in Chapter 12.)

Rita: When I was in fifth grade and Elizabeth (Betty) taught, the time frame was not so strict. We also took more time to do art work, listen to music, and learn a few words in Spanish. However, with both Elizabeth and Grace, we did follow the county's curriculum, and we always finished in seven and a half to eight months instead of the standard nine months. Learning was something that came easily to all of us, so I do not remember anyone's struggling. Learning just happened. In fact, the first time I realized that kids had trouble learning was when a little boy named Jackie came to school for a short time. His parents worked at Three Forks Ranch. I remember Jackie was in first or second grade. He had badly decayed teeth, and I think we were not very kind to him. He really struggled with his lessons, and I remember that Grace had to spend a lot of extra time with him.

Rita: I suppose my fondest memories involved recess. We would go outside and play. Grace would call us in when the exact number of minutes were up. If the weather was nice, Elizabeth would let us stay out and play longer, sometimes up to an hour longer. There was a swing set on which we played occasionally, and there were a few balls, but none of us really took up the standard team sports. Instead, the patch of willows right next to the school was the perfect place to play cowboys, Indians, horses, ranchers, bandits...you name it. We would make stick horses by cutting a willow to the right length, tie a twine string (bridle) at the top, straddle the stick, and run around pretending we were riding horses. A "pinto" was made by stripping only spots of the willow bark away; a "baldy" was made by stripping a few inches of bark only from the top of the stick. We would make elaborate corrals, houses, and forts by cutting some willow branches and weaving them among the standing ones. Occasionally, we would get really fancy and bring some bailing twine from home and weave that among the willows. (Our dads would get really disgusted with us because when they were trying to round up cattle among those willows, they would always be encountering our structures!) Besides the willows, we would climb the hill across the road from our school and play on the sandstone rocks. Those were perfect Indian dwellings, and many an imagined tribe took up residence there. We would use crayons and make petroglyphs (until the woodchucks found our crayons and ate them). That was also a good place to hide if we had robbed a stage or been caught in a winter storm. One winter Daddy left a big berm of snow on the road, and we dug tunnels into the berm and played Eskimos for several weeks.

Rita: We were really quite insular. I do remember Hungary's revolution and it being totally crushed. Elizabeth was teaching, and I for the first time realized that there were really dangerous places in the world. We all grew up.

Rita: All of our parents had different imperatives. Older kids needed to attend high school, so slowly, Willow Creek School dissolved. I'm sure we took sides, had fights, and the like, but my memory mainly distills down to the beautiful freedom we all had, the fresh air we breathed, and the security that we all experienced and took totally for granted.

Chapter 11

4-H

At the age of ten, we were eligible to join the Savery Savers 4-H club. Although we lived in Colorado, Savery, Wyoming, was much closer than clubs in Craig or Steamboat. Aside from the once-yearly joint Willow Creek and Battle Creek School Christmas program and an occasional dance that we were allowed to attend at either the Dixon Hall or the Pep Hall, 4-H was our only youth-centered, local, organized social outlet. It was a very big deal to us.

Each year, we would choose and somehow sign up for one or more semi-supervised projects that would require planning carefully, displaying the outcome at the county fair, and submitting our paper records for the entire project(s). With only three exceptions—one involving sewing and cooking for Rita and another featuring electricity for me—all of our 4-H projects involved animals. David turned ten first, and his initial project was chickens, where he bought hybrid white layers that eventually became a mainstay at the ranch. After that, we all showed Suffolk sheep including fat lambs, ewes and lambs, ram lambs, or a full-grown ram. Suffolks are a meat breed of sheep, ideally with no wool on their pure black heads and lower legs. Of course, we sheared their wool, but it was not high quality like that of Rambouillets or Columbias. Pure-bred Suffolks, to me, were the most elegant breed, especially compared to the shorter and stockier Hampshires, with which they were often crossed. For each project, we were required to turn in a record book at the end of the season explaining the entire project, its expenses and receipts, and what we learned.

At the end of the chapter are excerpts from my 4-H record books in my first year (1955) and then five years later (1960).

We selected the 4-H project animals early in the summer and worked every day to tame them, break them to lead easily, and to be maneuvered easily without a halter with one hand under the mouth and the other over

Rita with the skirt she made for 4-H.

the tail. They had to be trained to stand still, after each leg was placed squarely under each quarter, and even to stand still while a knee was placed in their brisket while holding the wool on each side of the neck. This was to "buck them up" so that when a judge felt their back for conformation, they would appear solid and wide across the back.

Their wool was carded frequently to pull out the ends of the wool into a fine mesh. This would essentially pull the wool together to eliminate any natural separations in the fleece. The ends of these pulled strands were then trimmed with shears to "block" the animal. Each sheep was "blocked" several times in the summer to gradually make it appear as rectangular and wide as possible.

After our second year of 4-H, we bought four bred old ewes from the Millers who lived between Baggs and Craig. We ended up with 11 lambs, four sets of twins and one set of triplets. We bottle fed one set of twins and one of the triplets, a ewe lamb we named "Jenny." After maturation, she gave birth to many of our best lambs in the growing flock over the years. Motivated by the expanding 4-H projects and our getting older and more independent, our parents decided to open a savings account for each of us to keep the money we earned from the sheep.

Subsequently, for more 4-H projects and our own "businesses," we decided to expand the purebred flock with 50 more bred old ewes from Warren Cogdill, who lived up Slater Creek. The ewes were really old, but as long as they had their teeth and reasonably good udders, we bought them. From these we raised Suffolk lambs. The rams we sold, for at least a few years, at the annual Ram Sale west of Craig. We kept the ewe lambs to build our herd and to replace the original old ewes that we sold within a year or two. Also, we would improve the future offspring by buying a good ram at that sale.

We kept these sheep separate from our family's "band" of sheep that summered variously at the Fleming Place and BLM land on Beaver and

Suffolk ewes in the winter.

Piney Mountains, or the Forest, and wintered on the desert near Wamsutter. We fed them alfalfa hay in the winter. Those we chose for 4-H projects also got carefully planned rations of molasses rolled oats, wheat bran, and other supplements. We kept the 4-H animals at the ranch along with 12–20 bum lambs that we raised on excess cow's milk.

In her last year, Rita decided to have a fat steer project. Dad purchased a well-proportioned but temperamental black angus calf, who must have

skipped several hundred genetic years of domestication. He never really settled down to an easily manageable state.

Returning to the social aspects of 4-H, we met one evening a month at the Savery Schoolhouse basement, an event we all eagerly waited for. The meetings began with the 4-H pledge: "I pledge my head to clearer thinking, my heart

New lambs in the early spring.

to greater loyalty, my hands to larger service, and my health to better living, for my club, my community, and my country."

We had 4-H barn dances from time to time in Harry Russell's barn, an annual awards banquet, and various other events. But two really big social events occurred each summer.

The first was the four-day 4-H camp. Harry Russell would put hay in the back of his 20 to 24-foot flatbed truck with the double high stock rack.

Starting in Baggs, he would come up the Little Snake River and pick up all "us 4-Hers." Our family was typically the last to board. Harry and Sinc as chaperones would open the rear gate, let campers climb in along with their sleeping bags and suitcases, and then lock the gate from the outside. We truly loved the ride "over the hill" past Columbine and Hahns Peak into Steamboat. Then, over the old Rabbit Ears Pass road to Walden, and then into Wyoming and shortly to the camp located at a place called Mountain Home in the alpine mountains southwest of Laramie.

The four days seemed like two weeks. We had sports (volleyball), target competition and rifle safety, nature studies, crafts, and baseball. As new 4-H members, this was our first acquaintance with group living, organized activities, skits, and a big dance. After adolescence, it morphed into boy-meets-girl activities wherein we sneaked out of our cabins at night to meet each other and "neck." The county agent and chaperones would be out until very late trying to find us and get us back into our sleeping bags. Some of our first kisses or "loves" occurred at 4-H camp.

The way home was often less noisy but exciting nonetheless. Often, we stopped in Steamboat and all swam in the wonderful pool there. No doubt, we left a lot of dirt behind in that pool.

The second and most exciting event of the year was the County Fair in Rawlins, Wyoming. Each family would load up the 4-H animals raised, trained, and groomed by the young 4-Hers and haul them to Rawlins. The assigned pens or stalls in the sheep and cattle barns were our places to set up our often decorated "show boxes" —large solid lockable chests that held our halters, wool cards, shears, brushes, combs, hoof trimmer, blankets, and anything else needed to show our projects. We also brought hay, buckets for water, and grain. According to the prescribed schedule, we showed our sheep (or rooster or steer), in classes of similar animals of other 4-H kids around the county to determine how each animal would place: first (blue or purple ribbon), second (red ribbon), third (white ribbon), fourth (yellow ribbon), fifth (pink ribbon), or sixth (green ribbon), or not placed (no ribbon). Champion ribbons had rosettes at the top and one, two, or three streamers.

Cattle were washed before show, brushed until their hair raised in all the right places and gleamed in the sun. Sheep were "blocked" again with any necessary touch ups. Additionally, they were often kept covered with burlap bags cut and tied to keep their backs and sides free from manure or dirt. All the straw and manure "tags" had to be carefully trimmed off their bellies before show with sharp shears.

In later years, we also showed our best-trained animal in a showmanship class, not to judge the animal but our own skills in showing the animal.

For market lambs or steers, the Fair always culminated in an auction where they were sold, often for very high prices. Selling the animals for a nice profit was always a positive experience for me, but Rita was often very sad parting with her sheep. She learned from Lexie to turn that sadness into crying and tears at the sale. Buyers would feel sorry for those sad little girls and pay even more for their animals.

From a social standpoint, County Fair was also a wonderful experience. We always stayed at the Ferris Hotel, which for us was one of the only times we were able to ride in an elevator. While at the hotel, our parents did not usually accompany us as we walked to the fair grounds. It was also a time to see other 4-H club members in all the other settings one could imagine in the "big city." The Fair was also a major social outlet for our dad and uncles, where considerable carousing and drinking occurred. We all enjoyed the parade and annual rodeo as well.

Beginning at about the age of 15, we also participated in another major summer event in 4-H, that is, livestock judging. It worked each year like this. Early in the summer, anyone interested from any of the clubs in Carbon County would come together for a judging competition. From that event, those individual 4-Hers with the highest scores were selected for the judging team that was to go to the County Fair. Arranged by Dick Hiser, our county extension agent, that team traveled both within and out of the county three or four times for more practice judging. The team went to ranches that had good breeding stock or show-quality cattle, sheep, and occasionally dairy cows or hogs. A running

Kenneth with a young ewe ready for the Fair.

David teaching his ram to show.

Kenneth blocking a lamb.

One of several grazing ewes kept clean for showing with a burlap bag blanket.

Various County Fair ribbons earned for 4-H sheep.

Ribbons earned at the County and State Fairs for Jinx, Kenneth's Suffolk ram.

Kenneth's livestock judging ribbon.

tally over the summer trips was kept such that, by Fair time, we knew how we had stacked up compared to the others on the team. The top three places for each club that entered the competition in the summer trips constituted that club's team at the County Fair. Thus, at the Fair, a club competition ensued, with individual and team awards at stake. The best team was chosen to compete with other counties at the State Fair.

David and I made the county team for two or three years; Rita did not. The actual judging proceeded as follows: Similar animals would be lined up and we had to rate them from best to worst and then explain our ratings. Each "class" consisted of four animals each, such as Angus bulls judged for beef, Rambouillet ewes judged for wool, Hampshire rams judged for meat, or Holstein cows judged for milk. We would have 15 minutes to "place" the class of four, numbered left to right, one through four, from best to worst, for instance, 2, 4, 3, 1. Thereafter, we had to prepare "reasons" for why we placed the class as we did. Typically, we would judge several classes in the morning and, after lunch, be obliged to individually give our "reasons" or rationale for why we placed the class as we did. These "reasons" were formal speeches, usually lasting about five minutes, and had to follow a prescribed format. For each animal, they began with, "I placed number two first, and over number 4 because..." "Correct" placing matched the placing of an "expert" judge. In our case, the expert was Dick Hiser.

MEMORIES

. David: My first 4-H project was chickens. I chose white hybrid layers and ordered about 50 one- or two-day-old chicks from a catalog. They were delivered by mail.

4-H judging team Laurie Hayes, Linda Sheehan,[unknown], [unknown], Gordon Hayes, Kenneth, and David. The county agent is squatting.

Judging a class of Hereford calves—Among the 4-Hers are Beverly (sleeveless blouse), Kenneth, David, and Frank Sheehan (shielding his eyes).

After they were grown, Mom killed and butchered the roosters, except for the one I took to the Fair. The pullets turned out to be our best layers. Since I was the first person in 4-H, we did not know we had to do anything to get ready for Fair. Mom found out that we did, so I remember cleaning up the rooster the night before we left for the fair with Jean and Shirley.

Kenneth preparing to give reasons for judging livestock.

County 4-Hers at a judging: Gordon Hayes, Frank Sheehan, Alan Peryam, and Beverly St. Louis.

David: Beginning with our 4-H projects, we went into the Suffolk business. Our sheep weren't registered, but we sold ram lambs to sheep companies at the yearly Ram Sale in Craig to put into their flocks the next year. For the first two years, we got really good prices, but after that, the prices fell. One year, Kenneth and I went to Ram Sale to buy one or two rams for ourselves. Dad was not with us for some reason. We began bidding, and the auctioneer stopped and asked us, "Can you pay for it?" Of course, I said "Yes!" We bought a ram, and one of the sheep men was upset at being outbid by two kids.

David: Four things stand out for me thinking about 4-H Camp. It was really cold riding in the back of Harry Russell's truck to 4-H camp. I really liked the rifle target practice; I could hit the targets and earned the NRA badges. We also learned to make cattle and sheep halters out of twisted rope by untwisting the rope at the right places to make loops through which we would then thread the lead end. I had my first date to a dance there with Kathleen Sheehan.

David: For the summer practice judging trips, we would all ride in one vehicle, usually a van that could accommodate the driver and up to eight of us. One year, the group included Jean and Shirley, Linda and Kathleen Sheehan, and Kenneth and me.

David: I remember going to Afton, Wyoming, in the Star Valley on one of the judging trips. I always wanted to go back there and finally, in 2019, did so after a trip to Yellowstone National Park.

David: Having been on the judging team and learning to give reasons helped me become a pretty good public speaker. Later, at Colorado State University, I was asked to be on the University judging team after an introductory beef cattle science course that involved judging cattle. I usually placed the classes perfectly, and I gave an excellent set of reasons. The other students had never heard a good set of reasons before, so the professor asked me to stand up in front of all of them and show them

Kenneth blocking Jinx.

Jinx's wool being kept clean with a burlap bag (gunny sack) blanket.

Kenneth winning grand champion Suffolk ram at the Carbon County Fair. Linda Sheehan's ram was the reserve champion.

Kenneth at left "bucking up" his lamb as the expert judge evaluated the class at the County Fair.

how to give reasons. Apparently, I gave a good demonstration, but I declined to join the judging team.

Kenneth: I remember not knowing how to block a sheep in the first year of 4-H. Dad was no help either because, so far as he was concerned, a sheep should just be sheared in the spring. I got better and better at it, especially after I learned that you could not card a sheep enough. Blocking was much easier after repeated carding, a process of hooking the hundreds of curved wires of the card to the wool and then rolling the card away and pulling out the strands. People had different ways of blocking in those days, and we were in the era of making them look as square as possible for the meat breeds. But some 4-H members simply made their sheep's wool follow their body conformation, as in the wool breeds. The ram I showed my last year, "Jinx," was huge. We actually

CHAMPION SUFFOLK RAM—The champion Suffolk ram at the 1954 Carbon county fair is shown by Kenneth St. Louis of Slater, the proud owner. It was one of 34 animals sold Friday afternoon in the 4-H and FFA sale. (Photo by Meyers)

A newspaper clipping featuring the grand champion ram at the County Fair.

sheared him into a block at shearing time, so he was the most "blocked" sheep in either the County Fair, where he was Grand Champion ram, or the State Fair in Douglas, where he was Reserve Champion. Not long after we quit 4-H and went to Steamboat, they stopped "blocking" Suffolks and, instead, sheared them close and carded the wool up to a uniform soft covering over their actual body conformation.

Kenneth: Jinx was mean if he had a chance. He butted me hard several times when my back was turned. I ended up not showing him at the State Fair because, just before my class, I was hurriedly trimming tags from his belly. In a rush to put the "keeper" (a strip of leather about two inches long with about an inch slit in it to slide over the shears to keep them closed) on the shears, I ran my right index and middle finger over the keeper and down the over-extended cutting edges closest to the handles. I sliced both fingers deeply and had to go to the emergency room for stitches while Linda Sheehan showed my ram. I still have the scars on both fingers.

Kenneth: At 4-H Camp, I also liked the rifle training, but I was not as good a shot as David. Still, I was proud of my bronze NRA marksmanship medals. One of the last years I went to camp, another camper and I sneaked out to meet up with girls. Dick Hiser was about to catch us, so as we ran down the hill in the dark toward the cabin, I hit a telephone pole guy wire at my neck and "clothes lined" myself in the process. That was the end of my sneaking out that year.

Kenneth: We did not have parents who bought expensive animals for our 4-H projects like some we knew about. Neither did Dad take care of the animals for us in the summer, like other fathers did, except when we needed to be gone for judging trips. I guess I was always a little upset about the fact that the playing field in the animal competition was not really level.

Kenneth: Because I stuttered, especially when I could not rearrange my words, I had a hard time with giving reasons on judging trips. I ended up coming in second or third once or twice and was always a bit surprised that I did. I remember that I could score best in dairy cows but placing them for beef and then just reversing the ratings. I never could figure out how to judge pigs.

Kenneth: I really enjoyed the practice judging trips in the summer. The weather was usually warm and dry, so more than once, we would stay at a community building, church, or something. The boys would sleep outside under the stars in our sleeping bags; the girls would sleep inside.

Rita: At 4-H camp I remember in rifle practice I did so poorly that my bullet did not even hit the paper target. I found out many years later that I was (and am) left-eye dominant. I was shooting right-handed but looking down the sights with my left eye.

Rita: I did not make the judging team because all of the animals looked pretty much alike for me, so I usually placed them in a totally wrong order. Furthermore, my reasons really did not make sense to me, let alone to anyone listening to my reasons.

Rita: The one who gave the strangest reasons was Joyce. Dick Hiser really liked to hear her reasons, such as "I placed number 2 at the top because she was the nicest heifer..." Dick loved it and acted serious as he listened but had a hard time not laughing.

Rita: At the County Fair, we enjoyed the carnival where rides cost 25 cents each. What some of us enjoyed even more was to find people who were drinking really heavily and say, "I'll buy you a ride." We would put them onto one of the really twirling rides, and they would get sick and spew vomit all over—if in an enclosed space, all over the little car and themselves, if not in an enclosed space, centrifugal force would spew it even farther.

Rita: Every year at the Fair, they gave a "Herdman's Award" to the 4-H club that kept the cleanest area. Several in our club, the Savery Savers, were determined to win that award one year. We kept our areas totally neat; as soon as an animal got up, we would smooth the straw around it; anytime an animal pooped, someone was on patrol to clean it up. A few of us bossy ones assigned club members to be on patrol during intervals in the day. Someone was on patrol all day long from early morning to late at night. A bunch of us were washing our cattle in a little room at the side of the large pavilion. As often happened, we got into a water fight. Jack Lorrigan, whom everybody knew as "Packsaddle," was helping us and joined into the fight. He had a full five-gallon bucket of water and threw it from the inside at someone near the door but missed. Instead, Mildred Hayes just happened to be walking by, and he drenched her. She turned us in, and, suffice to say, we did not get the Herdsman's Award that year.

Rita: My animals never did place very high at the fair, but I did win showmanship award one year with my fat lamb.

Rita: At my last year of 4-H, I wanted to show a fat steer. From some ranchers on Elk River who had really good stock, Daddy and I bought what could have been a prize-winning black angus in terms of his conformation. And he fattened out perfectly to the desired weight of about 800 pounds. The problem was—he was virtually untrainable! He tried to fight Daddy when he was just a small yearling. He never led well, he was always really jumpy, and he would not stand still when I tried to teach him to show.

Rita training her steer to show one week after he trampled her.

Since I fed him only grain rations and a little hay, the steer could not be turned into the pasture to graze with the other cattle. On hot summer days, I kept him in a little pen that Daddy built near the house so that he could be in the shade. I was always rather afraid of him. One evening when everyone else was inside the house, I was leading him from the pen to the barn. He balked at the entrance to the barn. So, to really lean into the rope and pull him, I wrapped the rope around my waist and really gave him a jerk. He pulled back, threw me off balance, and I fell. That startled him, so he began running. The problem was that the rope was in a sort of a half-hitch around my waist, so instead of coming loose, it just tightened down. As he ran, the rope was just the length that I was being dragged directly under him and stomped all to heck. I remember calling "help"; I remember coming to after passing out. I remember Daddy and Kenneth's turning up and wrestling him to a stop and getting me untethered. I only had some broken or pulled ribs, but my whole body was bruised. I remember a perfect hoof-mark across one eye.

What happened in the house was that Daddy and Kenneth heard me yell, and both came running to the rescue. When they crossed the slough to the barn, the steer was backing up next to the brooder house with me in front of him and was about to drag me over a spike-tooth harrow between us. Dad went to grab the steer. Kenneth took out his pocket knife and cut the halter rope; yet, later, he said that he had no specific memory of deciding to do that. Kenneth was not hurt at all, but Daddy was barefoot. Running to grab the steer, he stepped on a tooth of the harrow, which hurt his foot really badly. He limped for a couple of weeks.

We had to tranquilize the steer to take him to the County Fair and to show him. Even so, during his class, the tranquilizer apparently wore off enough for him to pull loose and run away. That was one animal for which I did not cry when he was sold.

THE STORY

Your achievement story is the final and most important part of your record book. You need not review the questions already answered in the preceding section. The story may include such points of interest as to why you became or continued to be a member this year, experiences in starting your club, its organization and plans, a description of the management of your project, the improvements you have made, important practices you have learned, how the project and club activities have helped you, your club and your community. **The main part of your story should deal with your project.** Perhaps you would like to acknowledge the help that has been given you by different persons and how you feel about such aid. You need not fill all of the next pages, but only as much as you care to write.

Club members carrying more than one livestock project can write separate stories as a combined story covering all project work. In this case you should designate in each project record book in which book the story will be found.

MY EXPERIENCES IN MY 4-H CLUB PROJECT

4-H Project Summary and story for a Suffolk ewe lamb project in 1955.

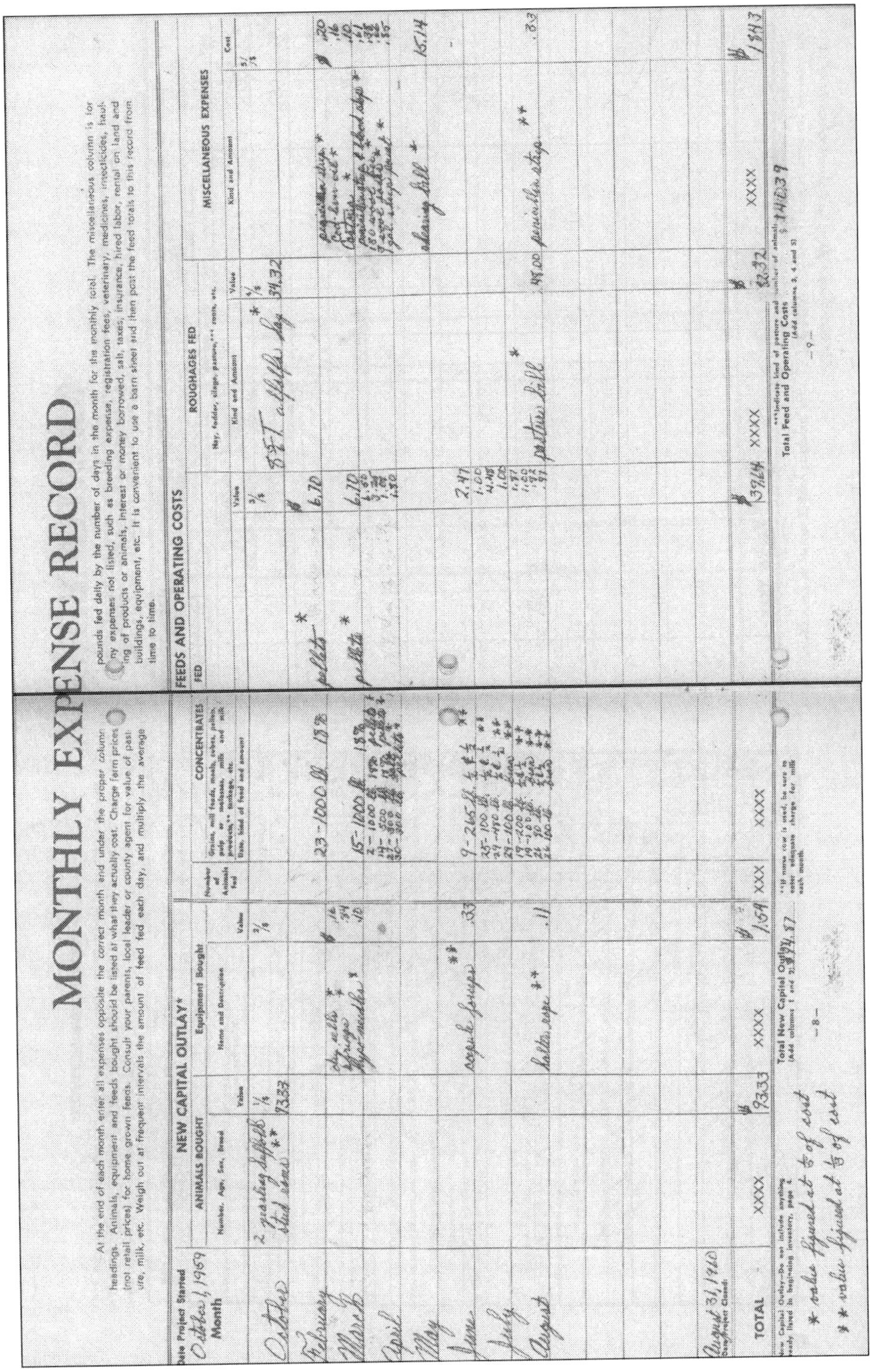

MONTHLY EXPENSE RECORD

At the end of each month enter all expenses opposite the correct month and under the proper column headings. Animals, equipment and feeds bought should be listed at what they actually cost. Charge farm prices (not retail prices) for home grown feeds. Consult your parents, local leader or county agent for value of pasture, milk, etc. Weigh out at frequent intervals the amount of feed fed each day, and multiply the average pounds fed daily by the number of days in the month for the monthly total. The miscellaneous column is for any expenses not listed, such as breeding expense, registration fees, veterinary, medicines, insecticides, hauling of products or animals, interest or money borrowed, salt, taxes, insurance, hired labor, rental on land and buildings, equipment, etc. It is convenient to use a barn sheet and then post the feed totals to this record from time to time.

Date Project Started: October 1, 1959 — Month	Animals Bought: Number, Age, Sex, Breed	Value	Equipment Bought: Name and Description	Value	Number of Animals Fed	Concentrates	Value	Roughages Fed: Kind and Amount	Value	Miscellaneous Expenses: Kind and Amount	Cost
October	2 yearling Suffolk stud rams **	93.33						8 & T alfalfa hay *	34.32		
February						23-1000 lb. 18% pellets *	6.70				
March			dry salts *, syringe *, hypo needles *	.16, .34, .10		15-1000 lb. 18% pellets *	6.70			penicillin strep. *, cod liver oil *, castrating *, penicillin strep. & blood strep *, 180 wool bags *, 9 wool sacks *, 1 gal. sheep paint *	.20, .16, .10, .61, .98, .66, .50
April						2-1000 lb. 18% pellets; 14-500 lb. 18% pellets; 27-300 lb. oats; 30-300 lb. pellets *	[illegible]				
May										shearing bill *	15.14
June			staple forceps **	.33		9-265 lb. **	2.47				
July						[illegible]	1.00, 4.45, 1.00, 1.97, 1.00				
August			halter rope **	.11		[illegible]	.97	pasture bill *	48.00	penicillin strep. **	.33
August 31, 1960 — Date Project Closed											
TOTAL	XXXX	93.33	XXXX	1.54	XXX	XXXX	39.64	XXXX	82.32	XXXX	18.43

New Capital Outlay—Do not include anything already listed in beginning inventory, page 4.

Total New Capital Outlay (Add columns 1 and 2) $94.87

**If nurse cow is used, be sure to enter adequate charge for milk each month.

***Indicate kind of pasture and number of animals.

Total Feed and Operating Costs (Add columns 3, 4 and 5) $140.39

* value figured at ⅓ of cost

** value figured at ⅓ of cost

—8— —9—

4-H Monthly Expense Record, story, and completion certificate for small farm flock and ewe and lamb Suffolk sheep projects in 1960.

4-H completion certificate for a ewe and lamb project.

Chapter 12

Interludes

Aside from needing to move to attend high school, four short-term moves for some or all of us occurred in the family. The first was a three-month stint where David went to the Shriners Hospital for Crippled Children in Salt Lake City. The second was the family's spending most of a school year in La Sal, Utah. The third and fourth involved my living away for three months to get help for my stuttering in Maricopa, California, and several years later, for six weeks in Laramie, Wyoming.

DAVID: FINAL SOLUTION FOR HIS ARM AT SHRINERS HOSPITAL IN SALT LAKE CITY

Mentioned in several previous accounts, David's accident happened when he was eight years old on Christmas Day 1951. He was lying down on the new sled we had just received for Christmas and being pulled on our snow-covered road by a long rope tied to a neighbor's Jeep pickup. Two others on skis were being pulled (ski-joring) behind the same vehicle. I was sitting in the back of the pickup. As the Jeep went around a curve between Oliver's and Perry's places, David went under a passing pickup and was hit on the back of the head and shoulder. He was immediately taken to Denver by Mom and Dad while Agnes, Sharon, and Joyce stayed with Rita and me. The accident rendered his left arm completely paralyzed. Dad returned after several days, but Mom stayed with David. After about a month in a hospital in Denver, Mom brought David home. Damage had been done to the nerves in the brachial plexus, injuring both motor and sensory nerves. Quite soon, his left arm began to go into contractures such that his fingers were mostly flexed, and his arm was somewhat bent at the elbow. For the next several years, Mom had to extend and flex his fingers and arm every night for about 15 minutes. Since David could not feel anything below the middle of his upper arm, he had to be careful not to injure the arm or hand. In the winter,

View of the Shriners Hospital for Crippled Children in Salt Lake City in the 1950s.

he wore a sock or sleeve over the arm and hand to protect it from frostbite. In those first few years, he acquired some ability to flex his arm (using the biceps) but could never push down or back (using the triceps). Also, some feeling of touch returned and progressed down his arm to about the elbow.

About two years after the accident, Mom took David by train to the Mayo Clinic in Rochester, Minnesota, for the best expert opinion in the country. The specialists there recommended that he should wait to see how much feeling and muscle control he might acquire over time. And both before and after the Mayo Clinic evaluation, David variously was evaluated and treated by chiropractors and osteopathic physicians. Finally, when he was 13, our parents took him to the Shriners Hospital for Crippled Children in Salt Lake City to decide the next step. About five months of his eighth grade was spent there in the hospital, which also included attending school in one room of the hospital. It is important to note that all care at the Shriners Hospital was provided at no cost to our parents.

The reason for the long duration of the stay was three-fold. First, the doctors were uncertain whether they should amputate part of the arm or recommend continued waiting for spontaneous improvement. Repeated testing for sensation and movement was carried out over the course of at least two months. Second, the eventual decision to amputate was slowed as they decided exactly where to amputate the arm. The third factor in the long hospitalization was the recovery time after the amputation. The arm was amputated about three inches below the elbow so that the remaining stump could be fitted into a movable prosthesis with a dividable hook at the end. After the swelling subsided and healing of the stump took place, David was taken to a Salt Lake City business where prostheses were made and fitted. His biceps muscle could flex the elbow joint of the prosthesis. A harness across his back and over his right shoulder, when tightened with shoulder muscles, would separate the top and bottom halves of the hook for grasping. Following the fitting of the prosthesis, more weeks were spent in physical and occupational therapy, learning to use it to do such things as tie his shoes.

MEMORIES

David: That first year after the accident, I remember that I was going to keep doing everything that I could do before. We were still little, but I remember that I could lift the crowbar over my head with my right arm and Kenneth couldn't.

David: I really hated all those chiropractor and osteopath treatments I had to go to. They hurt, and I never thought they did any good. Later, I concluded they were "quacks."

David: The Shriners ward I was on had kids with lots of different problems, but mostly club feet or polio. The boys slept in a big room at one end of a very long hall, and the girls slept in a similar room at the other end. Our beds were on both sides of an aisle, with the heads of the beds up against a ledge on either side. We had wheelchair races down the aisle. I couldn't go really fast with only one hand on the wheel, but I could do pretty well by pushing the right wheel and holding my foot against it to keep it going straight.

David: One boy at the hospital with polio had no use of either of his legs, but he had a very strong upper body and arms. He was amazing, winning all the wheelchair races. He could actually "run" on his crutches without his feet even touching the floor. He could also "walk" on his crutches while doing hand stands with his feet up in the air.

David: Several times, I had to stand in the middle of a group of doctors. One of them would take a pin and repeatedly prick up my arm to see where I could feel it. They would ask, "Does that hurt?" When they hit a place that I could feel the pain, I'd let them know loud and clear, "Yes, it hurts!"

David: I was just getting to the age when girls started to interest me. We watched the Mickey Mouse Club on TV, and I really liked Annette Funicello. I also remember that I thought the nurses in the hospital were sure pretty!

David: After Mom brought me to Shriners and stayed a few days, I was there alone. I don't remember for sure, but I believe Mom and Dad came a few times to visit before they came to take me home. I do know Mom was there for the amputation, and Jean came to visit me right after the surgery. The only time I left the hospital was the time they took me to be fitted for the prosthesis. A man there had two hooks, and he did beautiful paintings.

A box David wood-burned brands for Grandpa, Dad, and himself at Shriners Hospital.

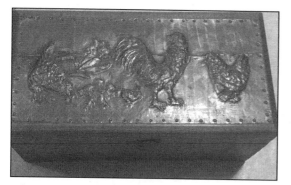

The pounded copper top David made for the box.

Inside the felt-lined box are David's 4-H and high school pins.

David: After they amputated my arm, I remember that Mom had bought some toys for me to play with in my bed. I also remember that someone dressed up as Tarzan, along with his chimpanzee, came to visit all the kids there one day. I got his autograph.

David: After I got the prosthesis, I went to occupational therapy and physical therapy where they were supposed to show me how to do all kinds of things with it. Heck, they didn't know any more about it than I did. They did teach me how to tie my shoes with it, but it was not the way a shoe should be tied. I figured out on my own how to do it much better. Much of the time, I was showing them how to do things.

David: I have a clear memory of decorating a wooden box in therapy. It was about a foot long, five inches deep, and four inches high. I wood-burned the sides with all the St. Louis brands and gave the box a "French finish," which was a mixture of linseed oil and shellac. The inside was lined with green felt. The top was a copper sheet, and before tacking it to the box, I made an image of a rooster in it by pounding it on a mold. They wanted me to hold the punch with the prosthesis and use a small hammer to make the indentations in the copper. I didn't do it the way they wanted, but I did make it nice. I have kept this box all my life and still have little keepsakes in it, mostly 4-H medals.

David: I did go back to the prosthetic business in Salt Lake a couple of times by bus alone from Steamboat to get adjustments or new prostheses. On one trip, I bought a cornet because I could play it with one hand. I took lessons in high school, but I didn't practice very much and, thus, never got very good at it. Benson took the cornet with him to college to play in the marching band, but he was mainly interested in Karol at the time, who was the drum major. I once asked him, "Do you still have my cornet?" Not knowing the history of the instrument, he replied, "It's mine." I said, "I bought it when I was a kid."

THE FAMILY: A YEAR IN A URANIUM MINING CAMP IN LA SAL, UTAH

Beginning in early November and lasting through the rest of the 1955–1956 school year, our family moved to the Homestake uranium mine camp a few miles from La Sal, Utah, so that Dad could work in the mine there. Gus, Doris, Darrell, Larry, and Clifford Ranch lived in a 36-foot mobile home there at the time, and Gus ran the hoist at the Homestake mine. Mom drove us three kids to the Ranch trailer, and we moved in with them for two weeks. Subsequently, Dad joined us and started to work in the mine. We soon moved into a dilapidated, fixer-upper house located at the feed mill in the little community of La Sal proper. Amazingly, Mom quickly made it reasonably livable. We lived there until Christmas but then moved back to the

Location of road down to the Homestake uranium mining camp.

The line of silver mobile homes (trailers) in the main part of the camp.

Dad and Mom in front of our trailer.

Mom, David, Kenneth, and Rita dressed up at the trailer.

Interludes / 263

Post Office at La Sal with Melinda and Mom in the 1980s.

The old schoolhouse at La Sal and a new addition.

Homestake camp into a company trailer that had just been vacated. It was at the top of a hill lined with at least ten identical, silver-colored trailers on either side of the road, all angled in the same herring-bone pattern.

From the Homestake camp, we rode the school bus, driven by Gus, to school at La Sal. There, Rita attended fourth grade, I, sixth grade, and David, seventh grade. First, second, third and eighth grades were in the school house. Our classes were in the Mormon "Church House" a few yards away. David and I were in a combined sixth- and seventh-grade class; our teacher was Mr. Bowles. Rita needed to walk through our class, past a temporary partition and some church chairs, to get to her class. The ten or so fourth graders used the early antique school desks in which one's fold-down seat was the front of the person's writing surface behind him or her. Next to Rita's class, up on a stage, was Larry's fifth-grade class. This was our first experience in a "big" school, and, somewhat surprisingly, we adjusted with little difficulty. All three of us were soon recognized for our academic abilities.

Dad worked in the mine until about May of 1956 but then returned to the ranch to begin spring work. The rest of us stayed there until school was out. Sinc had taken care of the milk cows and horses during Dad's absence.

MEMORIES

David: While we lived in the trailer at Homestake, we learned about "bad" kids. Once in a fight, one of their leaders hit me in the cheek with a BB gun. It made me so mad, BB gun or not, that I punched him in the face. He wasn't so much of a bully after that.

David: Several times, on the weekends in the spring, Darrell, Larry, Kenneth, and I (and sometimes Rita and Clifford) would pack wieners, bread, and ketchup and hike a couple of miles to some cliffs west of Homestake. We'd climb until we were tired and then go onto a ledge or into a little cave, build a fire, and then roast the wieners.

David: Darrell had an automatic Remington .22 rifle with plastic stock. He and I often took it away from the camp to shoot birds.

David: On the first day of school at La Sal, another kid, Sammy Johnson, made fun of my arm. I got into a fight with him and punched him in the face several times with my right fist. He backed down, and he never said another word to me about it.

Cliffs around the mining camp where we hiked.

David: Two memories come to mind from our combined sixth- and seventh-grade class with Mr. Bowles. Once, someone turned "horny toads" (horned toads) loose on the floor. Also, the seventh grade studied Utah history, which did not interest me because I tired of hearing about Brigham Young.

Kenneth: In addition to the hikes and wiener roasts in the cliffs, I often got involved in riding my bike down paths into gullies and over jumps we would make for them in the mining camp. Once we climbed the long hill coming into Homestake and coasted down the hill to the camp. I had never gone so fast on a bike. On the gravel road, if I had slipped, I'm sure I would have been hurt.

Kenneth: I was also involved in several instances of kite flying from a little knob close to our trailer. One time I remember, the wind took our kite farther than we had ever been able to accomplish. The wind died down, though, and the kite settled down about a quarter of a mile away. The terrain was rough and mostly filled with scrubby pine trees. We never did retrieve all the string and probably not the kite either.

Kenneth: La Sal was the first time we had been in anything larger than a one-room school. I remember we started every day with singing several songs from a book of folk songs.

Kenneth: I did well in school and remember making friends with one of the smartest and most popular kids in my sixth grade class, David White. His family either owned or was involved in running the only commercial operation in La Sal itself, a pellet feed mill, close to our first dilapidated house.

Kenneth: At Willow Creek School, we never learned to play sports. I remember joining a group of classmates in La Sal playing baseball. I did not know how to throw, catch, or bat, so I played way in the outfield. I did not have a mitt at that point, so I picked up a board to stop the ball if it came my way. As it would happen, someone hit a long high ball straight to me. I went to hit it with the stick, but the ball hit my index finger on the side of the board. I don't think I cried, but I can still remember the extreme pain that lasted for hours. And I remember the humiliation I felt. I lost my fingernail from the smashed finger, but more serious, I lost my desire to learn to play baseball.

Rita: I had a bicycle that David and Kenneth had lent to someone, and got it all covered in mud. I then rode the bike down that steep road that did a hard left at the bottom, and I had no hand brakes because the brakes were all full of mud. I crashed, of course, and I remember ruining my bike and driving the handle bar into my stomach and having a big knot there for a while.

Rita: We played on the rocks, and I remember Larry's standing at the bottom protesting because he was afraid to climb the places we went to. Clifford and I were not very understanding and called him hurtful names.

Rita: On these and other hikes, we would gather "Brigham tea" leaves and boil water and make tea. We told ourselves that it tasted good, but it was really quite bitter.

Rita: I remember going to Cortez with Daddy and Mom after they bought a two-toned 1956 Pontiac. It was sort of a mauve and white, I think. We had that car until 1963 when they bought a light green Chevrolet.

Rita: My birthday present was to go to Moab to the movies. It was about Tarzan, and I absolutely loved it. On a different occasion, we went to a different movie with the Ranches where everyone had to wear 3-D glasses. I remember Gus and Daddy "ducked" as arrows were shooting at them, and they cracked their heads together.

Rita: When we first went to stay at the Ranch trailer, they had some neighbors who had a little girl named Willa. Willa and I would play in their "yard"—actually just a space of about 15–20 feet from the next trailer. Her dad and uncle hung around, and I remember when they bent over, one could see substantial "plumber cracks." I was fascinated, because I had never seen a man's butt crack before. It grossed me out, but I could not resist taking another look.

Rita: Daddy worked really hard in that mine, and it was dangerous. He would work two weeks at day shift, then two weeks at night shift. He would come home every night absolutely filthy from hat to shoes. He hated working there, but I'm sure the money was welcome. I remember being awakened a time or two with Mom's calling for Daddy to wake up because he was having nightmares. One time, he was trying to drag her out of bed to get her out of the way of an ore cart.

Kenneth: A Missed Speech Therapy Experience in Maricopa, California

The third and fourth interludes were designed to do something about my stuttering. It happened that Dad had begun to guide deer hunters in the fall, and one of our first group of hunters came from areas near to Leonard, Doris, and Kathy's residence in Bakersfield, California. One such hunter, Gordon Holmes, who lived outside Maricopa, California, owned an oil rig service and repair company. He was president of the local school board and told Mom and Dad that, after a recent earthquake, they had built a brand new school. They had also hired a speech therapist. He offered to let me come and live with his family for a school year so that I could get help for my stuttering.

Plaque with Gordon Holmes's contribution to building the new school in Maricopa.

It was the next year, about October 1957, in the seventh grade, I rode out with Perry, Grace, and Beverly by car and train to Bakersfield. After a day with Leonard, I was driven to Maricopa and to the Holmes household. They had three boys, Fred, who was in the seventh grade and two older brothers, Bruce and Mike, who were in high school. I was welcomed into the family and participated in all their activities. The older brothers drove, but Fred and I rode the school bus each day to the school, a very long ride in and out of little roads going to various oil-related settlements, considering that the school was only about four miles away on the main road.

Maricopa School, 2011; built, 1956.

Location of the Holmes residence and oil well service company in 1957. The house was torn down by the time of the photo in 2011.

Location of the Holmes residence and oil well service company in 1957. The house was torn down by the time of the photo in 2011.

I fit in quickly in classes but did not play football, as Fred did. I excelled in school and made friends with some of the other "good" students. Unfortunately, it was only possible for me to get to see the speech therapist one time, and during that visit, I did not stutter at all, leaving her somewhat mystified. In fact, I don't remember stuttering at all during my entire stay with the Holmes family.

When the Christmas break arrived, the Holmes family took me to the train station in Bakersfield or Taft and bought a ticket for me to Rawlins, Wyoming. This two-day train ride involved changing trains in Fresno. Mom and Dad met me in Rawlins. My stuttering inexplicably returned on the 100-mile drive back to the ranch. I had not been homesick at all during the two and a half-month California stay, but I experienced some homesickness at the prospect of going back. Regrettably, I did not return.

MEMORIES

Kenneth: After a couple of days with the Holmes family, we got up in the morning and everything was covered with fog. I was fascinated; it was the first time I had ever seen fog.

Kenneth: The family had two lever action .22 rifles. I remember hunting rabbits or target practice with Fred in the tumble weeds and little gullies around the Holmes property.

Kenneth: The school was new, and I was taken by how big the campus was. It seemed that it would take a long time to get from one end to the other. I was especially impressed with the size of the gymnasium and football field. (Seeing it again after more than 60 years, it was not nearly as large as I remembered it.)

Kenneth: I immediately made a name for myself in the class (with Fred) for getting a 100% on a spelling test. I don't think that endeared him to me, nor me to him,

Fred Holmes and Kenneth standing in front of a memorial to the oil workers in Maricopa.

Bruce Holmes, Mike Holmes, Fred Holmes, Kenneth, and Rae Jean at lunch in Maricopa, 2011.

because he was not a strong student. (As I learned later, he had dyslexia and later set up a foundation to help children with dyslexia.)

Kenneth: I don't remember what I thought about my stuttering basically being nonexistent during my stay in Maricopa, and I don't recall the reason why I only saw the speech therapist once. In retrospect, it is surprising that Gordon Holmes did not intervene with her. In any case, in her interview with me, she asked me to talk about my stuttering. We both were surprised that I answered all the questions with complete fluency. She was baffled and told me that she did not see a problem. (At this time in my life, I wish I had a dollar for every time I've heard a similar story from a stutterer who did not receive therapy because they did not stutter during a first session with a speech-language pathologist.)

KENNETH: FIRST REAL SPEECH THERAPY AT THE UNIVERSITY OF WYOMING SPEECH CLINIC, LARAMIE, WYOMING

The fourth interlude occurred between my junior and senior years of high school. The stuttering had become more and more a burden, especially in making telephone calls, giving oral reports or speeches at school, and asking a girl for a date. I asked Mom to help me find some help. She called around and found out that I could be enrolled in speech therapy at the University of Wyoming's Speech Clinic in a six-week summer program. I decided to attend in the summer of 1961 and lived in Wyoming Hall, a college dormitory, for the duration of the program. It involved individual speech therapy, relaxation training, group therapy, and various other activities along with a host of other clients with the entire spectrum of speech and language disorders. I excelled in the program and learned to control my stuttering on the way to becoming almost completely fluent. It was during this time that I decided that I would become a speech therapist and solve the problem of stuttering.

Wyoming Hall at the University of Wyoming campus where Kenneth stayed during the six-week speech therapy program in the summer of 1961.

MEMORIES

Kenneth: I liked Wyoming Hall, the dormitory where I stayed. I especially liked the variety of food that they served in the cafeteria.

Kenneth: I pretty much stuck to myself in the evenings after the speech clinic activities during the day and on the weekends. Most of the other residents were not typical college students, but graduate students and adults who had come back to campus for continuing education. After a few weeks in the dorm, an older student approached me and asked if he could practice an intelligence test on me for a course he was taking. I told him, "Sure," if he would tell me my IQ. He gave me the *Stanford-Binet* and let me know that my IQ was somewhere around 130, pretty good I thought, but not as high as I would have wished. He was surprised because he thought my being so quiet suggested that I might not do so well.

Kenneth: I had not been an avid reader, but I thought that I should use the extra time I had on my hands to do more. I read *Gone with the Wind* and an entire book on psychology that I checked out from the library.

Kenneth: I believe I was the oldest of all the hodge-podge of clients in the intensive speech clinic that summer. I was arguably one of only two or three who could carry on a "normal" adult conversation with the graduate student clinicians or their supervisors. Accordingly, I made friends with several of the students, and was no doubt flattered to be surrounded by such a group of very attractive women. One of the male students invited me to his home more than once and, one weekend, drove me to the Cheyenne Frontier Days Rodeo 45 miles away.

Kenneth: It was in Laramie that, for the first time in my life, I felt I had some control over stuttering instead of waiting for it to happen. I became completely fluent and was exhilarated by it.

Chapter 13

Moving to Steamboat Springs for School

Willow Creek School only went through the eighth grade. Thus, just as our fathers and uncles experienced, when any of us reached the ninth grade, it was necessary to go somewhere else for high school. Jean, Shirley, and Beverly went to St. Mary's of the Wasatch Catholic School in Salt Lake City. Sharon began high school in Baggs and finished in Craig. Joyce completed all of her high school in Craig. Lillyan and Lexie started high school in Craig but finished in Steamboat. David, Rita, and I all went to Steamboat at once when David entered the ninth grade.

As children, we were more familiar with Craig because it was where we typically "went to town." Dad also had many connections in Craig. Our

Kenneth standing in front of Joe Ireland's cabin on the lake three miles southeast of Steamboat.

David, Kenneth, and Rita dressed up in front of our house on Park Avenue near the hospital in Steamboat.

parents looked for housing in Craig, but nothing was available in their price range. Fortunately, our Granddad, Joe Ireland, had moved back to Steamboat and offered to let us live in a cabin on his property about three miles from town. The main issue, however, would be the long drives home in the winter, which would be more than 120 miles versus 50 miles.

As noted in Chapter 7, Mom moved with the three of us while Dad stayed on the ranch. Mom worked first in a drug store during the school year. In the seven years until Rita graduated, she rented five different houses or apartments and purchased one house.

The three of us again quickly distinguished ourselves as good students, David in high school, I in junior high school, and Rita in elementary school. Additionally, we all were accepted easily and made friends. During our respective high school years taking the college preparatory track, we all were inducted into the National Honor Society. I was the valedictorian of my class; David and Rita were the salutatorians of theirs.

We also took mathematics courses from Gertrude Campbell: algebra, plane geometry, trigonometry, solid geometry, and advanced algebra. We took English, biology, history, and the other standard courses from such excellent teachers as Lucille Bogue, Marjorie Coulter, George Sloan, and Ted Rogers. Rita took Spanish, art, and some home economics. I enrolled in a year of French as well as one term in vocational agriculture and one in metal working. David took several courses in vocational agriculture.

Recognition for other activities and achievements were shared by all of us as well. We sang for at least a few years in the school chorus and became members of DeMolay or Rainbow Girls through the

The house on Oak Street where we lived the longest in Steamboat. Deep snow was a part of life.

House on 3rd Street where Rita lived with Mom and Dad for her senior year.

Shriners and Eastern Star service organizations. We were members of MYF (Methodist Youth Fellowship). David was most successful in track, especially the half mile, and was a member of FFA (Future Farmers of America). He also was very active in his class offices as well as Student Council. He was student body president in his senior year. I lettered for four years in high school wrestling and was also involved in class offices. Rita was also a class officer throughout high school. David and Rita attended Boys State and Girls State, respectively. I missed that opportunity because it coincided with my speech therapy program at the University of Wyoming.

We learned to ski at the local Howelsen Hill, but it was David who pursued it and became an accomplished skier in packed snow or deep powder. With his friends, David Bedell and Roy Tuffly, he made numerous weekend jaunts that involved climbing various mountains and skiing down or trekking across miles of deep snow. My wrestling coach, Carl Romano, strongly discouraged skiing among the wrestlers for fear that we would break a leg.

Rita was only a beginning skier, at best, because she could not afford both skiing and boarding horses. Thus, she did not pursue skiing. She arranged to board her horse, Gypsy, at the Elkins' property and would often ride with Steve Elkins to help Steve's father, Marvin, with his cattle, or just to ride for fun and enjoy such things as scaring tourists who were camping at Fish Creek Falls.

Despite the commonalities, we typically enrolled in other unique courses, pursued different extracurricular activities, or used our leisure time differently. It would not be uncommon for one of us not to know what the other

Kenneth's first date with Josephine Davis during the 8th grade.

Kenneth sporting a Mohawk haircut. Several other wrestlers apparently did so as well.

Kenneth (left) sparring to look for a take down.

Kenneth dancing, most likely with Vicky Elkins, at a school dance while others, including Jim Chesney on crutches, look on.

Foreign exchange student, Razelyn Nafiah, from Indonesia cutting a birthday cake. Judy Iacovetto is behind on the left. Katy Maguire and Chrisine Cox on the right.

Kenneth and Rita practicing the jitterbug at home at the ranch for Christmas.

David (left) and Kenneth (right) at the Oak Street house on the occasions of their high school graduations.

Inducted into the National Honor Society. Back: Clela Rorex, Sarah Sauer, Ed Neish, David, and Jim Maguire; front: Marsha Brown, Mary Lu Ellis, Dick Gardner, John Wither, Jim (Moose) Barrows, and Kenneth.

High school portraits of David, Kenneth, and Rita.

two were doing on any given day, except for jointly getting ready for school in the morning or eating dinner and doing homework together in the evening. In other words, there were few activities we did together, excepting MYF, occasional DeMolay/Rainbow Girls parties, and rare instances when David and I would have the same advanced algebra class. For example, I was always late getting home after the first two years playing football in the fall and all four years wrestling in the winter, as was David in the spring running track. It was clear that we three siblings were very clearly beginning to make our own ways in Steamboat.

We did need to come together to cooperate on those weekends when everyone would drive back to the ranch together or during one or two hunting seasons when Mom went back to the ranch to cook for the hunters for about four weeks. At that time, the three of us were expected to work together to fix their meals, maintain the house, travel to the ranch together on the weekends, and stay out of trouble.

As was the case on the ranch, daily, weekly, or seasonal chores included making our beds, cleaning the bathtub after our use, helping to clean the house, helping with dishes, filling the basement bin with coal for the furnace (first shoveled twice a day in large blocks but later small nut-sized coal shoveled once a day into a hopper wherein an augur would feed the furnace), shoveling snow in the driveway and sidewalk, picking up the mail a few blocks away, and doing whatever else needed to be done. A list from Mom was usually waiting on the table when we returned from school.

We all held various odd jobs for pay. David's first job in the ninth grade was to move the sprinklers and water the football field. During the winters when Granddad had moved to Aspen Street in Steamboat, he paid David to shovel his sidewalk and fill the hopper with nut coal. David also shoveled snow from sidewalks and driveways for various neighbors. Jim and Audrey Temple, who lived several blocks away, hired me to fill their coal hopper with coal each day. They also paid me to haul coal from a nearby mine to fill the storage room several times. Rita babysat occasionally in the sixth and seventh grades. In high school, she worked variously at the Kinney Drug Store, where Mom had worked in prior years, and at the El Rancho Café. Some work was not for pay. For example, as a junior, I volunteered to paint our three-story house and its steep metal roof. Borrowing a heavy wooden extension ladder and building a ladder-like structure to hold me on the roof, I did the entire job by myself during the spring final examination week as my grades had exempted me from the testing.

Antlers from a huge buck that Kenneth shot while helping out with hunters on a weekend at the ranch.

One day's deer season harvest of bucks with Fran Krugh, Sinc, another hunter, and Dad.

At the end of each school year, our routines changed dramatically. We all moved back to the ranch initially in the early years and worked on the ranch for what our parents could afford to pay us. David helped with riding and haying. I fixed fence, irrigated, and worked in the hayfield. Rita kept track of sheep or cattle on horseback, while avoiding as much domestic work as possible. One year, at the ages of 16 and almost 15, David and I, with help from no one else, "ricked" all of Shorty Temple's hay and made it ready for pickup in 18-wheeler trucks, all in about three weeks. This involved David driving Shorty's Jeep pickup pulling the "slip," a five-foot wide series of planks bolted together at the front, which I loaded. After about 30 bales were loaded three high, the slip was pulled to one of several collection points. We unloaded it as follows: I inserted a crowbar into the ground as deep as possible between the planks to hold the hay and then held the bar with my shoulder while David pulled the slip out from under the load. We also stacked a small percentage of the hay. Our uncles planned to help us finish this enormous amount of haying after they finished on the St. Louis ranches, but we finished first. Another summer we only stacked hay for Shorty, with Clifford driving the tractor and loading the elevator while David and I loaded the slip and stacked. In both of these summers, we got paid by the ton. It seemed to David at least that Shorty would weigh the lighter bales to calculate tonnage. Even so, relative to what we might have made helping Dad and our uncles, we made a lot of money for those weeks of very hard work.

Moving to Steamboat for School / 277

David, Rita, and Kenneth in the summer of 1960.   *Kenneth and Rita at the ranch in the summer of 1962 working for L-O-N Corporation.*

In 1961, after his final year of high school, David worked for Harry Russell. That summer, Rita worked at the Saddle Pocket dude ranch, helping with cleaning and cooking. I spent much of that summer at the University of Wyoming getting speech therapy. (See Chapter 12.) The next summer (1962), Mom stayed in Steamboat to continue her new job at the bank and Rita came to the ranch to allegedly cook for Dad and me, as we built fence. Mostly, though, she rode or did any available outside work instead. The following summer, after our ranch was sold but Dad was hired as ranch manager (see Chapter 14), Rita's job was to care for 700 steers and 70 cow-calf pairs. She loved it because it meant that she had to ride almost all day every day and, in so doing, to earn $70 per month.

Through 1962, we all continued in 4-H, so summers included all the care and training of animals required for showing them at the County Fair in Rawlins. For David and me, it also included several two- to three-day livestock judging trips. Twice, we had parties at the ranch for our DeMolay and Rainbow Girls friends in Steamboat.

In mid-September, the routine would go back to Steamboat during the week and the ranch on weekends. This, however, gradually diminished as we became more and more involved with sports and extracurricular activities. Dad frequently drove to Steamboat for home wrestling matches, and of course came for graduations and award ceremonies. We became very familiar with the 52 miles of gravel road "over the hill" to and from Steamboat. We would drive it as long as possible in the fall and begin again driving it as early as possible in the spring. Since the road was not kept open (by Dad) past Three Forks Ranch in the north and past Clark in the south, it was impossible to drive between these locations beginning about early December through mid-April. Accordingly, it was necessary to drive the 120 miles around to Baggs, Craig, and then Steamboat. As explained in Chapter 9, we learned to drive very early, with David and I driving alone by the age of ten on the roads near the ranch. (We drove tractors at the ages of six and seven years.) We were never aware that policemen monitored traffic on the gravel road. Thus, from the time we moved to Steamboat, David or I would frequently take the wheel from Mom as soon as we got out of town or relinquish it when approaching Steamboat from the ranch. By contrast, Mom was a poor driver. She did not like driving and was constantly afraid that an accident might be imminent. Once we learned to ignore her literal white knuckles and long inhalations on the ssss sound, it was a good arrangement. Everyone knew that we could do a better job than she could. Of course, once David reached the age of 16 and got his driver's license, Mom rarely drove at all on these trips.

On these trips, we honed our skills at changing flat tires on the road, driving on snow, ice, or mud with and without chains, and calibrating speed according to conditions. In a word, we became very good drivers, a skill that has served us well throughout adulthood.

Rita continued and finished high school in the two years after David and I had left for college at Colorado State University. For her junior year, she and Mom lived together in the Oak Street house, and she took over much of the driving. The house was sold in the summer of 1963 after the ranch had been sold late in 1962. Mom, Dad, and Rita moved to a rented house on 3rd Street between November and early January of 1964 and then to the main house at Granddad's lake property. Rita also lived at times with Elizabeth, Lillyan, and Lexie, who had all moved to Steamboat by that time. Clifford Ranch helped out at the ranch the next summer while Rita worked at the El Rancho Café. It was in that summer that Mom and Dad purchased the laundromat in Boulder from Jim Temple.

All three of us had social interactions with the opposite sex during the high school years, both in Steamboat and on the Little Snake River. David dated a number of his high school classmates but never became too serious with anyone. He still stays in touch with some of them. I had my first date with a classmate during the eighth grade. I took another classmate to the prom in my sophomore year on a weekend when Mom was at the ranch. I also had short romances in the summer with dudes at the Focus Ranch. In my junior year, I invited Judy Iacovetto to the prom, and that relationship lasted all through that and the next year. We ended up "going steady" with the exchange of class rings worn around our necks. Rita had a few short romances with dudes or dude wranglers as well at the Focus. She had male friends in high school that were not officially "dates," and she also had a steady boyfriend, Jim White, for a time as a junior.

MEMORIES

David: In spite of my experiences in La Sal and Salt Lake City, going to high school in Steamboat was the first time I experienced culture shock—the change from eight students in grade (elementary) school to 40 students in my graduating class, from country kids to city kids, from living in the country to living in the city, and from just having my arm amputated and a new prosthesis. In order to adjust, I tried everything that was offered. I quickly learned that I was no good at basketball, having never played before and having one arm. Although it was not true, I did my best to show anyone that revealing my naked stump did not bother me. Over time, I came to not think at all about having one arm. I suppose that is part of the reason that I was elected to positions in student government.

David: I first started learning to ski in high school PE class. Some of my classmates were on the ski team, but they had been skiing since grade school. After I learned to ski, racing did not appeal to me, but I loved to ski and would head to the slopes whenever there was snow. Three or four friends and I would ski every afternoon after school and also do night skiing twice a week. Then, we would ski all day Saturday and Sunday. We could buy a season ticket very cheaply and leave our skis at the ski hill, which was walking distance from home. On Sundays, we would wear our ski clothes to church before going to the hill.

David: Track was the only sport that made any sense to me. Unfortunately, I could not jump very high, could not throw very far, nor run very fast. The coach decided I would make a good miler. I tried running a mile, but decided that the coach was trying to kill me. I eventually learned that I was better suited for the half-mile even if I was slow. I never learned how to do the "kick" at the end of a race, so I would fall back before the finish. I did finally get a letter in track.

David: Even though we lived in town, my best friends were classmates who lived in the country, particularly David Bedell and Roy Tuffly who lived at Clark. In the winter, we often climbed mountains, such as Sand Mountain, and skied down in the powder.

David: The skills I learned in vocational agriculture have carried me throughout life—especially welding and parliamentary procedure. I am surprised how many people have never heard of Roberts Rules of Order.

David: My experience at Boys State helped me hone my skills in student government. I believe I did a good job in these offices.

Kenneth: After returning from California in the seventh grade, I finished up at Willow Creek School with Elizabeth as the teacher. I was a pretty good speller, so we decided that I would enter the county spelling bee to be held in Steamboat. I studied and studied and studied. I remember Mom and Elizabeth driving me to Steamboat. I stood up there with all those other junior high kids and was given the first or second word to be spelled. I heard and immediately spelled it "s-e-p-e-r-a-t-e." The teacher said wrong, and I sat down, humiliated. Ever since then, when I see that word it looks in my mind like "sepArate." I wondered how I would be remembered when I enrolled there in that same fall. The next year, I was in the same spelling bee. I did not win but was one of the two or three finalists.

Kenneth: All three of us got involved early with DeMolay and Rainbow Girls because we had friends who were involved. None of us had a clue about what all the ritual was about, and I suspect neither did our parents, but we went along with no questions. The dances and parties were the real reasons we stayed in these organizations as long as we did.

Kenneth: David had begun to be recognized in high school for success at running for class or student body offices. I wanted to as well, and I became our class treasurer for a couple of years. I did run for something on student council but lost. I remember that Jim Maguire helped me with an idea. We bought large packages of gum (Spearmint, Doublemint, or Juicy Fruit), we removed the colored wrapper from each piece but not the aluminum foil, we replaced the cover with a typed wrapper reading "Vote for Kenneth St. Louis" on one side, we glued the other side of the new wrapper together, and we handed them out to classmates.

Kenneth: I always liked mathematics, and I took Gertrude Campbell's classes for three years: two algebra classes, two geometry classes, and trigonometry. Calculus was not offered. I had a love-hate relationship with these courses. I was good, but I made transposition errors far too often, such as calculating "4835"and then copying it as "4385." For Mrs. Campbell, there was no such thing as partial credit. It was 100% right or it was "wrong." In plane geometry, if you spelled one word incorrectly in the proof, it was wrong. And for grades, she, especially, abided by the prescribed grade guidelines of 93–100% = A, 85%–92% = B, 78–85% = C, 70–77% = D, and below 70% = F. Each year, the high school gave out A and B medals at the end of the year at an awards assembly. To earn an A medal, every single quarter and semester grade had to be above an A. The same was true for a B medal. I got the B medal twice because, for one quarter grade in one of Mrs. Campbell's classes, I ended up with a B+. In one year, my average was higher than 92 1/2% but lower than 93%, and she did not round the grade to an A–.

Kenneth: Gertrude Campbell's courses helped to persuade me not to major in engineering in college, which is what I thought I would do. Little did I know that in those days before hand calculators that my tendency to transpose numbers would have had virtually no effect on a technical, mathematics-related career. However, Mrs. Campbell's positive in' ∂nce was much stronger. Because my later speech-language pathology departm was in a speech and theater department, I was not required to take mathem By the time I realized that I should have done so, it was too late. Importantly, I have carried out a successful research career with no other basic mathematics than what I learned in high school. Those courses gave me what I needed to do statistics, the only other math courses I ever took.

The United Methodist Church across the street from our house on Oak Street where we all attended church essentially for the first times in our lives and joined the Methodist Youth Fellowship (MYF).

Kenneth: I remember lots of times in high school when I sang with my guitar, at DeMolay meetings, in French Club, at MYF, and at home. As a senior, I received a "one" (excellent) for a solo at a high school vocal competition. I was always proud of my ability there, and of course I never stuttered at all when I sang.

Kenneth: I played basketball in the eighth grade and went on a few trips with the team, but I have almost no memory of that. I remember that I was not good at any part of the game, dribbling, shooting the ball, or rebounding. I also went out for football during my freshman and sophomore years of high school, and although I was very small, I was assigned to play the guard position because I could not throw or catch the football well. I did not like the experience and was hit far too hard by the larger players on the line. I sat on the bench in the games except for perhaps one or two times. I did not continue for my last two years of high school.

Kenneth: I have many good memories of being on the wrestling team. They started when I was in the eighth grade and I traveled on our school's athletic bus with a junior high team to Rangely to a one-day tournament. My weight class, if I

Kenneth riding his opponent.

Kenneth about to pin his opponent.

recall, was 100 pounds. I had two or three matches and won the championship. I did not say much on the way home, but I held that little trophy with more pride than I can ever remember. Later, in high school, I was proud when I made the team or earned letters. From the ninth through twelfth grades, my weight classes were 95, 103, 112, and 120 pounds. I felt especially good when I could beat a tough opponent at a match, especially when Dad and the family would be able to watch. I liked the wrestling trips we took to other towns: Hayden, Craig, Meeker, Rifle, Rangely, Oak Creek, Grand Junction, Paonia, Saratoga, and other places.

Kenneth: I also experienced a great deal of stress with wrestling. I had to diet for three to four months every year, and for someone like me who loved to eat, it was especially hard. The whole family would lose weight, as we often had broiled deer steak every night or two. The weekly weigh-ins were the culmination of a week of eating far less than I wanted, but more disturbing, not drinking water for the last couple of days in order to dehydrate the weight off. Even more stressful for most of my four years was making the team each week. We would have try-outs every week to determine who was the best in each weight class. I beat Jim Bartholomew almost every week, but he beat me out for the first team on one important team match. And the next year, John Holscher beat me once for the first team, so I had to wrestle two opponents on the second team that week. (I pinned them both.) I started worrying about the next week as soon as I made the team for any given week. Finally, I never performed at the district tournament in Meeker as I did during the season. I never won first place and, thus, did not get the chance to go to the state tournament in Denver. This happened twice although I had beaten both district champions earlier. And my senior year, the person who beat me in Meeker, and whom I had beat earlier, became the state champion.

Kenneth: I have so many memories of us driving back and forth "over the hill" from the ranch to Steamboat. I memorized the road and could anticipate every

Moving to Steamboat for School / 283

First date with Judy Iacovetto before leaving her house to Kenneth's junior prom.

Ken and Judy about ready to leave for a ride on the ranch.

Judy at her home at Dream Island Motel and trailer park in Steamboat.

grade, turn, and pothole (and still can). Each serious or memorable event became associated in my mind with a specific place on that road. One example is when Mom, Rita, and I were hauling Rita's horse, Gypsy, to Steamboat in the pickup one rather late Sunday evening in the rain. I was driving. We were fine until we had just come over the rise after Smith Creek and there were a few horses in the road. As we approached, they ran away from us, and Gypsy decided she wanted to join them. She climbed up the front of the stock rack (made of pine boards) and broke two or three of them with her front hoof coming through the back window and narrowly missing Mom's head in the middle of the seat. We got Gypsy back down into the pickup bed, and I had to scrounge some posts and boards from the old barn nearby and wire the stock rack together with some baling wire in order to continue on to Steamboat. The glass cut in Gypsy's leg became infected, and she spent days or weeks at Dr. Pinky Smith's veterinary hospital as a result.

Kenneth: While dating Judy Iacovetto, I would go to visit her at the Dream Island Motel, and her dad, Angelo, would typically put me to work. I'm quite sure they liked me, probably because I seemed so "safe" to them for their attractive daughter. Mom also seemed to like Judy as well, although she once asked me if I was getting too serious. Rita was not so charitable. She called me "Quiver Lip" because I had a habit of wrinkling my mouth at various times, and she called Judy, "Swivel Hip." I'm not sure it ever led to a fight, but I was not happy with these names.

Kenneth: Two funny stories stand out in my mind with Judy. Once, as the deep snow was melting in late March or early April, we had a lake of sorts in front of our Oak Street house. I had put about a ten-foot long, ten- or twelve-inch wide plank in order to walk over the water that had pooled from the melting snow banks. As more melting occurred, the plank would get wobbly. Well, one afternoon, Judy and I were coming to our house and I crossed the plank first. I was nearly across, and she was in the middle. I don't recall the conversation or the reason, but I must have warned her that it could tip, and she must have said she had excellent balance. So, I stepped hard on one side of the plank, causing her to fall on her butt into about four inches of water.

Another time, it was late spring and wrestling season was over. For once, I did not have to go to at least two hours of practice after school. It was an unusually warm day with bright sun, and we were walking slowly up 7th street on the sidewalk near the Junior High building. We were holding hands and not saying much as I recall. About three sidewalk panels ahead of us an ant started across the sidewalk. And as we approached the panel the ant was on, he would be directly in front of us. Without saying or signaling anything, the following sequence occurred: Judy casually but rather quickly put out her foot to step on the ant and I suddenly raised my foot higher than normal to stomp on the ant. The ant was completely smashed but so were Judy's toes.

Kenneth: During work on the ranch in the summers, as I took over some of the irrigation at the Fleming and Hackmaster Places, I started searching for four-leaf clovers as I walked through the hayfields. I found myself looking at the ground for hours, and eventually found about a half dozen. Perhaps this was a prelude to searching for "nuggets" of new information in huge databases later in my life.

Photo Kenneth took of a four-leaf clover that he found in the hayfield.

Rita: I mostly really liked high school. While I was not one of the popular girls who were athletes or cheerleaders, I had good friends. I liked most of my classes, but some of them were not what I "should have been taking." In the second year I signed up for Ted Rogers's art class, Gertrude Campbell marched up to me and informed me that I was to drop that class and take her advanced algebra class. When she demanded something, you did it! I really should have taken her Latin class too, but instead I chose Spanish, which was a total waste of time because Mrs. Butler knew Spanish about as well as I know Hindi.

Rita: I did love singing and I was good at it. I was always in the choir. During my junior and senior years I sang solos and in several groups, and we competed throughout the state. I remember one of the judges from Adams State wanted to offer me a music scholarship if I would go there. I also acted in a few one-act plays.

Rita: I went to MYF, mostly because it was a social gathering for me and an excuse to cross the street to the Methodist Church one evening a week and be with friends. It was through MYF, however, that I went in November of 1963 to New York and Washington, DC, on the train. I'm sure it would have been a memorable trip anyway, but it was more so because we were in Washington DC one week after Kennedy was shot. I remember snaking along in a very long line to walk past his fresh grave.

Rita: I think I was a freshman running for class president. People wrote signs, and posted them around school, asking that others vote for them. One day Kenneth came to me totally mortified and said I must take one of my signs down. You could not easily see an apostrophe on one of my signs which said, "1 2 3 4 Who're You Going to Vote For? Rita, that's who!" Instead, because the apostrophe was not well written the sign said, "1 2 3 4 Whore You Going to Vote For..."!

Rita: Every year during lambing, I would take a week off of school to help Daddy on the ranch. I loved it. It was a time that just Daddy and I were together, and that was special. Also, I was good at lambing. I could get a ewe to claim her lamb. Often-times, especially if a ewe had twins, one lamb would be abandoned and not allowed to suckle. I was usually really successful in getting her to realize that it was her baby and that she had to take care of it.

Rita: Throughout most of high school I worked at Kinney Drug Store. Don Kinney was kind of a hard-ass, but he really taught me that if you are going to expect to be paid, you needed to work to earn that pay. He insisted on being at work on time, on not standing around chatting with friends while on the job, and on finding work to do without being asked. He was pretty strict, but always totally fair. It would be good if other high school kids had such a boss or mentor.

Rita: In high school I did not date much. While I would not consider it "dating," Ray Selbe and I would often load into his Model A car and go to the car races. I did have a couple of memorably horrible dates. One was with an acquaintance of Kenneth who had asked him to ask me to the prom. I went with the guy, and most of what I remember is his stepping on my feet repeatedly and constantly fussing over and rearranging the orchid corsage that he had given me. Another date was with a classmate of mine with whom I had nothing in common except that we were both from ranches. He was in FFA, and he invited me to the Sweetheart Dance. I had been chosen as one of the candidates for the FFA Sweetheart, so I really couldn't tell him that I had other plans or anything. I agreed to go to the dance with him, but I mainly remember him constantly wanting to dance really closely and to kiss me. I spent that very long evening dodging his advances.

Rita: As a junior, I "went steady" with one of the young men, Jim White, from the new college in Steamboat. Jim would come to the drugstore where I worked, and I would make him milk shakes. We started dating, and at first, I thought he was really cool because he was in college and he had pretty eyes. He would come to our house for dinner several nights a week, but he was a really picky eater. Poor Mom put up with him too. After Christmas vacation when I went to Mexico with Elizabeth, Sinc, Lillyan, and Lexie, Elizabeth recounted to me several instances in which Jim was pretty cruel to another one of the students who had a speech defect. That, along with my realizing that he really was not who he said he was, made me less and less interested in him. (It turned out that the college had to accept anyone who had a warm body and enough money to pay tuition. Jim probably could not have gotten into another college.) However, to that point, I was too chicken to break up with him. But, finally, the clincher came: I invited him to the ranch in the spring and we took a horseback ride. At one point we went through a barbed wire gate, and he did not have enough strength to close it. That was the deal breaker! While I stayed with him into early summer, and even went to Colorado Springs to meet his parents right after Girls State, I broke up soon after I got home.

Rita: The other person I dated in high school and into college was Bob Deurloo. He was a really nice person, and we had a lot of fun together. In addition to everything else, he helped me get through advanced algebra. It was I who was the jerk in that relationship. There are several instances that I did things that were not nice to him, and I have since felt bad about my behavior.

Chapter 14

Higher Education
at Colorado State University

After graduation from high school, there was never a question if all three of us would go on to college. The questions were "Where?" and "For what degree?" Each of us deliberated on these questions and our thinking is further fleshed out in Chapters 15, 16, and 17 explaining major influences and turning points in our lives.

David applied and was accepted at Colorado State University (CSU). He was leaning toward an agriculture field, and it was only at CSU that agriculture majors were available. Also, Fort Collins was reasonably close and inexpensive. He also considered majoring in engineering or geology, but late in his freshman year, he decided on animal science in the College of Agriculture.

Prior to starting in the fall of 1961, David had bought a large Chrysler 1950 sedan, which he drove to Fort Collins. He moved into a dormitory, Ellis Hall, with a roommate, Dick McNitt, for his first year. During the second (winter)quarter, he pledged one of two agricultural fraternities, FarmHouse Fraternity.

The second year, he roomed with Benson McClaren from Ohio, who became a lifelong friend. Benson had pledged the other agriculture fraternity, Alpha Gamma Rho (AGR). They jointly decided not to move into the respective fraternity houses during their sophomore years, but to stay in Ellis Hall. In that year, David was elected as Ellis Hall president and president of the Inter-Hall Council. For his junior and senior years, he moved into FarmHouse.

Of course, David's course of study was heavily based in life and agricultural sciences, that is, biology, botany, zoology, crops, soils, and animal science. A foreign language was required as were several electives in speech and discussion as well.

As explained in Chapter 12, I had decided between my junior and senior years of high school that I would major in speech therapy, and a new program had been opened at CSU. I had learned that the field had begun in Iowa, so I had also applied to Iowa State University, not realizing that it was the University of Iowa that was famous for speech therapy. I had also applied to Harvard (mainly to see if I could get in) and for a prestigious Colorado Boettcher scholarship but was accepted for neither. For these reasons, CSU seemed like the best option.

David and I jointly purchased a brown 1957 Ford Fairlane in summer 1962. The Chrysler used so much oil that it had to be sold. We drove together to Fort Collins, and I moved into Newsom Hall, next to Ellis Hall. To my disappointment, I had been assigned a roommate from my Steamboat Springs High School class, Jim Marshall, whom I knew but did not consider a close friend. I wanted to room with someone from someplace I was not familiar with. Jim had apparently asked for me. After one quarter, I requested another dormitory placement and was assigned to Ellis Hall with a pre-veterinary major, Rick Robbins from Texas. Almost immediately, both Rick and I were "rushed" and decided to join FarmHouse Fraternity. At that time, a pledge needed to have either an agricultural major or an "agricultural interest." Clearly, Rick met the first criterion, and I, the second.

As for the Ford, it became increasingly unsightly. The paint on the hood peeled off more and more each year until it was almost entirely the orange color of rust. The car did run pretty well, however, but the engine burned up (fortunately in the last few miles from Fort Collins to Snake River) because the engine oil had all leaked out. A new engine was put in over the summer.

Our '57 Ford (right) and our parents' '62 Chevy (left) at the Steamboat house on 3rd Street.

The car then lasted two more years until I was about to graduate. I couldn't sell it, so I drove it to a junk yard in Fort Collins, sold it for fifteen dollars, and then walked back to the fraternity.

David, as well as Rick and I, moved from the dormitory to FarmHouse the next fall. David lived there two years until he graduated, and I lived there three years. Assigned rooms and roommates changed each quarter so that we rotated through the best and worst rooms and got to know most of the men in the house much better than if we had stayed in the same room with the same roommates. The fraternity brothers met every Monday night for a meeting and ate evening meals together, including Wednesday evenings when we were required to wear coats and ties. On those evenings we "rushed" new prospects all year long, unlike most fraternities and sororities in the Greek system that did so only for one week.

I majored from the beginning in the new major of hearing and speech science (also known then as speech correction, speech therapy, or speech pathology and now as speech-language pathology) where both baccalaureate and master's degrees were getting underway. My stuttering had gradually relapsed over the previous year, so not only did I take all the classes, I was enrolled in speech therapy. The major I had chosen was part of the Speech and Theater Department. So, in addition to typical courses taken by speech-language pathology majors, I was obliged to take courses in public speaking, group discussion, and introduction to theater as part of a core of common courses, including English and history. Nevertheless, the course of study was extensive, involving anatomy and physiology, psychology, sociology, anthropology, and all of the various speech, language, and hearing disorders. Surprisingly, it did not include a mathematics requirement, with only the physics of sound as a physical science course.

FarmHouse Fraternity house.

Kenneth's mentor, Bill Leith, at the Speech and Hearing Center.

Four of Kenneth's speech pathology classmates boarding a bus for their first American Speech-Language-Hearing (ASHA) Convention in Chicago, 1965. Posing are Mary Ann Berger, Janet Johnston, Joysa Post, and Martha Berger.

The entire FarmHouse chapter, 1961. Kenneth is far left in the back row, and David is far left in the third row.

Cort Van Riper and David (at the right) with two fraternity dignitaries.

Chuck Ault, David, and Rick Robbins looking at a fraternity scrapbook.

I chose to take a number of non-required courses: two years of French, university chorus, comparative religion, and two years of Air Force ROTC. As a sophomore, I became a member of the Color Guard and carried the American flag in parades. I also attended the Methodist student group,

Wesley Foundation, which had a house near campus and featured weekly worship services, groups, and other events. In addition, I entered the campus intramural wrestling tournament each winter quarter.

As a result of serious religious discussions, reading books on theology, various Wesley Foundation retreats, and spring break work camps to Yuma, Arizona, and San Luis, Colorado, I became more and more convinced that I had made a mistake joining ROTC. Seeing films each week of various "weapon systems" and seeing the growing evidence that the war in Viet Nam was not going well, I decided to quit. It was not to be as easy as that because I had won a scholarship at the end of my freshman year as a result of earning the highest GPA in the first-year basic program and also being in the Color Guard. Yet, after a formal hearing with actual Air Force officers at the end of the second year, I withdrew and did not enter the advanced program, from which resigning would be extremely difficult. Thereafter, I began soul searching about what I should do after graduation. I considered becoming a Methodist missionary who would serve in an underdeveloped country in actual social service. I also thought about going to seminary to become a minister. And I thought about the Peace Corps, which was then three years old. Interestingly, the idea of the Peace Corps was from David, who, during his senior year, also considered that as a post-graduation option. (David, instead, joined the International Voluntary Service, a similar, private organization with many of the same aims.) I decided on the Peace Corps and was eventually accepted into an "advanced" (meaning early—not more difficult) training program between the junior and senior year of college. See Chapter 16 for details.

Kenneth as a Basic Air Force ROTC cadet.

Kenneth St. Louis

Ken St. Louis Selected For Advanced ROTC

Press release about Kenneth's joining the Advanced level of ROTC. In fact, it did not happen.

I graduated "with high distinction" from CSU in June 1966. I had been inducted into the Phi Kappa Phi scholastic honorary, was voted the "outstanding student" in my major for the year, and was awarded one of CSU's twelve "Pacemaker" awards.

Rita entered CSU in the fall of 1964. She chose her major of liberal arts because she did not have a clear direction in mind. She had been assigned to Winkenwerder Hall, which was a co-educational dormitory. In those days, "co-ed" meant that men stayed in one wing, women in the other, and they shared a dining hall and commons area. Rita roomed there one year with a senior, Jan Gilbreath, who majored in speech pathology. Rita and her good friend from high school, Marveen Elkins, rented an apartment for their sophomore year.

Rita was interested in English, writing, and psychology for her two years at CSU, after which she married Chris Maser and went overseas. After returning from overseas, she enrolled at Oregon State University in Corvallis and majored in English. A year later, she switched to general science, mostly zoology and botany. She and Chris moved to Bandon, Oregon, where she completed her student teaching requirement. Actually, it was more like just taking over a classroom because the teacher was never around. Rita received her baccalaureate degree in general science education in 1970.

Summers during college brought us back to the family in increasingly diverse ways. At the end of his freshman year in 1962, David began working for the Forest Service in Routt County. He did many jobs, including campground maintenance, opening and clearing trails in the wilderness area, and fighting fires. The next summer in 1963, after my first year, things had changed dramatically when we drove our '57 Ford home. Dad and Mom had sold the ranch to the L-O-N Corporation; yet, Dad had stayed on as ranch manager, and Mom was a cook. David continued on with the Forest Service, but this time worked on the road crew. I was hired as a straw boss at L-O-N and put in charge of four high school and early college students from New York who had been recruited to come and work on a ranch. Being the same age, I had a lot in common with them, but I needed to show them how to do just about everything: fixing fence, irrigating, and haying.

In the next summer, 1964, Dad and Mom had given up working for L-O-N and had moved to Granddad's house with the lakes, southeast of Steamboat. David worked for Louie Gebauer on the farm near Akron, and I was hired by Shorty Temple at the Focus Ranch primarily as the irrigator. In addition to other chores and duties, I worked alone to irrigate all of the

HORIZONS 1966

Honor Night — May 16, 1966

"The world stands aside to let pass the man who knows whither he is going"
—Unknown

Pacemakers, 1966

Peter C. Boespflug, Minot, North Dakota

Joe L. Edgar, Rocky Ford, Colorado

Karen E. Grimaldi, Arlington, Virginia

Mary Ann Husbands, Littleton, Colorado

Sam W. Little, Gunnison, Colorado

Gail L. Manasil, Denver, Colorado

James A. McCambridge, Ault, Colorado

John L. New, Englewood, Colorado

Kenneth O. St. Louis, Steamboat Spring, Colorado

Roger A. Williamson, Rifle, Colorado

Top Profs

Maxine M. Benjamin, Professor, Pathology and Microbiology

Lester H. Stimmel, Professor, English

Who's Who in American Colleges and Universities

Arden, Ann
Betts, Susan Elizabeth
Biederman, Elizabeth Ann
Bilio, Paulette Elizabeth
Brogden, Elaine Leslie
Cundy, Dennis Roger
Curnow, Richard Dennis
Edgar, Joseph Lyman
Ervin, Frances Nicols
Rodgers, Linda Forstedt
Grimaldi, Karen Aileen

Hildebrand, Roger Lee
Husbands, Mary Ann
Keen, Morgan
Keepers, Susan Beall
Lohse, Jean Irene
McCambridge, James Adam
Nelson, Gerald Lawrence
Niebruegge, Janet Kaye
Puckett, Douglas Mitchell
Seymour, Robert Lynn

St. Louis, Kenneth Oliver
Welch, Charles Winfield
Welsh, Carolyn Jeannette
Welsh, Jack Robert
Williamson, Roger

SENIOR RECOGNITION

Black, David
Hoegh, Kristin
Manasil, Gail

THE QUESTION MARKS

While Yolanda Horgan entertai[ ]
us with a solo, Marilyn Drume[ ]
Lee Moeller, Barbara Keller, [ ]
Cathy Holcomb, Sandy Huffman, [ ]
and Claire Merle will enterta[ ]
us with a Las Vegas style dan[ ]

KEN ST. LOUIS

Ken is our western singer. He
has appeared in and around the
Fort Collins area. This is
Ken's first Green and Gold Re-
vue. He has been in one
Starfinder Revue.

A few of Kenneth's CSU awards and a booklet about a college-wide revue, 1966.

Rita's horseback Quadrille maneuvers at the 1965 "College Days."

Rita giving Gypsy a hug at the CSU "College Days" rodeo and celebration, 1964.

mesa and lower fields. Later, I mowed all the hayfields in the haying operation. Although I lived in the men's bunkhouse with young men and had regular contact with guests (dudes) and young women who worked there, this was the first time I had worked alone. Although it was an adjustment, I found that I enjoyed the hours of solitude. That summer, Rita worked as a waitress at the El Rancho Café in Steamboat.

The next summer of 1965, David moved to Laos, and Mom with Dad lived in Boulder to run their laundromat. I spent some time in Boulder, helped out for a few days in Denver after a devastating flood came through in the South Platte River, and then went to Portland, Oregon, for a six-week training program for the Peace Corps in Turkey. Rita lived in Steamboat at Elizabeth's house and worked at Harwig Saddlery. Over the 1965–1966 school year, Rita and I returned to CSU while our parents moved to Washington. Immediately after I graduated, Rita and I loaded up Dad and Mom's International Scout, picked up her horse in Steamboat, and drove to Washington. About two weeks later, I went to Turkey.

For Rita, a whirlwind chain of events happened that summer and early fall in 1966. Over the previous Christmas break, Rita had rekindled a relationship with Chris Maser, son of one of Elizabeth's friends who lived in Corvallis, Oregon. Several years earlier, Chris had stayed with Sinc and Elizabeth for a few summers and had worked on the ranch. In his last year

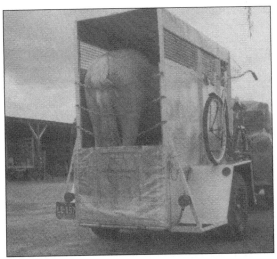 

Loaded up to leave CSU for Cusick, Washington, *Arrival in Cusick with Dad and Mom.*
a trip that took five full days with Kenneth, Rita,
Gypsy, and a puppy, along with an enormous load
for a Scout.

there, Dad and Mom had quashed a fling between the two of them because Rita was then only 14.

A few weeks after we arrived in Washington, Rita and Chris got married at the Cusick house. They made a quick trip to Chris's parents' home in Corvallis and then returned to Cusick. Shortly thereafter, Chris left to start an overseas commitment (see Chapter 17). As explained in Chapter 7, Rita stayed in Cusick to help Mom and Dad as they sold the Cusick ranch before departing overseas to join Chris.

Although not immediately matrimonial as with Rita, my relationships became more serious during the college years. Judy Iacovetto called an end to our previous "going steady" relationship during her senior high school year and my college freshman year. I dated several women briefly during my freshman and early sophomore years, including a relatively short relationship with Judy Smith, from Steamboat, who was studying at Colorado State College in Greeley. A longer, more serious relationship was with Nancy Starkebaum from Haxtun, Colorado, but she ended it after my junior year.

David dated regularly during college but did not enter any serious relationships.

MEMORIES

David: For the freshman year, everyone was required to take a full year (three quarters) of physical education (PE). To be exempt from taking swimming, everyone

David at his graduation from CSU, 1965.

Kenneth at his graduation from CSU, 1966.

was asked to swim a short distance in the pool. I sort of side stroked to pass the swimming test, so I could choose other courses. I chose bowling, ballroom dancing, and tennis for PE and got pretty good in all of them.

David: I was worried about getting good grades in college and wasn't sure I could do it. But, I quickly learned that, if I studied, I could get As. It surprised me after the first and second quarter how many students who had lived in the dorm were gone. They had a good time, as did all of us, but they flunked out. I slacked off in studying in my sophomore year and, as a result, I got a D that really disturbed me. (I hated organic chemistry!) After that, I was determined to get only As, and I did. All I had to do was read the assignments before class, take good notes, and be ready for a quiz on every day of class. I rarely had to cram at the last minute for a test.

David: Engineering was one of the options I was considering as a major. After taking advanced college algebra, even though I could do the work, I could not see myself spending the rest of my life crunching numbers.

David: In my academic track in animal science, a foreign language was required. Given that German was a scientific language at the time, I took it for one year. My first quarter's German teacher was a Vietnamese professor who had worked as an interpreter at the United Nations. The next two quarters were taught by a native-born German who taught German songs with his accordion on Fridays.

David: Dr. Tom Sutherland, an animal science professor, was my mentor and was instrumental in persuading me to go to graduate school. He suggested Iowa State University, Clemson University, and Cornell University as the best schools. Years later, when preparing for graduate study while in Laos, I applied to and was accepted by all three but chose Cornell.

Kenneth: I was ready to leave high school and was eager to get to CSU for college. I went along with having to wear a freshman "beanie" and enjoyed the orientation parties, where I met a few fellow freshmen with whom I kept in touch throughout my four years there. As noted above, I was not happy that my assigned roommate was Jim Marshall, my classmate from Steamboat. We got along OK, but I wanted a new experience. My second roommate, Rick Robbins, somehow "adopted" a crippled monkey, which we kept (illegally) in our dorm room for most of the spring quarter until the monkey's screaming caught the resident assistant's attention.

David and a date at a FarmHouse Spring formal.

Kenneth: I really liked my classmates in the Hearing and Speech Sciences Department. I remember being thrilled when, after the first year in an old barracks building, we moved to a brand new building. At the time, it was state of the art for a bachelor's and master's program. As a freshman, I was assigned to observe other students carrying out speech therapy with real clients. During my sophomore year, I was an assistant to a senior or graduate student. I started doing therapy with other clients myself as a junior and continued that as a senior. During all this time, I was a client as well. My clinicians were different senior or graduate students every quarter.

Kenneth: I really wanted to get the most out of college. As explained above, I was in the "Basic" Air Force ROTC program for two years. And, in this, I was made part of the Color Guard. (I carried the US flag.) Although not required, I sang in the university chorus, I took French for two years, I enrolled in a course in phonology, and I took a highly popular but difficult course in comparative religions. Beginning my junior year, I found I could audit courses just for the sake of interest. Two such courses were in Middle Eastern History, which I took after I learned I was going to Turkey in the Peace Corps. I did not like the required theater nor a few communication courses. In the major, I always liked the anatomy courses, especially the one which involved dissecting a human cadaver.

Kenneth: During my freshman year, I decided to participate in intramural wrestling. We only had to weigh in once, so I decided to try to go down two weights. I literally did not eat or drink anything for five days and lost 20 pounds! I weighed in once, and then proceeded to win my weight class easily over the next four weeks or so. I remember when I was at the gym practicing alone one day, doing shadow

CSU freshman beanie and "bible."

reverses and so on, the coach of CSU's team apparently had been watching. He approached me and asked my name. I told him and that I was from Steamboat, which he knew had the best or second-best high school teams in the state. He asked if I would do a few take downs with a well-known wrestler from Montrose, another state wrestling powerhouse. I complied and proceeded to take him down about five times in a row. (Maybe he just let me do it; I can't say.) The coach told me I should try out for the team. I was flattered, but I told him, "No," because I knew I did not have the time to do that and keep up with my studies.

Kenneth: I wrestled intramurals all four years, but never dieted like the first year again. The second year, I won easily again. The third year, as I got progressively out of shape, I won but with some difficulty. The fourth year, as explained in Chapter 16, I came in second but with probably lasting damage.

Kenneth: I have so many wonderful memories of Wesley Foundation, it's hard to know what to highlight. The two spring break trips, one to an Indian Reservation in the disputed area between Arizona (near Yuma) and California and another at San Luis on the Colorado-New Mexico border stand out. Combined with a chance to serve, I found them fun, educational, and adventurous all at once. There were also some practical jokes. On the second trip, one young woman had decided to bring methylene blue and serve it to the men in their grape juice for breakfast. We did not complain that the juice was kind of bitter, but we did notice later in the day that our urine was blue-green.

The trip to Yuma nearly turned disastrous, twice!

I was one of three men who acquired Colorado Chauffeur's Licenses so that we could drive the converted Wesley Foundation 35-foot re-purposed school bus. It had a large luggage rack on top, but, as we packed for the week trip, we did not want to put our suitcases or sleeping bags on top because it had recently snowed and was extremely cold just as winter quarter was ending. Instead, we loaded most of the luggage into the back of the bus. We were adults, but our brains must not have been completely developed because we stacked them all in front of two five-gallon plastic containers of gasoline that we took along in case we might run out somewhere on the 600-mile trip. It was stupid enough that we did not put the gasoline on top of the bus, but we also failed to notice that the main heaters of the bus were directly behind the gas containers.

We left late in the day and drove south through Denver, Colorado Springs, and Pueblo, where we turned west. I may have been the first or second driver, but it was below zero outside, the heater was on full blast, and nearly everyone was asleep on one of the seats of the bus. About half way between Colorado Springs and Pueblo, about 2:00 a.m., I heard a loud pop and hissing sound, followed immediately by screaming. I turned off the interstate onto the shoulder and opened the door while everyone ran out. The heat had caused the sealed spout of one of the gasoline containers to expand to the point it popped off and gasoline sprayed the entire interior of the bus. Everything was soaked with gasoline—our suitcases and clothes, our sleeping bags, our coats, the seats, everything! Nobody stated the obvious; if anyone had been smoking, we would all have burned to death in a terrible explosion. About 15 minutes outside in the below zero weather was about all anyone could stand. Thus, we moved the rest of the gasoline to the top, put on what clothes were not strongly smelling of gasoline from the closed suitcases, opened all the windows of the bus and continued on.

For the entire week, we endured the odor, especially in our sleeping bags (and many of us slept outside). My suitcase smelled of gasoline for at least a year.

The second near tragedy occurred the next day. We hit a terrible snowstorm as we were going up Wolf Creek Pass. Barry Cooper was driving at this time. It was so bad that he simply followed a snowplow up and over the pass, going about 20 mph. As we descended, the weather cleared, and gradually the road cleared as well. We were nearly off the mountains and coasting easily on long straight stretches of bare pavement. However, at one point the road went into a shaded area with trees and a suddenly snow-covered and potentially slick area that also had a dropoff on both sides of the road. Barry sought to shift from 4th to 3rd gear to slow down without using the brakes but, inexplicably, the gear box went into 1st or "compound." The rear wheels basically almost stopped while the bus careened first left, then right, then left again all in the middle of the road while Barry fought to keep from driving off either side. He succeeded and we went on, again no doubt with each of us thanking God that we survived.

I believe the bus was sold after the second work camp trip to San Luis, Colorado. But we did have a converted hearse that we used for other short trips and one long trip.

Kenneth: I thoroughly enjoyed and found great meaning in the numerous retreats

The Wesley Foundation bus on one of the trips we took.

Kenneth hauling a load of dirt at a spring break work camp.

we held with Wesley Foundation at a center west of Horsetooth Reservoir and the trips to conferences. I attended a Methodist Student Movement New Year's conference in Lincoln, Nebraska, with several other friends. He was not well known yet, but the keynote speaker was Martin Luther King Jr. who spoke of many people being like Rip Van Winkle, waking up after a revolution. On another trip, a number of us went to Sun Valley, Idaho, in August, this time driving the hearse.

Kenneth: I liked FarmHouse primarily because its strongest orientation was on becoming campus leaders and doing well academically. I was one who always brought the chapter grade point average up, so did not feel bad about never seeking an office. I did go to all the dances and parties. I especially liked the Silver Dollar Stomp every year, where we would dress up in costumes, as did our dates, usually with some Western theme. Photos were taken of each couple, and I enjoy reminiscing about how young I looked and how lucky I was to escort such beautiful young ladies.

Kenneth: Every year, FarmHouse would have a rodeo at a local rodeo arena with AGR, the other agricultural fraternity. I believe I only went to one and I rode a bareback bronc, the only time I ever did any rodeoing. I was the first one from Farm-House not to be bucked off, but I believe two riders after me did stay on for the eight seconds. I ended up in second place.

Kenneth: I did a lot of singing at CSU. I sang in the University Chorus, which had two concerts a year. I also led lots of sing-alongs at Wesley Foundation, FarmHouse, and other places with my guitar. I even entertained the CSU Rodeo Club once and sang a cowboy song as part of a traveling show that performed a few times. Finally, three fraternity brothers, Jim Ground (botany major from New Mexico), Jim Hage (agricultural major from near Fort Collins), Gene Matsurra (piano major from Hawaii), and I formed a singing group for about half of our senior year. The height of political incorrectness, we called ourselves "Peter, Paul, and Pineapple Pollock, Plus 1." We performed several times, but never for money. We were undoubtedly at our best with Simon and Garfunkel's "Sounds of Silence," which had recently been recorded.

Kenneth: David and I had relatively little interaction at CSU. The exceptions were for meals. I often ate lunch or breakfast with him and his roommate, Benson McClaren, in the cafeteria of Ellis Hall, after I moved there in my second quarter. We both moved into FarmHouse at the beginning of my second and his third year. We ate dinner together there every night, although I can't remember that we ever sat together. We also both attended a weekly meeting of the chapter on Monday nights. We did jointly own the '57 Ford that we drove to and from Steamboat. Most of our conversations had something to do with who would have the car on any given day or weekend.

Kenneth: I had even less interaction with Rita when she came to CSU during my junior and senior years. I was very busy in my major with classes, practica, and so on. Rita was not interested in joining me in my many activities at Wesley Foundation, and she was not interested in pledging a sorority. Again, our interactions typically centered around transportation.

Rita: Before I got to CSU, my roommate was already assigned to me. She turned out to be a senior, Jan Gilbreath, who majored in speech therapy. Jan was good for me because she was centered, generally knew the ropes,

The FarmHouse Silver Dollar Stomp with Nancy Starkebaum (under threat of a shotgun wedding).

Kenneth and Ann Arden at her Spring Formal.

and offered great friendship. My high school friend, Marveen Elkins, also lived in Winkenwerder, but she seemed to be more interested in exploring the possibilities

Higher Education at Colorado State University / 303

Kenneth riding a bareback bronc at the annual FarmHouse-AGR rodeo.

Our singing group: Jim Ground, Kenneth, Gene Matsurra, and Jim Hage.

offered by her own roommate, dorm friends, and boyfriends than to go to class or study.

Rita: I had a big awakening with the familiar "little fish in a big puddle" phenomenon. Classes were large, professors really did not seem to care much about freshmen, and other women in the dorm seemed foreign. I did not view that year as a bad experience, but I definitely did not relish it as anything special.

Rita: Marveen and I decided to room together in off-campus housing for our sophomore year. In those days, any woman under 21 was required to be in "approved" housing, which meant she had to live in a dormitory or agree to a 10:00 p.m. curfew on weeknights and a midnight curfew on the weekends. Furthermore, no men were allowed in our apartment without the approval of our landlady, Mrs. Roberts. Marveen and I agreed to this. We had an upstairs apartment and Mrs. Roberts would snoop through our dwelling while we were gone. She often would remind us that the sink needed to be cleaner, or the trash was overflowing. She also read through the envelopes as much as she could any letters we received. Mrs. Roberts's brother lived with her, and occasionally they would have heated arguments. Marveen and I would lie on the heat registers and listen to them. One night we decided to be naughty; we sneaked out of the house after ten p.m. and wandered the streets in our nightgowns and with our hair rolled up in great big curlers. After about a half an hour, we noticed a police car driving around slowly so we ran home before we were caught. Apparently, someone had called about the two strange females wandering around laughing.

Chapter 15

David—Where Did I End Up and How Did I Get There?

WHERE I ENDED UP

My Achievements

My Career

Most farmers or ranchers are the offspring of farmers and ranchers. It is no accident, then, that I ended up in the field of agriculture. As a boy and teenager, I had become intrigued with geology, probably related to Dad's and Gus Ranch's interest in prospecting. In fact, I strongly considered geology during my freshman year at CSU. The first course I took turned me off, so I decided on animal science as a major, and with that line of study, I continued through three academic degrees, BS, MS, and PhD.

My career in agriculture actually began immediately after my BS degree. As soon as I graduated, I traveled to Laos and served for two years with the International Voluntary Service (IVS). I taught animal science at the Teacher Training College near Vientiane, Laos. The college had tracks for French, English, and Lao speaking students, and they were taught in those respective languages. I taught beginning animal science to second-year students, so while learning the subject matter, they were learning a new vocabulary in nutrition, reproduction, and genetics. I overheard them jokingly calling me "Mr. Sperm." The college had a demonstration farm for the students to have hands-on learning, which included poultry, swine, and fish production as well as growing some feeds. The animal science teacher for the Lao section, who had studied in Thailand, lived on the farm, and we worked together closely. Often, we had local farmers tour the farm, which gave us the opportunity to teach improved production practices.

After the IVS tour, I stayed in Laos and accepted a position in agriculture with the United States Agency for International Development (USAID/AGR) a branch of the State Department working to help resettlement of refugees fleeing northern Laos. The location was Sam Thong, which was accessible only by air. My job was to help the villagers begin production of swine, poultry (chickens and ducks), and fish (tilapia). We obtained purebred pigs from Thailand that were kept on a farm at Long Tieng (LS20A). For each sow or gilt (female pig under one year) placed, the villagers were expected to return one pig from the litter so the program could be self-sustaining. The poultry and fish programs were successful in providing villagers with a protein source, but the swine program was not very successful because of poor nutrition and disease.

Most of the refugees were ethnic Hmong hill tribe people. A Hmong chief, Nhea Hur Lor, whom I called Nai Khong (the title for "chief") helped me in most of my work with refugees, mainly advising me of the situations in the villages. Besides helping refugee villagers, I was in charge of the farm in Long Tieng where we raised purebred pigs (Duroc and Large White). In addition to Hmong workers, a Thai counterpart, whose expertise was growing vegetables, stayed at the farm.

My third two-year tour was also with USAID, but with the Agricultural Development Organization (USAID/ADO), which had agricultural cooperatives in about four Lao provinces. I was the co-op manager for Khammouane Province in Thakek, Laos. We provided loans to rice farmers to buy improved rice seed, fertilizer, and tools. They paid back their loans at harvest with rice. Traveling on motorcycles to get to the villages, my job was to train local Lao co-op agents how to maintain strict inventory control, complete paperwork for all transactions, and maintain good bookkeeping. With all the "rough" (unmilled) rice we took in for loan payments, we negotiated with local millers to buy it. Throughout the process from the loans, inventory, bookkeeping, and rice milling, I had to stay on the lookout for constant skimming. This meant hiring and firing some of the agents, not an easy job for a foreigner with my personality.

Upon returning from Laos, I immediately began master's and then doctoral study at Cornell University in Ithaca, New York. I worked in Puerto Rico for 18 months for my doctoral dissertation research in collaboration with the University of Puerto Rico. The research was at four different branch experiment stations. At Lajas, I participated in research on corn and sorghum varieties with irrigated forage plot trials. At Corozal, the research focused on pasture grazing and supplementation trials with dairy heifers. At Gurabo, I conducted intake and production trials with various supplements for milking Holstein cows. And at the laboratory in Rio Piedras, I ran forage fiber analysis on samples from the trials in Lajas, Corozal, and Gurabo.

This training prepared me for a career in animal science, especially, my master's thesis in animal genetics and my PhD dissertation in ruminant nutrition. I was also well versed in tropical agriculture and agricultural economics. Not finding an academic position right away, my first job after graduation was with Glenelg Dehydrators of Ellicott City, Maryland, who had supported my research in Puerto Rico. The company raised corn and alfalfa that was dehydrated into feed pellets for cattle and horses. I enjoyed the work there for one and a half years but had no ambition to make it my career. I wanted to do research.

Nearly all of the rest of my animal science career was at two university stations in the southeast US. In 1978, I landed the first academic position as a research animal scientist at the Edisto Experiment Station of Clemson University in Blackville, South Carolina. It was there that I was project leader in beef-forage systems research in cow-calf production, backgrounding-finishing cattle, and replacement female development. I stayed there until 1984 but left because I did not make tenure. After about a year searching for another position, I accepted a research animal scientist position for Mississippi State University at the South Mississippi Branch Experiment Station (MAFES) in Poplarville. There, I continued the same type of research that I had done previously with Clemson University until I retired in 2008.

Whereas these experiment station positions were pure research positions, both had "extension" aspects as well. In South Carolina and at the beginning of my job in Mississippi, emphasis was primarily on research to help local farmers. Almost all of the research had an agricultural economics component, so farmers could see how adopting new practices would improve their standard of living. Unlike the South Carolina position, the Mississippi job was not a tenure-track position. Nevertheless, in both places, I was expected to design and carry out experiments and to publish the results in appropriate "in house" and national peer-reviewed journals.

Most of the research studies that I carried out had to be done with cattle owned or purchased by the university farm, and most of these required two to four years to complete the data-collection phase. Each experiment farm had hired assistants who were basically farm or ranch hands whose jobs were to carry out the strict requirements of the studies. Because these assistants did not understand research and I could not hire a carefully trained technician due to budget constraints, I took a leadership role in the supervisory tasks to be sure they were done right. I enjoyed the extension part of my job when I could meet with a group of farmers, one-on-one, and explain how the research could help them make better livings. On the other hand, I was not fond of writing articles.

In my opinion, the most important focus of my research was on economic viability of various production practices. For example, our research showed that fattening beef steers was not feasible in the Deep South for most farmers; in other words, it showed several ways to lose money in that endeavor. Negative results like this, though hard to publish, are beneficial to farmers. By contrast, we documented procedures that farmers could adopt to make more money with cow-calf and stocker cattle production by combining forage production and utilization practices, along with strategic grain supplementation and improved cattle management practices. Additionally, my research demonstrated that a complete mixed ration utilizing least-cost analysis and the latest ruminant nutrition models could produce animal gains as cheaply as ryegrass pasture. I was able to obtain a grant to utilize rice straw for ruminants; for that I hired a post-doctorate who did the research on campus and published in peer-reviewed international journals. Had I not retired, the most significant research would have been on year-round, economically feasible production of fat cattle for freezer beef in south Mississippi utilizing corn grazing, high-quality forages, and least-cost complete mixed rations.

I will say that while I have mostly positive thoughts about my research and extension career, it did not end well. In the wisdom of the administration, a new position of facilities coordinator was created so that the scientists could focus on their research and not be concerned with the day-to-day running of the stations. In 2004 I inherited a facilities coordinator for the beef cattle operations who did not understand the reasons for strict research protocols. She was more interested in a showplace for cattle and had the ear of my boss, a horticulturist by training. Her only focus was on my number of refereed journal articles, which had been compromised by policy changes at the station, both inadvertent and purposeful. In essence, she demanded that I be more productive while at the same time eliminating the resources that I needed to meet the demand. I knew the handwriting was on the wall.

David getting ready to check on a MAFES research project.

The Mississippi Agricultural and Forestry Experiment Station (MAFES) where David worked for 23 years until his retirement.

One of a number of bulls David purchased for several demonstration/research projects with the Barzona brand that could thrive in the Mississippi heat (a synthetic breed with African and American beef bloodlines).

Barzona cows in one pasture at the White Sands farm owned by MAFES.

David—Where Did I End Up and How Did I Get There? / 309

Somchai (Chai) at the time of her wedding to David. 1967.

Chai's siblings at their home in Ban Kwao, Mahasarakham, Thailand, 1968. Peegoon, Nupat, Chai, Sunthorn, and David. Chai's sister, Supee, was not present for the photo.

Chai and siblings in Thailand, 2016: Peegoon, Sunthorn, Nupat, Supee, and Chai.

I would have retired early then in 2007, but I stuck it out because I needed to wait five years until I was 65 in order to qualify for Medicare.

My Family

I knew instinctively that someday I would likely get married and have children, not to say that I had a clear goal or desire to have a family. I never thought seriously about getting married until I met Chai while working for IVS in Laos. The IVS volunteers lived in apartments called bachelor officer quarters (BOQs) inside an American housing compound six kilometers north of Vientiane. Chai did housekeeping for most of the volunteers and a few other Americans who lived there. Johnny Cash's song "Ring of Fire" comes to mind: "I went down, down, down and the flames burned higher."

Chai and I were actually married three times. The first time was in a nondenominational church in Vientiane by an American missionary who conducted the wedding in both Lao and English. To me this is the only marriage that truly counted. However, in Laos, the marriage was not legal unless it was performed by the mayor of the village. The mayor came with us to the American Embassy and performed the ceremony after which the Embassy gave us a marriage license. Chai did not have a Thai passport, so, as we later began the paperwork for Chai's visa, we discovered that our marriage was not legal in Thailand. Therefore, we were obliged to have another marriage ceremony in Mahasarakham in order to get the necessary Thai marriage license.

I had an instant family! Prior to our marriage, Chai had given birth to Robert Pyboon. After we were married, I immediately adopted him. Our son, Benson Petsamon, and daughter, Lisa Surilak, were born within the next two years. All three children were delivered at the Filipino's Operation Brotherhood Hospital in Vientiane.

Lisa was born with a unilateral cleft lip and palate. When she was about a year old, we flew to Colorado where both her lip and palate surgeries were performed at the Denver Children's Hospital. At the end of my work in Laos, Chai and the kids returned with me to the US. Chai and Robert became US citizens; Benson and Lisa were already citizens since their births were recorded at the American Embassy.

The Sam Thong position with USAID was my first good paying job; however, it meant being away from home for two weeks at a time, which was not good for family life, especially for a new family. While I was gone, Chai and the young children lived in government housing in Vientiane for two years. While separated, our communication was by spotily relayed radio messages through the USAID network. And, because of these poor communications, I did not know about Benson's birth until after he was born. Fortunately, Chai was not alone as her sister or cousin was staying with her and Robert. I was home when Lisa was born, so she was the first of my children whom I saw at birth. After those first two years of our marriage, I was never gone for long periods of time.

Upon returning to the US and becoming a student at Cornell, I did work long hours, often leaving home early in the morning and coming home late at night. The one and a half years in Puerto Rico was a difficult time for Chai and the children because they did not speak Spanish. (I did not

Robert, Lisa, and Benson in junior high and high school in Blackville, South Carolina.

David—Where Did I End Up and How Did I Get There? / 311

speak it well, but I had taken a crash course at Cornell before we left.) We tried sending the children to the public school, but they were so unhappy because of the language barrier, we enrolled them in a private school that taught classes in English.

In Maryland and at the two university research stations, my offices were very close to our house such that I could walk or drive home every day for lunch. It was easy to be involved in the kids' extracurricular activities and sports; I attended the baseball and football games for the boys and the cheerleading for Lisa. However, since Chai and I are not avid sports fans, after the children graduated from high school, we have rarely attended football or baseball games.

Chai and I have returned to Thailand about every two to five years to see her family. In 2016, Benson and Lisa (along with Joseph and Jeff) accompanied us for their only visit back since we left in 1971.

In 1980, Chai was very seriously injured in a head-on collision when we lived in South Carolina. With her left leg bone essentially shattered above the knee, Chai was in the hospital with her leg in traction for three months followed by three more months in a cast at home. After that, she had to have one kidney removed and now suffers from stage III kidney disease. She developed rheumatoid arthritis causing pain throughout her body, especially hands and back. She has had stress fractures in her spine due to osteoporosis. Because of kidney disease, medications for arthritis and osteoporosis are extremely limited.

My Lifestyle

From the time I was a boy, I have always wanted to be self-sufficient. I subscribed to the Boy Scout magazine, *Boys Life*, and particularly liked reading about bush craft and things I could make to survive in the wilderness. A good example is a "survival kit" I made when I was about ten years old. I carved a small slingshot from a forked willow branch, and I wrapped the handle with fishing line. Dad said if you had a fishing line you could always catch fish and never go hungry. I never got a good rubber band for the slingshot or a leader for the fishing line, but I had a good start for my kit.

My lifestyle was pretty much determined by the places I worked for most of my career. In Maryland and South

David's childhood "survival kit," a fishline and a sling shot.

Carolina, we lived on site at the dehydrator mill or experimental farm; in Mississippi, we lived essentially next door to the farm and had a large acreage behind our house in a relatively small development. I wanted to save money wherever possible, so we heated with wood in South Carolina, did most of our own mechanical maintenance on the vehicles, and bought used cars. I had a small herd of cattle for a time, have raised chickens, built solar panels to save on our electric bills, and even experimented with making charcoal.

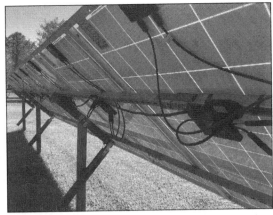

Underside of solar panels David built from scratch for his home in Mississippi.

I have always been aware of the cyclical nature of life, especially the life of farmers and ranchers. An overarching influence in my life derives from the fact that the seasons remind me what I need to do. On the ranch, spring meant repairing the fences, brushing the meadows, cleaning the ditches, lambing or calving. Summer meant branding or docking, getting the sheep or cattle on summer range, irrigating the meadows, and putting up hay. Fall dictated gathering the livestock and taking them to market. Winter meant repairing machinery, feeding hay, and managing animals during severe weather. And the next year, and the year after that, was the same cycle. In Laos and Thailand, the seasons were the rainy season and the dry season. The southern US experiment stations where I worked had the four seasons, but each one had its own necessary cycles. In hindsight, it is likely that without realizing it, because of the comfort afforded by the work cycles there, I was more drawn to the animal husbandry part of the life of the experiment stations than to writing up research results.

My International Experiences

Paraphrasing Seymour Martin Lipset's observation about the value of travel, "Those who know only one culture know no culture." I believe that one of my most significant achievements has been to learn and experience another culture, which has allowed me to know what it means to say, "I am proud to be an American."

When I was in college at Colorado State University, I was inspired by John F. Kennedy's statement "Ask not what your country can do for you. Ask

The office at Sam Thong, Laos.

Dirt airstrip at Sam Thong with a Helio airplane taking off.

Caribou airplane disabled after the left landing gear collapsed during landing.

what you can do for your country." With a forthcoming BS degree in animal science, I applied to the new Peace Corps as I was interested in going to Kenya to work with cattle. They did not respond for a long time, so I inquired at the university office where Peace Corps applications were received. Someone there suggested that I apply to IVS, which in fact had served as a model for the Peace Corps. I applied and was accepted within two weeks to go to Laos. Ironically, during a two-week, intensive language training in Lao, the Peace Corps did accept me as well, but I was already committed.

Once in country, I quickly learned to speak Lao, and immersed myself in the Lao culture. I extended my immersion with the Hmong culture in Sam Thong. It is important to remember that all of my stay in Laos was during the Vietnam War, which had spread to Laos. The famous or infamous Ho Chi Minh Trail, wherein the North Vietnamese moved soldiers, weapons, and materiel to South Vietnam, went through Laos, which bordered both North and South Vietnam to the west. The Ho Chi Minh Trail was bombed incessantly first by regular US Air Force B-52 bombers and later by the CIA's secret air force, "The Ravens." Air America contracted with the CIA to mostly deliver "hard rice" (ammunition and weapons) to Hmong soldiers on the ground. Suffice to say, living in Laos at that time was dangerous for Americans. Before I could take this job, I had to be granted top secret security clearance. I saw many things I could not talk about, but never knew exactly what was going on. I can say, however, some of those CIA men were nuts. For what really went on, I recommend reading the book *Shooting at the Moon*, an exposé by former CIA operative Roger Warner.

Long Tieng (LS20A) was the headquarters of the covert paramilitary operations of the Central Intelligence Agency (CIA) in northern Laos. It was situated just south of the Plain of Jars (Plaine des Jarres in French). The L in LS20A denoted one of the "Lima Sites" that had unimproved air strips and was meant for outsiders to believe it to be the same as Sam Thong (LS20). As noted, I would fly back to Vientiane to see my family about every two weeks. Sam Thong had a small two-level dirt runway on a ridge and was long enough to land a two-engine de Havilland Caribou aircraft. This small cargo plane brought fuel and supplies for this center of operation for refugee resettlement in northern Laos. Small airplanes (Helio and de Havilland Porter) and helicopters (H34) shuttled back and forth among about 50 refugee villages. The CIA secretly owned Air America, which contracted with USAID for all air operations. The Air America pilots were not happy with the smell of pigs, chickens, or ducks and their manure in their planes, although I thought it smelled better than when local passengers vomited in the plane. The farm where the animals were taken belonged to General Vang Pao and was about two miles downstream from Long Tieng. Nearly all the workers at the farm were sons of Nai Khong (the Hmong chief I worked with) as he had three wives.

Fast forward 25 years. While working for Mississippi State, I took a six-month sabbatical leave to Sakon Nakhon, Thailand. There I initiated research at the Sakon Nakhon Agricultural Research and Training Center (SARTC) on fattening of beef cattle. I trained SARTC staff in computer applications to beef and dairy research and production as well as consulted on the management and operation of the station beef, dairy, and forage operations and how it relates to economics of farming. Other international experiences, before retiring from Mississippi State University, were two-week voluntary assignments for Winrock International in their Farmer-to-Farmer program. These involved training farmers in Nicaragua to fatten beef cattle; training farmers in El Salvador in dairy cattle nutrition (two assignments); training farmers, extension workers, and feed manufacturers in feed quality for ruminants (beef, dairy, sheep, and goats) in Mali (two assignments); and training farmers in Ethiopia and Bangladesh in dairy cattle nutrition (one assignment each).

After retiring, based on the work I had done on my sabbatical in Thailand, I arranged to work as a research and extension advisor in animal science at two Thai universities—six months at Mae Jo University in Chiang Mai and nine months at Kasesart University in Khampaengsan. It

David listening at a dairy training seminar in Bangladesh organized by the Winrock Foundation.

David in Ethiopia demonstrating how to determine the condition (fatness) of beef cattle. The interpreter is on the right.

Farmers in Mali being trained to use urea to aid in forage digestibility for goats.

A cattle market in Mali.

was during these experiences that I learned to speak understandable Thai, which, though similar to Lao, has many differences. All told, I have been to 22 countries, living for two weeks in five of them and more than one year in three.

My Religion

At a very early age I knew God was with me. Once when we were knocking down swallow nests at the ranch, we were hilariously laughing at every curse word we could think of. It was hilarious until Mom came out. She said, "I may not know what you're doing all of the time, but God does." That stuck with me, not just mentally or fearfully, but that His presence was always with me. We went once in a while to the Episcopal Church in Dixon or a service at the Temple Ranch, and we had had Bible study sporadically at the Battle Creek schoolhouse, but I don't think I felt God's presence with me at those times. I remember thinking I wish I could talk to God and at other times I wished I knew how to pray. Prayer books did not seem to help. Looking back on it now, in those thoughts and wishes, I know God was listening, and He knew what I wanted. When I took the vows to join the Methodist Church in Steamboat Springs, I experienced a spiritual experience like nothing I had felt before.

At Colorado State University, Kenneth and I occasionally attended the Methodist church. The students in Wesley Foundation really turned me off with their know-it-all attitudes, so I stopped going. Several times, Farm-House fraternity went as a group to the Presbyterian Church. Those were the only times I felt the preacher was talking to me. Toward the end of college, I said to myself, "I am tired of trying to do right all the time." After that, a fraternity brother and I went to a movie with a bottle of whiskey and got drunk inside the theater.

Immediately after college, in Laos, I attended an American community church service in Vientiane a few times. Being a Christian and trying to immerse myself in the Lao culture at the same time did not seem to be a problem except when going into a Buddhist temple. Doing so made me uncomfortable as if my Christianity might become polluted. I came to know two men who both were strong Christians and missionaries. One, with a Baptist background and whose last name was Smith, was affiliated with Church World Services. He married Chai and me in both English and Lao. The other was Father Bouchard, a Catholic priest who worked out of Sam Thong and traveled everywhere on foot. He had been in Laos a long time, and all the locals knew and respected him. He had small congregations of converts on both sides of enemy lines and spoke a large number of the minority languages. I remember his taking medicine and supplies to a leper colony hidden away in the mountains where no one else went.

When we moved back to the States, I began attending the Methodist church in Newfield, New York. Even though Chai was Buddhist, I wanted the children to get a Christian education and thus encouraged them to go to Sunday school. Chai had no objection; in fact, she and I would join the kids after Sunday school for an hour of worship. I would drop the kids off for Sunday school and drive back home to get ready for church. One day it hit me like a ton of bricks, "There is something wrong with this." I decided to begin attending Sunday school as well. In our class of young adults, we took turns each Sunday leading the lesson. When my turn finally came, we were to study John, Chapter 3. Preparing and leading the discussion for that Sunday was another turning-point spiritual experience.

For about three years, we did not attend church because I could not find a church that suited me in Puerto Rico or Maryland. However, after moving to South Carolina, I began to grow as a Christian in the local Presbyterian Church, where I became a member. I volunteered to work on committees but would not commit to becoming a deacon. Chai joined as well. She had experienced a spiritual awakening and decided to become a Christian after the long hospitalization and recovery from the serious automobile accident that left her with a shattered leg and lots of internal injuries. When we moved to Mississippi, I visited a number of churches in Poplarville, but when I walked into the Ruth Memorial Presbyterian Church, I knew I was home. I have since become a Presbyterian deacon and elder. Our church had been without a permanent pastor since 1965, so different preachers came to deliver sermons. We celebrated the Lord's Supper once or twice a year when we had a Presbyterian minister. Sometimes we could not find anybody to preach, so the elders committed to delivering a sermon once or twice a year if needed. For these reasons, when a class was offered, I took a yearlong course to become a Commissioned Lay Minister so I could improve my preaching skills and do the sacraments. Since then, I have been invited to preach in Presbyterian churches in the area when their pastors are absent.

A good friend encouraged me to join the Gideons International. I resisted for a long time. He said to let him know any Sunday we did not have a preacher, and he could have a Gideon fill in for us. I was impressed! A local Gideon gave an excellent message, and other Gideons came to support him. The Gideons hold an annual pastors' appreciation banquet to acknowledge the efforts of pastors from all the local churches. Since Ruth Presbyterian did not have a pastor, I was invited and thought I needed to go to represent our church in the community, perhaps needing to vote on something. The purpose was only for pastor appreciation, and there was no voting. Although impressed, I was reluctant to join because I had no interest in joining any organization, such as the Lions or Kiwanis, just to look good or to pad my resumé. If I joined, I planned to work. After attending Gideon meetings for several years, I did decide to join. My experience with them has accelerated my growth as a Christian. I have never prayed so much in my life, with a prayer breakfast every Saturday morning. I have qualified to speak in churches and become friends with people and pastors from all denominations. I have come to better understand the core values of a Christian.

In 2015 I was in the intensive care unit after a laproscopic repair of acute appendicitis failed, and I quickly suffered sepsis. (To me, that means a septic tank has been dumped into your belly!) One of my Gideon brothers is the coroner. He came to visit me in the ICU where the nurses knew him. They asked him what he was doing there, and he said he had just come to visit me since he had to pick up a body on the seventh floor. They pointed to me and told my friend, "You can come pick him up tomorrow." I don't remember how many days I was in ICU, as I drifted in and out of consciousness, possibly in a medically-induced coma. I do know that I had excruciating pain in my whole body every time I awoke. The nurses would give me an injection for pain, and I would go back to sleep or lapse into unconsciousness. I remember telling them to stop giving me morphine because I was having weird hallucinations. It seemed I was connected to every medical gadget imaginable—a ventilator, intravenous feeding and hydration, and kidney dialysis through a cerebral artery and vein. I remember the nurses' having problems keeping all the tubes and wires untangled. Suffice to say, recovery was very long and difficult.

What does all this have to do with my religion? In ICU, while drifting among coma, sleep, and consciousness, I had a vision. I know it was not a dream because this was much different, and I can remember everything clearly. In my vision I was in a huge vat up to my neck in a black foamy liquid. It was pulling me down and backward. I knew that if nothing changed, I would die. I was anxious but not fearful, wondering what it felt like to die. While wondering, I saw something like a three-prong pitchfork emerge very, very slowly out of this black stuff. On the tip of each tine appeared bright, shiny heart-shaped, silver arrowheads that were sharper than any razor blade. The center tine was above the other two, and they shined as if they had a light of their own. Slowly, more and more of these pitchforks arose around me. Suddenly I knew, "I am not going to die!" and I was no longer being pulled down. I knew that I did not have enough strength or power on my own to make this happen. I was wondering where this power came from when it dawned on me that it was coming from these pitchforks. It took me a while to realize that the power in these pitchforks was coming from others' prayers. I know now that if it was not for the power of prayer, I would be a dead man. I know that God could have taken me if he wished, but he wanted me to live a while longer for some mission He has for me. Every day since then I wonder why He wants me alive and what His mission is for me.

David—Where Did I End Up and How Did I Get There? / 319

That experience determined, in part, how I have lived my life since. I ran across a quote at the beginning of the COVID-19 shut-down that rings true to my heart. It says, "Fear does not stop death, it stops life. And worrying does not take away tomorrow's troubles. It takes away today's peace." I believe that God has always provided the fullness and power that He desires for me, even though I did not realize it until recently. It has always been more power than I desire. He provided and created situations for me to fall or step into, whether it was my desire or not. The constant challenge has been for "me" to get out of the way of what He wants to do with me.

To summarize my faith journey, "God leads the way. I must simply step into it and not back off." Another way of saying it is, "By the grace of God, I am what I am."

My Entrepreneurial Efforts

As a child, I heard Dad talk about this or that person being or becoming a "millionaire." He often dreamed of that for himself and for our family as well. He would get a pencil, sharpen it perfectly with his pocket knife, and then start "figuring." This would involve what he would pay for a steer, a cow, or a ewe, how much it would cost for hay or grain, and what the expenses would be for transportation, shipping, and so on. After selling the animals, the profit he would figure always showed what a good deal buying the cattle or sheep might be. Of course, with one or two rare exceptions, it never did work out that way. Dad would also talk about becoming a millionaire from minerals. He prospected for copper, molybdenum, and uranium. As I explained in a Chapter 7 memory, he could have become rich once when he and Lewis Morgan staked uranium claims west of Baggs. Another missed opportunity to be a millionaire was failing to buy Granddad's property in Steamboat Springs, which ended up as the location of dozens of condominiums. In that possibility, he did a lot of figuring and said, "You can't pay off forty dollars per acre with cows."

Dad also talked a lot about "making a living." This was also about money, the amount one would need to run a ranch at sufficient profit to have enough for all the necessities of life as well as enough for modest luxuries once in a while. He sold the ranch after figuring because he said, "You have to get bigger or get out. I can't get anyone around here to sell to me."

From these stories and influences, as a boy, I suppose that I wanted to be rich or at least to have no financial worries when I grew up. It was partly for that reason that Dad and Mom wanted us to go to college, for they believed that this would be the best way for us to make a better living than they could. After I became an adult, I realized that becoming rich was not the best goal. I was already rich in so many ways. Even so, I continued to focus on making a better living and studied some economic theories and influences. I earned a lot of money (compared to what I had earned earlier in life) in Laos working for USAID, and I invested that money in mutual funds. I used those mutual funds as collateral to finance our first house in Newfield. It was a four-apartment house wherein we lived in one apartment and rented the other three to pay the mortgage. Even though I broke even financially when I sold the apartment house, my "profit" was being able to live rent free for six years. I spent a few years as an Amway salesman and distributor, but that did not make as much income as I had hoped. When my children were about to enter college, I was sure they would need student loans. For them to qualify, I could not have too much money. Therefore, when we moved to Mississippi, I bought cattle with our savings, which did not count in the applications. When I needed money, I sold a cow. For the pasture, I leased 40 acres adjacent to our home. The landowner decided not to renew my year-to-year lease so he could start a housing development. That did not happen, and the property now is a jungle. I rented other pastureland in other locations, but no one would give me a long-term lease. Eventually, I sold the cows because I was tired of building fences and corrals for other people. I was lucky to sell when the prices were high, but it did no good because the stockyard was caught "kiting" checks and, after the courts got involved, I did not get paid all I was owed.

I gambled with leveraged positions in various markets (such as futures and stocks) and was doing okay until the 2008 crash when I was on our Continental Divide pack trip without communications. I could not know what was happening in order to liquidate my positions to prevent margin calls and further losses. I don't leverage investments today because of too much market rigging by large institutions who are experts at fleecing small investors. The only investment I consider as a gamble (with no leverage) is crypto currency. My one gold mining stock is not much of a gamble and should do well.

I have tried to make money through various real estate investments over the years. In addition to the house in Newfield, New York, I purchased 80 acres of pine trees in South Carolina where, after selling, I essentially broke even. Then, starting in 2007 I bought 43 lots of tax forfeited land near Poplarville, Mississippi. Because of the 2008 downturn in real estate, I still have

Chai feeding cows behind their home in Poplarville.

Poplarville home at Howard Heights before Hurricane Katrina.

22 lots as of July 2020. It is possible, but not a sure thing, that I will eventually break even with these.

Living with Only My Right Arm and Hand

The accident that paralyzed my left arm, which was eventually amputated and replaced with a "hook" prosthesis, as explained in Chapter 12, was the major turning point in my life. Yet, learning to live well with one arm was one of my most important life achievements. I decided very shortly after I recovered from the accident that, as far as I was able, I was going to do everything everyone else could do with two hands. And I was going to do it better! That may have been unrealistic to most people, but for the most part, I succeeded.

All of this required ingenuity, and I constantly thought of alternative ways to do things. I learned to halter, saddle, mount, and ride a horse with one hand. I learned to open and close barbed wire gates with one arm. I learned to drive a car and truck, plus operate a tractor, forklift, road grader, combine, forage cutter, and wind rower. I could fly an airplane if I had to, but the landing might be a little rough. I have trouble with skid steer loaders. With my prosthesis, I can worm or snell a fishhook, tie my shoes, operate a chainsaw, and castrate a calf. In a fistfight, I followed Dad's advice to get in the first blow as hard as I can. In rodeos I was bucked off of bareback broncs, saddle broncs, and bulls. I did complete one really good bareback ride, but I didn't win any money. I could ski cross-country and downhill, including climbing a mountain on skis. I could change brakes in a car or rebuild a transmission. As an older adult, I even decided I did not need to wear a clip-on tie, so I learned to tie a long one.

I tried and failed to be an acceptable basketball player in high school, and I was embarrassed. Yet, I determined not to be self-conscious, and to prove it to myself and others, I went into student government activities, which continued into college. And I did well at it.

My Social Interactions with Others

I always seemed to have an innate ability to figure people out. By that I mean, like Mom, I could size people up fairly quickly and know how to interact with them. I learned how to get along with almost anybody and have used this ability most of my life both for entertainment and for serious business. As a kid, I could almost always get Kenneth, sometimes Rita, and usually Lillyan to react in certain ways if I set them up. As I wrote in a memory in Chapter 9, I put cow manure in a little hole in the darkest part of the woodshed and told Lillyan not to dare touch what I put in the hole.

David getting ready for a local social event.

Of course, that is exactly what she did and became raging mad. Of course, I could say I told her not to do it, and it was her fault for doing it anyway. In similar ways I can often say something that seems outrageous and get someone to disagree. Then I challenge them to a bet knowing I will win. Those who know me seldom bet against me.

On the serious side, I have learned to follow an anonymous quote: "Do not argue with a fool because bystanders do not know which one is the fool." On the other hand, if I know someone who has a strong bias, I enjoy "jerking their chain." I have a strong belief that no one should take themselves too seriously. They are my favorite targets and social media works well for this. For some outrageous Facebook quote I say, "Does anybody still believe this?" I disarm them before they react, and I do not have to declare my side on the issue.

I like to perform, and I have found that most people like my performances. I learned a fairly convincing Scottish accent for some songs I often sing a cappella at social events, very much like Dad and Grandpa did. I also learned songs and monologues that both of them used to entertain at family and community events. I see the light side of things, so I like to tell and hear jokes and stories. In fact, I have honed my ability to tell stories in the Poplarville Storytellers Guild, where we meet and refine both new and past stories. Two stories I have told many times relate to our childhood: the moving of the schoolhouse and how I learned what it felt like to fly when my horse stepped in a hole while running at full speed down a steep hill. "... After the launch I soared like a kite, or like a ski jumper, as I sailed down the hill until the tops of the sagebrush slowed me down to a safe, un-scratched landing...."

My Personal Happiness

I did not particularly expect happiness in my life. But, on the whole, I have been happy and have taken life as it came to me without expecting something different. When people have high expectations, like Kenneth does, they set themselves up for disappointment. When thinking of times when I am the happiest, they are usually when I am doing something adventurous. The most unhappy were the several years before I retired where the stress of my job affected my health.

My Disappointments

I cannot say that I have disappointments in my family and career. I have regrets that some situations could have turned out better. I know the many mistakes I have made, many of them forgotten. But even knowing some of my mistakes, I would probably do them over again given the same circumstances.

HOW DID I GET THERE?

Characteristics and Values from Childhood and School

Conscious Decision to Accept Life as It Comes

My philosophy is that if you can't do anything about a situation, then there is no use worrying about it. So, for that reason, I don't get overly stressed about anything. I suppose that if I stressed more about getting things done, I would have achieved more in my life, but I am satisfied with what I have done.

Being Independent and Making My Own Decisions

Since early childhood, I have been a very independent person. I also believe that people should take care of themselves. This tendency has got me in trouble in my life in that some people who are dependent have found me overbearing.

Having What I Call "A Mean Streak"

I have always liked to test people and even make them uncomfortable, especially if I think they are taking themselves too seriously. Kenneth says I like to "agitate." I also have always had a tendency not to change my mind easily about something I have thought about or feel strongly about. Mom said she finally had to accept when I was very young that I would have the "last word" even if it meant I would be punished for it. Maybe it means, like the old cigarette advertisement said, "I'd rather fight than switch."

Wanting to Get Closure on Things

I think logically about things, but I don't like to over-think things. When a decision has to be made, I look at the facts as I see them and make the decision. There is no way of knowing until after the fact if it was the best decision. So, after making a decision, I have no regrets. I probably have some blind spots when I think I have dealt long enough with a situation, but other people disagree. One example was when I was the guide for Kenneth, Rita, and John in Thailand. I did not feel like translating Thai conversations as much as they wanted because, in my opinion, it would take too long and was not necessary for them to understand the entire context.

TURNING POINTS

Following is a list of 12 influences, in hindsight and arranged from most to least powerful, which I believe served as major turning points in my life journey.

- Losing the use of my left arm and hand
- Experiencing a new culture in Laos and the Vietnam War first-hand for six years
- Marrying Chai from Thailand and raising a family
- Experiencing Dad's death and realizing his influence on my life
- Realizing that my life's goal was to help farmers make a better living

- Deciding to choose agriculture with animal science as a major

- Deciding to go to graduate school after taking a six-year break from school

- Being ordained as an elder in the Presbyterian Church and being a member of Gideons International

- Spiritual experience in ICU from appendicitis

- Accepting life as it comes

- Working at two university research station jobs and subsequent consulting work

- Assuming the role of caretaker for Chai

Chapter 16

Kenneth—Where Did I End Up and How Did I Get There?

KENNETH: WHERE I ENDED UP

My Achievements

Peace Corps

I applied for and was accepted to become a Peace Corps Volunteer, and soon after college I spent nearly two years working in rural community development in Turkey. Members of our group were assigned in male-female pairs to rural villages in western and central Turkey with the goal of helping the villages align their perceived needs with their real needs (as determined by local government officials), and then to assist them in best making that happen. The idea was that the female volunteers could work with the women, and the male volunteers could work with the men since unmarried men and women did not have much interaction in the conservative Muslim society otherwise. It did not work well and was extremely difficult for the women volunteers; they were essentially a "third sex." My site partner left the village for a city job after about five months and then left the country a few months later. In fact, about half of our group left after the first year. Basically, we did what we thought we could achieve. I was one year in the Black Sea province of Bolu in a very poor village and the second year in a more progressive village in the Aegean region in the province of Denizli, very near the touristic site of Pamukkale. In Bolu, I worked with government officials to try (unsuccessfully) to get villagers to enclose or "sanitize" their human waste, which came down a chute to the ground from a hole in the boards of the second floor of their houses. I also tried to persuade them (with limited, and much later, success) to switch from less than subsistence farming of wheat raising to a cash crop of potatoes. I also did a fair amount of first aid (with my handy-dandy Peace Corps medical kit) and helped with a small tree-planting project. In Denizli, ostensibly I was to work with a USAID project of raising a Mexican variety of high-yield wheat that would be resistant to "lodging," or growing up and then falling over from the weight of the grain such that the wheat would rot on the ground. I never worked in this project, but it was a dismal failure. The wheat lodged anyway! Instead, I pursued poultry raising and persuaded two villagers to carry out demonstration chicken projects in the village, wherein hybrid chicks were purchased, raised separately in fenced yards and ventilated coops, and then sold for meat at restaurants in Denizli. Vaccination against Newcastle's Disease was key to the success as most of the other chickens running around the village carried the disease. For a short stint in Bolu, I taught English to middle school students in a nearby town, and in Denizli, I held a regular English class at a local textile factory and with a village school teacher (who later emigrated to Australia).

A summary of my Peace Corps experience would not be complete without pointing out that the fluency I had acquired at CSU disintegrated while learning Turkish in our months of training. While speaking Turkish—but not English—for the entire two years I was in the Turkey, my stuttering returned. Sometimes, it was as bad as ever; other times, I was completely fluent. I persevered despite my stuttering, but it was arguably the hardest obstacle I had to overcome during my assignment. My previous fluency returned when I came home and spoke only English.

In all of this, I discovered that I could not only survive in the Peace Corps, as many of our group did not, but even succeed. My Peace Corps experience, which involved living and working in a foreign land with another dominant religion (Islam) and at the same time learning their language, dramatically changed my life. It taught me that people are essentially the same around the world and that we are all global citizens. I tell people that "Turkey is my second country." I have gone back there almost every year since 2006, and each visit renews me. Moreover, we have had 11 Turks (all practicing or nonpracticing Muslims) come and stay at our home for at least three weeks in the past decade.

My Career

My life career goal, which I adopted at the University of Wyoming Speech Clinic in the summer after my junior year of high school at the age of 16,

Arriving in Ankara, Turkey, with the Turkey X ("Ten") group of rural community development volunteers, 1966. Kenneth is second from the left in the front; his future site partner, Margo Jones, is next to him on the right.

Istanbul. Suleymaniye Mosque.

Istanbul. The Egyptian or Spice Bazaar.

Istanbul. Ferryboat and rowboats in the Bosphorus.

Kenneth—Where Did I End Up and How Did I Get There? / 329

A winter view of Kenneth's first village in the province of Bolu in the Black Sea region of Turkey.

Sitting on logs cut for firewood.

Photo of a Bolu villager and her son, whom she would send to her husband working in Germany. She placed her gold dowry on the boy.

Kenneth's second village in the province of Denizli near Pamukkale in the Aegean region of Turkey. Talking with a villager about chickens.

Kenneth giving his only speech in Turkish at the Children's Holiday.

Sitting on one of the travertines of Pamukkale.

was to solve the problem of stuttering. This had been my first real speech therapy experience, and it was dramatically successful in eliminating my stuttering, at least in the short run. As I have said and written many times, my goal was incredibly unrealistic, perhaps as unrealistic as completely understanding how the human brain works. Even so, most of my professional choices and a fair number of my personal choices were made with that goal in mind. As soon as I began to learn about stuttering, I long ago abandoned the desire to "solve the problem" of stuttering. But I have tried to improve the lives of those of us who stutter in any way that I could.

The only option I was aware of to work with stuttering was to do a PhD and become a university professor. I started as an assistant professor of speech-language pathology at the State University of New York (SUNY) at Plattsburgh for three years and then moved to West Virginia University, where I continued my career for 42 years, coming up through the ranks of assistant, associate and full professor. I retired in 2018 as an emeritus professor. Tenure-track faculty in my department are expected to do teaching, research, and service. I worked hard on all three of these job components for 45 years. And over the years, I was approved for five sabbatical leaves, including one at the University of New South Wales in Australia.

Mary Weidner and Kenneth at an American Speech-Language-Hearing Association's Annual Convention.

Increasingly, I focused on research. In my last six to eight years, I was able to reduce my nine-month teaching load to two or three courses per year. I did not work in the summers for a salary except for a few years. Seven years ago, I took on our department's first PhD student, Mary Weidner, a bright, competent, principled, charming, and extremely hard-working young woman. Getting her through the program in three years was among my most important and lasting achievements. I experienced, in the first and only time I took on this role, the incredible and rare satisfaction of sharing what I have learned as a mentor and watching a mentee grow into a valued colleague and friend.

Why did I focus on stuttering? Why not continue and improve the ranching business? Why not become a doctor, as Mom suggested at one point? Why not become a first-rate engineer, which is what I, like several of my high school classmates, had thought we would do? For me the answer is so obvious that it almost begs the need for an explanation. The reason was that I knew first-hand the suffering that can come from stuttering, and I had felt first-hand the freedom of fluency. Was this a good reason? Perhaps. Perhaps not. I had a caustic but brilliant professor who remarked that most of those who go into psychology are "screwed up." Those who become normal get out of psychology, leaving only those who are hopelessly disturbed as the helpers in that field. I would hope, at least, and I believe many would support me in this thought, that I have not let my own "issues" negatively affect my efforts to improve the lives of stutterers in my teaching, in my interaction with children and adults who stutter or their parents in therapy or self-help/support groups, or in my research.

Every stutterer is different, and every stuttering pattern is different. The glue that holds us together is the feeling of not being able to say what we know very well how to say and the repetitions, prolongations, and blocks that result from that. In mine and so many other cases, stuttering did not go away in childhood. Instead, it progressed and became associated with fears of certain speaking situations, certain listeners, and a host of "tricks" adopted allegedly to get through the stoppages. And over time, we came to see ourselves, to a greater or lesser degree, as "less than," as handicapped, as "not able to reach our God-given potentials." I have essentially recovered from stuttering. Yet, even though mostly stutter-free, I have always hated to make telephone calls to businesses, strangers, and so on. I am most likely to stutter on the phone but, even when I do not, I dislike calling all but close friends and family.

I wanted my students to understand this problem so well that they would eschew the "quick fix" approaches out there that simply distract the stutterer and generate temporary fluency. I wanted my clients—or the clients my students were assigned under my supervision—to get the best care, the best advice, the best understanding available. For that reason, I was a "hard ass" as a professor. I believe that there are no short cuts to being competent as a clinician. It takes intelligence, empathy, honesty, hard work, and perseverance coupled with solid information and knowledge.

Teaching initially energized me; I was eager to share my quite extensive knowledge with students. But my enthusiasm diminished over the years because I repeatedly had the experience that my students and colleagues nearly always liked me initially but all too often later turned less positive. I have had a very difficult time accepting the fact that I have not been widely regarded as a popular teacher. This was exacerbated over the years by our faculty's equating being a "good teacher" (which I strongly believe that I was) with a "popular teacher," defined as one who received virtually all "excellent" ratings on written post-course evaluations. The worst things that happened to me professionally were being ostracized and penalized for speaking the truth to colleagues about a hopelessly weak student and for supporting another teaching colleague who was being harassed for speaking the truth about a group of vindictive students to the point he left the university. By contrast, I was always regarded as a supportive, helpful clinical supervisor of graduate students doing speech therapy with various clients.

Aside from how my colleagues thought about it, for the long haul of life, I have always held that being a competent clinician or teacher takes the kind of ongoing curiosity and mental flexibility to be able to admit that what we did or what we taught was not necessarily correct—or just plain wrong—and after that to adopt entirely new approaches supported by research. So many of my excellent students and so many of my esteemed colleagues first learned brilliantly with open minds but then spent the rest of their lives justifying why what they learned were the only or best facts or approaches available. As a high school senior, my classmates and I were asked to come up with a motto for ourselves to accompany our senior picture in the annual yearbook. I don't remember where I saw it or why I adopted it, but mine was, "Minds are like parachutes; they only function when open." I must have been subliminally aware of one of my driving motivations at that young age.

As I reflect on my career, more than anything, I wanted to be a researcher. As tedious and frustrating as it can be—and often is—I have always been energized by searching for new understandings, undiscovered relationships, or novel results in a set of data. And when one emerges, it might be analogous to the thrill of finding a gold nugget in a river of gravel.

The year I left the Peace Corps, my first yearlong job materialized almost accidentally after being rejected to for the draft to go to Vietnam in the Army (see below). After traveling to Fort Collins to visit a former professor, I was offered a position to work on one of six traveling survey teams whose mission it was to determine the prevalence of speech and hearing disorders in the US public schools. I immediately accepted and worked on the National

The East Coast team: Krisan Fluckey, Sybil Piersma, Kenneth, and Bonnie Stenzel Legg.

Getting ready to test a child for speech in one of the three rooms in the van.

Our team's custom-built van for testing speech and hearing as part of the National Speech and Hearing Survey in 1968–1969. Six teams tested 39,000 children.

Speech and Hearing Survey from mid-1968 to mid-1969. Our task was data collection only, but I thrived on it.

For many years, I was not sure I was good enough to compete with the top-notch researchers in my field. I tried many times to get large research grants, but I never succeeded, partly because I chose to investigate what I wanted to investigate rather than areas where funding was more plentiful. So, I worked on studies that did not require grant funding, and after a slow start, I began to publish regularly.

I have made significant contributions in a number of areas: documenting and reducing negative attitudes or stigma toward stuttering, bringing a related fluency disorder known as "cluttering" into the mainstream of speech-language pathology, understanding the power of individual stories of stutterers in teaching and self-help, exploring the coexistence of many speech and language disorders, and developing several widely-used diagnostic or assessment measures used by speech-language pathologists. The last two decades of my career, and indeed the amount of life energy spent, were overwhelmingly determined by research into public

Just a few of the many international partners who collected public attitude data using the Public Opinion Survey of Human Attributes–Stuttering (POSHA–S).

attitudes toward stuttering. I developed an instrument to measure public attitudes worldwide, and it caught on successfully beyond my wildest dreams. I have permitted researchers and students around the world to use it for free in exchange for their sending me their raw data to build a database. With more than 300 samples from 45 countries and translations to 30 different languages representing more than 35,000 respondents, I have developed the only database that can be used to accurately compare attitudes around the world. And even though I am retired, I am still involved with about 50 ongoing, national or international projects. I am proud of the mentoring I have been able to do with hundreds of colleagues around the world, many of them students or new academics, and it also meshes perfectly with my desire to be a global citizen.

As a researcher, I feel like I retired near the top of my game. It can be said that successful people fail more than those who are failures, regardless of their field. I have failed and been rejected many, many times. Quantity does not equal quality in research, but I believe I have achieved a respectable degree of both. I have authored or coauthored more than 200 journal articles, chapters, monographs, or books, almost all peer-reviewed, as well as almost 350 peer-reviewed or invited professional presentations, about 75 invited workshops or lectures, and more than 50 unpublished studies. I was recognized as a Benedum Distinguished Scholar at WVU in 1999 (with a single award in the area of social and behavioral sciences given each year), and actually did more work of greater importance after that. Among the awards I have received outside the university include the Lifetime Achievement Award from the International Fluency Association in 2015, first Deso Weiss Award for Excellence in the Field of Cluttering in 2007, and an honorary doctorate from SouthWest University Neofit Rilski in Bulgaria.

I'd like to think that more important to me than the "numbers" is the recognition and respect of my colleagues. In the more than 100 professional conferences I have attended, at nearly all of which I also presented papers, I have come to understand that the hugs, the conversations, and the discussions at these conferences are extremely important in keeping me going, probably because my colleagues remind me that my work means something.

My Family

Karen and I met in our yearlong master's program at the University of Michigan. Although I dated a good bit during the first two-thirds of that year, we settled into a serious relationship and got engaged before leaving Ann Arbor. We moved to Minneapolis for me to pursue a PhD, and Karen got a speech-language pathology job at the University of Minnesota Hospital. We were married at the end of the first semester at the University of Denver chapel by my former Wesley Foundation pastor, Robert Hunter. We lived in Minneapolis for the remainder of my three years at the University of Minnesota and then moved to Plattsburgh, New York, for three years. Karen took a job in a local school district, and I worked at SUNY, doing everything from teaching, clinical supervision, scheduling, and even answering the phone. I had to get my necessary clinical certification at the same time because I had never worked only as a clinical speech-language pathologist. I did my so-called "clinical fellowship" part-time at the maximum-security state prison nearby in Dannemora, New York. Melinda was born during our last year at Plattsburgh.

Having been trained in two first-rate research institutions, I wanted release time to do more research. I therefore sought a position in good-sized universities located in small cities. I was offered a job at the University of Northern Iowa and West Virginia University and accepted the latter.

Delivering an invited lecture at West Virginia University upon receiving the Benedum Distinguished Scholar Award, 1999.

Receiving an honorary doctorate from SouthWest University (Neofit Rilski) in Blagoevgrad, Bulgaria, with nominator Dobrinka Georgieva and a university official, 2003.

After his keynote address, Kenneth posing with colleagues at the Third International Conference on Stuttering in Rome, Italy, 2018. Kenneth, Selma Saad Merouwe (Lebanon), Katarzyna Węsierska (Poland), Kurt Eggers (Belgium), and Joseph Agius (Malta).

Standing in front of a poster at an annual convention of the American Speech-Language-Hearing Association with Rhonda Walker and Robert Mayo, 2014.

Kenneth—Where Did I End Up and How Did I Get There?   / 337

Posing in front of DILKOM (Speech and Language Disorders Training, Research, and Information Center) at Anadolu University in Eskişehir, Turkey, 2014. Kenneth arranged a study abroad experience for five West Virginia University students, and Rita accompanied us. Back: Rita, Müge Tunçer, Elçin Tadıhan, Ali İhsan Kısıkkaya [mostly hidden], Sertan Özdemir, and Semra Selvi. front: Merve Nur Sarıyer, Seyhun Topbaş, Kenneth, Ashley Houchin, Tia Mancini, Bridget Bellardini, Olesya Egelova, Taylor Kieffer, Mary Weidner, and İlknur Maviş.

Celebrating after a conference at Medipol University in Istanbul, Turkey, 2019. Eda Uzuner, Merve Biçer, Safiye Tekkeli, Seyhun Topbaş, Kenneth, Evra Günhan Şenol, and Sertan Özdemir.

Kenneth and Rae Jean at home in the kitchen.

Rae Jean and Kenneth outside on the day of their wedding, 1994.

In 1976, after selling our house in Morrisonville, New York, we moved to the Morgantown area. We bought a small farm in Gladesville. We lived there for two years but soon began looking for something closer to Morgantown. In 1978, we sold our Gladesville farm and bought another farm near Cassville. The next year, we sold the house and a lot to Ron and Suzanne Smart, who have continued as next-door neighbors to the present. We built a new log house on our property nearby. Melinda rode the bus to kindergarten and first grade in the aging Cassville elementary school that was eventually closed due to mine subsidence damage. We then transported her ourselves to excellent elementary and middle schools in Morgantown.

Karen and I separated during Melinda's middle school years and eventually divorced. After two years, Karen moved to Pittsburgh, and Melinda moved there to attend high school, coming back regularly to the log home in a joint custody arrangement. I met and eventually became a partner with a woman from Fairmont, Margaret (Peg) Wolfe. We lived together for about five years.

After that relationship ended, and I lived alone at the Cassville farm, Rae Jean came into my life. We had previously met at a speech-language-hearing conference in the city of St. Louis because Rae Jean had been a former tenant of Rita and Hugh in Seattle, where she had been a speech and hearing student at the University of Washington. I called her in 1993 on the day of a horrendous blizzard in West Virginia. This began a short but active long-distance courtship, which ended in Rae Jean's moving to join me at the log home. We were married the next year and have lived in the same place for nearly 27 years.

In far from perfect ways, I try to be a good husband to Rae Jean. I have tried my best to be a loving, faithful, and loyal companion and friend. I also have tried to be a good father to Melinda: teaching her important life lessons as a young girl, helping her grow in virtues and experiences, and instilling a sense of honesty and integrity.

I marvel and am humbled by Melinda's drive for justice and fairness in the world. I would not have expected that I communicated such a degree of concern for the down-trodden, exploited people of the world, but it is likely that I played a role. And although I can take no credit for Rae Jean's ability to connect with people, remember their names and important facts about them, manage a multitude of projects simultaneously, and respectfully supervise employees, I am proud to be a part of what she has created with our small publishing company. (See below.)

My Lifestyle

It is clear from the foregoing that I have always been drawn to rural living, at least as rural as I could manage. In Plattsburgh, I built a "food shed," a room in the back of the garage where I raised rabbits and laying hens next to a greenhouse where I was going to raise vegetables year-round. Mysteriously, the greenhouse was a total disaster from "damping off" disease. I don't believe any plants made it more than a few weeks. We did have a successful garden there. I tried the chickens and rabbits again in both Gladesville and Cassville for a few years. The chickens again worked out; the rabbits did not, and I later found out that the fault was mine. The meshed floors did not permit them to eat and re-digest their own manure, so they did not thrive.

We had a large garden for several years and bought yearling heifers for summer grass feeding and slaughtering in the fall. This gave us a full freezer each year of meat and vegetables. We hosted a sheep and goat grazing project on our steep powerline carried out by a soil scientist colleague from WVU. It lasted for several years but fizzled after the colleague could not accept the fact that I got divorced. I bought a registered yearling Appaloosa filly at an auction, mainly because she was sold so cheaply. I wanted her for Melinda. I built a barn, corrals, fences, and kept her, Princess, for many,

House at the first West Virginia farm in Gladesville.

Log house, garage, and shed built near Cassville, West Virginia.

Princess in the field near the house.

Princess saddled at the barn with Jennifer Taylor and Melinda.

The road Kenneth and Rae Jean walk nearly every day.

View from the top of the walk in the fall.

Kenneth—Where Did I End Up and How Did I Get There? / 341

years. Unfortunately, due to a lack of time, an ornery streak in the horse, and Melinda's moving away after the divorce, Princess never was well broken to ride. She basically became a pet until she had to be put down at the age of 35.

Until the past five years, I cut oak, cherry, locust, ash, and maple firewood for our wood stove in the winter, our only source of heat while we were home. After owning three rather worthless Ford or Massey-Ferguson tractors, I bought a Kubota tractor that, when working properly, permits me to plow snow in the winter, mow nearly five acres of lawn and sloping meadows, maintain brush control on fence lines, and lift and move miscellaneous heavy objects.

We have lush greenery and huge hardwood trees surrounding our house and the surrounding countryside. I have grown accustomed to our daily walk around the two and a half-mile "loop" down our driveway, up the gravel road to the top of the hill, back across the ridge, and down the "paved" road section back to the turnoff to our gravel road, up that short section and back up our driveway. It reminds me of my life in some ways: downhill on the driveway symbolizing no responsibilities and no need to take care of myself. The quarter mile or so along the little hollow has some gentle ups, downs, and level areas, symbolizing my childhood and elementary years. The long half-mile climb represents the hard work of high school, college, early career, and a child to raise, followed by about three quarters of a mile of easy walking along the ridge when the child is on her own and I'm adding years to my career. The short, steep downhill does not quite fit, but could represent some late middle-age successes, and the next half mile or so downhill and level might be my phased and real retirement. The last mild climb, followed by the steep climb up the driveway, is analogous to getting close to the end and the final struggle followed by death.

Whereas I enjoy good music, good theater, and social events, I enjoy estate auctions as much as anything, especially farm auctions. Much of the furniture and "junk" in the house were owned by someone else and purchased for rock-bottom prices at auctions.

My Religion

As children, our family did not attend church. This is probably because we lived in such a remote area and the only church, St. Paul's Episcopal Church in Dixon, Wyoming, where I was baptized, was about 30–45 minutes away. We ordinarily worked seven days a week on the ranch. When we moved to Steamboat Springs (see Chapter 13), I began attending the Methodist Youth

Fellowship (MYF) and loved it. The First Methodist Church was just across Oak Street from our house, which we bought a year and half later.

In college, I went to church every week at the United Methodist Church in Fort Collins, and I became heavily involved in the Wesley Foundation (the university-level Methodist student organization) at Colorado State University for four years. I often remarked that Wesley Foundation was my second major. I was highly active in all aspects of the organization: weekend retreats, participation in "faith and life" groups, travel to regional and national conferences, and participation in two spring break work camps. I began to read books on theology and learned from theologians like Paul Tillich, Karl Barth, and Dietrich Bonhoeffer. This experience and study changed my life and was greatly responsible for my deciding to enter the Peace Corps instead of continuing in Air Force ROTC.

All this is to say that in college I came to realize that I have no interest in war. After two years in "Basic" Air Force ROTC, I became more and more convinced that I did not belong in the military. They had a major hearing with me when I announced I would not go on into the "Advanced" program (which would lead to a 2nd Lieutenant position in the Air Force), probably because I had earned a small ROTC scholarship as a freshman. During my last year of college, I began to become political in the sense that I openly opposed the initial US incursions in the Vietnam War.

I became drawn to international work, originally through the church. First, I briefly looked into becoming a Methodist missionary, not to save souls but to work in a service area. Eventually, as noted above, I decided to apply to the Peace Corps because I could serve my country, which I wanted to do, but in non-military service. After two years in Turkey, I came home in 1968 just as the Vietnam War was at its worst. Many of us were "drafted" into the Army right out of the Peace Corps. I had carefully planned and petitioned my local Draft (Selective Service) Board to serve instead in one of two alternative positions, both for which I had been accepted. One was a second two-year stint in the Peace Corps in Peru; the other was to work in a refugee resettlement program in South Vietnam. The Draft Board rejected both possibilities and started the drafting procedure with me. Fortuitously, I failed the physical exam (because of stuttering) and was given a rating of 1-Y, or eligible to be called up only in an emergency.

Also, as a result of the Wesley Foundation experiences, worship, and study, I gave up the family Republican orientation and became a Democrat because it was crystal clear to me that Jesus's admonitions to take the sides

Front of "The Shack" Presbyterian Church and
Neighborhood House, where Kenneth attended
church and did extensive volunteer work in the
community for more than 20 years.

The Shack swimming pool, which was the first
racially integrated pool in West Virginia.

The altar and front of the little church
or chapel at The Shack.

of the down-trodden were much closer to the Democratic platforms.

Karen and I joined a multi-denominational church during my doctoral work at the University of Minnesota, but we did not attend a church during our three years in Plattsburgh. Upon moving to West Virginia, we wanted Melinda to know the church, so we attended a local Baptist church in Gladesville for a few weeks. I really liked the people but found myself consistently appalled and angry at many of their fundamentalist beliefs and proclamations. Eventually, we found the Presbyterian Church in nearby Arthurdale and attended there until we moved to Cassville, whereupon we began attending The Shack Presbyterian Church and Neighborhood House in Pursglove.

On Palm Sunday of 1979 (or 1980), at an ordinary Shack service, I felt a "call" that I cannot explain except that I simply knew that after that day, I was going to stay in the Church, no doubt for the rest of my life. To this day, I can't remember anything else about the experience except that I know it was real. After several years, I joined and became an elder. I was also very active in the social service aspects of the Neighborhood House. When the Shack Church closed in 2002, Rae Jean and I joined the First Presbyterian Church in Morgantown, where we have attended since. I have served as an elder on the Session, and she has served as a deacon.

Singing with the choir (second from the left in the middle row) at the First Presbyterian Church in Morgantown, WV.

In the Peace Corps and thereafter, my overarching sense of "call" has been to work for peace through personal contact, international cooperation, understanding, and empathy with anybody who is "different" or "outside" the mainstream. From a Christian perspective, I pay far more attention to Jesus's many Biblical teachings that we should serve those who are most marginalized by society, regardless of their religion, than to the relatively few admonitions to seek converts. I believe much of the evil that Christians have visited on the world has come from trying to convert the unenlightened of the world to Christianity so that they can be "saved." I realize that such evangelism is based on Scripture, but it has nearly always, in my observation and reading, been carried out with the unstated and typically naïve assumption that the missionary's culture is somehow superior to that of the people they are trying to convert. The result has been some of the worst cultural oppression the world has seen.

I am a committed Christian and cannot imagine that I would ever change my faith. On a personal level, my faith and church activities have helped keep me going when my all-too-familiar discouragement sets in. Sometimes, my faith has helped me to put my research into its proper perspective. I assume that I am still in the process of uncovering a tiny bit of some master plan that, influenced by our human contributions (both good and bad), has brought us all to where we are at this point in the history of this planet. And, overall, when I take my faith seriously, which is not nearly as often as I aspire to, it helps make me a little bit more humble.

I am a firm believer in the separation of church and state, especially in our public schools and government operations. I have always kept my religion separate from my work and teaching. My faith in no way motivates me to try to convert anyone to my way of thinking; instead, I believe that my works will speak far louder than anything I might tell people. The hymn "They'll Know We Are Christians by Our Love" pretty much sums up my approach to evangelism.

My Travel

I like to travel, and most of my long trips outside of family visits have been combining sightseeing with national and international conferences. I find myself on long flights taking out the airline's magazine, turning to the maps at the back, and counting the number of countries I have visited, about 40 I believe. As noted, I have found great satisfaction in returning to Turkey to visit new colleagues and village friends (or offspring of friends) of more than 50 years ago. I absolutely enjoy speaking Turkish again, even though it is not as good as it was when I left the Peace Corps. On the other hand, I stutter much less in Turkish than I did at that time.

I have concluded that as much as we can benefit from reading and watching movies about other places in the world, we seemingly must rediscover through our own experiences the commonalities we have with other human beings around the world. It is in these experiences that we begin to see our own blind biases and self-centered views of the world. In these, we are forced to challenge our assumptions, prejudices, and beliefs, and in so doing, emerge with healthier, more accepting perceptions of ourselves and of our neighbors. Twice, I led a study abroad experience for four and then five students to Turkey (in 2013 and 2014) for three-week stints. I know from what they have told me that this was an eye-opening and life-changing experience for them, and I am sure that at least most of these female speech-language pathologists now understand what it can mean to be a global citizen. As a curious aside, it was fascinating to me that after the first group went to Turkey, all of my students at the University seemed to appreciate me more, and my course evaluations improved. The courses did not change, but maybe I changed.

I am also committed to traveling to Colorado, either by air or by car, at least twice a year to spend time in our cabin, which I named "Yayla," meaning mountain pasture or retreat in Turkish and rhyming with the name

Ayşe (far left), who lived with her grandmother and Kenneth and who taught him a great deal of Turkish in Aşağısayık. Here she is with her mother and other relatives, 1966.

Ayşe (right) with her own daughter, 2009.

Kenneth's landlady, Ayşe Korkmaz, making tomato paste, 1968.

Hasan Korkmaz at 2 years of age, 1968.

Kenneth along with two of the Korkmaz children with their mother, Ayşe: daughter, Ayşe Kolku, and son, Hasan Korkmaz, 2008.

Yayla from the river.

Yayla from the road.

The lower deck and river from the cabin.

"Myla." I am energized by the Rocky Mountains every time I am there, and I am thankful to be able to walk outside of our three-quarter-acre lot and sit on huge, rounded glacial boulders, gaze at and listen to the swift Upper Elk River about 30 yards away, walk through lodgepole pines, service berry bushes, choke cherry bushes, sage brush, and wild flowers and grasses. Except for cottonwood trees and aspen groves, this little lot gives me the pleasure of experiencing almost all of the plants I admired as a child on the ranch.

My Entrepreneurial Efforts

I was never overly motivated to make a lot of money, although I often imagined it. It became clear to me early in my adulthood that the amount of available money people had seemed to relate far more to the amount they spent rather than the amount they earned. I was never a spendthrift and always considered seriously whether I really needed or wanted something before I bought it.

I did, however, want enough money for good investment opportunities, for unforeseen emergencies, or for a nest egg later in my life. To me, real estate always seemed like the best investment, perhaps partly because Dad nearly had a fortune several times in our early years but sold too soon or too low. Or maybe I remembered Mark Twain's advice to buy land because they are not making any more of that. I dabbled in buying land when I was working on my PhD in Minnesota. Karen and I bought 40 acres and a one-room cabin for an incredibly low price in the Arrowhead country of Wisconsin. We went there many weekends for the second two years of our stay in Minneapolis.

In the third year, we purchased 20 acres of raw land for $500 in central Minnesota. We rented the cabin and 40 acres for a couple of years after we left but sold it because it had been broken into and vandalized a couple of times. I kept the 20 acres for about 20 years, and eventually sold it. We (I) held a land contract on these sales, but none of them made much money. In the interim, I bought several lots sold at a tax delinquent auction in Routt County in the defunct Steamboat Lake Development (now called the Willow Creek Development) between Clark and Hahns Peak. Over the next 20 years, I bought, sold, and consolidated lots in order to own at least five acres that could be replatted and rezoned. With a limited partnership involving several other owners, we replatted and sold one five-acre lot. We held the other for a possible building site after retirement but put it on the market when we purchased our cabin on the Upper Elk River. It has not yet been sold.

The cabin and outhouse with 40 acres near Grantsburg, Wisconsin, while living in Minneapolis.

Our lot location (from an aerial photo) at the Willow Creek Pass subdivision north of Clark, Colorado.

With Karen and later Rae Jean, I have owned homes or small farms in Morrisonville, New York, and after moving to West Virginia, in Gladesville and Cassville. The Cassville log home became a model for Real Log Homes, and Karen and I became local dealers for the company for three years. A few years later, we bought two houses in Morgantown, remodeling one into a speech and hearing center, and renting the other. Our Communication Disorders Center, jointly owned by another couple and us, lasted only two years. This occurred about the time Karen and I separated; thus, it had to be sold.

Rae Jean and I still live in the log home with 21 adjoining acres. Shortly after our marriage in 1994, we inaugurated Populore Publishing Company. After renting offices at two sites, in 2008 we negotiated to buy two commercially zoned houses in greater Morgantown that could become

Building the house, which was a Real Log Home model.

One of a number of log homes sold under the business name Natural Shelter.

The "Mini-House" Kenneth built on a trailer, to advertise by pulling it to home shows and parades.

potential homes for Populore. Assuming we very well might not successfully close on either house, with a partnership arrangement with a relative, we ended up closing on both. We rented the ranch-style remodeled home in Star City to families and moved Populore to one end of the 1855-built home in Westover. The historic house had three apartments as well, so we were landlords renting four units for ten years. We tired of being landlords, so we sold the Westover house in 2018, and remodeled the Star City house for our Populore office. Populore, under Rae Jean's management, celebrated its 25th anniversary on January 2020. It has become a well-established small business.

In the arena of salary, I did not make any of my professional decisions based on the amount of money I would make. I took a pay cut to come from SUNY Plattsburgh to WVU. And I began at WVU on a 12-month contract, which was a rare opportunity even then and potentially much more lucrative over many years than the far more common and later sole option of a nine-month contract. Still, I gave up the 12-month arrangement after one year, and even accrued a penalty for doing so because I wanted summers to be able to work on the farm. As it turned out, I did not work much more on the farm, but my university summer work was mostly my own choice, that is, research, rather than teaching and clinical supervision. Additionally, I rarely spent any time and energy watching my

The current Populore office in Star City, West Virginia.

Rae Jean, 2020, in conference room at the office. The bookcase here is full of books produced by Populore.

TIAA-CREF university retirement account; I just assumed it would take care of itself. And I gave up half of it when I divorced.

Another serious hit to my financial situation occurred midway through my WVU career. Our consensus departmental position had been *not* to evaluate ourselves for raises, believing that doing so would constitute a conflict of interest. However, in determining how to allocate a one-time substantial raise to the faculty, our college administration decided that if faculty members did not evaluate themselves, they would receive no raises. Importantly, all the discussion of this occurred while I was away in Colorado. Upon returning, I learned that everyone else had "caved in" and evaluated themselves for the raises. I had held to our previous principle rather than give in to personal expediency. As a result, everyone but me received the substantial one-time raise to their base salary, upon which all future raises would be calculated.

Finally, I did not even fully understand that at age 70, I was obliged to start taking Social Security or lose it. But, when I did respond to that reality and began in the past five years to work with a financial planner (mainly fostered by Rae Jean), I found that we have enough money to retire and live in reasonable security. I credit this "achievement" mostly to luck and to working almost as long as possible, because I wanted to.

My Disappointments

A clever Peace Corps colleague told me once that my motto was "Regretsio. Ergo sum." (I regret. Therefore I am.) I have always had a pessimistic streak, so it would be no surprise to those who know me that my list of failures would rival my list of successes. This tendency to do something and then regret that either I should have done something else, or that it did not work out as planned, may come from a childhood script playing over and over in my mind that perhaps I don't measure up. Following are some of the disappointments or failures in my life.

My Family

Perhaps my greatest family failure was that my first marriage did not work out. This book would not be the place to explore the reasons, but since the divorce, I have struggled to find the right balance of holding on to or letting go of Melinda. Of course, that balance is challenged in any family because children grow up, become adults, have families of their own, and choose paths that their parents either did not want or did not anticipate.

Part of this disappointment no doubt harkens back to my drive to accomplish. That has led me to limit the time I allocate to family members. I envy those who are able to easily spend time visiting, telephoning, relating, or otherwise interacting with spouses, children, grandchildren, and friends. As a result, I frequently am disappointed when my "quality time" is not viewed as such by others. This is also augmented by the fact that I am by nature an introvert who has been surrounded by extroverts, except for Rae Jean.

My Personal Happiness

In terms of personal life, I am not sure if I have achieved true happiness. I'm not even sure what happiness is. Of course, it includes positive feelings or thoughts like comfort, satisfaction, familiar routines, love, optimism, novelty, and belonging. But it also includes feelings or thoughts of sacrifice for the better good, overcoming difficult obstacles, and finding out later that "unhappy" months or years were in fact part of one's happiness. All told, I would have to give myself a C for achieving happiness.

I also have some regrets about my almost insatiable drive to achieve. One of my personal mottos is "Giterdone" (Get it done). I have not found the ability to savor an achievement very long before feeling the impulse to get started on the next project. Along with that and partly fostered by the numbers game in academia, I wish I was not so focused on the number of publications or presentations I accomplish in a year. I know, deep down, that quality is far more important than quantity, and that relationships are more important than arbitrary achievement, but I update my vita every time something new is complete. And, as I wrote earlier, I count the added entries. Maybe I'm addicted to these numbers, like some people are addicted to earning more money when they clearly have enough.

My Health

In 1978, I injured my back while carrying a heavy barrel. This devastated me because I had always defined myself by the amount of physical work I could do. A re-injury in 1979 led me to a treatment called "auto traction" where I did not sit down or drive for an entire year. I had to work in the office standing up or lying on a cot. I removed half of the car's back seat and had to lie on a cot there while Karen did all the driving. This was one of the most difficult periods in my life. At the time, we sold log homes, but I later gave that up partly because I never felt confident that I could carry logs safely. My back has "gone out" (beset with spasms) many, many times since, and it has taken me 20 years to mostly accept them without experiencing quite serious depression for several days at a time. Thankfully, in the past decade, I have been able to make the two- to three-day drives to and from Colorado and numerous cross-Atlantic or Pacific Ocean flights with minimal difficulty.

Prior to and through my divorce, I sought help from a counselor and was introduced to a body approach known as "Radix." I learned that many of my physical and emotional problems were related and due to chronic muscular "blocking" of emotions. The counselor helped me get through the separation and eventual divorce but also helped me understand and deal with my back spasms with greater success than anything I ever tried. Unexpectedly, the Radix work changed me fundamentally in other ways. I discovered that I no longer had any desire to hunt and kill animals, as I did as an adolescent and young man, even though I could still do so if necessary. Relatedly, I became more attuned to—and disturbed by—suffering in animals. I became more aware of my and others' feelings than before, which probably made me a better clinician. I also discovered that I had increased awareness of psychological blind spots in others, which perhaps made me less optimistic about people's ability to change in basic ways.

My Leisure

I do not believe I ever learned how to relax. As with family "time together," I find myself at loose ends within a few hours of doing "nothing." My enjoyment of spending time at the beach, for example, is usually limited to a day or two. After that, I get bored and want to do something, such as take long walks or search for shells.

This is very likely related to the fact that I am not a reader, another failing in my life. While I read comic books and short novels normally as a child, I remember deciding that reading was a waste of time, and, after that, I only read what I needed to for school. Later, in college, I read non-required books for purpose, such as books related to theology. It was only in the Peace Corps, when evenings alone in my room were empty, that I could light my kerosene lamp, hook it onto a nail by my bed, and read novels, biographies, and other "normal" books that were provided in our Peace Corps book locker.

As an adult, I have always preferred watching television to reading. Perhaps one reason is that I find my mind less likely to wander and that it is simply easier. Another reason is that since my back problems, which began in my 30s, I have never been able to lounge on a couch or curl up in a comfortable chair for very long without pain, leg numbing, and so on. I have had to lie on the floor with a pillow or sit on a hard chair, the latter I typically did for the eight to ten hours at work. Holding a book up in the air on the floor was tiring, especially when I needed bifocals or trifocals. These made watching television even more preferable to reading.

A final reason for not being an avid pleasure reader is that, in the past 20 years, I have spent most of my time writing. No doubt there have been in excess of 100,000 emails, many of them back and forth with coauthors and editors. Additionally, I have increasingly spent the majority of my time writing and rewriting journal articles, chapters, presentations, and class outlines.

My Hobby Farm

"You can do anything. You cannot do everything." I dreamed of having a hobby farm that would bring in much of the food the family needed as well as an outlet for me to stay connected with my agricultural background. While partly successful, with all the research projects I chose to pursue in addition to my absolutely more-than-full-time job, there simply was not enough time left for gardening and caring for animals. Most of my "farm" time was spent cutting/hauling/splitting firewood in the summer, mowing, and getting hay for Princess (the Appaloosa who lived for 35 years). I lacked the time for necessary jobs such as fence building or upkeep, and I lacked the money necessary to buy all the machinery or pay for the help to develop a serious agricultural sideline.

I also consider it unfortunate and sad that I never did break Princess to ride sufficiently. Because of her ornery streak, I did not trust her implicitly enough to let Melinda ride her, the main goal of buying her in the first place. As a result, my daughter had a horse for most of her early life but never learned to ride.

My Entrepreneurial Efforts

I have succeeded in not making as many mistakes as Dad had made in his many failed enterprises to make money, such as cattle deals, sheep deals, prospecting, or real estate purchases. None of my land purchases have made the kind of money that seemed to be the rule rather than the exception in many parts of the country. This is no doubt due to the fact that I do not share the majority opinions on what makes property valuable. To most people, unique small farm on a bad road is not as valuable as a cracker-box tract home in a new development. Even so, I have not lost money on my real estate ventures, as my parents did in most of theirs.

As for the businesses, a log home dealership, a private speech and hearing clinic, and a publishing company, they have not made me rich either. Nevertheless, I believe that you don't get a chance to succeed if you don't try.

A counselor once told me that I probably am not enough of a sociopath to be a successful entrepreneur. He might be correct, but I have always assumed that one could be a caring, generous, religious person and still be successful in business. Perhaps I was more committed to being ethical than to being profitable.

I regret not being more thoughtful and strategic about my salary, pursuing every possible raise, and managing my TIAA-CREF retirement portfolio for most of the years I worked. If I had done so, I am certain that we would have a great deal more money for retirement than we do.

Other

I am not good at staying in touch with people unless I have something pressing to communicate or accomplish. I find it very hard to write "thank you" cards or notes, and so, most often, I do not. I rarely send Christmas cards, and when I do, I write a form letter to go with the card. Related to this, I regret not taking the time to write to so many former friends, relatives, classmates, colleagues, and former mentors and teachers. I am so appreciative of all of them, but they do not know that. I wish I had taken the time to write to or arrange to visit with my first-grade teacher, Laura Lee Beeler

Dodds, when she was alive. I wish the same for my close high school friends or teachers and many of my Ireland relatives. But I didn't.

How Did I Get There?

Characteristics and Values from Childhood and School

Internalization of a Strong Moral Compass

Of course, I have told occasional lies or distorted the truth in my life, but at an early age, I adopted as much as possible an unbending value of telling the whole truth. I believe this came from Dad's frequent statement that "A man is as good as his word." Mom, too, was always honest. I have a very negative reaction to willful lying and experience a great deal of guilt if I do myself.

Seeking Harmony and Freedom from Worry or Stress

While I have never been pegged as timid, I was not one to seek out potentially fearful or stressful experiences. In retrospect, I believe this resulted from being traumatized, and to some extent guilt-ridden as a young child, by David's accident. That morning, I had been very upset that I did not get to ride on the sled. I also brought to adulthood a desire to stay out of trouble and no doubt a sense of helplessness as a result of Dad's failures with sheep or cattle and our parents' fights. I did not want to experience suffering or observe it in other people. (During childhood, this did not consistently generalize to most animals.) I remember that every time it became especially windy, I used to worry that the trees on the west side of the house might blow over onto the house. In my later years, I have concluded that I only enjoy watching close sporting events if I don't care who wins. In cases where "my team" is playing and not winning by a wide margin, the uncomfortable stress I usually experience motivates me to simply not to watch or not attend the event.

Being Independent and Able to Make My Own Decisions

I was accorded a great deal of independence by both parents, and while I was never told not to take advantage of that trust in me, I understood that I could not abuse the privilege. I never purposely took extremely dangerous chances and have been mostly a rule follower when those rules made sense to me. Even so, I generally was never afraid to try new things (that were not inherently dangerous), even those that many people would not try.

I came to discover and then develop a confidence that my own insights were often more likely to be correct than those that may even have come from "experts." I also discovered that I had the ability to figure out how to do simple and complex things efficiently and well on my own and, therefore, often wondered why others did not develop the same insights that seemed so obvious to me.

Being Curious about the Thoughts and Actions of People (Myself Included)

I wrote a naïve—but to me, serious—paper in high school on "analysis," or analyzing ourselves. During high school, I greatly enjoyed my first book on psychology, which I had checked out from the University of Wyoming library during my residential speech therapy program. Over my undergraduate and graduate schooling, I sought out and took numerous courses in psychology. My curiosity about why David, Rita, and I ended up different as we did is a major motivation for my writing this book.

TURNING POINTS

Following is a list of 22 influences, arranged from most to least powerful, which I believe served as major turning points in my life journey.

- Seeking harmony and freedom from worry

- Having a success-oriented, driven personality

- Being independent and able to make my own decisions

- Wanting to be a good husband and a good father

- Being the middle child

- Enjoying learning, imagining, and creating

- Having the ability to excel academically

- Internalizing a strong moral compass

- Being drawn to wanting to understand people (including myself) and to helping people

- Wanting what I know and what I say to be right

- Wanting fun and excitement

- Being fascinated with religion, later being drawn to social gospel Christianity

- Being committed to peaceful international relations

- Experiencing life more "intensely" than most

- Being changed through counseling/psychotherapy

- Being fascinated with speech and language

- Enjoying analyzing research data

- Having a good singing voice

- Feeling pride about my family, lifestyle, and home

- Lacking abilities in many other activities of my boyhood classmates and friends

- Achieving considerable success in wrestling

- Giving high priority to reconnecting with my past

Chapter 17

Rita—Where Did I End Up and How did I Get There?

WHERE I ENDED UP

My Achievements

My Overseas Experience

Chris and I went to Nepal where Chris had a contract through the US Navy to collect birds and mammals and their parasites. The Navy had an interest in the parasites because they were the same ones that carried certain diseases in Vietnam. Being in Nepal was an interesting experience, but I was totally unprepared for it. Chris and I were newlyweds, and in truth we really did not know each other. Looking back, I think each of us was more in love with an "ideal" than we were with each other, and the commitment it takes to be married. From the start, Chris totally dominated the decisions in our marriage, and I sort of went along.

Chris had been hired to do a job, but when we got to Nepal, none of our equipment was there, and support from the Principal Investigators—one in Beirut, Lebanon, and one in Cairo, Egypt—was almost nonexistent. So, Chris tried to resurrect the project as best he could by getting support from the American Embassy and USAID personnel. It was difficult, to say the least. On top of those difficulties, Chris contracted amoebic dysentery, West Nile fever, and malaria. It was a very chaotic time, and we were not easy on each other. I was very dependent, and he in turn went to visit various people who worked at the embassy or for the airlines. Of course, that made me even more clingy.

I hated Kathmandu. It was filthy, full of diseases, and it stank. People stopped to poop and pee wherever the urge struck, so one had to constantly

Rita and David in Kathmandu when David traveled to Nepal from Laos on his way home, 1967.

watch where feet were placed. Children had snotty noses and fly-covered eyes. Feral dogs, including those with rabies, ran everywhere. While in Kathmandu, I did teach English as a second language to young men who were really eager students.

Chris and I did take a few trips outside of Kathmandu, and those were really special. One was to the Terai, a region near the Indian border, and another into the Himalayas in the Lang Tang region. Our camp was at an abandoned Buddhist temple at 12,000 feet elevation. The nomadic Tamang people were in the area at the time herding their half-yak cattle. They lived in little huts consisting of permanent "skeletons" of bent-over sticks over which they would throw skins to make shelters. When they moved on, they would take their skins and leave the skeletons behind. We traded for some of their yoghurt-like milk, which was delicious. While in the field, we had a crew of three or four people who interpreted, cooked, and helped with our field collecting. Our main food was dahl baht (rice and lentils), but we ate a lot of the animals we collected as well including deer, mice, birds, and monkeys. Monkeys were the hardest to eat because their little carcasses looked just like little people hanging there.

The main thing I took away from living overseas was how very fortunate we are to live in a country where there is not such abject poverty, where people literally starve to death in front of your eyes. I never was a person who wasted a lot of food, but after living in Nepal, I really do not like throwing away food.

My Family

After Chris and I returned to the US in late 1967, we moved to Corvallis, Oregon. Chris was accepted into a PhD program, which he later decided not to finish, and I finished my bachelor's degree in general science with a teaching credential at Oregon State University in 1970. We moved to the coastal town of Bandon where we lived for about two years. There, we were doing a survey of the land mammals of the Oregon Coast. I finished my teaching degree by student teaching in the local high school. While I very much enjoyed student teaching, life circumstances never resulted in my teaching again in a school except for occasionally substitute teaching much later in Alaska. While we lived on the Oregon coast, Erik was born.

Chris and I then moved to Tacoma, Washington, where he worked on a book about our work on the Oregon Coast, and I studied for one semester at University of Puget Sound, pursuing a master's degree in mammalogy. That was cut short because we moved back to Corvallis, where, again at Oregon State, I completed my master's degree in biology and environmental education in 1974.

Then we moved to La Grande, Oregon, where Chris had a position with the Bureau of Land Management. Shortly after we had moved, Chris decided that he no longer wanted a family, and we separated and eventually divorced in 1976. I left La Grande with Erik, and we moved in with Mom in Steamboat for the summer.

It was in Steamboat that I connected with Hugh Richards, who had been one year ahead of me in high school. We fell in love, and moved back to the Northwest, to Seattle. We married two years later in 1978. Erik took Richards as his last name.

I was in Seattle to pursue a PhD at the University of Washington in wildlife biology and, as explained below, the doctorate never came to be. In the process, I did get another master's degree, in that field, in 1981. Hugh worked at odd jobs and then got a Master of Fine Arts degree in film making.

Before we were together, Hugh had had some wonderful experiences floating down the Yukon River with friends during their college days. After we were together, Hugh always talked of wanting to return to Alaska. I did not necessarily want to move to Alaska, but we made a deal: We would go to Alaska for one year. Then we would return to the real world, make real friends, and get real jobs. That was in 1981. We all ended up loving Alaska, and it became our home. At first, it was really hard to be so far away from family and friends, but as the years went by, communication was easier, travel was easier, and I guess we just got used to being far away.

I worked for ECS Computer Systems, and Hugh pursued a master's degree in resource economics at the University of Alaska. He later partnered with an established economist in a business that estimated lost earnings and financial assets after serious accidents or deaths. Eventually, Hugh took over the business. We lived in Alaska for all of Erik's remaining school years but gradually drifted apart. At my initiative, we separated and eventually divorced.

I built a house on a beautiful lot above Fairbanks with a view of the Alaska Range, the Tanana River, and Mt. Denali. I met, became friends with, and in 2005 married John Swan. While I believe that was a good thing for both of us, we were both pretty much set in our ways, and hard-headed, so we both have had to adjust in ways that we probably would not have, had we been younger. We both enjoy the outdoors and outdoor activities. We are pretty much like-thinking politically and fiscally, so ours is a good, comfortable, loving relationship.

Upon reflection, family has been for me a mixture of great delights and great disappointment. "Family" at times seemed to be elusive to me. Because of our ranch's being sold when I was in high school, I felt quite adrift. Family seemed to elude me. My brothers were gone to college and were—at least in my mind—being successful but not part of my life. Mom and Daddy were struggling to discover who they were and what their future should become.

When I became part of the Maser family, I thought I discovered what a good family really was. But even then, the cracks and tears of its dysfunction kept appearing and eroded my view of family. On rare occasions, I felt that Chris and I were a real family after Erik was born. I suppose the real feeling of family was most prevalent after Hugh Richards and I married. Together we made a living, raised Erik, and shared common interests.

Also, by that time, Hugh's family, the Richards, became really important to me, as did my own blood family: Mom, Daddy, David, and Kenneth. I had grown up enough by then to really appreciate who they all were and how precious they were to me. And through it all, Erik was the most important person in that mix. I'm sure it was partly because he is my son and partly because I wanted to shield him from the hurt of Chris's leaving us when he was four years old.

Now in my later years, being married to John, family has yet another meaning. I believe we each care deeply for one another's kids and their families, but ours is not a blended family. His daughter, Amara, and my son, Erik, barely know each other, so it's more like "your kids and my kids."

While Erik still remains the most important person in my life, "importance" has expanded to Amy, Evan, Camden, Scott, and of course, John. Also, I am comfortable with a very dynamic adopted family, which includes Amara's family, and other young people we know. Whenever I see nieces and nephews, I feel such warmth and delight to know them and to see who they have become. They are really important to me, although I do not interact with them much at all.

My Career

My career just sort of happened. My marriage to Chris Maser was probably the "fork in the road" that put me on a trajectory that stayed with me. Chris was an outstanding naturalist, and I became very interested in ecology and natural history, especially of mammals. Working with him, I gained a knowledge that I would never have gotten otherwise. After we divorced, I continued my interest in ecology of mammals and pursued a PhD in wildlife biology at the University of Washington, Seattle. Because of many circumstances, including my not being assertive enough and my major professor's belief that women should not work in wildlife biology, I lacked the will to persevere after roadblock upon roadblock, which he repeatedly put in front of me. As a result, I did not finish the PhD.

By then I was so discouraged about my abilities that I took a job as a receptionist at the small computer company ECS Computer Systems. That job evolved into a programmer job. While I was decent at programming, I was never really good at it. My greatest strength was customer relations. I was good at helping customers fix the messes that they got themselves into with the computer programs that they bought from our company.

While I remained at ECS for 23 years, that job was never my passion. I had applied for a job at the Alaska Department of Fish and Game in 1981 when I first got to Alaska. In those days, it was really a good-old-boys club, and I was told that without a PhD, I was virtually unemployable.

Fast forward 20-some years, and I read of a job involving coordinating meetings among Fish and Game advisory committees. I applied for and got the Advisory committee coordinator position. In that position, I went to many villages in Interior Alaska. In the process, I got to see a whole lot of Alaska that would not have been possible otherwise. Plus, there were lots of dangerous and wonderful adventures in small aircraft, not to mention being a small part of village life—such as being among the Athabaskan and Eskimo Native people, seeing their humor, sleeping on schoolhouse floors, and wondering whether the plane would leave in bad weather.

Exhausting as the job was, I really liked seeing the country and meeting so many wonderful people of rural Alaska. But then, the regional planner-guy, Randy Rogers, was looking for an assistant. Randy was active in pursuing the reintroduction of the wood bison to Alaska. He asked me to consider the position. I applied and was offered that job. Randy died of cancer in 2013, but I continued in the planning capacity, and in 2015 through a huge team effort, 130 wood bison were released in western Alaska. The big

Rita getting ready to fly to a village for the Alaska Fish and Game Department.

Posing with an anesthetized wood bison bull, which was being moved to a cargo box and would then be reawakened. The cargo boxes, with 30 bulls, were barged to the release site 1000 miles away.

issues Randy and I worked on were getting user groups to agree on moose hunting allocations and bison-farmer conflicts with the Delta bison herd. Also, in the wings was the slow process of reintroducing the endangered subspecies of wood bison to Alaska.

That reintroduction effort was the highlight of my career. We had a great team, and everyone worked really hard, and because of so many setbacks— mostly involving the Endangered Species Act—we all had to continually "keep our eyes on the prize."

My Religion

I would say that I am not a very religious person. I have gone through various stints in my life when I attended, and even belonged, to churches, but I was never really struck by the need to identify with one group or another. In high school, I attended the Methodist church and was active in Methodist Youth Fellowship. In Seattle, I was pretty active in the Quaker church. Since living in Fairbanks, I have not attended church very often.

I guess my religion is more of a spirituality that embraces Nature as much as it embraces human beings. Some of my most spiritual experiences have been outside, and mostly where other people were not around.

My Lifestyle

I'm not sure I selected a lifestyle; it probably selected me. Mostly, I love the out of doors, and I avoid cities and crowds, so my lifestyle reflects that. I think I go on certain "binges" for a while, then merge into another and leave that one.

Alaska offered great outdoor experiences. Probably among the most important to me were some hikes in the wilderness in the Brooks Range. Most people do not understand wilderness. There are no roads, no communication, no connection except for the pilot who has agreed to pick you up at a certain place on the map on a certain date. One is left to one's own resources. If you screw up, or if luck turns, the wilderness does not care. You can be a good dinner for a bear. That reality spooked me when we went on our first trip. Erik was in middle school, and it was a great experience to share with him. Years later, David joined Hugh and me for another incredible hike.

Rita playing with a litter of puppies, 1991.

For about 15 years Hugh and I had a dog team, and that took a lot of our time, finances, and energy. For several years we were partners with our friend, Dick Barnum, who ran both the Iditarod and the Yukon Quest dog races. We helped him train, and by default, had the use of the dogs to take camping trips. We saw a lot of beautiful Alaskan country just by virtue of taking trips with our dogs.

Erik attended college in Fairbanks at University of Alaska. As a result of living in the same town, the two of us spent a lot of time in the same gym and became really active in powerlifting. That was a good sport because it helped us get strong, get in shape, and have fun with other lifters. I got pretty good at it and entered two or three national contests as well as local contests. I was able to go to Hungary with the USA masters team to compete in the World Championships. While not a threat to the really top lifters in the world, I did finish tenth in my weight class of 132 pounds.

As Hugh and I started drifting apart, I became interested in Native American spirituality, and I attended several gatherings. While that was an interesting journey, I got tangled up with a Native guy who turned out to be really bad for me. Aside from that "entanglement," I also came to realize that the Native American spiritual gatherings were not for me. While I totally respected, and still respect and endorse, many of the tenets of the gatherings, there are just too many really needy, dysfunctional people who attend.

A loaded sled being pulled up a steep hill, 1990s.

Rita riding the sled through an Alaskan spruce forest, 1990s.

Rita with her lead dogs, late 1980s.

Hugh and Rita on a camping trip, 1990s.

View from the sled traveling along a frozen river, 1990s.

Rita at a powerlifting meet in Hungary, 1997.

Somewhere along the way, I realized that being around them just is not for me.

But it is because of being on the organizational side of the gatherings that John and I met, and after a year or so, started dating. We have been together close to 20 years now, and they have been good years. We both like the outdoors, and hunting and fishing, and hiking. As the years pile upon us, though, we realize that we cannot do as much as we would really like to do. But we still really enjoy family, and travel adventures.

John and Rita on the Oregon coast, 2000.

My Travel

Travel has been something I have always enjoyed. Some travels are close to home but have remained the most memorable trips, most notably, two fantastic hikes in the total wilderness within the Brooks Range. On one of them, in which my brother David had joined us, a plane dropped us off at one lake and picked us up at another ten or so days later. In between, we were totally on our own without communication of any kind with the outside world. Additionally, we took lots of two- to seven-day dog sled trips not toofar from Fairbanks in the White Mountains. As well, we took several one- to three-week trips into Denali Park and into the Brooks Range. Again, we were totally on our own and had to rely on our own resources in all situations. Once I nearly cut the tip of my index finger off but was two days away

Hiking in the Brooks Range in Alaska, mid-1990s.

Camping on about 50 miles north of Fairbanks, mid-1990s.

from any road and three from any medical facility. A lot of blood and a good patch job kept me going.

Nowadays, people rely on cell phones and satellite phones "just in case of emergency." While I do see the wisdom of that, I firmly believe that for me, instant communication takes away from the adventure. If one is a button-push away from help of some sort, one never leaves civilization, even for a week or two. Leaving civilization, and totally depending on one's own resources is really important to how I view the necessity of getting away from it all. To quote my friend Charles Bradford, I would rather "pay my quarter and take my chance."

As is clear from the chapters all through my childhood and early adulthood, I have loved riding horses. It is no surprise then that I have greatly enjoyed our family trail rides in Colorado. Since then, in recent years, I have had the opportunity to help a friend take her horses into her camp on the Wood River in the Alaska Range where she guides hunters. I eagerly await the four-day trips across mountains and wild rivers with the sturdy horses.

I love traveling to see family and to see new places. However, because of owning a house, I always feel the pull of needing to be home to do chores and to ensure that all is working correctly. Sometimes I would like to be a total vagabond with no house to be in charge of. But I do balance that to some degree by traveling both home and abroad.

Traveling abroad has great appeal to me, but not to really poverty-stricken countries. I think my stint in Nepal cured me of wanting to spend a lot of time in third-world situations. Nevertheless, I have enjoyed trips with my brothers to Turkey and to Thailand.

Crossing a river on the way to the Alaska hunting camp, 2018.

Riding at Van and Mary Sybrandt's Place on Elk River near Clark, 1990s.

Rita—Where Did I End Up and How Did I Get There? / 369

Visiting Kenneth in West Virginia, about 1980.

My Entrepreneurial Efforts

I would say that my entrepreneurial efforts were a combination of some good sense and mostly luck. Chris and I bought dwellings together because we believed—as most people did at the time—that owning is better than buying. When we divorced, I used my share of the money from the sale of our house to buy another in Seattle while going to graduate school.

In Seattle, two things happened that started my trajectory toward owning real estate. One was buying a home with a tiny down payment and with collateral that Hugh and I put together. It is pretty astounding that the bank lent us money for a $30,000 home based on no income but with equity such as "canoe, VW bus, BMW car, jewelry..." all of which were either really old or had no quantifiable value. The second thing was that we sold that first house within six months because Hugh wanted a different place in which he could build a basement apartment and have extra income. We just scrubbed the first place up, gave it a good coat of paint, and ended up with an $8000 profit. With that profit we bought another for about $35,000. A very wise real estate lady told us about leveraging money. She advised that we make a minimum down payment and buy two other houses too with minimum down payments. So, there we were with three houses, two we rented out and one in which we lived and in which Hugh built a basement apartment to rent. As luck would have it, renters covered most of the mortgage payments, and real estate began really appreciating in Seattle. After Seattle, Hugh and I invested in real estate in Fairbanks. When we divorced, we split our holdings.

The "good sense," if any, has been a result of pretty successfully reading the real estate market. It has also been a result of consciously never spending beyond my means—except for the first house in Seattle—so I have accumulated very little debt over my life. The rest is simply luck.

My Personal Happiness

For me personal happiness comes first from being with family and loved ones. As I get older those contacts and time shared become more and more important to me. Second, personal happiness comes from interacting with other relatives and non-relative friends, both new and old. I realized a few years ago how important it is to nurture relationships, especially among younger people. I now have several young friends, mostly women, whom I really value as friends. The value of having young friends is their outlook on life, their vitality, and the fact that their health issues are not the main subject of discussion.

I also find personal happiness in accomplishing things that I feel need to be done. Those include long-term goals as well as short-term goals. Interestingly, the happiness comes after the task is accomplished, not in the doing! (It's great to have the shed oiled or the cupboards cleaned, but happiness comes after the fact.)

My Leisure

For me leisure is not a natural thing, if leisure means "not doing much." I do like to read, although I do it mostly at night in bed. I do like to knit and paint with watercolors. I knit because I feel watching television every night is a waste of time, so I knit so that I have "something to show for the time I spent." I paint because it is a source of joy to me. Painting is rewarding and disappointing at the same time. It is exhausting too. But the artistic part of me really blooms when I paint. There is something about painting that is satisfying in a way that I have not felt anywhere else.

I think if I lived by the sea, I could watch the water forever. I suppose that is what leisure really is. But instead I do enjoy being outdoors and soaking in whatever Mother Nature has to offer. Mostly, though, I would classify that as "adventure" and not leisure.

My Disappointments

My disappointments mostly revolve around not choosing good relationships. I've had two failed marriages, which I find disappointing on some real level.

Another disappointment was not to have stood up to my major professor at University of Washington. I believe had I been more assertive, I could have obtained a PhD. He thought women should not have doctorates in wildlife management, and his actions proved to be a greater obstacle than I was prepared to overcome at the time.

A third disappointment, which was in some ways my greatest, was when our parents sold our ranch. I felt that my soul was sold.

A lesser, but very real disappointment was when I realized my singing voice had vanished. I used to love singing, and I was quite good. (Fort Lewis College actually offered me a music scholarship as a result of the many singing contests I entered in high school.)

HOW DID I GET THERE?

Characteristics and Values from Childhood and School

I believe that early childhood is a prime mover that determines what kind of a person someone will be. How was one motivated? How was one encouraged? How was one discouraged? What lessons came from parents, siblings, and other people in one's life?

Feeling Safe from a Secure Childhood

I would classify my childhood as really ideal. While our family did not have extra money, and occasionally I would overhear conversations or arguments about money, I never felt deprived in any way. The entire country was our playground, and we were allowed to go far and wide playing our games. (The only forbidden spot was on the sandstone cliff above our garage, so of course that's where we really wanted to play!) We were encouraged to travel or to play with at least one other person, so that one of the two or more could go for help if necessary. We were required to say which direction we were headed, but beyond that we were allowed to go as far north-east-south-or-west as we chose. Lillyan, Lexie, and I would take off on our horses and wander for entire days with no worry about whether we should be home. (Mom told of her and Elizabeth's commenting to one another, "I wonder where the kids are..." but not really wanting to know because they believed there were enough of us that someone would be left to fetch help if necessary.) We ate good meals, we had clean clothes, and a warm home.

In spite of this we had essential discipline. I think Daddy was more indulgent than Mom. I have no memory of his ever spanking me. Mom was more strict, but again, she was in charge of us way more than Daddy was in our early years.

Coming from a Family Where Affection Was Not Expressed Openly

Earlier than my own memory, Mom told me that I was a difficult baby. I did not cuddle like little babies; I did not relax like little babies; I did not sleep like little babies. I do know that I had difficulty thriving. Mom nursed

Rita's water color painting of a creek.

us very little if at all, and the bottled formula at the time did not "sit well" with me. Thus, I was sickly, and was told at one point that I nearly died. Mom and Daddy raced to Denver on bad winter roads and got me to the Children's Hospital. Apparently, the formula was changed to a rice-based formula, and things looked up from there. Mom told me that I would cry and cry, and after she knew of nothing else to do, she would just leave me in a room to cry. All of that is understandable, given the times (remember Dr. Spock said you should not spoil your baby), and given that she had two other little people who needed care. Furthermore, Mom was not a demonstratively loving person herself. I believe she really did not know how to really show affection while we were little. Her own upbringing suggests that she certainly did not learn such behavior from her family. Toward the end of her life, I believe she taught herself—or should I say trusted herself—to be more demonstratively loving. While not ones to demonstrate their love with kissing, hugging, and saying "I love you," I do believe that Mom and Daddy loved me and my brothers, and I have no doubt they did the best they could.

Believing that Keeping One's Word Is Fundamental

Mom and Daddy engendered some key values in me, even though I did not realize it at the time. For instance, Daddy often stated, "A man is as good as his word." He did not need signed contracts; he just needed a word. (That was one of his downfalls, too, because he would believe someone's word, and then get taken to the cleaners because there was no signed contract.)

Internalizing the Value of Working and Budgeting

Our parents both demonstrated daily the necessity, and hopefully the reward, of hard, honest work. While we got a ten-cent, then later a 20-cent allowance every week, we were taught that we could not expect to get paid for doing our chores. Furthermore, if we were sick, someone else did our chores, but everyone still got the same allowance. (Of course, later on, David and Kenneth were paid to work in the hayfields, but that was different.) We were taught that when the money was gone, there was no more, so we learned to save and to budget for the things we wanted that our parents did not buy. We raised bum (orphan) lambs for pocket money. Of course, Mom and Daddy furnished the milk cow's milk and the pasture, but we did the work. In the fall we sold those lambs, and with that money, we paid for our bicycles, saddles, boots, and other things we wanted.

When we went to Steamboat to school, each of us had a checking account with a certain amount of money to buy our clothes, luxuries, and school supplies. So from sixth grade forward, I knew that I would have to budget my funds because more money would not be forthcoming if I spent it all. Any other money had to be earned from working. I babysat some, although I hated it because most of the kids were little hellions—I especially remember the Green and the Temple kids to be hellions—and I was not old enough to set them straight. Later, in high school, I worked after school and weekends at Kinney Drug Store, El Rancho Café, and Harwig's Saddlery.

TURNING POINTS

Following is a list of 10 influences, arranged from most to least powerful, which I believe served as major turning points in my life journey.

- Selling the ranch on Snake River

- Deciding to marry and follow Chris Maser to Nepal

- Giving birth to my son, Erik

- Moving to and living in Alaska

- Marrying Hugh Richards

- Marrying John Swan

- Failing at getting a PhD at the University of Washington

- Working for Alaska Department of Fish and Game

- Being a part of the team that released 130 wood bison into western Alaska

- Becoming interested in dog mushing in Alaska

Chapter 18

A Long Look Back

REFLECTING ON LIFE INFLUENCES

I pointed out in Chapter 1 that the life journeys of my brother, sister, and me were at once both ordinary and extraordinary. In their ordinariness, they are but one miniscule example of the stories of billions of families who have inhabited this planet. How could our stories in any sense be extraordinary? The simple answer is that every person's life story, every family's life story, is unique. Just as every person's DNA is different, so too, every person's story is unlike that of any other person, living or dead. I was fully aware of this before even contemplating a book such as this one. Yet, it was, for reasons I cannot fully articulate, important for me to try to understand why I became the person I did, which is so unlike the persons David and Rita became. In that sense, for me, the book is an autobiography of my own search for understanding of how this all came about.

We did not follow the odds. If someone in 1950 would have predicted where we three siblings would end up, barring some economic or environmental upheaval, it would likely have been that we would become ranchers at or near our home or that we would work in one of the small towns nearby. That is what happens with the vast majority of children who grow up in rural areas such as the Little Snake River Valley. But that did not happen. Like most of our St. Louis cousins, we excelled in school and pursued higher education. And, we kept going. For starters, in 1966, in just five years after David began college at CSU, we all three found ourselves working in Asia: Laos, Nepal, and Turkey. One of Mom's friends reportedly remarked to her at that time, "Nobody told them they couldn't do it." Except for about a year with Rita, we never went back to Colorado to live. After Laos, David lived in New York, Puerto Rico, Maryland, South Carolina, and Mississippi. He looked for work all over the Southeast and even in Ethiopia. After Turkey, I traveled all over the East Coast for a year and then lived in Michigan, Minnesota, New York, and West Virginia. Rita made her homes in Washington, Oregon, and Alaska. This might have been expected had we been "military brats" who moved all over the world every few years as children, but not for rooted northwest Colorado ranchers.

The question is, "Why did we three siblings, who as children were early exposed to such similar influences, end up so different, and at the same time remain as connected as we are?" This book does not answer the questions in any definitive way but perhaps sheds light on some of the important dynamics.

The Men and Women Who Influenced Us as Children

From the perspective of people who did not know them intimately, the St. Louis Boys were the epitome of the cowboys, the rugged individualists, the work-hard ranchers, the Saturday night carousers, the larger than ordinary life romantic ideal of men who showed how the West was won. They were our heroes and role models. From their ability to rise to almost any occasion and do what had to be done, we learned a work ethic second to none. From their gregarious and often loud celebrations, we absorbed an unapologetic desire—and perhaps imperative—to stand up and make a splash in our entertaining and storytelling. From their values of speaking the truth, supporting one's entire family, and acting with a certain chivalry toward ladies, we emerged with unquestioned principles (at least through adolescence) for our own lives. And from what we experienced in our play and later work on the ranch, we all three developed a remarkable sense of self-confidence and self-sufficiency that pervaded our futures.

Yet, because we were hands-on and close in—not observers from a distance—we also became aware of inconsistencies and weaknesses in our dad and St. Louis uncles. As children, we watched helplessly the financial disasters that resulted from the acts of God or foibles of nature (the livestock illnesses, the droughts, the early spring storms, the sheep-killing coyotes). We also witnessed the effects of lack of knowledge, too much alcohol, poor judgment, or lack of business acumen that ended in failed cattle or sheep deals, vehicular accidents that should have been averted, and hasty decisions that should have been more carefully considered.

In many ways, it could be argued that our external personas that most people would see came from our dad and uncles. We would be less ostentatious than the Boys, but their influence would be just under the surface.

The amazing women who brought the world to the Little Snake River as young mothers, Grace, Doris, Elizabeth (Betty), Dorothy Grace (Dot), and Agnes.

Agnes, Grace, and Elizabeth (Betty) in their golden years.

And as much as we all three have tried, with only intermittent success, to be entrepreneurs, we somehow lacked the shrewdness or desire to get rich, a trait much more apparent in our Granddad Ireland.

Our mom and St. Louis aunts, however, were most likely much stronger influences on our internal motivations than our dad and uncles. It was the initial influences of the wives of four of the five brothers who first propelled our lives, and those of our St. Louis cousins, in the amazingly divergent directions that resulted in our widely different careers and world views. Speaking only for myself, the chronicles and stories in this book convince me that we would not have taken such widely divergent paths without these incredibly strong women.

Mom, of course, was the most important adult female influence for us. She did not achieve more than a high school education largely because she had neither the financial means nor the family support to go on to college. Nevertheless, she was extremely bright and resourceful. She was a very strong student, being the valedictorian of her ninth grade class in Greeley, Colorado, after bouncing around for years from school to school. Mom—and Dad—made sure that we were all treated as fairly as humanly possible. But she—not Dad—was the one who made sure that we had books and encyclopedias to read and use for school research. And, although Dad was supportive, it was Mom who in myriad ways over the years communicated to us, very matter-of-factly but firmly, that we would go to college. It was

Mom who taught us frugality and responsible money management. At her direction and support, we earned a weekly allowance from our very early years; we opened individual savings accounts to keep our money from the 4-H and other sheep; we had our own checking accounts in high school for our clothes, school supplies, and luxuries; and we had larger allowances for college. Although true of Grandma and all the aunts, it was Mom who provided the three of us with the clearest instruction of maintaining our homes. We all had daily and weekly chores both outside and inside the house. Our house might get messy, but we learned to vacuum, to dust, to clean up after ourselves, and to make our beds.

Elizabeth, who was among the most highly educated persons on the Little Snake River, was without a shadow of a doubt the strongest influence in my life in terms of launching me in the direction of international endeavors. And, although the early memories are dim, "Betty" is the person I most remember simply loving me. She was arguably equally important in Rita's decisions to love animals; appreciate art, music, and language; and wish to see the world. Elizabeth also taught us at Willow Creek school for most of one year, and it was our first introduction to learning some words in another language—Spanish.

With a few exceptions, by virtue of teaching David from the third through sixth grades, me from the second through fifth grades, and Rita from kindergarten through third grades, our aunt Grace was essentially "our teacher." Although none of us became unusually close to her emotionally, her constant steady presence, her order and structure, her unstated but somehow clearly communicated expectations of excellence, and, in retrospect, her unflappable and fair-minded treatment of all of us, gave us the academic readiness and tools that propelled all three us eventually into advanced doctoral study. It is likely that her influence similarly propelled our cousins toward their further higher education.

Agnes had less direct influence on our young lives than either Elizabeth or Grace. Yet, she clearly gave us nurturing when we needed it, as when David's accident occurred. Had she been our teacher instead of Grace, I am sure that we would have received the same excellent education, but Agnes did not play that role for us. Instead, she was the aunt who was always so happy to see us when we arrived in Wamsutter, Dixon, or Craig. She was the woman who, like our grandmother, made beautiful quilts appear from scraps of cloth and whose house was always inviting and intriguing.

Long distance did not permit us to be influenced nearly as much by Doris St. Louis, because she, Leonard, and Kathy only entered our lives for about a month each summer. Still we observed from them that one could leave the Valley, succeed in ways that those who stayed could not, and yet come back to savor its wonderful qualities.

Thus, if our faces to the world more resembled those of the St. Louis men, the essential skills to make our ways in foreign countries and in new occupations or professions came from the St. Louis women. Most early settlers, the McIntoshes, Morgans, McCargars, and Oliver St. Louis brought the outside world to the Little Snake River. But then for a generation, the Valley became its own little world for our dad and uncles. As Elizabeth once said, it was like Camelot, but perhaps without knowing it, our mom and aunts were the ones who, again, brought new ideas and powerful outside influences to bear in our few miles of the Valley.

We were much less influenced by our aunts and uncles on Mom's Ireland side, except the Ranch family. No doubt, Mom's older sisters and brother taught their families in many of the same ways she taught us. Suffice to say, that, for reasons that would be far beyond the scope of this book, our family's life trajectories would appear to most resemble those of the children of her oldest sister, Ruby Lawler, than any of the others.

Effects of Our Life Circumstances

Without question, the planned and unplanned life circumstances powerfully influenced the trajectories of our individual lives. Most people, and perhaps David and Rita, would explain the differences among the three of us, or major differences in most families, in this way.

It goes without restating that our Little Snake River ranching heritage and early life experiences affected all three of us indelibly and deeply. That, of course, is one of the reasons that this book focused so much on those early years.

One common trait that emerged for all of us is to strive for self-sufficiency. David designed and built his own solar collectors to save money and also to be able to have useable electricity if the grid were to fail. He also has experimented with making charcoal. Rita and I both built houses with wood stoves as a primary heat source or a backup. I heated entirely with wood until a few years ago, using electric heat as a backup only when we were gone. Now, the rarely used wood stove is the backup. Our West Virginia house has access to both natural gas and electricity, in case one fails, and the electricity is backed up with a whole-house gas generator. All three siblings, with our families, have had gardens intermittently for food as well as chickens. Rita places great value in getting food off the land from fishing and hunting. For a I time, I bought gasoline in bulk. This trait most likely comes from what we experienced as children, but also from a desire to shield ourselves as much as possible from budgetary crises, real or possible. Life in agriculture is unpredictable, so successful farmers and ranchers must have backup plans and contingencies. We no doubt adopted that principle for our lives.

But what of the life circumstances that happened—or were chosen—by the three of us that were not the same?

The fact that I began stuttering at an early age and continued into adulthood affected my relationships, my self-image, and my life's work. An unwelcome bad back for years along with a series of psychosomatic annoyances have colored many of my decisions in later life. So, too, did my decisions to spend two years as a Peace Corps Volunteer in Turkey, to pursue a career in academia, to marry two women who were reared in cities, and to successfully find a job in West Virginia where I could try to live in both my rural past and my more urban daily reality. The decision to pursue a divorce, and all that followed from that, impacted me deeply as well. My less-than-successful to moderately successful ventures into real estate and businesses have certainly affected my outlook and later life choices.

For David, growing up and living his life with one functioning hand affected him deeply. He allowed in a moment of candor that he "has a mean streak" and that, if he had not lost his arm, he might not be as helpful or accommodating as he turned out to be. The importance of deciding to go to Laos in the International Voluntary Service, and then deciding to marry a foreigner, Chai, cannot be underestimated either. After long job searches, landing positions at Clemson University and Mississippi State on experimental farms led David to a career of livestock-centered research and consulting. Living in the southeast US was important. He resurrected his earlier weekly practice of church-going in a mix of Presbyterian reformed theology and an evangelical, conservative Christian milieu. David's life, too, has been affected by his entrepreneurial pursuits, the majority of which have not worked out as hoped. In recent years, his health has dramatically affected his life, most powerfully his near-death experiences following a failed appendectomy, but also a mysterious cardio-pulmonary syndrome.

Rita's decision to marry and follow Chris to Asia and then to the Northwest US, as well as her later decision to marry Hugh and follow him to

Alaska each ended with dramatic life changes. So did the two divorces. The fact that she and Hugh purchased houses at just the right time in Seattle, and later real estate purchases, propelled Rita to a degree of financial security that might not have otherwise occurred. Clearly, taking a job in Alaska that did not align with her training or affinity resulted in seeking satisfaction elsewhere, such as travel, treks, and powerlifting. Marrying John and deciding to live out her golden years in Alaska led to a dramatically satisfying contribution to reintroducing wood bison to that state in a job she always dreamed of having.

Effects of Our Personalities

My siblings may disagree, but it is my conclusion after collating all the material for this book, including two self-report measures, that our individual personalities overshadow the life circumstances, both planned and unplanned, as determinants of the dissimilar destinations of our life journeys.

It certainly appears to be the case for me, as these and other self-completed inventories nail me! No doubt, my driven nature to accomplish and succeed, and my perfectionism were critical in becoming a reasonably accomplished social scientist. However, the inevitable "side effects" of such a personality (sometimes referred to as a "Type A" temperament) tend to foster more than typical reactivity, aggravation, impatience, and stress. The first three of these have not endeared me to family, friends, and colleagues nearly as much as would be the case if I were more "laid back." The fourth, stress, has taken its toll on my body in the form of back spasms, hypertension, and other conditions.

Socially, I have been given the message my entire life, in subtle or direct ways, that I should be different than I am or ever was. I know that life would be smoother if I were calmer, gentler, more patient, or less time conscious. But intense, direct, and on-time is what I am and have been since I was a young child. This is why I have tried for at least half of my life to find a balance between expressing my emotions or containing them. In either case, I experience the emotions. When I express them, I suspect my body is healthier, but those around me are less comfortable. When I stuff them, other people enjoy being around me more, but I find myself suffering from stress and psychosomatic symptoms.

As I have thought about what make me tick, I am convinced that my personality overshadows all the other influences, even the very strong influences

Keirsey Temperament Sorter

The Keirsey Temperament Sorter (derived from the Myers-Briggs Type Indicator) divides the population into 16 different personality types based on answers to lists of either-or questions such as "In company, do you (a) initiate conversation or (b) wait to be approached" (Extrovert [E] versus Introvert [I]), "Do you go more by (a) facts or (b) principles" (Sensing [S] versus iNtuitive [N], "In making decisions do you feel more comfortable with (a) standards or (b) feelings" (Thinking [T] versus Feeling [F], and "Are you more comfortable (a) before a decision or (b) after a decision" (Perceiver [P] versus Judge [J]). Of course, few people score all or none for any of these dichotomies, but most people have a natural preference for one over the other. Thus, based on personality a person could be identified, for example, as an INFP (Introvert iNtuitive Feeling Perceiver).

These 16 types are also grouped into four basic personality temperaments. For example, "Artisans" are stronger in Sensing and Perceiving (SPs) and make up about 30% of the population. The other three temperaments are SJ "Guardians" (45% of the population), NF "Idealists" (15% of the population), and NT "Rationals" (10% of the population).

On this measure, David is an ENTJ (Extrovert iNtuitive Thinking Judge). He has an NT "Rational" temperament, but more specifically, ENTJs, who make up 5% of the population, are often called "Fieldmarshals" or "Commandants." They are born leaders, even at a very young age. They simply find themselves in control partly because they have almost an innate ability to translate ideas into concrete strategies that are clearly communicated. When they identify a vision, they bring together whatever resources are necessary to achieve it. Being practical and efficient and maintaining focus on the big picture, ENTJs are also ready to abandon any action that does not align with their goals.

On the Keirsey, I am an INTJ (Introvert iNtuitive Thinking Judge), often labeled as "Scientists" or "Masterminds." INTJs are among the most rare, at 1% of all people. They are said to love challenges and contingency plans but dislike duplication of effort or inefficiency. They tend to be hard driving to excellence and superiority and thus push themselves very hard, even more than they push others. They are known to be self-confident and will not yield easily to others' ideas unless they see evidence that requires a different way of approaching a problem.

Rita's scores on the Keirsey Temperament Sorter were highly variable over two attempts, an unusual result. Therefore, she read the descriptions of the four basic personality types and rank-ordered herself from most to least matching the descriptions. Her rank order was "Artisan" ("by far"), "Idealist," "Guardian," and "Rational" ("definitely not").

Rita has characteristics of the first three of these, but most likely strongest for "Artisans." And of those, since both of her previous scores were Es for Extrovert, she is most likely an Extrovert Sensing Feeling Perceiver (ESFP) "Performer." She also likely has tendencies of the Extrovert iNtuitive Feeling Perceiver (ENFP) "Champion."

ESFPs are highly engaging people with contagious good humor and a joy for living. They are optimistic, generous, and charming. They want to and can live in the present, and they seek exciting possibilities. They may, however, defer to others instead of pursuing what is best for them. To the extent Rita also has strong tendencies of an ENFP, she is passionate about seeking novelty, exploring new things, but also in doing people-to-people work as in arranging meetings and conferences. On the other hand, ENFPs often lose enthusiasm when projects are established and become routine.

International Personality Item Pool (IPIP) Big-Five Factor Markers

Other aspects of personality are measured by the International Personality Item Pool (IPIP) Big-Five Factor Markers. It features a five-point Strongly Disagree to Strongly Agree scale to rate various items (such as "I have a soft heart") from which profiles are generated for five dimensions.

Compared to the entire population, David's scored highest in the five dimensions for Emotional Stability, followed by Extroversion, then by Intellect/Imagination, then by Conscientiousness, and finally by Agreeableness, which was relatively lowest. By contrast, I am highest in Intellect/Imagination, followed by Conscientiousness, then by Agreeableness, next by Extroversion, and last by Emotional Stability. Rita's rank order was highest for Agreeableness, followed in order by Conscientiousness, Intellect/Imagination, Extroversion, and Emotional Stability. Rita's scores were considerably less variable than David's or mine, suggesting, as in the Keirsey, that she has developed all aspects of her personality in a more balanced fashion than we have.

of my childhood and later environments and life circumstances. The major, minor, and imperceptible choices I have made propelled me to focus on solving problems, carrying out research meticulously, and becoming involved in causes that have tangible outcomes. I do not believe I would have succeeded as well as I did in school and work without a hard-working, driving nature. On the other hand, the down sides of my temperament have exacted tolls on my success, health, and life satisfaction.

I have always been introspective and curious about why I am as I am. In high school, I wrote an essay for English class on analyzing oneself and how difficult that can be. Based essentially on my own introspection, it was naïve and simplistic but reflected an early interest in self-searching. If such an orientation could be inherited, it clearly came from Mom whose only college correspondence course was in psychology and whose self-acquired insights are revealed in her Discoveries essay in Appendix E. Although I had no prior inclination at all to pursue a career in a psychology-related field, or even a medical field, my success in at least temporarily overcoming my stuttering in the six-week summer therapy program at the University of Wyoming changed all of that. I could have been thrilled to gain some control over this fluency problem and use it as a springboard to do whatever else I wanted to do. Instead, I decided that speech-language pathology was what I was going to pursue. More than that, unlike most recovered or semi-recovered stutterers who choose this field with the goal of helping others struggling with stuttering, I had a larger goal. I wanted to solve the problem of stuttering. It is no accident then that I always was more intrigued with understanding the whys of stuttering more than the whats. At my undergraduate advisor's suggestion, I was pleased to do a major independent study and to write a paper on "The Stuttering Personality." Later, as an academic, I was always more in my "zone" planning and carrying out research studies than supervising clinical treatment of stutterers or teaching courses to college students.

In preparing this book, I read numerous saved letters that I had written to our parents (but directed to Mom mostly) during my Wyoming therapy and during my last year at Colorado State (after they had moved to Washington state). Though my letters then sound extremely pompous to me now, much of the content related to how my views of my past had changed in simple and complex ways. They described what Christianity meant to me and why I changed in college from a moderately conservative Republican to a very liberal Democrat. They gave my views of what higher education should be all about, that is, learning new information or skills to get a good-paying job, using the college experience to seriously test oneself, and becoming self-actualized. I was concerned that so many of my fraternity brothers only wanted a career from their education.

Had I gone into any other field, even engineering or agriculture as I had thought I might, I have little doubt that I would have gravitated, most likely in a university setting, to seeking answers to complex questions, carrying out research, and constructing layers of backup plans. After all, that is what INTJs (introverted-intuitive-thinking-judges) do.

The Keirsey profile of the "Fieldmarshal" fits David pretty well, especially the leadership tendency. He does not like being in a position where nobody will decide what to do, and he senses that he can make the necessary decision better than most people. When we were kids on the ranch, Rita and I typically followed David's lead when he wanted us to. It seemed he expected that of us. Even as adults living far apart, when we get together, David gravitates to arranging things but has seemed surprised sometimes when we have not acquiesced.

David regards losing his arm as the most potent influence in his life. I cannot argue with his perception, but I believe that he would likely have ended up in similar life circumstances if he had had two normally functioning hands, had pursued a different career, or if he had not gone to Laos. David has always tended to "size things up" and decide whether or not it is worth trying to intervene and change an undesirable circumstance, potential or actual. In my opinion, he has always taken the path that, to him at the time, was the least disruptive to his life or to those he cares about. Beyond that, he operates on the assumption that "If you can't change it, there is no use worrying about it." And he decidedly does not worry about it! Additionally, David is highly self-sufficient. He takes care of himself and expects that those around him will do the same.

Whereas, for me, introspection (and even regret) has characterized many of the key choices in my life, practical outcomes have characterized David's choices. With an almost innate sense of power, his personality has guided him into leadership positions most of his life. He likes to take charge and seems to expect others to recognize that. He made a decision as a child that one arm was not going to limit him, and it did not. He calmly recognizes his mistakes, even serious ones, but has few regrets. For David, "What is, is."

David also enjoys adventures just enough on the wild side to experience an adrenalin rush but still come out reasonably unscathed. Who else in high school would join in an escapade to climb a long steep hill on skis, run a bull elk through the deep snow until he was too exhausted to go on, and then figure out a way to put a cowbell on him and turn him loose?

David no doubt has questioned and discarded some of the values or ways of living we all absorbed as children, but among the three of us, I believe he has done so the least. He has been satisfied to maintain his adolescent and early adult orientation and would likely have fit into the Little Snake River Valley lifestyle with ease, if that is where he had stayed. For example, although most recently he has gravitated to a Libertarian perspective, he continues to vote mostly Republican as did our parents and virtually all of our uncles and aunts. He, like they did, holds a profound dislike for most government regulations. If he had become a geologist, as he thought he might, prospecting and doing outside work would have suited him as much as the hands-on, practical research he did as an extension specialist in animal science. In his career, David focused far more energy on the outdoor work with cattle than on the indoor desk work of analysis, writing, and publishing. And he still refers to the noon meal as "dinner" and to the evening meal as "supper."

Rita's personality, in my opinion, has determined her life choices at least as much as any external influences. As her preferred Keirsey profile predicts, she has always been an adventurer. As a child, nothing gave her greater joy than going on long rides with Lillyan and Lexie. She was never afraid to cross the river during high water, to ride to a place where she might get lost, or to worry much about her horse stepping in a badger hole while racing through the sagebrush at a full gallop.

With some reluctance—and as she admits, a healthy dose of gullibility—Rita chose to follow her first two husbands' dreams, the first to the third world countries of Egypt and Nepal, and the second to Alaska. Both involved striking adventures, and she treasures those experiences, but there were downsides. The negatives of daily life outweighed the adventurous positives for her in Nepal. And in Alaska, she took and stayed in a mostly unsatisfying job at a computer programming company for decades. Nevertheless, she adapted and grew to love the state. Dangerous dog sled trips involving blizzards or bone-chilling cold did not deter her from seeking longer and potentially more dangerous treks into the wilderness.

Rita dearly loved our two trail rides in Colorado and Wyoming. And her recent pattern of helping a friend take horses into and out of a hunting camp each year in Alaska continues the adventure. The four-day trip each way involves fording swift rivers, sleeping in essentially abandoned cabins, and lack of communication with the outside world for the ride's duration.

She always had a soft spot in her heart for animals, and horses were among her favorite. Rita's horse, Gypsy, even went to college with her, where they participated in a mounted drill team. Yet even as the youngest of us, Rita was the one who could nurse an orphan lamb back to health after being dropped off at the ranch just a few days old and nearly starved to death. She and Hugh had two dozen sled dogs for a number of years after they moved to Alaska. They shared a deep empathy for those animals and cared for them as members of the family, even as they got old and eventually died.

Rita also has always gravitated to the role of the family caretaker. She was decidedly never drawn to domestic pursuits, but throughout our lives has been the one who has unselfishly kept us in touch through cards, letters, and family visits. Rereading my saved letters while I was at the summer speech therapy program in Laramie, it was she who was by far the most generous in corresponding with me. This may be related to her penchant for writing. She initially studied English and became an accomplished chronicler of numerous Alaska adventures in beautiful prose. And she insists on calling herself the British version of "Rita," where the /t/ is aspirated ("exploded") as in the word "top."

These qualities clearly did not lead her to seek a job as a computer programmer; that job was to pay the bills. Yet, even there, she gravitated to customer relations, where her skills and preferences emerged most strongly. Her last career move, to the Alaska Department of Fish and Game, brought all of Rita's strongest skills and preferences to bear. She interacted with Natives in the bush, typically by flying in less than ideal circumstances in small planes, organized difficult meetings and guided negotiations, and played an important role in re-introducing wood bison back to the Alaska wilderness.

Politically, whereas I have become a liberal Democrat and David, remaining a conservative Republican—but leaning toward Libertarian—like virtually all of our childhood relatives, Rita chose to be a left-leaning Independent. Our joint religious views are somewhat parallel to our political views but not quite so far apart. David and I are now Presbyterian elders, and he is also a lay minister. As well, he is a Gideon. I favor a strong social gospel version of Christianity. David practices his faith in social action too, but also adheres to a much stronger evangelical, personal salvation orientation. Rita is not a church-goer, but she has found great spiritual meaning and support in nature. I would argue that our individual personalities—much more than our life circumstances—led us in these different directions.

Envelope for the November, 1956 election supplies mailed to Dad and, very likely, a copy of the results of the election. Not surprisingly, Republican Dwight Eisenhower received 16 votes versus only one for Democrat Adlai Stevenson. (David remembers that everyone "knew" the Democrat was our teacher, Grace.) Dad received one write-in vote for Justice of the Peace, while Mom got one for Constable. Notable is that the Precinct was in the town of Honnold (location of a bygone US Post Office at or near the Honnold Place).

GROUNDED IN A PLACE

We three did not stay where we grew up, but I, at least, have always felt more centered, more grounded, more in tune with the world in Routt County than anywhere I have lived. I always thought I might retire there, so I bought some random lots at the county tax-delinquent sale of the previous bankrupt Steamboat Lake Development (now called the Willow Creek Pass Association). For decades, I bought, sold, and traded lots to acquire enough to build on. Rae Jean and I achieved that, but then stumbled onto a cabin on the Upper Elk River on the Seedhouse Road. We bought it during the downturn of 2008 for a good price and have gone there every year since for five to eight weeks in the summer.

Over most of our adult lives, before our parents died, Steamboat Springs, the Little Snake River, or surrounding areas were the places we siblings all came together. Various members of our families regularly met there for

Christmases, summer vacations, funerals, and family reunions. After Dad and Mom were gone, it has been our cabin where the majority of our get-togethers have occurred. So, it could be said that we all continue to hold an affinity for the places of our early and later childhood unlike that for anywhere else.

I still have vivid dreams of our ranch. The mountains live forever in my memory: Three Forks, Piney, Twin Buttes, Squaw, Sheep, Mule, Beaver, Columbus, East Gibraltar, West Gibraltar, and Battle. And each time I drive by, I take long looks at the sandstone cliff that caved in over our garage, the cottonwood trees that backed our log house that has been torn down, the sloughs where we played, the vacant location where Willow Creek School stood, and the only remaining refurbished horse barn and deteriorating log shop at Grandpa and Grandma's Home Place. I so would like to walk up the old Hackmaster ditch to its head in Roaring Fork. I would have liked to go into the Pep Hall and maybe hang for a moment on one of the bars across the ceiling before it was razed (as confirmed by Google Earth). I would love to coast down the Temple grade again on a sled. I would enjoy climbing around the rocks at Pine Scope one more time.

The Elk River, where our cabin is located, is not the Little Snake River, but it gives me the same feeling, better in some ways than the childhood ranch because I am not reminded of how much our Little Snake River "Camelot" has changed. It is also near my favorite mountain, Hahns Peak. In the course of researching our past relatives, I discovered, to my surprise and great satisfaction, that Hahns Peak, both the mountain and the village that bears its name, is the capstone in the arch of our heritage.

How did the mountains get their names?

"...Robert McIntosh named many places that appear on our present maps. In the very early days he ranged many horses on the Snake river range and was familiar with every hill and creek. Near the present Columbus mountain he found a lad, as he said, herding cattle. He found the lad to be a Columbus Kelley, so Mr. McIntosh painted on a board a finger pointing to the mountain and the words "Columbus mountain" on it and Columbus mountain it is. He named East and West Gibraltar from their appearance of solid rock, and Beaver mountain from a nearby creek that was a favorite place for beaver. Bears Ears was his suggestion from the twin peaks resembling ears. It is known by this, but Hayden's map has it Anita peak. The origin of the name Sand mountain is not known, but it may be of interest and a surprise to some to know it is twelve feet higher than Hahns peak. Sheep mountain, with a ledge of rocks almost around it, was a natural home for mountain sheep. Here they made their last stand for an existence and their passing from here marked a closing era. Piney mountain, covered with pine timber, but as a whole the mountain resembles a pine tree by its tapering shape. Three Forks mountain is where the three streams came together that form Snake river. Slater park was named for Bill Slater, a trapper, and California park was a name given by Ben Yackey with no particular significance...."

Excerpt from "Early History of Northwest Colorado Presents Endless Anecdotes and Star Features" by Mrs. J. J. Jones, Historian of Routt-Moffat County Pioneer Association in the *Craig Empire*, Number 24, July 6, 1921.

Twin Buttes down the Valley in winter.

Sheep Mountain with sheep in the foreground.

Piney Mountain.

Three Forks Mountain.

Columbus Mountain.

Beaver Mountain.

West Gibraltar with Beaver Mountain in the background.

East Gibraltar with Three Forks and Piney mountains in the background.

When Joseph Hahn discovered gold in 1862 on what Rose Marie Wheeler called "God's Mountain," he set into motion a series of events that came together to greatly define us long before we were born. Hahn died a few years later in a snowstorm, and later, our second great-grandfather Alfred McCargar came to make his fortune in gold at the new mining camps later to become known as Hahns Peak. William Tecumseh (Billie) Morgan, upon being discharged from the US Army Cavalry in Wyoming, found himself at Hahns Peak as well, where he met McCargar's daughter Sarah Mariah, whom he later married. Billie and Sarah were our great-grandparents whose children included Onie Morgan, our grandmother.

Another gold seeker, Robert McIntosh from Quebec, Canada, also came to Hahns Peak, and it was his placer mining operation that constituted the most successful extraction of gold from any of the mines in the area. When the amount of gold no longer justified the expense of extracting it, McIntosh decided to raise horses for the US Army and pasture them in the land south of the Little Snake River. He opened a trading post of sorts and eventually a store in the current location of the Slater Post Office that we knew as children.

Oliver St. Louis, who grew up on a farm just one or two stone-throws from the farm on which close relatives of Robert McIntosh were reared near the little town of Ormstown, Quebec, traveled west to work for McIntosh, herding his horses on the open range. Oliver met and married Onie Morgan and settled about 12 miles up-river from Slater. And, of course, that is where our dad, George St. Louis, was reared and only a half-mile from the place we siblings occupied as children.

On the other side of our family, Joe Ireland, after having given up a homestead in the northeastern part of Colorado near Sedgwick, with his son, Elmer, bought an earlier homestead about a quarter mile northwest of the village of Hahns Peak. This was no doubt because his cousin, Rose Wheeler, had moved there with her husband years earlier. Our mom, Dorothy Grace Ireland, did not grow up in Hahns Peak but had nieces who spent several young childhood years there. Mom did finish high school in nearby Steamboat Springs and also spent two summers at the house still standing at the Ireland Place at Hahns Peak. It was because of her living and going to dances there, at the Wheelers' dance hall, that she somehow met Lucy Temple and, later, Dad.

Hahns Peak also intersected our family's life and heritage in other important ways. The village was the location of many dances in the 1920s to

Magnificent Hahns Peak from a variety of angles.

1950s that Dad and his brothers eagerly attended. The peak itself is the only mountain that everyone in our family has climbed, including Mom. Our own childhood home was a former log saloon in Hahns Peak village that Dad somehow acquired, dismantled log-by-log, hauled by hayrack and sled to our ranch site, and reassembled. My earliest memory of our ranching was Dad running cows and calves at the Frye Place just east of Hahns Peak village, now mostly under water from Steamboat Lake. Dad and Gus Ranch worked for part of one summer opening an old molybdenum mine just southeast of the mountain. Dad talked about buying 160 acres of deeded land in the middle of the Routt National Forest in the middle of Big Red Park, which is directly on the north side of the mountain. (Regrettably, no such negotiations ever happened.) When we moved to Steamboat for high school, we drove from the ranch to Steamboat, or the other way, "over the hill," directly past Hahns Peak hundreds of times. I chose to do a junior high theme on Hahns Peak, and went to the local library to do research on its early history.

As important as all of these direct or oblique connections to Hahns Peak are to us, there is the raw captivating beauty of "God's Mountain" itself. It has an almost perfect volcanic, inverted cone shape with a tiny fire lookout station on the top. Although not the highest mountain in the area at 10,843 feet, it stands out singularly among numerous others in Routt County. A friend from Japan once told me it looked like their famous Mount Fuji. All five of us, Dad, Mom, David, Rita, and I, have stopped numerous times over the years to take yet another photo of the mountain from a more perfect spot. Rita recently painted a water color image of the mountain that sold handsomely at a recent Ireland family reunion. And although we cannot see it from our cabin, which is only a few miles southeast as the crow flies, one of our first side trips each visit to the cabin is to drive up Colorado 129 to take in the view of this magnificent mountain.

WISDOM TO PASS ON

The "legacy letter" or "ethical will" from Jewish tradition is often written by people in their twilight years to pass on what wisdom they have acquired in their lives. That was one purpose of this book. We could each have written lists of our individual pearls of wisdom to pass on to our descendants. But such wisdom—if it can even be called wisdom—must certainly come mainly from the choices we have made and our adaptations to the circumstances simply handed to or encountered by us as we lived our lives. Accordingly, a large part of the individual and joint life stories of David, Rita, and me simply are that wisdom. In our individual ways, we have been successful. And we have lived full lives. Thus, the achievements that got us to our mid-70s are worth considering for someone who might want to take something important from our lives. So, too are our mistakes, regrets, and tragedies, because no one gets very far in life without experiencing suffering and loss.

Humbly, then, we dedicate these pages to our children, grandchildren, great-grandchildren, and anyone else who might find themselves reading the stories, perusing the photographs, discovering that they might be related to us, or even doing some of their own genealogical research. If wisdom jumps out at anyone, or even percolates up later, we are pleased.

A FINAL TURNING POINT

As this book is nearing completion, the entire world finds itself suddenly in a calamitous upheaval, caused by a virus known as SARS-CoV-2 (novel coronavirus) that results in the disease called COVID-19 (Coronavirus disease in 2019). More than a million people worldwide have died from COVID-19, and possibly one of us will be among the final count. This coronavirus pandemic will become a major defining moment in the lives of most young people in the world henceforth. It is less likely, but possible, that it will become for us a major life-changing event as well.

At this point, the pandemic reminds me that all of our lives are transient. Certainties turn out not to be certain. Reclaiming my life of just a few months ago will be impossible. In fact, no one has ever been truly able to relive the past. The pandemic reminds me that finishing this book for my descendants is important, and I am confident that my brother and sister would agree.

Appendix A

Native Son—Obituary for George Edwin St. Louis

He was born and lived most of his life in a small valley by a little river. A river that begins in minor mountains and flows in a narrow strip through high desert. An unknown river, really, except to those lucky enough to live along its course.

He was not a famous person. He did not make a mark in the world of business, of science, of politics, of art. And yet, in the ways that matter, George St. Louis was rich.

He was rich in the company and honor of his friends: rodeoing, boxing, working, horseplay as a young man; Valley-wide doin's and help for others in maturity; visiting, cards, reunions, still working long into the age of retirement.

He was rich in heritage. Arising from pioneer stock, he grew in a new land where the cowboy legend had been born and was being turned into one of the vital myths of the land. The richness of the West is for us to inherit—he lived it.

He was rich in work—the mark of the man, performed with honor and dignity, meaningful in the word's root sense, and, yes, he was rich in work simply because there was a joy in its doing.

He was rich in courage. How many were the disappointments he met, the sorrow he bore? How many the battles he entered with a proud fighter's heart?

And can we possibly forget? He was rich in song. In the songs of his father, his Valley, his life. In rhymes for family; in ditties for dudes, in ballads for Valley doin's; and in real songs of the West for children halfway around the world. In songs that tripped the tongue, in songs full of love and devils and broncs and punchin' the dough. In the song of life.

For George was rich in life. He made and shared eternity through every moment lived in fullness, in acceptance of the hurt and pain and hardship that are our common lot. His strength, the spirit that brought him through the hard times with honor and dignity and through the good times with pleasure for all who knew him to share, was this very richness in the moment, richness in connection with Creation.

And yet, perhaps George St. Louis was richest in family. In his wife Vivian who shared many of his last years. In his wife Grace, who, although long divorced, deeply honors both him and herself by her friendship and grief at his passing. In brothers, who shared pranks beyond count on the old home place, who shared hours of work that would stun many people today, who shared the growing up of their families, dispersal as the world and the Valley changed, and finally a coming together again at their roots. In nieces and nephews—visiting for a taste of the ranch, and leaving with lessons on how to work and how to live. And George was rich in his children and grandchildren. They are his special bequest. Patient parent, teacher: he showed how to live with dignity, with respect toward others, with humor, and yes, by God, with joy in living. His children carry his legacy in their hearts to undreamed of places and achievements, and his grandchildren will carry him to yet even more undreamed of triumphs.

We celebrate today the fullness of the life of this man, lived in a little valley, unimportant in the large affairs of men and states. But a life filled with the glory that God gives to a man and rich in the glory he returned to God through his complete connectedness to the life given him. May we honor him and praise him with the company of our friends, in the joy of our heritage, in our work, in our songs, in our families—in our living.

—Hugh S. Richards, January 1, 1991

Appendix B

Native Daughter—Obituary for Dorothy Grace Ireland St. Louis

Dorothy Grace Ireland St. Louis was a native daughter of the pioneers who settled the Centennial State of Colorado. Born in 1922 in the great plains near the North Platte River northwest of Sedgwick, Colorado, she grew up on a dryland farm homestead with her parents, four sisters, and one brother. (Another brother and sister had died of scarlet fever before she was born, and a baby sister born five years later lived only three days.)

Grace went to school in Sedgwick, Evans, Akron, Greeley, and Steamboat Springs (graduating as valedictorian of her class in 1940). She lived two summers in Hahns Peak and, after high school, worked at a dude ranch. There, she met and eventually married George St. Louis in 1941 and moved permanently to the mountains in the Little Snake River Valley, an area that could not decide if it belonged to Colorado or Wyoming. On a ranch in that corner of Routt County, she raised her own children, two sons and a daughter.

The years were hard and steady: preparing the daily three large meals on the wood and coal stove in the kitchen, doing laundry that took an entire day to complete, hosting yearly visits from families of relatives from the "Eastern Slope" who were seeking a fishing trip after their wheat harvest, serving huge helpings of fried chicken or steaks to the hay crew when it got around to stacking the hay at George's "place," keeping a vegetable garden, raising and cleaning chickens, arbitrating fights and meting out appropriate punishments for her children and for whatever other St. Louis and other cousins might be present, fixing lunch for her children who walked to the one-room schoolhouse just down the road, driving to 4-H meetings, using the twenty-one-family party phone line, getting ready for the county fair in Rawlins, Wyoming, doing Christmas shopping from the Wards and Sears catalogues, struggling not to get snowed in or having the water freeze during the long winters, joining family dinners at the St. Louis "home place" for holidays, making infrequent trips to Craig or Steamboat to shop, dressing up for dances at the nearby "Pep Hall" or in Dixon, Wyoming, and helping out with the yearly school programs.

This misnomer of a "routine" was further punctuated by events and experiences such as organizing the women of the Valley to bring in the REA (Rural Electrification Association) or gravel for the road, a brief but failed attempt to "sell out" and move to Montana, numerous cattle and sheep operations, a serious automobile accident affecting her older son, cooking for hunting camps, a winter in La Sal, Utah, at a uranium mining camp, and a trip to California for her younger son to see a speech therapist. During her children's high school years, she managed a home on the ranch and a house in Steamboat, and—at the same time—worked in town, first as a drugstore clerk and then as a bank employee.

Beginning in 1963, Grace's and George's lives changed dramatically. They sold the ranch but found that staying on as caretakers did not work out. They looked elsewhere: ranch work near Steamboat...a stint operating a laundromat in Boulder...a new ranch and move to Cusick, Washington, followed by a crushing depression for Grace and subsequent return to Steamboat.... After the return, Grace and George drifted apart and eventually divorced. They both remarried but, in spite of their separate lives, continued to care deeply about each other until their deaths.

In 1967, Grace bought a house in Steamboat and worked there for twenty-one years until she retired. She became a mainstay at the bank, working her way up through several positions, with the reputation for being friendly, helpful, thorough, accurate, and discreet with her customers. It was during the two decades in her red house on 7th Street that she came to know (in limited visits) her grandchildren and her son- and daughters-in-law. Intermittently, she traveled widely in North America to visit her scattered children and other vacation spots.

After retiring from the bank in 1988, Grace moved to Grand Junction to a beautiful little house on a cul-de-sac with lots of flowers and windows. Grace enjoyed her volunteer work at the Chamber of Commerce and Senior Citizens Center. It was during this time that she made several quilts and afghans for her children and grandchildren. Early on, she traveled to visit her children (once overseas to the Netherlands) and faithfully attended family reunions, but the family, including several new members, typically came to visit her. She lived in—and truly enjoyed—her own home until November 1997, but her advancing lung disease became too severe for her to stay alone. She spent her last six months in assisted living, nursing home, and hospital care.

Grace was a rugged individual, survivor, devoted mother, and passionate student of life. She was a private person; thus most people knew only a little of this complex and remarkable woman. She never sought nor accepted easy answers, though she longed for meaning in her existence. Hardened by formative years during the Depression and by the death of her mother when she was only ten, she knew poverty and adversity, perhaps even despair, firsthand. No doubt influenced by these experiences, she knew, expected, and taught the value of hard work, perseverance, and taking responsibility for one's own choices. Grace always seemed to rise to whatever challenge faced her. She was a master organizer and took great pride in her household; everything was clean, organized, and functional. "Always in control" was often used by others to describe this woman, even in irony, as when she might declare, "I don't get sick!" during a bout with the flu. She took charge of her own affairs, and her five-feet, two-inch stature stood much taller at those times when she firmly resisted controlling suggestions from others.

There was a soft side to her as well. As a young girl at her mother's side, she experienced the healing that comes from song, the perspective that comes from a sense of humor, and the lesson that "poor" means neither "dumb" nor "second class." Grace maintained a warm but proud dignity about her, visible in her walk, her clothes, her home. She was known in elementary school by her smile, and by many who later knew her as a person with uncommon compassion, generosity, and tolerance. She loved dancing, the works of artist Vincent Van Gogh, good books, windmills, serving her famous homemade dinner rolls, and, yes, even figuring out IRS forms for people. And, in rare instances of "giving in," she forgave with a smile those who might dare to change her identity to "Dot" or even "Auntie Mac."

Her acquaintances were many, but she especially valued her deep friendships wherein she experienced an easy reciprocity. When given or taken freely, she loved to help others and to learn from them as well. Her friend and sister-in-law on Snake River, Elizabeth ("Betty") St. Louis, provided intellectual and artistic gifts to her from the best Europe had to offer. In turn, Grace gave Elizabeth the perspective and skills to cope with the rigors of cooking for hay crews and finding stimulating conversation in an isolated valley. Grace always had a warm empathy for her sisters-in-law, Agnes

Russell, and Grace (Burkardt) St. Louis, both schoolteachers and outsiders who—like herself—married into a St. Louis family with strong expectations of what wives should be or do. She always liked and respected Lucy Temple, her first employer at the nearby dude ranch and later devoted neighbor. She valued her Steamboat friends—several of whom moved to Grand Junction for retirement as well: Earl ("Pinky") Smith, DVM, Barbara Hudspeth, Judy Bagley, Don and Eileen Lufkin, and Ernie Anderson, Ralph Selch, Ellen Winchell, Charlie and Bob Swinehart, and many others. Over the years, but especially during her twilight years in Grand Junction, she appreciated and valued the help of her sister Doris Ranch. She treasured the relationships built up with her next-door neighbors, Mr. and Mrs. Melecio Martinez, and her niece and close friend, Maxine Forrest.

Most of all, she loved her children. Near death in a moment of unusual candor, she commented that her daughter, Rita, was her "best friend," that her son David was her "religious and financial advisor," and that her son Kenneth was her "confidant." After a courageous rally to say "Goodbye" to each of her children and her sister, Doris, she died peacefully in the presence of her niece on June 8, 1998, at St. Mary's Hospital in Grand Junction. Grace died knowing that she was not alone. After leaving the Little Snake River well behind her for more than thirty years, Grace experienced a change of heart; she chose to be buried at the Reader Cemetery near Savery, Wyoming, next to her former husband, George. May she find in death the meaning and peace that, by their very nature—and her own, were destined to elude her in life.

—Kenneth O. St. Louis, June 8, 1998

Reprinted with permission. Original reference: St. Louis, K. (2000). "Native Daughter." In R. J. V. Sielen, N. E. Weber, & J. A. Ross (Eds.) *One Among Many: America Stories of the People.* (pp: 133–134). Morgantown, WV: Populore.

Appendix C
Early Memories

Dad (Joseph "Joe" Otto Ireland) was from St. Elmo, Illinois, and Mama (Laura Frances "Fannie" Galvin Ireland) was from Nevada, Missouri. My older sisters did not know how they met. Around 1910, they left Illinois with their children, Elmer and Ruby. They stayed with Grandma Ireland's sister, Belle Hodges, in Kenesaw, Nebraska. They were on their way to Colorado to claim their homestead rights under the Homestead Act of 1862, a dryland farm six miles north of Sedgwick in Sedgwick County in the northeastern part of the state.

Mama had her babies at home. When it was time, the children were sent to the neighbors or to school. Aunt Delilah (Dad's sister-in-law) or someone would come to look after Mama. Velma remembers that if the doctor got there before the children were gone, she and Violet wondered how he could carry a baby in his little satchel.

Ruby recalled that their first house was built in the side of a hill with a roof sloping to the ground. As a little girl, she remembered the dog howling from the rooftop. By the time I came along, Dad had built a two-room house over a concrete basement. He built a pantry (a luxury at the time) and then attached a porch to the kitchen. He also added a parlor and a second bedroom. I was the youngest of six living children. Doris and I used the bedroom, and Mama and Dad used the parlor as their bedroom. Dad also added a half story upstairs that included one large bedroom for Velma, Violet, and Ruby (when she was home) and a smaller room for Elmer. I remember that the downstairs had hardwood floors and plenty of windows. Mama kept the windows spotless. They had dark green roller window shades but no curtains. The upstairs had dormer windows.

The dining room was filled with a large table, many chairs and a buffet with a mirror. I liked looking at a few "beautiful" dishes in the buffet and I remember climbing on a chair, looking in the mirror and saying, "I think I pretty."

Dining rooms and kitchens were the center of social happenings such as playing cards or just reading. Neighbors who had a living room that did not have to be a bedroom sometimes gave dances. The grownups danced in the living room to a fiddle and banjo or such and the kids danced in a bedroom. Doris and I demonstrated the Schottische.

The upstairs rooms had sloping ceilings with fascinating storage places under the eaves. Clothes closets could be a shelf with a flowered "cretonne" curtain around it to hide the contents. There was not much need for large closets. Probably, women and girls had about two everyday dresses and one good dress which was the newest cotton dress. When an everyday dress wore out or was outgrown, a new one became the good dress and the preceding good dress became an everyday dress. Children had one pair of shoes and adults may have had two pairs.

I played with my one doll and with cats. I remember cutting the long sleeves from a worn-out adult dress and making dresses for cats from them.

Elmer, the oldest of the siblings, was sixteen when I was born. To me he was a grown man as was Ruby a grown woman. Elmer took a man's place on the farm and Ruby was away teaching and then married. Elmer teased me and I was sort of afraid of him when I was little. Of course, we were all afraid of Dad. On rare occasions when we really wanted to go to a movie (picture show) or a circus if one was in town, it was Doris who had courage enough to ask Dad to take us. You may believe I didn't ask.

We had a black mare "Old Nell" at Sedgwick, and Violet was mainly the one who rode her to bring the milk cows in from the pasture.

I vaguely remember Dad's Model T Ford. I think the gas was fed with levers on the steering column. He later got a car with a gear shift that caused a great deal of cussing to be emitted. Elmer had a one seat "roadster" that had faulty brakes. When Mama would see him coming from a distance, she would send someone out to open the gate into the area where the car was kept. Elmer would drive through the gate and go around and around a shed until resistance helped the car stop.

Dad somehow provided a lovely pump organ for Mama who had an extraordinary gift for music. She could hear a tune once and pick it out on the organ. She sang while performing regular tasks and played an organ for Sunday school when it was held at the schoolhouse. Sometimes everyone— except Elmer and Dad—gathered around and sang. Dad used to ask Doris and me to sing certain songs for him after Mama was gone. As I have been told, "Let Me Call You Sweetheart" is the first song that I learned to sing.

That tune and many others learned through the years roll around in my being even though I can no longer sing.

Back then, older sisters and mothers (brothers and fathers in some families) obtained sheet music from which to learn the new popular songs along with learning those that were being passed down from different generations. The "affluent" must have purchased the sheet music and passed the song around to friends.

My mother, as I remember, played mostly church hymns, but she apparently had sheet music for "Three O'clock in the Morning" and "Silver Threads Among the Gold." Probably she had a book of church hymns. Eventually Ruby taught school and had money to buy a few luxuries. (One could qualify to teach grade school after a session of summer school at a teacher's college.) She sent home a beautiful tone on tone blue portable wind-up phonograph and one or two records. One of the records (perhaps the only one) was "My Blue Heaven."

Some songs I learned from Mama were "Bluebell" (my most favorite), "Christine Leroy" (which I did not understand about someone losing her man to Christine), "Yankee Doodle," "Rock of Ages" (how could you hide yourself in a rock?), "The Old Rugged Cross" (I think it had slivers in it), "Higher Ground" (going up a hill), "Old Black Joe" (I thought Dad was old Black Joe since his whiskers were black and his name was Joe)...the list could go on. Fortunately, I have a copy of a notebook in which Violet wrote down the words of the songs sang.

In spite of predawn hours, many cows to milk twice a day, chickens and eggs to be taken care of, and helping with household work, the family always made some fun—what Ruby called "home-spun fun." We squirted milk in the pocket of someone milking next to us, we squirted milk into others' faces, and we sang. Once I was singing so loudly that I couldn't hear others telling me to shush because someone was coming. So, Ed Lyons walked in the barn to my concert.

I don't know from whom I learned cowboy songs, which were usually deliciously sad.

When there was a chautauqua (a musical or variety show) near enough, Dad and Mama took us to it. We also went quite a distance to house dances. Mama often chorded (seconded, as it could be called) to what the dance "band" was playing. The "band" was often a fiddle and a banjo. The adults waltzed, two-stepped, or square danced. They also performed the Schottische and the heel-toe polka.

Dad square danced but Velma did not know if he did the waltz or two-step. The children had their dancing corner, and we all learned to dance at an early age. Later, when Elmer was a young man, he would take Velma and Violet with him when he went dancing.

Velma took music lessons from two different school teachers, but she essentially taught herself to read notes and play. I still remember her keyboard rendition of "Falling Waters" with its trills. Ruby sent sheet music home for us. Velma and Violet both had notable singing voices. They sang duets at community gatherings—Violet singing a lovely soprano and Velma singing alto.

It was perhaps at a chautauqua in 1918 that our family was exposed to scarlet fever. Clarence, age eight, Gladys, age six, and Velma, age three, became gravely ill. Mama moved into the schoolhouse across the road with the well children—Elmer, age twelve, Ruby, age ten, and Violet, age one. Dad stayed in the main house and took care of Clarence, Gladys, and Velma. A nurse from Omaha eventually came to help. Gladys died and then Clarence died four days later. Velma was seriously ill, but recovered. The dead children were put in the cellar until they could be buried at the Sedgwick cemetery, where baby Mary Lois was later buried. Velma said Mama did not talk about these tragedies—not one word.

Mama made all the clothes for the girls and herself with a Singer treadle sewing machine. Underpants, called bloomers, came almost to the knees with elastic encased in the bottom of each leg. These were made from sateen, a shiny soft cotton fabric. Bras, called brassieres, were made from bleached or unbleached muslin. Underskirts, or slips, were made of lawn, a fine cotton cloth. Nightgowns were made of cotton outing flannel. Sheets and pillowcases were made from unbleached muslin. Dish towels were made from opened and hemmed flour sacks and sugar sacks. Toweling was bought by the yard, cut, and hemmed.

Mama never cut her hair. She arranged it into a soft bun and curled the shorter stray hairs around her ears. She let all of us comb her hair, which was black streaked with white.

Two of Mama's sisters, Addie and Minnie, lived in the Sedgwick community. Addie was married to Oren Chezum, and they had four children: Lillian, Ralph, Wilbur, and Sylvia. Both Ralph and Sylvia died at an early age. Aunt Addie was little—so tiny she wore children's shoes. Velma and Violet wondered how she had babies. Uncle Oren was a little thin man with crippled feet—a barber by trade. Occasionally Dad would say, "Let's go to

Addie's today." They lived only a mile away. Often the menu was wonderful chicken and noodles, especially if it was Sunday. Sometimes Velma and Violet were each given a quarter to get a haircut from Uncle Oren. Aunt Minnie was married to Elmer Williams, and they had two children: Carl and Lucille. They lived several miles north of us toward Lodgepole. Dad's brother, Bob Ireland, and his wife, Delilah, also lived close to Sedgwick with their children: Lloyd, Glen, Opal, and Nola. Uncle Bob was a policeman. Opal and Ruby were not only cousins but good friends as were Velma and Nola.

I remember the last baby, Mary Lois, who was born when I was five. It was December 23, and I had gone to school and been part of the traditional Christmas activity. Doris and I bounded into the bedroom to show Mama what we had received. When we were through, she turned back the sheet and said, "Look what I got for Christmas." It was a baby sister. Sadly, the baby died three days later. I remember the little dress that Ruby made for the baby's burial.

I attended the Sedgwick one-room country school for first and second grades. My recollections of those two years are few. Violet taught me the Schottische on the way home from school (a one-mile walk). Another memory is of the billy goat. Someone who lived close to the school had goats. The big kids, which included Velma and Violet, would call the male goat over to the school at recesses and noon and tease him so he would chase them around the schoolhouse. Of course, I did not have the courage to join in or to go to the toilet when the goat was there. I wet my pants.

Velma and Violet were both good students, but Velma took the eighth grade for a second year. For some reason she could not be sent into Sedgwick for high school. The next year she did go into town and stay with some folks so she could do ninth grade.

When Velma was a freshman in high school she stayed in town with a family and worked for her room and board. In the spring Velma saw a wagon go by and thought it looked like Dad and his team of horses. She soon learned that Dad had bought a place at Akron and was finishing some business in Sedgwick. Dad moved the family to the farm southwest of Akron. By that time, Ruby was married to Louis Lawler, who had been hired by Dad to shuck corn, and was living in Paxton, Nebraska.

We moved to a farm thirteen miles from Akron, Colorado, when I was seven. We went to Akron town school for one school year so that Violet and Velma could attend ninth and tenth grades in high school. Dad rented part of a house for the four of us for the school year while Mama stayed on the farm with Elmer and Dad. That was the last year of school for Velma and Violet because Velma did not want to go anymore and Dad would not let Violet live in town without Velma. Also, the next fall Dad said he just did not have enough money for high school. (He had bought 320 acres for $1,600 with a loan from Federal Land Bank, and payments had to be made on it.) I don't think Violet ever quit resenting the fact that she had fewer years of school than any of us. How tragic since she was a natural scholar. I will add that she did become educated even if it was not in school.

Fourth and fifth, and probably part of the sixth, grades were spent in a one-room country school at Akron. Doris and I rode the horse "Old Nell" four miles to school. The old plug, pretty as she was, would trot but she almost refused to gallop. It took about an hour to ride the distance. In the winter the prairie winds and snow can be terribly cold. Sometimes we turned around backwards on the horse so as not to face the stinging cold if it was coming from the frontward direction. In good weather, we were quite creative on those long horseback rides. We would sing songs, give plays, speak pieces and entertain the cornstalks and prairie dogs, which were our audience.

Long underwear, bloomers, long heavy stockings, a flannel petticoat under a dress and all were encased in bib overalls and coats for riding the horse in winter. The bib overall—over a dress—were also summer riding gear. The newest bib overalls were for riding to school, and the old ones for milking cows, feeding calves and other farm chores. Of course, the overalls were taken off for the school day and for hours in and around the house.

Velma remembers Dad taking Mama to a doctor in Sterling, which meant she must have been quite ill. She had high blood pressure. Early one morning in 1933 she had a stroke. Dr. Crawford came and did what he could. Mama was taken to Denver where she died about ten days later. It was just a few days before her forty-fifth birthday.

It is strange what one remembers. Upon hearing of Mama's death, we four girls, Velma, Violet, Doris and I, congregated in the outdoor toilet, with my crying and my sisters comforting me. I remember our being with Aunt Delilah when a dress was picked out to bury Mama in. A grey crepe dress with a decorative jeweled oversized safety pin. I was puzzled by the purchase of ready-made clothes since the clothes I had seen were made by Mama. Velma and Violet also bought dresses for the funeral. Doris and I wore some new cotton dresses that Mama had just made. I had never been to a funeral. Aunt Delilah brought and shared a supply of handkerchiefs. How did she know we would need them?

I suppose I missed my mother more a few years later. At the time I was sad, but I don't think I felt abandoned. I am thankful to have known her as long as I did. Ruby, Elmer, Velma, and Violet knew her better than Doris and I did since they had more years with her. From what I have heard and what I know, she must have been kind and gentle and special. Her life had to be everything but easy. She was a refined lady. Somehow, we did learn what is proper and not proper, at least in our limited environment. Of necessity, we grew up creating our own fun, and we did not lose our penchant for "home-spun fun." Mama had to have known some of the things we did in the name of fun. There is no doubt that she had a good sense of humor.

Not long after Mama's death Dad had a succession of housekeepers. He would put an ad in the Denver paper for a "housekeeper for a mother-less home" and stay in a Denver hotel for interviews. This was during the Depression; women had very few choices for work, and some were enough in need to try whatever was offered. I wonder how many housekeepers came and went from our home. Dad instructed them not to do the work because it would spoil his girls, and they needed to do the work. Each woman stayed a few days, a week, a month, or maybe more.

I would say some would not tolerate the farm conditions with no water in the house, an outside toilet, and the relatively crowded quarters. Of course, personality clashes could be a reason. Whatever the reason, it did not take any one long to quit or get fired. Velma later admitted that she worked at making them miserable so they would leave.

Becky came as another housekeeper with her son, Charles, who was little older than Doris. She convinced him that one could get milk from a cow by pumping her tail. He tried. Charles didn't stay long. I suppose he went to Denver and lived with his sister or to Illinois to live with a brother. Becky came and went more than once.

Velma and Violet were dating brothers, Joe and Louie Gebauer. They, including Joe and Louie, were very good to Doris and me. They took us to the barn dances, which were special, and included us whenever they could. Can you imagine brazen little sisters inviting them to the barn on Sunday evening and telling them we had lots of extra buckets and milk stools?

There were about thirty milk cows and everyone except Dad and the housekeeper helped with milking, feeding calves and pigs and separating the milk. The cream was sold in ten-gallon cans. It was taken into town, left at the depot to be transported to Denver to a processing place and the check would come in the mail. Statistics with the check stated the pounds and butterfat content of the cream which ultimately determined the amount of the check. The cream checks probably paid all expenses including one of two hired men's wages. It runs in my mind that a good man got fifteen dollars plus room and board per month. There would have been some pigs, calves and old cows to sell which would supplement the cream check and maybe contribute to a savings account.

Dad, Doris and I went to live with Aunt Dema for a short while when I was eleven. Aunt Dema was Dad's sister and she lived close to Evans, Colorado, a small town close to Greeley. I mostly remember that Aunt Dema made us each a dark dress from some old dresses and made us wear that dress to school for a week before it could be washed. That bothered me because I was always prone to get my clothes dirty fast. Mama had just given me a clean cotton print dress to put on. They were happy dresses by contrast. Another memory of living with Aunt Dema was the comb honey of which Doris and I stole a mouthful every time we set the table.

Well, that didn't last long. Dad and Aunt Dema couldn't get along so Dad, Doris and I moved into Evans in a house owned by an old man who kept one side of the house for himself but came to eat with us. That is probably how the rent was paid. How that old coot stunk. We had to sit at the table with him while he gummed his food. It was impossible to keep the bedbugs under control because they would come from his side of the house no matter how hard we worked at killing them on our side.

We lived in various houses in Evans and in the country close to Evans. Sometimes we went to Evans town school and sometimes a rural school. We obtained novels from the school library which was the evening pasttime. We would sit at the dining table with a kerosene or gasoline lamp to read by.

We were aware that other girls did not have underwear lumps under their stockings. (Underwear lumps are the legs of long underwear folded over so the stockings could be pulled up over the underwear.) The stockings were heavy cotton and we had to darn the holes in them as they occurred. We walked to school and when we lived in the country, we wore boys four-buckle overshoes in wet weather over our boys high-top shoes. (Boy's clothes lasted longer.) Some other girls had lighter zipper overshoes, low cut shoes and no underwear lumps.

Of course, there were the blessed cow(s) to milk most of the time. Doris and I would be up first in the morning, build the fire, go do the milking, tend the chickens and then go in to cook breakfast for Dad and whatever housekeeper, if any, who was there before going to school. Breakfast was cooked cereal, eggs and bread. We may have washed dishes and milk utensils too before going to school.

At some point Dad married Becky. She had been there as a housekeeper a few times prior to the marriage and like other housekeepers we felt it was just one more person to cook for. Actually, in spite of what seemed to be innate laziness, she taught us quite a lot such as how one gets pregnant. Our information was sketchy. She would tell Dad that the groceries cost more than they really did so she could buy us stockings more like other girls wore. She saw that I had a nice dress for ninth-grade graduation. But her nagging nearly drove me to desperation.

For ninth grade, the last year of junior high school from which one graduated, we lived in town at Evans. Dad owned and operated a liquor store and leased out the attached filling station that came with the purchase. We lived in some rooms of the same building. By this time, Doris had graduated from ninth grade in the three-room country school wearing a pretty dress, which our older sisters got for her. She went to Greeley High School for the first year of high school, which was tenth grade. I went to the Evans school. This situation had its pluses since we could wear each other's clothes and appear to have more than we did.

Sometime previous to this, the lumpy legs and boys shoes had been phased out. When Dad would ask us if we had enough winter underwear, the answer would be yes. Well, we had them, but we didn't put them on.

I did well in school and was the valedictorian of the ninth-grade graduating class. I was a good student. I guess I have always compensated for less than desirable circumstances by trying to be the best. (Exclude athletics here. If I was not good, I refused to try.)

When Doris and I were teenagers, I loved the summers we spent at Akron with Violet and Joe and with Velma and Louie. One of us would stay at one place and one at the other. They paid us to help with housework and chores, which I doubt they could afford. The money provided for bus tickets and a few clothes. The wage was about two dollars fifty cents a week. They still took us to the dances, taught us how to drive a car, and generally filled in as parents. Violet taught me the requirements for a balanced meal, instructed me when I made my first dress, taught me about etiquette, and showed me how to fix my hair. Violet could sew any kind of garment, including tailored jackets and coats. She had an extraordinary sense of humor and sometimes had difficulty reprimanding her children when they needed it because she would "get so tickled" over what they did.

David, Velma and Louis's firstborn, was the busiest little boy I have ever known. That little two-and-a-half-year-old could get from one place to the other faster than is imaginable. I remember going out the back door and a quarter of the way around the small house, glancing in the window, and finding that David had pulled a chair up to the water bucket and started dipping water onto the floor. Another of David's favorite jobs was to use any receptacle available and dip water out of the chicken trough onto the ground. If he got spanked, he would just say "ouch" and carry on.

Charlotte, the fifteen-month-old sister toddled around and tried everything David did. Once, after a search, I found them both in the chicken house, sitting innocently under the chicken roost where the chickens perched at night. They looked so little and cute, but there were broken eggs all over them as well as on the wall and floor of the chicken house.

For church on Sunday and going to town on Saturday everyone got dressed up—Charlotte in her pretty little dress, her little white shoes that I had just polished, and her freshly washed white hair. David had dress-up outfits too, and he got scrubbed up for the occasions. It was a challenge to keep them clean until we got them into the car.

Velma recently asked me if I remembered the time when David got into the hired man's car and patted axle grease all over the seats. I said, "Yes, I remember."

No matter how much work we had to do, we always seemed to make lots of fun. Velma recalled how she and I started playing outside when we were supposed to be catching some young chickens to fry for the harvest crew and almost forgot to get dinner on time. She was hauling me around in the wheelbarrow like she had when I was really little.

She and I would sing "opera," which meant our faces were about four inches apart, and we sang "Ahh" in our highest and loudest soprano. We said we were looking at each other's tonsils. When I had to go to the doctor and he told me to open my mouth and say "Ahh," we both nearly lost it.

There was an abundance of giggles and belly laughs along with cooking; cleaning; carrying water; milking a few cows; separating milk; feeding chickens, pigs, and calves; and washing and ironing. Velma taught me a lot about sewing, too.

In those days, even though I lived and went to school in Evans, Akron still felt like home.

After coming and going as housekeeper several times and coming and going as Dad's wife a few times, Becky divorced Dad a second time from their second marriage to each other.

Now, enter Sylvia. She was a simple girl of about 25 and Dad married her. She came from a very fundamentally religious but financially poor family who, I think, encouraged the marriage. This was placing one of several girls as well as maybe feathering a nest or two since Dad was relatively rich, but Dad nipped that with what we now call a pre-marital agreement.

Dad's life was mostly taken up by a lawsuit in Illinois where he and his brothers and sisters were trying to get a share of the mineral rights from his father's farm. He and his siblings did win some shares of a producing oil well. He bought a small ranch at Hahns Peak. Elmer and Lillian were partners and lived at the place all year. Dad and Sylvia spent a summer there, and Doris and I were introduced to the mountains. We enjoyed the summers there because of the fun dances at Pinedale dance hall. (Pinedale is now submerged by Steamboat Lake.) The Wheelers had built the dance hall on part of their place, they furnished the music and they sold midnight buns, wieners and cake. I'll never forget those sourdough buns that Rose Wheeler made, and I'm not remembering them because they were good. But when a fellow bought your supper, that was romance, and the food did not matter. Rex Wheeler sort of courted me and it was OK because I had a reliable means of getting to and from the dance each Saturday. Since he played in the family dance band, I didn't have to dance with him very much. Dad would not have let us go with just anyone. The ultimate was to get to dance every dance with someone. Doris and Gus became an item at those dances.

My tenth and eleventh grades were spent at Greeley High School. How thankful I am for those two years at progressive Greeley High. A biology teacher allowed and encouraged his students to study what most interested them and make whatever form of report they chose from their study. I did a complicated research on intelligence and heredity, which led to learning about chromosomes and genes. In English literature class, I learned to appreciate Shakespeare. I learned some basics of public speaking which we were taught in conjunction with our reports on what we were studying. I thoroughly enjoyed drama class, even if I did not get any leads in plays. French was fun. I was good at it, and I learned lots of grammar because of it. I can't say much for my talents with geometry and history. I had been good in arithmetic, but I could never fathom geometry and algebra. During those two school years I stayed with Harley and Ethel Smith and their daughter, Lois. I worked for my room and board doing cooking, dish washing, house-cleaning and sometimes bringing in the wood and coal for fires. Ethel, Harley and Floyd, a nephew who stayed there, worked. Lois, a little girl of ten, and I were the first ones home in the evenings, so I prepared most of the dinner. I would start homework rather late. I remember standing up to study so I could stay awake. The real compensation was having Floyd as a friend. He was fun, kind and good. I suppose he was my first love even if he did not know it.

Doris stayed with a family in Greeley, and we saw each other only during noon hour and at French class, which we both attended except for rare occasions.

After eleventh grade I worked as a hired girl for an old couple in Greeley for a short while—just long enough to save up bus fare. It was a gloomy quiet place and in desperation I asked Elmer and Lillian at Hahns Peak if I could come spend the rest of the summer with them. I think Doris was living with Ruby and her family in Scottsbluff. She had graduated from high school. While I was at Hahns Peak, I decided to go to Steamboat Springs for my senior year.

I had more fun than I ever had during that last year of high school. I tried skiing, I skipped school (and got caught) for the first time and got the first D that I ever had, and it did not bother me. The D was in algebra. All was rewarding because at last I was overcoming some complexes. There, I could shine in public speaking and drama fields because I had training that was not offered in Steamboat. I could out figure the physics teacher by using arithmetic (not algebra), I did not hesitate to point out his errors every chance I got. What does that tell you about his ability to teach physics? Actually, he was the principal of the high school.

I must have stayed at Elmer's after the twelfth grade because Lucy Temple asked Doris and me to come help at the dude ranch for a month in the fall.

From there I went to Scottsbluff and lived with Ruby and Louis but applied to work at the Temple ranch the next summer. I got the job as cook's helper, waitress and cabin cleaner.

Enter George! We had great times that summer dancing, George going to entertain Easterners at the Perry Mansfield School close to Steamboat, Steamboat Fourth of July rodeo, and going to the cow camp during the fall round-up.

I had lots of money to buy my wedding dress. I had made thirty dollars a month during the summer, and forty-five dollars a month after the cook left in September. I was then cook and cook's helper. Lucy made the bread and rolls, but I cooked for about thirty people at the age of not quite nineteen. I also inherited seventy-five dollars from my mother's father, Grandpa Galvin. Forty-five dollars of that bought the "good" silverware, which is yet the good silverware. Lucy gave a bridal shower for me, and I can still point to a few things I got at that time.

On November 9, 1941, George and I were married at the First Christian Church in Greeley. That church, the minister, his wife and other young people had helped me shed some negative complexes. I especially wanted Reverend Cecil to perform the marriage ceremony.

I had thought George was going to go to Denver and get work, but he didn't. We lived with Onie, Oliver, Grace, Perry and Alfred in the big house.

Sometime after Pearl Harbor Day, December 7, 1941, George got a notice to report for military recruitment. Oliver obtained a deferment for him to do necessary agricultural food-producing work. If we were not already stuck on the family ranch, I suppose the deferment was good reason to stay there.

I soon decided to move into the Bunkhouse. We fixed it a bit and moved in about six months later. In spite of declarations that it was extravagant, I got some wallpaper to paper over the magazine-covered walls and ceilings. Plain red scalloped oil cloth on shelves and on the table was the focal point of the decor. We carried water from the big house and used the outside toilet. We lived there about two years. In the winter in cold weather the mop would stay frozen behind the kitchen stove, which was the source of heat. David thrived in spite of the cold. David was about a year old when we moved to the log house that George had purchased at Hahns Peak. He disassembled the house at Hahns Peak, moved it with a team of horses and a sled, and reassembled it on its permanent site.

We had no closets nor cupboards nor radio nor toilet nor water there when we moved, at my insistence so that we could be "settled" by the time Kenneth was born.

George dug a hole from which we dipped water and later put a hand pump on it. The toilet started out being a seat with one north side and a west back, which shielded its occupant from the house. One could take in all the scenery while sitting there.

This was during World War II and building material was difficult to obtain. The floors of most of the house were "wainscoting" turned upside down. Wainscoting as we knew it then was boards about three inches wide with grooves. It was used to line the bottom half of kitchens and dining rooms so that there was a paintable finish for rooms that needed it. George did get enough oak flooring from a neighbor in payment for some badly needed hay with which the living room was floored.

Eventually we got kitchen cupboards, some clothes closets and acquired more furniture. I don't know when we got a spring piped into the house, but it was after all three kids were born. The water line from the spring to the house was prone to freeze in December and thaw out in May, and it did just that for two winters. We got electricity in 1949. Prior to that time, we used gasoline and kerosene lamps. George and his brothers put blocks of ice from the river in storage to use in an ice box in the summer. I used irons heated on the cook stove or a gas iron. In due time as we could we got an electric refrigerator, iron, vacuum cleaner, and mixer. We never did get a gas or electric cook stove there because there were always other places to spend the money.

My life with George was a definite improvement over what I had known earlier. As you know, he was a good, good father. I repeat myself when I say that I am not sorry for most that I experienced, but I would not want to do some of it again. It is good that the positives out-weigh the negatives.

A Post Script

Ruby was fourteen years older than me. She was grown and gone from home before my memories began. I remember that it was a special treat to have dinner with her and Louis and to stay with them. They lived on a farm close by with their oldest three children: Maxine, Lawrence, and Frances.

Elmer, too, had always been grown. He and his wife, Lillian, lived close by also. I knew him well as an adult, and my best memories of him and Lillian are when I stayed with them at Hahns Peak and his being my guardian when I went to school my senior year in Steamboat Springs.

Of course, I knew Velma and Violet as children, as teenagers, and as adults. Doris and I grew closer together, sharing everything possible, and we still do.

Sisters and brothers grow together, then grow apart, but tend to become more important to each other with the passage of years. Those of us who are left still have wonderful giggles over our shared memories.

—Dorothy Grace Ireland St. Louis

Appendix D

Country Life in the Forties

Today I can press my clothes that I washed yesterday in the automatic washer and dried in the electric dryer. My ironing board is usually set up, and, of course, an electric steam iron is always right there—but I do have to bend over a bit to plug it in. This is quite a contrast to the days before we had electricity and water piped into our house on the ranch.

George, my husband, worked long hours outside, but he was most helpful with indoor tasks and with the children when he could be. Three children, ages one, two, and three, can manage to interrupt anyone's routine.

Tuesday was ironing day. I always hoped to get it finished before it was time to fix the noon dinner for the five of us and whoever else might be around. No matter how hot or cold the weather, I heated the three irons on the coal cook stove. The handle fit any one of the three irons. I would use one iron until it was no longer hot enough and then replace it with another from the stove. I turned an iron skillet upside down over the irons if they were not heating fast enough to keep the iron sufficiently hot. I had to keep the stove stoked with just the right amount of coal and wood. We had no wash-and-wear fabrics, so dresses (which women wore—not pants), pajamas, shirts, pants, pillowcases, and handkerchiefs needed ironing. Some people even ironed underwear, sheets, and dishtowels. (We used dishtowels to dry all of the dishes.)

As an alternate, I had a gas iron that got too hot and was more likely to "scorch" clothes than the irons heated on the stove. I had to iron extra fast with the gas iron to keep the heat usable.

Ironing day was easier than Monday's wash day when I carried water from a hand pump outside to fill a large wash boiler and other large pans. I'm not sure of the capacity of the boiler, but it must have been about fourteen inches by twenty-four inches and eighteen inches high. While the water was heating, I washed, rinsed, and dried the dishes from a breakfast of coffee, juice, milk, cooked cereal, pancakes, and eggs. I had heated the water for the after-breakfast cleanup while cooking. This cleanup also included making beds and sweeping the kitchen.

I used the rinse water from the dishes as a pre-rinse for the cream separator, milk pails, and four-piece milk strainer because the soap and water would mix with the milk and end up being slimy. After the pre-rinse, I washed the milk things in soapy water, rinsed them by pouring scalding water over them, and left them to air dry. No doubt I found a use for the rinse water some place.

The cream separator had a large tank into which fresh milk was poured. It was powered with a hand-turned crank. There were perhaps twenty-five or thirty parts that included a series of disks through which the milk was spun causing the cream to rise and come out the top spout and the skimmed milk to come out the bottom spout into a different container. This was food for the pigs and chickens. The cats usually raided whole milk at the cow barn. The relatively small quantity of cream was used on the table for making butter, and any excess was sold.

When the wash water was hot, I was ready to do the laundry. On lucky days the gasoline motor on the washer would start. I sorted the clothes—whites first and progressed through pastels, medium, and dark colors. Blue denims were always last. Each washer load was agitated for as long as it took me to go outside and hang the previous batch on the line to dry. I took each piece from the washer one at a time and put it through a wringer attached to the washer that would swing to the desired position over the rinse tubs. I put each piece through the wringer into a second rinse water then wrung it out and put it on the clothesline.

If the wash water got too dirty before I was finished, I threw it out and put the first rinse water into the washer or held back some good clothes and used fresh wash and rinse water. The second wash water would be relatively clean so I might use it to scrub the outside toilet. (Our concept of "running water" was that you run in with clean water and you run out with the used water.)

I usually did not get all the wash done before it was time to cook the midday dinner of meat, potatoes, gravy, salad and/or vegetable, and dessert. Homemade bread, butter, jam, or jelly was a part of every meal. So I would finish the wash after cleaning up the dinner dishes. There was time for a short rest before I had to take the clothes from the line, fold them, put them away, and sprinkle what was to be ironed tomorrow. I could sit down to fold most of the clothes at the dining table.

While the children were little, wash day was repeated on a lesser scale on Thursday. On the other non-wash days, I pre-rinsed the diapers, boiled them in a large kettle with soap, rinsed them twice, and hung them out to dry. I used the soapy water from the boiling for cleaning and set aside the rinse water for soaking and pre-rinsing more diapers.

I spent the rest of the week baking bread and other goodies, churning cream for butter in a hand-cranked glass churn, mending, and catching up on whatever else there was to do. I spent some time changing beds, sweeping, dusting furniture, and dust-mopping floors.

On Sunday, I could usually do a few special things, such as reading or going some place. I would wait to see what Sunday would bring.

My weekly routine was altered when we made a trip to "town."(Craig, Colorado), which was seventy miles away. Part of the trip was on a surfaced road and part was on a dirt road. On these days I fixed the baby formula earlier than usual, did the after-breakfast cleanup earlier, and got everyone dressed up. We hoped to complete the almost two-hour trip by eleven in the morning. At the doctor's office we would go and wait our turn. Buying an indefinite supply of groceries took an hour or two. Shopping for clothes, machinery repair parts, and odds-and-ends needed for a ranch home was time consuming.

Dinner in town was special because I could order and have dinner carried to the table and not have dishes to wash. The children were fascinated with the jukebox and its changing colors. It was usually dark by the time we got home after stopping at Dixon, Wyoming, for a rest. We'd have a beer or Coke and put a nickel or so in the slot machine. The kids thought that money came from a slot machine—all you had to do was put money in and more money came out.

We classified time as BW (before piped-in water and a bathroom in the house), AW (after piped-in water and a bathroom in the house), BE (before electricity), and AE (after electricity). AW and AE did not come at the same time, however. The three pre-schoolers were well beyond the toddler stage when water was piped in the house and only later did the Rural Electric Association come to our valley. However, the water line from a spring one-half mile away froze on two different winters around New Year's and did not thaw until late May. We put in an electric pump for the nearby well AE.

An electric washer, a refrigerator and freezer, a toaster, electric churn, and an electric iron made a difference. A vacuum cleaner eased the dusting and dust mopping of the uncarpeted floors. We continued to use the coal cook stove because we needed its warmth in the winter.

We expanded our annual chicken-raising project to 100 and later to 200 baby chicks raised to fryer size and stocked in the freezer. We sold excess fryers. The freezer made an enormous difference in the year-round variety of available food.

I suppose this sounds as though life on the small, somewhat isolated, ranch was only drudgery. It wasn't. We read magazines and books and listened to the radio. We visited with neighbors, and we danced every chance we got. I can remember lots of singing during work and leisure, and we all sang together during car trips. We also played cards and board games.

We quarreled plenty. Ours was not like the life television's Waltons depicted. Sometimes things didn't work out the way we hoped. Of course, I tried to change some situations and not necessarily with the wisdom of St. Francis of Assisi—knowing the difference in what can or cannot be changed. Call it lack of maturity or impatience. But I was not resentful—the situation just was as it was.

A quote from a book I read, *Border Music* by Robert James Waller, reads:

"But time is an old lens of amber, and as you look down the barrel of it, good things get remembered and bad ones left behind. The good images stay, as if they were suspended somehow in a mason jar, like Jack had said about sunrises one time. She keeps them in a jar and sometimes in late Octobers, especially the late Octobers, takes them out and looks at them."

The relatively short phase of my life on the ranch when the children were babies, toddlers, and pre-schoolers is a time I would not want to repeat, but, as with most of my life, I'm glad I experienced it.

—Dorothy Grace Ireland St. Louis

Reprinted with permission. Original reference: St. Louis, D. G. (2000). "Country Life in the Forties." In R. J. V. Sielen, N. E. Weber, & J. A. Ross (Eds.) *One Among Many: America Stories of the People.* (pp: 115–117). Morgantown, WV: Populore.

Appendix E

Discoveries

It was my job to identify, sort, and dispose of the contents of some boxes labeled "mementos." Nothing was categorized, so one by one I defined the paper contents.

The five- by six-inch, once-white envelopes caught my eye first. Inside each, of course, was the second envelope housing the real contents—wedding invitations and high school graduation announcements from nieces and nephews.

A sizable hunk torn from what had been a standard sheet of paper advertising the merits of a savings insurance plan had this written in longhand on the back side:

"Certainly you should not abandon nor avoid the abstract and the daydreams. From them, new ideas can evolve and eventually become realities by one means or another. How dull it would be if we did not have the adventure of dreams and daydreams. But, of the ones that cannot be realized or fortified with enough concreteness, just label them daydreams that were fun while they lasted."

There were dozens of small envelopes with contents announcing the births of nieces and nephews. I wish that each family could receive back the graduation, wedding, and birth notices.

A heavy, large brown envelope contained a certificate of merit for Palmer Method handwriting, some elementary and high school diplomas, a senior autograph register with messages from classmates along with happenings and ambitions, and a prom dance book with its own little pencil attached.

A three-ring loose-leaf notebook contained some fictional compositions and what looked to be written reports that must have culminated in some projects.

Within one box was a proud wooden box with a metal clasp to fasten the hinged lid. The top of the box had an engraved coat of arms surrounded by impressive foreign adjectives describing Roberts Tampa Tops—no ordinary wooden cigar box. The contents were mostly newspaper clippings of special achievements of the family.

There was an unattached piece of paper with some fading pencil writing:

"Remember how good you felt when you knew that your son or daughter was an individual with his own power to take care of his own problems? Remember how you freed him—gladly—and with love for him? Remember the freedom you felt when you no longer needed to shoulder his needs?"

"Love is non-possessive. It frees the loved one. Probably the loved ones will 'touch lightly' often since there are no restrictive nor possessive nor dependency ties. Each can possess the love, not the person."

Another reflection:

"Just because one is sorry for or about a situation does not necessarily mean that he should or can do something about it."

There were letters banded with lifeless rubber bands and some not banded because the rubber bands had given up. A pre-adolescent away from home had sent "Dear Mommy and Daddy" letters recounting new places, faces, and experiences. Another youngster away for an extended time had sent "Dear Daddy and Mommy" letters bravely saying all was well. However, as the dates progressed, so did the lines saying, "I'll be glad when I can come home." More cohesive letters were headed with "Dear Mother and Daddy" from a teenager who told what was going on, but with some loneliness creeping in between the lines. There were letters from college discussing curriculum, activities, grades, and sometimes apartment living and getting the laundry done. There was a whole separate box with "Dear Mother and Dad" letters from abroad. They were informative and educational, and they conveyed that hardships were being transformed into adventures while living in underdeveloped countries.

The bottom of one box had some intermixed Mother's Day, Father's Day, and birthday cards as well as more paper with this written in longhand:

"In my reaching out or searching I have found a few persons who keep me from being as much of an introvert. I hope that I can recognize and respond to some other lonely ones who are searching for what I call a 'brother' or a 'friend.'"

And this:

"Profit by past mistakes and experiences. It is all right to have made mistakes, but don't make the same ones over. Repeatedly making the same mistakes is an indication that you are refusing to recognize your limitations and that you are coloring 'things' the color you want them to be instead of what they are."

Another:

"A routine of work is good therapy. There is a sense of security in a routine. It is helpful to have things that one has to do."

There were several more handwritten observations too lengthy to repeat here. Here is just one more:

"The older one gets, the more alone one becomes. A baby receives assistance from his mother and physician while being born. He is cared for by his parents throughout childhood. He gradually seeks and gains independence, but with this independence he knows his parents or someone is there to 'rest on' if he wants to. He or she marries and each expects support from the other. Idealistically, each has that support—leaning on each other and depending upon each other—resting on each other.

"If for one reason or another, it turns out that one has no real support, that he is the leaning post and there are too many and too much leaning on him, he can crumple as a post might that is holding up too much fence alone. Perhaps he did not know that he no longer had the strength (reserve) to do as he had been doing. He is no longer a support nor is he supported. This is when he is truly alone.

"He picks himself up alone, starts over alone, and finds that he is free because he is alone.

"From this freedom he can begin to grow again. He stands alone with no one depending upon him, and he is not dependent upon others. He is only responsible for himself. After providing for obligations and responsibilities for himself, he has a surplus of himself to give to others, but he remains alone. Alone even if he is with another person or persons.

"As years go by, he continues to be alone. That is all right. He will die alone—no human can go with him.

"More (and perhaps opposing) insight, thank God: I have not been able to find what others call 'Faith.' Along with my faith in the reality that the sun rises, the snow comes, the snow melts, trees and grass become green, and along with saying that 'Faith' is the actual unquestioned authority of my experience, perhaps I can say that I could not have been that crumpled post that picked itself up if there had not been some unseen help. I guess I wasn't alone. I just said I am alone now—alone and free. That unseen help came through understanding friends. Perhaps I am not alone—there still must be the unseen help who is God. How could I say 'Thank God' if He were not there then and there now?

"I shall pursue this thought further..."

Dispose of? Oh yes, that I must do. Most of this will be thrown away. Actually the value of the contents was in the memory of the one who stored these boxes. One can remember the person, but he cannot know the undocumented memories of that person.

—Dorothy Grace Ireland St. Louis

Reprinted with permission. Original reference: St. Louis, G. (2000). "Discoveries." In R. J. V. Sielen, N. E. Weber, & J. A. Ross (Eds.) *One Among Many: America Stories of the People.* (p 135-136). Morgantown, WV: Populore.

Appendix F
The Big Blizzard

It was late 1947 or early 1948 and Gus was working in Craig, Colorado, for Moffat County, when we were invited to move to the rural area named Great Divide, thirty-five miles northwest of Craig. This was wheat, sheep, and cattle ranching country. The town consisted of a post office, a mercantile store, and a few homes. We were offered a beautiful two-story home, rent free except for cleaning and fixing it up—no one had lived in it for ten years except mice and pack rats! It had a well, a huge barn, and a coal shed. I imagine that at one time it had been a wheat and cattle ranch. It was quite isolated with no phone and no neighbors nearby. After a lot of cleaning, washing, and sanitizing, the five of us moved in. Darrell was four, Larry was two, and Clifford was only one month old. We enjoyed living there.

One night it started snowing and soon the wind began to blow. A good blizzard was in progress, but Gus's snow equipment was in Craig. He left to go to Craig without knowing if the roads were passable or not. The snow and wind kept at it all day. The boys and I were fine—I had the cook stove and the coal heater for heat. When night came it was getting colder outside as well as inside of the house. The blizzard was still raging.

I pulled the big easy chair up to the heater, put the boys in the chair with me, and covered up with a blanket. We stayed warm, but bedtime was coming and I wondered what was the safest thing to do. I didn't want the house to burn. Should I stay up and keep fires going or bank the stoves with coal and go to bed? The beds won out! We went upstairs and I put blankets all around Clifford's crib and snuggled him in. The other two boys went to bed with me and I piled on extra covers. My thoughts once more turned to what I would do in case of a fire. If there was time, I would throw bedding, hopefully a mattress, out the window and we could jump to safety. We would stay warm while the house burnt. Then we could get into the coal shed or the barn. Thank God that didn't happen!

Morning came and the storm was over, but it was so cold! Brrrr! I was going to have to get up and start the fires to get the house warm before the boys got up. I was listening to the outside quiet, trying to gather my courage to get up. The bed was so comfy and warm. All of a sudden I heard another sound. It sounded like a motor! It couldn't be because we were snowed in! Lo and behold, it was a motor. We were going to be rescued! The sound came closer and closer. Soon it came into the yard and stopped. It was Gus and his two helpers. He had his big FWD with an A-frame on front as well as the blade underneath for plowing snow. They had worked all night to come to our rescue. They were about frozen too! I didn't have to get up in a cold house and build fires after all. I cooked them a big breakfast a while later.

Gus had to go back into Craig that day. No way were we staying there by ourselves again, so the kids and I loaded up and went with him.

I look back and think it is more scary now than then. I guess I wasn't quite the pioneer person I thought I was.

—Doris E. Ranch

Reprinted with permission. Original reference: Ranch, D. (2000). "The Big Blizzard." In R. J. V. Sielen, N. E. Weber, & J. A. Ross (Eds.) *One Among Many: America Stories of the People.* (p 128). Morgantown, WV: Populore.

Appendix G

My First Trip to the St. Louis Ranch

I arrived in Steamboat Springs, Colorado, in the fall of 1947, an aspiring veterinarian. I struggled to gain the confidence of the ranchers who were famous for their independence. They were fiercely proud and capable individuals—what they could not do for themselves did not get done. I was only twenty-four, and looked even younger, so they had no good reason to trust me with something as important as their livestock.

My gross income for the first year was only $2,000, which forced me to live off the land. My single-shot 22 was my constant companion in hopes I might be able to shoot a duck, a grouse, or a rabbit. When things were really tough, I even resorted to shooting woodchucks and porcupines.

In mid-June 1949, northwest Colorado was in all its splendor. The meadows were full of cows and calves, and every living thing was flourishing with the warm sunshine and the moisture from the long, snowy winter. This was what every cattleman lived for; it was as close to heaven as a rancher could get.

I was milking our prize possession, a Guernsey cow, when Bertie, my wife, came out to the shed and said the St. Louises had called from up on Snake River. They could not get in touch with their regular vet and wondered if I could help them with a sick cow. My heart jumped into my throat at the mention of the name St. Louis. This was a family with five boys who had established a reputation for being wild and unruly. I had heard local cowboys relating experiences they had with the St. Louis boys. They could drink, cuss, and fight with the best. They were close-knit—if you were foolish enough to pick trouble with one, you had to contend with all of them. I also detected from the cowboys a great deal of respect for the St. Louis boys' hard work and abilities as cattle ranchers.

By 7:00 a.m. I had as many drugs in the back of my Studebaker pickup as I thought I would ever need. I loaded my gun, fishing pole, and a gunnysack just in case I happened to see something edible along the way. My five-year-old daughter, Judy, was begging to go along. I explained that I didn't know these people yet and I didn't know if they liked little girls getting in their way. The fact was I wanted to make a good impression and didn't want any distractions.

Finally, with a great deal of anticipation, I headed for the St. Louis Ranch on Snake River. Just out of Steamboat to the west, I turned north on the Elk River Road. I went twenty miles up the beautiful winding river, all the way to Clark. The Valley was quite wide in places, and the meadows reached out for a mile or so beyond the river. Every few miles there were ranch houses with beautiful green meadows dotted by mother cows grazing and their calves bucking and playing with each other. I could see a little snow on the very top of Hahns Peak, which was at the end of this pictorial valley.

Just past Clark, I crossed a bridge over the Elk River. With the spring snow melting, the river was at its peak for the year. Most rivers filled with runoff are muddy and full of dead trees and debris—not the Elk River. It was clear, and where each large rock rose above the surface, it was frothy white. The origins of the Elk River are far to the east on the Continental Divide at Mount Zirkel, which is mostly untouched wilderness in the Routt National Forest. That explained the crystal clear river.

I proceeded north up this winding gravel road toward Hahns Peak, which was an old gold-mining town that served as the Routt County seat for years around the turn of the century. It had deteriorated into complete disrepair with just a few diehards who insisted on living there in 1949. Just to the west of the town, I could see evidence of the gold operation. The area south of Hahns Peak was rolling meadows with a mountain stream winding through the center with large clumps of willows growing all along it. The peak itself was like a tall black cone more than 11,000 feet tall [sic 10,843 feet] standing sentinel over the whole area.

The road from Hahns Peak north to the Snake River was more like a dirt trail that would accommodate two cars in most places for passing. It was closed all winter, and after it is opened it takes several days to dry sufficiently to travel it in anything but a four-wheel-drive vehicle. I was pleased to find it not only had been cleared but some attempt had been made to smooth out the deep ruts. As I drove through the canopy of green aspens, I went by a few cabins that were built for summer use. Next was a summer forest station as I wound my way down the north side that opened up into vast open areas of sagebrush. There was evidence along the way that sheep were put on this land for summer grazing. However, I didn't see any. The only place I saw any wildlife was off the north side as I was going down toward the Snake River. There were a few woodchucks and an occasional quail. Also off in the distance I could see a few deer, mostly does. I couldn't tell if they had fawns hidden among the sage or not.

I was now less than five miles from the ranch. I soon arrived at the river and noted it was flowing quite full and was not clear like the Elk River had been. I crossed the bridge and soon spotted the entry to the ranch. My heart was beating full tilt by now. As I walked toward the house I noticed that it looked like no one was around. I wondered where the sick cow was and who would show up to help. Just as I started to rap on the door, it was opened by a nice-looking woman. She smiled and said, "You the vet?" I nodded and said, "You Mrs. St. Louis?" She said yes, and brushed by me saying, "The cow is out here in the barn." As she walked briskly toward the barn, she said, "We are very sorry to bother you, but our regular vet is Dr. Utterback and we couldn't find him this morning. This cow is in very bad shape and we think she needs immediate attention." I looked around and said, "Are there any menfolk around to help?" She replied that there were not because everyone was needed to move the cattle off the meadow toward their summer pasture. She indicated she would be glad to go get a neighbor, but even they were busy this time of the year. I got the message loud and clear that I was to handle this myself.

She opened the barn door, and just inside was a milk cow stretched out flat and breathing very erratically. Foam was coming out of her mouth, and she looked more dead than alive. Just as I was about to ask a few questions, Mrs. St. Louis volunteered that they thought she had the calving fever. I looked into the closest stall and saw a one-day-old calf. Being a high-producing milk cow nursing her calf in the season of lush grass, I concluded the cow did, in fact, have "milk fever." A condition common at this time of the year, it is caused by calcium being released too fast from the bloodstream when the udder is relieved of its milk. The treatment was to replace the blood calcium by giving the cow calcium gluconate in the jugular vein. Normally one 500-cc bottle will get a cow back on its feet in fifteen minutes. This response is spectacular, and I was hoping it would leave a favorable impression so I might be called back another time. However, Mrs. St. Louis indicated she had plenty to do in the kitchen without standing around the barn. I administered the medicine and sure enough the cow was on her feet soon after I completed the intravenous injection.

With no one to impress or to admire my fine work, I went to the house and reported on the condition of the cow. I started to tell Mrs. St. Louis how much the bill was, and she said very quickly, as if she were reading my mind, "Doc never charges over fifteen dollars to come up here, and nothing extra for the treatment if he has other patients to see in the area." She caught me so off guard that I mumbled something about that sounded like a fair charge and added on another five dollars for the treatment of the cow. She paid me and I started to give her instructions about not letting the calf nurse and keeping the cow from going into the meadow. But she felt I had done my job and it was better that I go. I was hurried out the door and back to my truck.

One day many months later I was at a vet meeting with Dr. Utterback, and he made a great point to tell me that what I had done for the St. Louis family cow had not done much good. He had been called the next day to go back and really fix that cow up he said. I asked him if she had gone back down, and he told me he had to go clear out into the meadow where she was flat on her side and her calf was trying to nurse.

Needless to say, my first trip to the St. Louis ranch as a veterinarian proved also to be my last. However, I have gotten to know some of the family quite well and am pleased to call them friends.

—Earl (Pinky) Smith, DVM

Reprinted with permission. Original reference: Smith, E. (2000). "My First Trip to the St. Louis Ranch." In R. J. V. Sielen, N. E. Weber, & J. A. Ross (Eds.) *One Among Many: America Stories of the People.* (pp: 119–122). Morgantown, WV: Populore.

Appendix H

Births, Marriages, Children, Deaths, and Burials of the St. Louis Relatives

The following St. Louis listing contains known relatives on our dad's side of the family. They go back as far as records were located and as far ahead as relatives were able to identify their children, grandchildren, and great-grandchildren. The first section, *Ancestors from Our Grandparents' and Earlier Generations*, provides as many ancestors as possible who preceded our grandfather Oliver St. Louis (carrying the St-Louis name), that is, his paternal side. Little information was available to me on his maternal side, the Sinclairs. However, following the St-Louis ancestor listing, are ancestors of our grandmother Leone (Onie) St. Louis's mother, Sarah Mariah McCargar. Little is known of her paternal side, the Morgans.

The second section, *St. Louis Family: Uncles, Aunts, First Cousins, and Their Children*, begins with our grandparents and proceeds next to the generation of our parents, aunts, and uncles, then to our generation and that of our first cousins. Next, it progresses to our children's generation, then their children's generation, and so on. (See Notes to Readers for additional clarifications.)

The St. Louis listing is followed by photos contributed by relatives. After those, two alphabetized indexes appear for all the St. Louis relatives, one for the listing and one for the photos.

Ancestors from Our Grandparents' and Earlier Generations

St-Louis Ancestors

René Filiatrault dit St-Louis (Born: 1642 in France; Died: 1699) *Married to* **Jaquette Genicau** Filiatrault dit St-Louis (Born: 1646 in France; Died: 1699) (6th great-grandparents)

> **Louis Filiatrault dit St-Louis** (Born: 1688; Died: 1752) *Married to* **Marie-Madeleine Labelle** Filiatrault dit St-Louis (Born: 1681; Died: [year]) (5th great-grandparents)

> > **Francois Filiatrault dit St-Louis** (Born: 1707; Died: 1776) *Married to* **Thérèse Gravel** Filiatrault dit St-Louis (Born: [year]; Died: [year]) *Married to* **Marie-Veronique Bonhomme-Beaupre** Filiatrault dit St-Louis (Born: 1722; Died: [year]) (4th great-grandparents)

> > > **Paul Filiatrault dit St-Louis** (Born: 1746; Died: 1841) *Married to* **Marie-Louise Filion** Filiatrault dit St-Louis (Born: 1748; Died: 1827) (3rd great-grandparents)

> > > > **Marie-Louis F. St-Louis** (Born: 1772; Died: [year])
> > > > **Marie-Thérèse F. St-Louis** (Born: 1773; Died: 1773)
> > > > **Paul Filiatrault dit St-Louis** (Born: 1774; Died: 1803)
> > > > **Joseph Filiatrault dit St-Louis** (Born: 1776; Died: 1826)
> > > > **Antoine Filiatrault dit St-Louis** (Born: 1777; Died: [year])
> > > > **Marie-Veronique F. St-Louis** (Born: 1778; Died: 1778)
> > > > **Marie-Victoire F. St-Louis** (Born: 1779; Died: 1799)
> > > > **Louis Filiatrault dit St-Louis** (Born: 1780; Died: 1829)
> > > > **Marie-Thérèse F. St-Louis** Lavictoire (Born: 1781; Died: 1839) *Married to* **Pierre Lavictoire** (Born: 1767; Died: [year])
> > > > **Francoise Filiatrault dit St-Louis** (Born: 1783; Died: 1783)
> > > > **Francoise Filiatrault dit St-Louis** (Born: 1784; Died: 1769) *Married to* **Victoire Ethier** St-Louis (Born: 1787; Died: 1826) *Married to* **Marie Helena Mennie** St-Louis (Born: 1799; Died: 1880) (2nd great-grandparents)

> > > > > **Marie-Élie Filiatrault dit St-Louis** Lanthier (with first wife) (Born: 1810; Died: 1900) *Married to* **Basile Lanthier** (Born: 1810; Died: 1852)
> > > > > **Victoire Filiatrault dit St-Louis** Sauvé (with first wife) (Born: 1811; Died: [year]) *Married to* **Jean-Baptiste Sauvé** (Born: 1805; Died: [year])
> > > > > **Christine Filiatrault dit St-Louis** Mennie (with first wife) (Born: 1813; Died: 1900) *Married to* **John Mennie** (Born: 1807; Died: [year])
> > > > > **Marie Filiatrault dit St-Louis** Godmer (with first wife) (Born: 1814; Died: 1901) *Married to* **Pierre Godmer** (Born: 1800; Died: 1901)
> > > > > **François Filiatrault dit St-Louis** (with first wife) (Born: 1815; Died: 1872) *Married to* **Françoise Paquet** St-Louis (Born: 1815; Died: [year])
> > > > > **Francois Filiatrault dit St-Louis** Lagarde Carrières (with first wife) (Born: 1816; Died: 1889) *Married to* **Antoine Lagarde** (Born: 1809; Died: 1861) *Married to* **Louis Carrières** (Born: [year]; Died: [year])
> > > > > **Scholastique F. St-Louis** Lebrun Proulx (with first wife) (Born: 1816; Died: [year]) *Married to* **Janvier Lebrun (Laforest)** (Born: 1810; Died: 1841) *Married to* **François Proulx** (Born: [year]; Died: [year])
> > > > > **Emery-Jérémie F. St-Louis** (with first wife) (Born: 1819; Died: 1909) *Married to* **Genevieve St-Aubin** St-Louis (Born: 1820; Died: 1909)
> > > > > **Paul Filiatrault dit St-Louis** (with first wife) (Born: 1822; Died: 1822) *Married to* **Angéle Lapointe** St-Louis (Born: 1833; Died: [year])
> > > > > **Moïse Filiatrault dit St-Louis** (with first wife) (Born: 1824; Died: [year])
> > > > > **Anselme Filiatrault dit St-Louis** (Born: 1825; Died: [year])

François-Xavier F. St-Louis (with first wife) (Born: 1825; Died: [year])
Louis Filiatrault dit St-Louis (with first wife) (Born: 1825; Died: 1826)
Diana Dolphin St-Louis Barrington (with second wife) (Born: 1831; Died: 1867) *Married to* **Thomas Barrington** (Born: 1822; Died: [year])
Oliver (Olivier) St-Louis (with second wife) (Born: 23 JUN 1833 in Saint-Andrews, Quebec, Canada; Died: 20 APR 1924 in Ormstown, Chateauguay, Quebec, Canada; Buried: Union Cemetery, Ormstown, Quebec, Canada) *Married 26 NOV 1864 to* **Sophia Sinclair** St-Louis (Born: 28 SEP 1844 in Ormstown, Chateauguay, Quebec, Canada; Died: 11 Jan 1928 in Ormstown, Chateauguay, Quebec, Canada; Buried: Union Cemetery, Ormstown, Quebec, Canada) (Great-grandparents)

Alfred St-Louis (Born: 1865; Died: [year])
Francis James St-Louis (Born: 1866; Died: 1952) *Married to* **Elizabeth Barr** St-Louis (Born: 1870; Died: 1960)
David Porter St-Louis (Born: 1868; Died: 1902) *Married to* **Laura Isabella Hunter** St-Louis (Born: 1865; Died: [year])
Elizabeth Brown St-Louis (Born: 1870: Died: 1891)
Lorina Sophia St-Louis Rember (Born: 1872; Died: 1907) *Married to* **Alexander Pringle Rember** (Born: 1867; Died: 1943)
Oliver St-Louis [Changed to **St. Louis**] (Born: 15 MAR 1875 in Ormstown, Chateauguay, Quebec, Canada; Died: 15 MAR 1965 in Meeker, Colorado; Buried: Reader Cemetery, Savery, Wyoming) *Married 20 FEB 1901 to* **Leone Morgan** St. Louis (Born: 26 MAY 1879 in Slater, Colorado; Died: 11 AUG 1979 in Craig, Colorado; Buried: Reader Cemetery, Savery, Wyoming) ∩-1-∩ ; ∩-2-∩ (Grandparents: see below)
William Alfred St-Louis (Born: 1877; Died: [year])
John St-Louis (Born: 1879; Died: 1924) *Married to* **Frances (Annie) Fulton English** St-Louis (Born: 1879; Died: [year])
George St-Louis (Born: 1882; Died: [year])
Annie Louisa St-Louis Cooper (Born: 1884; Died: 1928) *Married to* **Merrill Alexander Cooper** (Born: 1867; Died: 1926)
Rosalie St-Louis Moreau (with second wife) (Born: 1828; Died: 1860) *Married to* **Gédéon Moreau** (Born: [year]; Died: [year])
Francis St-Louis (with second wife) (Born: 1847; Died: 1869)
Marie-Archange F. St-Louis (Born: 1786; Died: 1852)
Pierre Francoise Filiatrault dit St-Louis (Born: 1787; Died: 1819)
Marie-Catherine F. St-Louis (Born: 1790; Died: 1790)
Marie-Marguerite F. St-Louis (Born: 1791; Died: [year])
Marie J. St-Louis (Born: 1747; Died: 1749)
Joseph F. St-Louis (Born: 1750; Died: 1834)
Marie Filiatrault dit St-Louis (Born: 1748; Died: [year])
Françoise M. St-Louis (Born: 1752; Died: 1774)
Marie M. St-Louis (Born: 1755; Died: [year])
Marie V. St-Louis (Born: 1758; Died: [year])
Marie Madelaine St-Louis (Born: 1700; Died: 1700)
Marie Anne St-Louis (Born: 1701: Died: 1722)
Pierre Filiatrault dit St-Louis (Born: 1703; Died: 1786)
Michel Filiatrault dit St-Louis (Born: 1705; Died: 1745)
Louis Filiatrault dit St-Louis (Born: 1708; Died: 1708)

| Jean Filiatrault dit St-Louis (Born: 1710; Died: 1710)
| Louis Filiatrault dit St-Louis (Born: 1710; Died: 1756)

McCargar Ancestors

Thomas McCargar (Born: 1758 in Glengary County, Antrim, Ireland [or much less likely, Aberdeen, Scotland]; Died: [year] *Married ~1780 to* **Sarah (Sallie) Thomas** McCargar (Born: 1761 in Halifax, Vermont; Died: [year] *Left and married to* **Rebecca Nowlin** McCargar (Born: 1770; Died: 1852) *Widowed and married to* __ **Stoughton (or Stoten)** McCargar (Born: [year]; Died: [year]) (4th great-grandparents)

  Mary (Mollie) McCargar Barton (with first wife) (Born: 1781; Died: 1861)
  Thomas William McCargar (with first wife) (Born: 1783: Died: 1855)
  __ **(Son) McCargar** (Died: young)
  Joseph McCargar (with second wife) (Born: 1785; Died: 1867)
  Mollie McCargar (with second wife) (Born: [year]; Died: [year])
  Robert McCargar (with second wife) (Born: 13 Aug 1791 in Albany County, New York; Died: 15 JUN 1858 in Faribault, Minnesota; Buried: Denison Cemetery, Faribault, Minnesota) *Married to* **Jane Hunter** McCargar (Born: 1796; Died: 1879) (3rd great-grandparents)

    Joseph McCargar (Born: 19 May 1815; Died: 5 AUG 1815)
    Philander McCargar (Born: 21 JAN 1821; Died: 5 DEC 1874)
    Catherine McCargar McDermott (Born: 25 MAY 1817; Died: 8 JUN 1876)
    Mariah McCargar Campbell Harrington (Born: 8 MAR 1819; Died: 14 JUN 1896)
    Samuel E. McCargar (Born: 7 FEB 1824; Died: 18 JAN 1881)
    Alpheus McCargar (Born: 8 DEC 1825; Died: 9 DEC 1825)
    Hannah McCargar (Born: 12 MAR 1828; Died: 25 APR 1828)
    Erastus McCargar (Born: 18 MAR 1829; Died: 19 NOV 1879)
    Alfred Henry McCargar (Born: 7 FEB 1831 in Leeds and Grenville, Ontario; Died: 22 FEB 1898) *Married 20 JUL 1955 to* **Elizabeth Gibson** McCargar (Born: 31 MAY 1831 in North Gore, Quebec; Died: 1930 in [city], Colorado; Buried: [city], Colorado) (2nd great-grandparents) ⋂-3-⋂

      Caroline Jane McCargar Hinman (Born: 12 MAR 1857 in Faribault, Minnesota) *Married 24 DEC 1880 to* **Frank Hinman** (Born: [date]; Died: [date] in Battle Creek, Colorado)
      Robert Henry McCargar (Born: 12 MAR 1857 in Faribault, Minnesota)
      Sarah Mariah McCargar Morgan (Born: 16 MAY 1858 in Faribault, Minnesota; Died: 9 AUG 1930 in Denver, Colorado; Buried: Reader Cemetery, Savery, Wyoming) *Married 5 OCT 1876 to* **William Tecumseh Morgan** (Born: 21 AUG 1846 in Tioga, New York; Died: 5 JUL 1912 in Slater, Colorado; Buried: Reader Cemetery, Savery, Wyoming) ⋂-4-⋂ ; ⋂-5-⋂ (Great-grandparents)
      Margaret Elizabeth McCargar Humphreys (Born: 9 MAR 1860; Died 1937; Buried: Reader Cemetery, Savery, Wyoming) *Married 12 OCT 1879 to* **William Humphreys** (Born: 1851; Died 1907; Buried: Reader Cemetery, Savery, Wyoming)
      Alfred McClellan McCargar (Born: ~1870 in Dunlap, Iowa; Died: [year])
  Garner McCargar (with second wife) (Born: [year]; Died: [year])
  Hugh McCargar (with second wife) (Born: [year]; Died: [year])
  Philander McCargar (with second wife) (Born: [year]; Died: [year])
  Milo McCargar (with second wife) (Born: [year]; Died: [year])
  Barnabus McCargar (with second wife) (Born: [year]; Died: [year])
  Lottie McCargar (with second wife) (Born: [year]; Died: [year])

|Sarah McCargar (with third wife) (Born: [year]; Died: [year])
Joseph McCargar (Born: ~1750 Glengary County, Antrim, Ireland [or much less likely, Aberdeen, Scotland]; Died: [year])

St. Louis Family: Uncles, Aunts, First Cousins, and Their Children

Grandparents
　Aunts, uncles, parents
　　Cousins, siblings
　　　Nieces, nephews, children
　　　　Grandnieces, grandnephews, grandchildren
　　　　　Great-grandnieces, great-grandnephews, great-grandchildren
　　　　　　Great-great-grandnieces, great-great-grandnephews,
　　　　　　　great-great-grandchildren

Oliver St. Louis (Born: 15 MAR 1875 in Ormstown, Chateauguay, Quebec, Canada; Died: 15 MAR 1965 in Meeker, Colorado; Buried: Reader Cemetery, Savery, Wyoming) *Married 20 FEB 1901 to* Leone (Onie) Morgan St. Louis (Born: 26 MAY 1879 in Slater, Colorado; Died: 11 AUG 1979 in Craig, Colorado; Buried: Reader Cemetery, Savery, Wyoming) ∩-6-∩

　William Oliver Sinclair St. Louis (Born: 19 Jan 1903 at home in Slater, Wyoming; Died: 22 NOV 1996 in Steamboat Springs, Colorado; Buried: Reader Cemetery, Savery, Wyoming) *Married 8 JUL 1938 to* Lila __ Heikkila St. Louis (Born: [date/location]; Died: [date/location]; Buried [location]) *Divorced and married [day] JUN 1944 to* Elizabeth Maria Lucia Miozzi St. Louis (Born: 17 JUN 1918 in New York City, New York; Died: 18 JAN 1999 in Mesa, Arizona; Buried: Reader Cemetery, Savery, Wyoming) *Divorced and married 1969 to* Deloris Marie Grudzinksi Adamek St. Louis (Born: 18 JUN 1919 in Ashton, Nebraska; Died: 3 APR 2015 in Aurora, Colorado; Buried: Craig Cemetery, Craig, Colorado)

　　Lillyan St. Louis Walter St. Louis (Born: 11 MAY 1945 in Dixon, Wyoming; Living) *Married 15 OCT 1972 to* Stanley Joseph Walter (Born: 23 OCT 1935 in Las Cruces, New Mexico; Living) *Divorced*

　　　Sara Elizabeth Walter Murphy Bear (Born: 18 FEB 1973 in Steamboat Springs, Colorado; Living) *Married [day/month] 2001 to* Bradley Stuart Murphy (Born: 19 JUL 1972 [location]; Living) *Divorced and married [date] to* Matthew Elton Bear (Born: 5 NOV 1979 [location]; Living)

　　　Cameron Sinclair Walter (Born: 16 JAN 1975 in Steamboat Springs, Colorado; Living) *Married [day/month] 1999 to* Ayako Toyama (Born: [day] AUG 1971 in [city], Japan; Living)

　　Alexandra (Lexie) St. Louis Siegal (Born: 14 APR 1947 in Corvallis, Oregon; Living) *Married 1 AUG 1973 to* Warren Barry Siegal (Born: 26 APR 1943 in Chicago, Illinois; Died: 5 JUL 2001 in Steamboat Springs, Colorado; Buried: Reader Cemetery, Savery, Wyoming) *Widowed and partner with* Stephen Larson Brown (Born: 20 MAY, 1946 in Steamboat Springs, Colorado; Living)

　　　H. Morgan Siegal (Born: 1 APR 1977 in Phoenix, Arizona; Living) *Married 10 JUL 2009 to* Courtney Elizabeth Lanning Siegal (Born: 22 MAY 1972 in Wheatridge, Colorado; Living) ∩-7-∩

　　　　Sydney Elizabeth Siegal (Born: 13 MAR 2015 in Bryn Mawr, Pennsylvania; Living)

　　　　Alexandra Morgan Siegal (Born: 24 NOV 2016 in Cheyenne, Wyoming; Living)

Wyatt Alexander Siegal (Born: 20 SEP 1978 in Phoenix, Arizona; Living)

Brett St. Louis Siegal (Born: 31 JUL 1980 in Phoenix, Arizona; Living) *Married 21 DEC 2007 to* **Kelly Ann Finnegan** Siegal (Born: 5 FEB 1981 in Brooklyn, New York; Living)

> **Scarlett Ann Siegal** (Born: 2 MAY 2011 in Scottsdale, Arizona; Living)
>
> **Ivy Elizabeth Siegal** (Born: 5 JAN 2014 in Scottsdale, Arizona; Living)

Alfred Chester St. Louis (Born: 10 OCT 1904 at home in Battle Creek, Colorado; Died: 28 MAR 1982 in Craig, Colorado; Buried: Reader Cemetery, Savery, Wyoming)

George Edwin St. Louis (Born: 26 JAN 1906 in Battle Creek, Colorado; Died: 1 JAN 1991 in Hattiesburg, Mississippi; Buried: Reader Cemetery, Savery, Wyoming) *Married 9 NOV 1941 to* **Dorothy Grace Ireland** St. Louis Magill St. Louis (Born: 7 DEC 1922 in Sedgwick, Colorado; Died: 8 JUN 1998 in Grand Junction, Colorado; Buried: Reader Cemetery, Savery, Wyoming) ∩-8-∩ *Divorced and married 13 JAN 1978 to* **Vivian Mary Johnson** Hunt St. Louis (Born: 27 MAY 1912 in [city], Utah; Died: 4 APR 1989 in Dixon, Wyoming; Buried: Reader Cemetery, Savery, Wyoming)

David George St. Louis (Born: 28 JUL 1943 in Hayden, Colorado; Living) *Married 4 DEC 1967 to* **Somchai Khamsayin** St. Louis (Born: 23 FEB 1939 in Ban Kwao, Mahasarakham, Thailand; Living)

> **Robert Pyboon St. Louis** (Born: 7 DEC 1965 in Vientiane, Laos; Living) *Married 5 JUL 1986 to* **Nereida R. Padilla** St. Louis Collins (Born: 31 DEC 1962 in Bronx, New York; Living) *Divorced and married 18 SEP 1998 to* **Shannon Lee Pike** St. Louis (Born: 3 APR 1970 in Yukon, Oklahoma; Living) *Divorced and married to* **Karen Sue Smallwood** Garrett St. Louis (Born: 2 JUN 1959 in Jefferson City, Tennessee; Living) ∩-9-∩
>
> > **Tai Francisco St. Louis** (Born: 1 APR 1988 in Orlando, Florida; Living) *Partner with* **Ebony Bates** (Born: [day] JAN 1992; Living)
> >
> > > **Mia Elizabeth St. Louis** (Born: 6 JUN 2010 in Kissimmee, Florida; Living)
> > >
> > > **Navy St. Louis** (Born: 20 OCT 2017 in Kissimmee, Florida; Living)
> >
> > **Jourdan Robert St. Louis** (Born: 14 OCT 1990 in Jacksonville, Florida; Living) *Partner with* **Anne Ayala** (Born: [date/location]; Living) *Partner with* **Ivonne Guillen** (Born: [date/location]; Living)
> >
> > > **Uree St. Louis** (Born: 25 MAY 2010 in Kissimmee, Florida; Living) (Mother: Anne Ayala)
> > >
> > > **Avaleah Enid St. Louis** (Born: 16 NOV 2012 in Kissimmee, Florida; Living) (Mother: Ivonne Guillen)
> >
> > **Kaeden Leland Lucas** (Born: 23 JUN 2005 in Jacksonville, Florida; Living) *Step grandson; Full custody*

Benson Petsamone St. Louis (Born: 29 JUL 1968 in Vientiane, Laos; Living) *Married 29 AUG 1992 to* **Karol Leigh Scott** St. Louis (Born: 6 OCT 1968 in Hattiesburg, Mississippi; Living) ∩-10-∩

> **Griffin Scott St. Louis** (Born: 23 APR 1995 in Tupelo, Mississippi; Living)
>
> **Spencer Morgan St. Louis** (Born: 23 MAR 1998 in Hattiesburg, Mississippi; Living)

Lisa Surilak St. Louis Knight (Born: 13 JUL 1969 in Vientiane, Laos; Living) *Married 25 JUL 1992 to* **Joseph Odell Knight** (Born: 29 JUL 1969 in Philadelphia, Mississippi; Living)

> **Jeff David Knight** (Born: 14 APR 1999 in Meridian, Mississippi; Living) ∩-11-∩ ∩-12-∩

Kenneth Oliver St. Louis (Born: 9 NOV 1944 in Steamboat Springs, Colorado; Living) *Married 27 DEC 1970 to* **Karen Helen Waterman** St. Louis Teaman (Born: 13 MAR 1947 in Schenectady, New York; Living) *Divorced and married 26 FEB 1994 to* **Rae Jean V. Sielen** Farfsing Cousineau Sielen (Born: 30 DEC 1954 in Santa Monica, California; Living) ⋒-13-⋒

> **Melinda Joyce St. Louis** (Born: 14 AUG 1975 in Plattsburgh, New York; Living) *Married 14 JUN 2002 to* **Pablo Javier Benavente Gonzalez** (Born: 14 FEB 1965 in Managua, Nicaragua; Living) *Divorced*
>
> > **Lila Grace Benavente** (Born: 2 OCT 2007 in Washington DC; Living) ⋒-14-⋒

Rita Grace St. Louis Maser St. Louis (Born: 11 FEB 1946 in Dixon, Wyoming; Living) *Married 2 JUL 1966 to* **Christopher Ottmar Maser** (Born: 13 OCT 1938 in Bronxville, New York; Living) *Divorced and married 17 JUN 1978 to* **Hugh Strane Richards III** (Born: 13 SEP 1945 in Danville, Pennsylvania; Living) *Divorced and married 23 DEC 2005 to* **John David Swan** (Born: 6 JUN 1945 in Murphy, North Carolina; Living)

> **Erik Maser Richards** (Born: 22 DEC 1971 in Coos Bay, Oregon; Living) *Married 2 JUN 2007 to* **Amy Barnes Stoyles** Richards (Born: 22 OCT 1973 in Syracuse, New York; Living) ⋒-15-⋒
>
> > **Evan McKinley Richards** (Born: 11 APR 2008 in Bradenton, Florida; Living)
> > **Camden Taylor Richards** (Born: 9 MAR 2010 in Annapolis, Maryland; Living)
> > **Scott Douglas Richards** (Born: 7 JUL 2011 in Las Cruces, New Mexico; Living)

Francis James St. Louis (Born: 28 MAY 1907 at home in Battle Creek, Colorado; Died: 27 MAY 1951 in Slater, Colorado; Buried: Reader Cemetery, Savery, Wyoming) *Married 10 FEB 1940 to* **Agnes Ellen Caswell** St. Louis Russell (Born: 6 SEP 1911 in Upton, Wyoming; Died: 24 SEP 2007 in Craig, Colorado; Buried: Reader Cemetery, Savery, Wyoming) *Widowed and married 3 OCT 1956 to* **Forrest Adrian (Mike) Russell** (Born: 24 FEB 1907 in Dixon, Wyoming; Died: 10 JUN 2001 in Craig, Colorado; Buried: Reader Cemetery, Savery, Wyoming)

> **Sharon Lou St. Louis** Andrew (Born: 28 NOV 1941 in Craig, Colorado; Living) *Married 8 JUN 1960 to* **Stephen Robert Andrew** (Born: 3 JUN 1939 in Rawlins, Wyoming; Died: 22 FEB 2018 in Denver, Colorado; Buried: Reader Cemetery, Savery, Wyoming)
>
> > **Kirsten Ann Andrew** Remmick Andrew (Born: 21 MAR 1961 in Craig, Colorado; Living) *Married [date] to* **Clayton Carl Remmick** (Born: 13 OCT 1981 [location]; Living) *Divorced and common law marriage with* **Santos Nava** (Born: 21 SEP 1956 in Kerrville, Texas; Living)
> >
> > > **Mark Andrew Nava** (Born: 20 AUG 1998 in Steamboat Springs, Colorado; Living)
> > > **Maya Anna Nava** (Born: 24 APR 2003 in Steamboat Springs, Colorado; Living)
> >
> > **Julia Beth Andrew** Elliott (Born: 19 MAR 1968 in Craig, Colorado; Living) *Married [date] to* **Shawn William Elliott** (Born: 19 SEP 1967 [location]; Living) *Divorced*
> >
> > **Carrie Ellen Andrew** Arambel Cook (Born: 1 FEB 1964 in Craig, Colorado; Living) *Married 12 JUL 1986 to* **Robert Paul Arambel** (Born: 6 JUN 1961 in Rock Springs, Wyoming; Living) *Divorced and married 11 SEP 2013 to* **Marshall D. Cook** (Born: 24 MAR 1966 in Lamar, Colorado; Living)

Logan Robert Arambel (Born: 27 OCT 1988 in Craig, Colorado; Living)
Tanner Edwin Arambel (Born: 1 OCT 1990 in Craig, Colorado; Living)
Joyce Ellen St. Louis Miranda (Born: 6 MAY 1948 in Hayden, Colorado; Living) *Married 21 DEC 1970 to* **Clifton James (Jimmy) Miranda** (Born: 25 JAN 1949 in Lampahoehoe, Hawaii; Living)

> **Russell James Miranda** (Born: 19 JAN 1970 in Hilo, Hawaii; Living) *Married [day/month] 2003 to* **Joelle Amundrud Tafoya** Wilson (Born: 23 MAR 1985 in Waimea, Hawaii; Living) *Divorced and partner with* **Evelia Alexis Thalia Aguilar** (Born: 15 MAY 1994 in Lihue, Hawaii; Living)
>
>> **Savannah Faith Miranda** (Born: 24 DEC 2009 in Waimea, Hawaii; Living)
>> **Ryder Jay Miranda-Aguilar** (Born: 28 June 2020 in Waimea, Hawaii; Living)
>
> **Marti Ann Miranda** Snyder (Born: 31 OCT 1974 in Pahala, Hawaii; Living) *Married 14 AUG 1999 to* **Robert Earl Snyder III** (Born: 18 JAN 1966 in Los Angeles, California; Living)
>
>> **Justice James Truth Snyder** (Born: 20 MAY 2003 in Lihue, Hawaii; Living)
>> **Alexandra Kalina'oe Snyder** (Born: 23 DEC 2004 in Lihue, Hawaii; Living)

Perry Alberta St. Louis (Born: 11 OCT 1910 at home in Battle Creek, Colorado, Died: 8 OCT 1962 in Baggs, Wyoming; Buried: Reader Cemetery, Savery, Wyoming) *Married 7 JUN 1939 to* **Grace Mary Burkardt** St. Louis (Born: 23 JUN 1909 in East Brooklyn, Illinois; Died: 9 JAN 2007 in Craig, Colorado; Buried: Reader Cemetery, Savery, Wyoming) ∩-16-∩

> **Jean Alberta St. Louis** Ely Ely-Landini (Born: 18 SEP 1940 in Sioux City, Iowa; Living) *Married 23 JUN 1962 to* **Donald Eugene Ely** (Born: 19 JAN 1934 in Brush, Colorado; Died: 6 FEB 2017 in Slater, Colorado; Buried: Sheep Mountain Ranch, Slater, Colorado) *Divorced and married 2 SEP 2006 to* **Carlo (Carl) Sante Landini** (Born: 17 FEB 1936 in Fruita, Colorado; Died: 10 AUG 2018 in Fruita, Colorado; Buried: Elmwood Cemetery, Fruita, Colorado) ∩-17-∩
>
> **Shirley Elaine Ely** (Born: 14 NOV 1962 in Lamar, Colorado; Living)
> **Shana Leone Ely** Morris Bunker (Born: 20 NOV 1963 in Craig, Colorado; Living) *Married 27 JUN 1987 to* **Zane Ray Morris** (Born: 23 MAR 1964 in Laramie, Wyoming; Living) *Divorced and married 24 JUL 1992 to* **John Lambert Cadwalader Bunker** (Born: 14 APR 1961 in New Orleans, Louisiana; Died: 9 AUG 2011 in Wheatland, Wyoming; Buried: Wheatland Cemetery, Wheatland, Wyoming) *Married 29 SEP 2012 to* **Jeffery Wayne Switzer** (Born: 14,1961 in Adams, New York; Living)
>
>> **Marel Elyse Morris Bunker** Ross (Born: 9 APR 1991 in Wheatland, Wyoming; Living) *Married 22 DEC 2010 to* **Zach Adams** (Born: 1991 in Wyoming; Living) *Divorced and married 8 JUN 2019 to* **Scott Andrew Roth** (Born: 12 JUL 1990 in Cheyenne, Wyoming; Living)
>>
>>> **Raela Rose Roth** (Born: 25 JUN 2020 [location]; Living)
>>
>> **John Merit Bunker** (Born: 1 JAN 1993 in Wheatland, Wyoming; Living)
>> **Muira Grace Bunker** (Born: 4 JAN 1995 in Wheatland, Wyoming; Living) *Married 8 SEP 2018 to* **Ryan James Madsen** (Born: 4 JAN 1994; Living)
>>
>>> **Mya Marie Madsen** (Born: 17 JUN 2019 in Wheatland, Wyoming; Living)
>
> **Dean Paul Ely** (Born: 4,1964 in Craig, Colorado; Died: 19 SEP 1967 in Slater, Colorado; Buried: Reader Cemetery, Savery, Wyoming)
> **Jona Margarite Ely** Kohpay Kainz Ely (Born: 15 APR 1969 in Craig, Colorado; Living) *Married 4 SEP 1993 to* **Theron Phalen Kohpay** (Born: 27,1970 in Pawhuska, Oklahoma; Living) *Divorced and married 10 MAY 2011 to* **Shawn Vernon Kainz** (Born: 6 MAR 1965 in Cheyenne, Wyoming; Living)

Remmington Dean Kohpay (Born: 2 JUL 1997 in Craig, Colorado; Living)
Raeann Ely-Kohpay (Born: 20 JUN 1999 in Steamboat, Springs, Colorado; Living)

Grady Oliver Ely (Born: 23 DEC 1970 in Craig, Colorado; Living) *Married 30 AUG 1997 to* **Wanda Dee Ashbaugh** (Born: 23 MAR 1970 in Steamboat Springs, Colorado; Living) *Divorced and partner with* **Suzanne Michele Meyer** Campbell Meyer (Born: 12 JUL 1968 in Cheyenne, Wyoming; Living)

Jonathan Perry ("JP") Ely (Born: 17 DEC 1997 in Craig, Colorado; Living)
Peyton Shaye Ely (Born: 2 AUG 2008 in Craig, Colorado; Living)

Shirley Marie St. Louis Schultz (Sister Grace Marie, CSC/Sister Shirley Marie, CSC, 1959 to JUN 1971) (Born: 17 NOV 1941 in Craig, Colorado; Living) *Married 25 SEP 1975 to* **Richard William Schultz** (Born: 30 NOV 1935 in Santa Monica, California; Died: 29 NOV 2013 in Lincoln, California; Buried Sacramento Valley National VA Cemetery, Dixon, California) ∩-18-∩

Beverly Ann St. Louis Runnion Rave (Born: 4 JUL 1946 in Hayden, Colorado; Living) *Married 10 SEP 1966 to* **William Frederick Runnion Jr.** (Born: 28 SEP 1941 in Douglas, Wyoming; Died: 27 SEP 1978 in Casper, Wyoming; Buried: Converse County Cemetery, Douglas, Wyoming) *Married 22 AUG 1979 to* **Elwood Leroy Rave** (Born: 21 NOV 1938 in Dell Rapids, South Dakota; Living) *Divorced* ∩-19-∩

Bryan Douglas Runnion (Born: 8 MAR 1969 in Casper, Wyoming; Living) *Married 20 MAY 2006 to* **Danielle Nicole Monnia-Runnion** (Born: 11 JUL 1977 in Hicksville, New York; Living)

Coulter William Runnion (Born: 19 JUL 2009 in Steamboat Springs, Colorado; Living)
Cassidy Grace Runnion (Born: 13 JAN 2011 in Missoula, Montana; Living)

Vickie Lynn Runnion Walker Steele (Born: 22 APR 1973 in Casper, Wyoming; Living) *Married 21 MAY 1992 to* **Steven Troy Walker** (Born: 29 SEP 1969 in Heppner, Oregon; Living) *Divorced and married 30 AUG 2018 to* **Douglas Allan Steele** (Born: 28 SEP 1969 in Craig, Colorado; Living)

Bryanne Nicole Walker Cossey (Born: 9 OCT 1992 in Pendleton, Oregon; Living) *Married 14 MAY 2016 to* **Daniel James Cossey** (Born: 28 MAR 1990 in Montrose, Colorado; Living)

Leonard Adrian St. Louis (Born: 12 APR 1916 at home in Battle Creek, Colorado, Died: 20 SEP 2004 in Grand Junction, Colorado; Buried: Reader Cemetery, Savery, Wyoming) *Married 12 JUN 1939 to* **Doris Helen Honnold** St. Louis (Born: 5 SEP 1911 in Slater, Colorado; Died: 18 DEC 2005 In Grand Junction, Colorado; Buried: Reader Cemetery, Savery, Wyoming) ∩-20-∩

Kathy Ann St. Louis Russell Ward (Born: 24 APR 1950 in Burbank, California; Living) *Married 8 JAN 1977 to* **John (Rusty) Wayne Russell** (Born: 18 DEC 1950 in Lubbock, Texas; Living) *Divorced Married 12 FEB 1994 to* **Thomas Harold Ward** (Born: 9 SEP 1950 in Lansing, Michigan; Living) ∩-21-∩

Cody Wayne Russell (Born: 12 AUG 1978 in Greeley, Colorado; Living) *Married [day] OCT 2004 to* **Joy Marie French** Russell (Born: 29 NOV 1979 [location]; Living); *Divorced and married [day] SEP 2015 to* **Mirjam Gramatzki** (Born: 15 APR 1976 in Hannover, Germany; Living)

Josephina (Josie) Fiona Gross (Born: 20 JUN 2003 in St. Albans, Vermont; Living) *Stepdaughter*
Avianna (Ava) Christel Gross (Born: 11 SEP 2007 in Montrose, Colorado; Living) *Stepdaughter*

Casey Wade Russell (Born: 11 APR 1980 in Greeley, Colorado; Living) *Married 5 FEB 2005 to* **Danielle Marie Riley** Russell (Born: 20 SEP 1978 in Eugene, Oregon; Living)

Ella Russell (Born: 3 OCT 2006 in Gilbert, Arizona; Living)

Taylor Riley Russell (Born: 20 JAN 2010 in Gilbert, Arizona; Living)

Tyrel J Russell (Born: 23 MAY 1981 in Greeley, Colorado; Living) *Married 17 SEP 2005 to* **Jessica Elaine Carlson** Russell (Born: 17 APR 1981 in Flagstaff, Arizona; Living) *Divorced*

Aubrey Elaine Russell (Born: 20 MAR 1999 in Scottsdale, Arizona; Living) *Adopted*

Christopher Zavier Ortega (Born: [day] DEC 2015 in Scottsdale, Arizona; Living)

Jayden Ortega (Born: [day] DEC 2018 in Scottsdale, Arizona; Living)

Isaac Ortega (Born: [day] DEC 2018 in Phoenix, Arizona; Living)

Tristian Jolene Russell (Born: 12 JAN 2005 in Phoenix, Arizona; Living)

∩-1-∩ *Portraits of Oliver and Sophia St-Louis.*

∩-2-∩ *Oliver St-Louis Sophia Sinclair St-Louis gravestone, Ormstown, Quebec.*

∩-3-∩ *Placing a flower on Alfred McCargar's gravestone on the hill above Slater, Colorado.*

∩-5-∩ *William T. Morgan and Sarah Mariah McCargar Morgan gravestone, Savery, Wyoming.*

∩-4-∩ *Studio photograph of William T. and Sarah Maria Morgan.*

∩-6-∩ *Oliver & Onie St. Louis's family: Oliver, Sinc, Alfred, Onie, George, Francis, Perry, and Leonard.*

∩-7-∩ *Sydney, Morgan, Courtney, and Alexandra Siegal, 2018.*

∩-8-∩ *George and (Dorothy) Grace St. Louis's extended family at Steamboat Springs, 1981. Back: Hugh, Rita, Mom (Grace), and Dad (George); Middle: Erik, Chai, David, Vivian, and Kenneth; Front: Robert, Benson, Lisa, Karen, and Melinda.*

∩-9-∩ *Karen and Robert St. Louis with their grandson, Kaeden Lucas.*

∩-10-∩ *Benson and Karol St. Louis with their two sons, Griffin and Spencer, 2015.*

∩-11-∩ *Lisa and Joseph Knight with their son, Jeff, 2006.*

∩-12-∩ *Joseph, Jeff, and Lisa Knight at Mississippi State University.*

⋀-13-⋀ Lila Benavente, Melinda St. Louis, and
Kenneth St. Louis at George and Dorothy Grace's
gravestone, 2019.

⋀-14-⋀ Pablo Benavente, Lila Benavente. and
Melinda St. Louis, 2018.

⋀-15-⋀ Erik and Amy Richards with their three sons,
Evan, Camden, and Scott, 2020.

⋀-16-⋀ Grace St. Louis at her 92nd
birthday party.

∩-17-∩ *Jean and Don Ely family, 1971. Grace (grandmother) with Shana, Shirley, Jean with Grady, and Don with Jona.*

∩-18-∩ *Shirley and Richard Schultz.*

∩-19-∩ *Beverly Rave's family. Vickie Steele holding Cash Lynn Steele, Allan Steele, Jake Steele, Jory Steele, Bryanne Cossey holding Harper Steele; front: Jasper Steele. Cash Lynn and Jasper are Jory's children, and Harper is Jake's son.*

⋂-20-⋂ *Leonard and Doris St. Louis family. Doris, Leonard, Kathy with Tyrel, Cody, and Rusty with Casey, 1981.*

⋂-21-⋂ *Tom and Kathy Ward with their two dogs, 2018.*

Index of St. Louis Relatives: Generational Listing

Russell, Forrest Adrian (Mike) 439
Russell, Jessica Elaine Carlson 442
Russell, John (Rusty) Wayne 441
Russell, Joy Marie French 441
Russell, Taylor Riley 442
Russell, Tristian Jolene 442
Russell, Tyrel J 442
Sauvé, Jean-Baptiste 434
Sauvé, Victoire Filiatrault dit St-Louis 434
Schultz, Richard William 441
Schultz, Shirley Marie St. Louis (Sister
    Grace Marie CSC/Sister Shirley
    Marie CSC) 441
Siegal, Alexandra (Lexie) St. Louis St. Louis
    Lexie 437
Siegal, Alexandra Morgan 437
Siegal, Brett St. Louis 438
Siegal, Courtney Elizabeth Lanning 437
Siegal, H. Morgan 437
Siegal, Ivy Elizabeth 438
Siegal, Kelly Ann Finnegan 438
Siegal, Scarlett Ann 438
Siegal, Warren Barry 437
Siegal, Wyatt Alexander 438
Sielen, Rae Jean V. Sielen Farfsing Cousin-
    eau 439
Snyder, Alexandra (Lexie) Kalina'oe 440
Snyder, Justice James Truth 440
Snyder, Marti Ann Miranda 440
Snyder, Robert Earl III 440
St-Louis, Alfred 435
St-Louis, Angéle Lapointe 434
St-Louis, Annie Louisa 435
St-Louis, David Porter 435
St-Louis, Elizabeth Barr 435
St-Louis, Elizabeth Brown 435
St-Louis, Frances (Annie) Fulton English 435
St-Louis, Francis 435
St-Louis, Francis James 435
St-Louis, Françoise M. 435
St-Louis, Françoise Paquet 434
St-Louis, Genevieve St-Aubin 434
St-Louis, George 435
St-Louis, John 435
St-Louis, Joseph F. 435
St-Louis, Laura Isabella Hunter 435
St-Louis, Marie Anne 435
St-Louis, Marie Helena Mennie 434
St-Louis, Marie J. 435
St-Louis, Marie M. 435
St-Louis, Marie Madelaine 435

St-Louis, Marie V. 435
St-Louis, Oliver (Olivier) 435
St-Louis, Sophia Sinclair 435
St-Louis, Victoire Ethier 434
St-Louis, William Alfred 435
St. Louis Agnes See Russell, Agnes
St. Louis, Alfred Chester 438
St. Louis, Avaleah Enid 438
St. Louis, Benson Petsamone 438
St. Louis Beverly See Rave, Beverly
St. Louis, David George 438
St. Louis, Deloris Marie Grudzinksi
    Adamek 437
St. Louis, Doris Helen Honnold 441
St. Louis, Dorothy Grace (Dot) Ireland St.
    Louis Magill Ireland Dorothy Grace
    (Grace) 438
St. Louis, Elizabeth Maria Lucia Miozzi St.
    Louis Betty 437
St. Louis, Francis James 439
St. Louis, George Edwin 438
St. Louis, Grace Mary Burkardt 440
St. Louis, Griffin Scott 438
St. Louis Jean See Landini, Jean
St. Louis, Jourdan Robert 438
St. Louis Joyce See Miranda, Joyce
St. Louis, Karen Sue Smallwood Garrett 438
St. Louis, Karol Leigh Scott 438
St. Louis Kathy See Ward, Kathy
St. Louis, Kenneth Oliver 439
St. Louis, Leonard Adrian 441
St. Louis, Leone (Onie) Morgan Morgan
    Leone (Onie) 437
St. Louis, Lila Heikkila 437
St. Louis, Lillyan St. Louis Walter St. Louis
    Lillyan 437
St. Louis Lisa See Knight, Lisa
St. Louis, Melinda Joyce 439
St. Louis, Mia Elizabeth 438
St. Louis, Navy 438
St. Louis, Oliver 437
St. Louis, Perry Alberta 440
St. Louis, Rita Grace St. Louis Maser 439
St. Louis, Robert Pyboon 438
St. Louis, Shannon Lee Pike 438
St. Louis Sharon. See Andrew, Sharon
St. Louis Shirley See Schultz, Shirley
St. Louis, Somchai Khamsayin 438
St. Louis, Spencer Morgan 438
St. Louis, Tai Francisco 438
St. Louis, Uree 438

Index of St. Louis Relatives: Photographs

Appendix I

Births, Marriages, Children, Deaths, and Burials of the Ireland Relatives

The following Ireland listing contains known relatives on our mom's side of the family. They go back as far as records were located and as far ahead as relatives were able to identify their children, grandchildren, and great-grandchildren. The first section, *Ancestors from Our Grandparents' and Earlier Generations*, provides as many ancestors as possible who preceded our grandfather Joe Ireland, that is, his paternal side. Little information was available to me on his maternal side, the Ritchies. Following the Ireland ancestor listing, are ancestors of our grandmother Laura Francis (Fannie) Galvin's father, Thomas Galvin. I was unable to learn anything about Fannie's mother's lineage.

The second section, *Ireland Family: Uncles, Aunts, First Cousins, and Their Children*, begins with our grandparents and proceeds next to the generation of our parents, aunts, and uncles, then to our generation and that of our first cousins. Next, it progresses to our children's generation, then their children's generation, and so on. (See Notes to Readers for additional clarifications.)

The listing is followed by photos contributed by relatives. After those, two alphabetized indexes appear for all the Ireland relatives, one for the listing and one for the photos.

Ancestors from Our Grandparents' and Earlier Generations

Ireland Ancestors

Thomas Ireland (4th great-grandparent)

Noble Ireland Sr. (Born: ~1795 in Ireland; Fought in the War of 1812; Died: 2 DEC 1869 in Loudon Township, Fayette County, Illinois: Buried: Loudon Township, Fayette County, Illinois) Married 30 SEP 1819 to **Mary Catherine (Caty) Vian** Ireland (Born: ~1797 in Pennsylvania; Died: [date] Loudon Township, Fayette County, Illinois: Buried: Loudon Township, Fayette County, Illinois) *Widower and married 25 APR 1867 to* **Nancy Walker** (Born: [year]; Died [year]) (3rd great-grandparents)

William H. Ireland Sr. (Born: 6 JAN 1824 in Knox County Ohio; Died: 30 APR 1961 in St. Elmo (Loudon Township, Fayette County), Illinois; Buried; Bob Doane Cemetery in Beecher City, Illinois) *Married 27 FEB 1853 to* **Jemima Jane Welker** Ireland Dial (Born: 6 AUG 1833 in Marion County, Ohio; Died: 29 AUG 1919 in Fayette County, Illinois; Post Oak Cemetery, Fayette County, Illinois) (2nd great-grandparents)

Noble Ireland Jr. (Born: 9 JUN 1855; Died: [year] in Peoria, Illinois) *Married 27 APR 1877 to* **Anne McKenzie** Ireland (Born [year]; Died [year])

Emanuel ("Man") Ireland (Born: 16 NOV 1856 in Beecher City, Illinois; Died: 29 APR 1934 in St. Elmo, Illinois; Buried: Post Oak Cemetery, St. Elmo, Illinois) *Married to* **Hannah J. Skeleton** Ireland (Born [year]; Died [year]) *Divorced and married 1 FEB 1892 to* **Phoebe Etta Kathryn (Katie) Bolds** Ireland (Born: 23 JAN 1874 in Fayette County, Illinois; Died: 4 NOV 1954 in Oceana, Illinois: Buried: Post Oak Cemetery, St. Elmo, Illinois)

Catherine Ireland Harding (Born [year]; Died [year])

Dinah Ireland Dayhuff (Born [year]; Died [year])

William Ireland Jr. (Born: 27 MAR 1861 in St. Elmo (Loudon Township, Fayette County), Illinois; Died: 14 FEB 1943 in St. Elmo, Illinois; Buried: Post Oak Cemetery, St. Elmo, Illinois) *Married 3 AUG 1882 to* **Eliza Jane Ritchie** Ireland (Born: 15 AUG 1861 in St. Elmo, Illinois; Died: 17 MAR 1944 in St. Elmo, Illinois; Buried: Post Oak Cemetery, St. Elmo, Illinois) (Great-grandparents) ☘-1-☘ ; ☘ -2-☘ ;☘ -3-☘

Joseph Otto Ireland (Born: 14 OCT 1883 in St. Elmo (Loudon Township, Fayette County), Illinois; Died: 26 APR 1963 in Akron, Colorado; Buried: Sedgwick Cemetery, Sedgwick, Colorado) *Married 17 SEP 1905 to* **Laura Francis Galvin** Ireland (Born: 3 APR 1888 in Little Blue (Near Nevada), Missouri; Died: 31 MAR 1933 in Denver, Colorado; Buried: Sedgwick Cemetery, Sedgwick, Colorado) *Married 13 NOV 1937 to* **Sylvia Mae Sanford** Ireland Hinshaw (Born: 18 SEP 1915 [location], Nebraska; Died: 29 AUG 1975 in Shoshone, Lincoln, Idaho; Buried: Shoshone Cemetery, Shoshone, Idaho) (Grandparents: see below)

Emma Lodema (Dema) Ireland Durbin Lyons Spencer (Born: 23 APR 1886 in St. Elmo, Illinois; Died: [year]) *Married to* **Hacle Durbin** (Born: [year]; Died: [year]) *Married to* **William Edgar Lyons** (Born: [year]; Died: [year]) *Married to* **J. P. Spencer** (Born: [year]; Died: [year])

Fred Eugene Ireland (Born: 12 OCT 1888 in St. Elmo, Illinois; Died: 21 OCT 1970; Buried: Post Oak Cemetery, St. Elmo, Illinois) *Married 7 NOV 1936 to* **Mandy Elizabeth Scholes** Ireland (Born: 19 NOV 1912; Died: [year])

Robert Lee Ireland (Born: 18 DEC 1890 in St. Elmo, Illinois; Died: 20 DEC 1960 in Oregon) *Married 19 FEB 1908 to* **Delilah Sides** Ireland (Born: [year]; Died: [year])

Lula Ireland Clow (Born: 23 FEB, 1984) *Married 18 APR 1014 to* **Johnson E. Clow** (Born: 18 AUG 1892; Died: 18 FEB 1980)
Nancy Ireland (Born: [year]; Died: [year] in infancy)

Galvin Ancestors

John Galvin (Born: [year]: County Limerick, Ireland; Died [year]: County Limerick, Ireland; Buried: County Limerick, Ireland) *Married to* **Mary Mahar** Galvin (Born: [year] County Limerick, Ireland; Died [year]: County Limerick, Ireland; Buried: County Limerick, Ireland) (3rd great-grandparents)

Cornelius Galvin (Born: 25 MAR 1829 in County Limerick, Ireland; Emigrated 20 OCT 1833 to 24 DEC 1833 to USA; Died: 28 JUN 1909 in Dederick, Vernon, Missouri; Buried: Mount Vernon Cemetery, Dederick, Vernon, Missouri) *Married 10 JUN 1850 or 1952 to* **Sarah J. Painter** Galvin (Born: 16 NOV 1833 in Bourbon County, Kentucky; Died: 23 OCT 1889 in Dederick, Vernon, Missouri; Buried: Mount Vernon Cemetery, Dederick, Vernon, Missouri) (2nd great-grandparents)

John W. Galvin (Born: 16 APR 1853 in Nicholas County, Kentucky; Died: [date]) *Married 17 FEB 1881 to* **Eizabeth E. Murphy** Galvin (Died: 23 JUL 1883; Buried: St. Mary's Cemetery (South), Independence, Missouri)

Thomas Henry Galvin (Born: 13 JAN 1855 in Nicholas County, Kentucky; Died: 19 JAN 1940 in Fort Scott, Kansas; Buried: Missouri) *Married to* **Elizabeth (Eliza)** __ Galvin (Born: 25 MAR 1855 in Missouri; Died: 31 DEC 1910 in Moundville, Vernon, Missouri; Buried: Welborn Cemetery, Moundville, Missouri) (Great-grandparents)

Addie Mae Galvin Chezum (Born: 3 MAY 1883; Died: 23 DEC 1966 in Sedgwick, Colorado) *Married to* **Orren Chezum** (Born: [year]; Died: [year])

Sarah Margaret Galvin Ricketts (Born: 5 SEP 1884; Died: 6 DEC 1971 in Fort Scott, Kansas) *Married to* **Fred Ricketts** (Born: [year]; Died: [year])

Minnie L. Galvin Williams (Born: 19 JAN 1886; Died: 3 SEP 1965 in Sedgwick, Colorado; Buried: Sedgwick Cemetery, Sedgwick, Colorado)

Laura Francis (Fannie) Galvin Ireland (Born: 3 APR 1888 Little Blue (Near Nevada), Missouri; Died: 31 MAR 1933 in Denver, Colorado; Buried: Sedgwick Cemetery, Sedgwick, Colorado) *Married 17 SEP 1905 in Moundville, Missouri to* **Joseph Otto Ireland** (Born: 14 OCT 1883 in St. Elmo (Loudon Township, Fayette County), Illinois; Died: 26 APR 1963 in Akron, Colorado; Buried: Sedgwick Cemetery, Sedgwick, Colorado) (Grandparents: see below)

Harrison Thomas or Thomas Harrison (Harry) Galvin (Born: 28 AUG 1890; Died: [year]) *Married to* **Myra Ford** Galvin (Born: [year]; Died: [year])

Robert J. Galvin (Born: 4 May 1992; Died: [year]) *Married to* **Nora Tallman** Galvin (Born: [year]; Died: [year]) *Married to* **Alberta Ruby** __ Galvin (Born: [year]; Died: [year])

Mary Elizabeth Galvin Wolfe (Born: 13 MAR 1896 in Fontana, Kansas) *Married 26 JAN 1916 to* **William Wolfe** (Born: [year]; Died: [year])

George D. Galvin (Born: 23 APR 1900; Died: JUL 1957 in New York City, New York)

Mary Alice Galvin Houser (Born: 13 OCT 1857 in Nicholas County, Kentucky; Died: 19 AUG 1904) *Married to* **Whit Wilson Houser** (Born: 27 MAR 1854 in Ohio; Died: 14 APR 1921; Buried: McGee Cemetery, Stratford, Oklahoma)

Robert Coleman Galvin (Born: 27 AUG 1859 in Nicholas County, Kentucky or Little Blue, Missouri; Died: 19 APR 1946 in Kansas City, Missouri; Buried: Fort Scott, Kentucky) *Married 22 MAR 1888 to* **Amelia (Millie) Gray** Galvin (Born: 3 DEC 1870; Died: 1947)

Cornelius Oliver Galvin (Born: 27 FEB 1862 in Farley, Missouri; Died: 10 MAR 1995 in Fort Scott, Kansas; Buried: Oakgrove Cemetery, Fort Scott, Kansas) *Married to* **Roxanna West** Galvin (Born: 13 JUBN 1872 in Illinois; Died: 13 FEB 1942 in Fort Scott, Kansas; Buried: Oakgrove Cemetery, Fort Scott, Kansas)

Sarah Margaret (Maggie) Galvin Vickers (Born: 27 FEB 1862 in Ohio; Died: 15 AUG 1896; Buried: Lone Tree Cemetery, Stuttgart, Arkansas) *Married 17 NOV 1885 to* **Aquilla (Quill) Converce Vickers** (Born: 20 MAR 1858; Died: 6 NOV 1929; Buried: Lone Tree Cemetery, Stuttgart, Arkansas)

George B. Galvin (Born: 1 JUN 1864 in Nevada, Missouri; Died: 29 AUG 1952 in Harwood, Missouri; Buried: Mount Vernon Cemetery, Vernon, Missouri) *Married 5 SEP 1887 to* **Sarah C. Dunaway** Galvin (Born: 9 OCT 1868; Died: 1943 in Dederick, Missouri; Buried: Mount Vernon Cemetery, Vernon, Missouri)

Elizabeth (Lizzie) Galvin (Born: 1 JUN 1864 in Nevada, Missouri; Died: [year])

Nannie Bell Galvin Vickers (Born: 3 FEB 1866 in Missouri; Died: 27 DEC [year] in Vernon County, Missouri) *Married 20 OCT 1865 to* **George Washington Vickers** (Born: 15 JAN 1849; Died: 31 MAY 1923

Joseph Alexander Galvin (Born: 3 DEC 1869 in Vernon County, Missouri; Died: 1939; Buried: Lone Tree Cemetery, Stuttgart, Arkansas) *Married 3 JUN 1896 to* **Cordelia Dell Harper** Galvin (Born: 16 AUG 1876; Died: 4 JUL 1947; Buried: Lone Tree Cemetery, Stuttgart, Arkansas)

Benjamin Franklin Galvin (Born: 13 OCT 1870 in Vernon County, Missouri; Died: 20 FEB 1949 in Dederick, Missouri; Buried: Mount Vernon Cemetery, Vernon, Missouri) *Married 26 FEB 1890 to* **Maggie Emma Duenkel** Galvin (Born: 4 DEC 1869 in Montgomery County, Missouri; Died: 10 MAY 1934 in Vernon County, Missouri; Buried: Mount Vernon Cemetery, Vernon, Missouri)

Ireland Family: Uncles, Aunts, First Cousins, and Their Children

Grandparents
 Aunts, uncles, parents
  Cousins, siblings
   Nieces, nephews, children
    Grandnieces, grandnephews, grandchildren
     Great-grandnieces, great-grandnephews, great-grandchildren
      Great-great-grandnieces, great-great-grandnephews, great-great-grandchildren

Joseph Otto Ireland (Born: 14 OCT 1883 in St. Elmo (Loudon Township, Fayette County), Illinois; Died: 26 APR 1963 in Akron, Colorado; Buried: Sedgwick Cemetery, Sedgwick, Colorado) *Married 17 SEP 1905 to* **Laura Francis Galvin** Ireland (Born: 3 APR 1888 Little Blue (Near Nevada), Missouri; Died: 31 MAR 1933 in Denver, Colorado; Buried: Sedgwick Cemetery, Sedgwick, Colorado) ☘-4-☘ *Widowed and married twice [~1934–1936] to* **Becky** __ __ Ireland *Divorced and married 13 NOV 1937 to* **Sylvia Mae Sanford** Ireland Hinshaw (Born: 18 SEP 1915 [location], Nebraska; Died: 29 AUG 1975 in Shoshone, Lincoln, Idaho; Buried: Shoshone Cemetery, Shoshone, Idaho) *Divorced*

 Elmer Thomas Ireland (Born: 23 AUG 1906 in St. Elmo (Loudon Township, Fayette County), Illinois; Died: 29 MAR 1958 in Fort Morgan, Colorado; Buried: Riverside Cemetery, Fort Morgan, Colorado) *Married 31 AUG 1932 to* **Lillian Francis Chabot** Ireland Chabot (Born: 22 APR 1912 in Essex, Iowa; Died: 3 JAN 2012 in Fort Morgan, Colorado; Buried: Riverside Cemetery, Fort Morgan, Colorado)

Hazel Mae Ireland Jess (Born: 21 JUL 1933 in Akron, Colorado; Living) *Married 13 JAN 1952 to* **Edwin Carl Jess** (Born: 6 JUL 1932 in Fort Morgan, Colorado; Living) ☘-5-☘ ☘-6-☘ ☘-7-☘ ☘-8-☘

Irwin Lee Jess (Born: 21 OCT 1952 in Fort Morgan, Colorado; Died: 9 MAY 2016; Buried: Jess Farm, Fort Morgan, Colorado) *Married 24 SEP 1977 to* **Susan Jane Kembel** Jess (Born: 20 MAY 1953 in Fort Morgan, Colorado; Living) *Divorced and married 29 OCT 1988 to* **Tamara Lynne Rehkop** Jess (Born: 15 OCT 1961 in Fort Morgan, Colorado; Living)

Chelsea Michelle Jess Riscoe *Married 24 MAY 2011 to* **Eric Robert Riscoe** (Born: 9 JUL 1983 in Littleton, Colorado; Living)

Christopher Carl Jess (Born: 14 DEC 1989 in Greeley, Colorado; Living)

Randall Wayne Jess (Born: 12 OCT 1956 in Fort Morgan, Colorado; Living) *Married 5 JUN 1976 to* **Robin Lyn Wulf** (Born: 24 SEP 1958 in Ft. Morgan, Colorado; Living) *Divorced and married 15 DEC 1979 to* **Rhonda Sue Koehler** Jess (Born: 23 JUL 1958 in Fort Morgan, Colorado; Living)

Jason Edd Jess (Born: 23 OCT 1980 in Fort Morgan, Colorado; Living) *Married [day/month] 2006 to* **Lisa Marie Dahl** Jess (Born: 18 DEC 1966 in Fort Morgan, Colorado; Living) *Divorced*

Kaylee Marie Jess (Born: 18 MAY 2004) in Greeley, Colorado

Jaxon Michael Jess (Born: 19 NOV 2014 in Fort Morgan, Colorado; Living)

Jeramy Randall Jess (Born: 22 MAR 1982 in Fort Morgan, Colorado; Living) *Married 6 MAY 2006 to* **Kathleen (Kati) Dale Templeton** Jess (Born: 14 JUN 1982 in Denver, Colorado; Living)

Brodin Randall Jess (Born: 20 AUG 2007 in Fort Morgan, Colorado; Living)

Brooklyn Elizabeth Jess (Born: 15 JUN 2010 in Fort Morgan, Colorado; Living)

Jennifer Sue Jess Eiring (Born: 14 JUL 1985 in Fort Morgan, Colorado) *Married 17 JUN 2006 to* **Kyle Robert Eiring** (Born: 21 OCT 1985 in Greeley, Colorado; Living)

Gracie Sue Eiring (Born: 2 JAN 2011 in Loveland, Colorado; Living)

Benjamin Kyle Eiring (Born: 3 DEC 2013 in Loveland, Colorado)

Jacob Dean Eiring (Born: 29 DEC 2016 in Loveland, Colorado; Living)

Lyle Stewart Jess (Born: 18 APR 1959 in Fort Morgan, Colorado; Living) *Married 22 MAY 1980 to* **Christi Lee Windsheimer** Jess (Born: 22 AUG 1958; Living)

Bryce Carl Jess (Born: 8 MAR 1988 in Greeley, Colorado; Living) *Married 10 APR 2013 to* **Sabrina (Bri) Dawn Lehman** Jess (Born: 19 JUL 1978 in Fort Morgan, Colorado; Living)

Chase Lyam Jess (Born: 20 SEP 2018 in Fort Morgan, Colorado; Living)

Blair Vernon Jess (Born: 28 AUG 1989 in Greeley, Colorado; Living) *Married 16 JUN 2017 to* **Cady Jo Frasier** Jess (Born: 1 JAN 1989 in Fort Morgan, Colorado; Living)

Norma Francis Ireland Parachini (Born: 29 NOV 1934 in Evans, Colorado; Died: 13 MAY 1997 in Denver, Colorado; Ashes at Elmer and Lillian Ireland grave, Riverside Cemetery, Fort Morgan, Colorado) *Married 12 APR 1958 to* **Ronald Joseph Parachini** (Born: 27 JUN 1937 in Denver, Colorado; Died: 13 JAN 1999 in Denver, Colorado; Ashes spread in Silver Plume, Colorado) *Divorced*

Terri Lynn Parachini Trujillo **Ireland** (Born: 12 FEB 1959 in Denver, Colorado; Living) *Married 25 MAY 1985 to* **Carlos Manuel Trujillo** (Born: 1 MAY 1959 in Havana, Cuba; Living) *Divorced and married 2 SEP 1997 to* **Jeffrey Craig Clack** (Born: 6 APR 1959 in Rapid City, South Dakota; Living)

Ryan Castle Presnell (Born: 7 MAY 1993 in Denver, Colorado; Living)

Debra Kay Parachini Jones (Born: 19 MAY 1960 in Denver, Colorado; Living) *Married 25 FEB 1980 to* **Randall Bruce Jones** (Born: 22 JUL 1957 in Laramie, Wyoming; Living)

Amanda Michelle Jones Belden (Born: 12 AUG 1987 in Laramie, Wyoming; Living) *Married 17 JUN 2018 to* **Mitchell William Belden** (Born: 23 AUG 1989 in Vail, Colorado; Living)

Addilyn Rose Belden (Born: 7 JUN 2018 in Grand Junction, Colorado; Living)

Finnegan Randall Belden (Born: 21 JUN 2020 in Grand Junction, Colorado; Living)

Darlene Louise Ireland Hellmuth Dunning (Born: 5 JUN 1936 in Akron, Colorado; Living) *Married 3 OCT 1954 to* **Jerry Walter Hellmuth** (Born: 3 SEP 1934 in Milwaukee, Wisconsin; Died: 1 FEB 1974 in Fort Morgan, Colorado; Buried: Riverside Cemetery, Fort Morgan, Colorado) *Divorced and married 15 OCT 1977 to* **Gilbert "Gib" Duane Dunning** (Born: 3 MAR 1925 in Dillon, Colorado; Living) *Divorced*

Ricky Dee Hellmuth (Born: 15 OCT 1955 in Fort Morgan, Colorado; Living) *Married [date] to* **Shanna C. Farish** Hellmuth (Born: 9 OCT 1955 [location]; Living)

Chelsea Louise Hellmuth Luna (Born: 15 APR 1984 [location]; Living) *Married [date] to* **Lionel Lonnie Luna** (Born: 17 AUG 1983 [location]; Living)

Christopher Jay Hellmuth (Born: 28 JUL 1959 in Fort Morgan, Colorado; Living) *Married 25 AUG 1977 to* **Wendy Kay Scofield** Hellmuth (Born: 6 MAR 1958 in Fort Morgan, Colorado; Died: 16 FEB 2014 in Salina, Kansas; Buried: Riverside Cemetery, Fort Morgan, Colorado) *Widowed and married 14 OCT 2017 to* **Michelle Catherine Wiegel** Salas (Born: 24 MAY 1970 in Colby, Kansas; Living)

Stephanie Rae Hellmuth (Born: 3 JUN 1978 Fort Morgan, Colorado; Living)

Ariana Marie Hellmuth (Born: 16 NOV 2001 in Colby, Kansas; Living)

Raela Ann Rose Davis (Born: 1 JAN 2006 in Salina, Kansas; Living)

Daevon Lamont Malcolm Davis (Born: 19 MAR 2007 in Salina, Kansas; Living)

Brandon Jay Hellmuth (Born: 21 MAY 1980 in Fort Morgan, Colorado; Living) *Married 27 AUG 2002 to* **Amanda Marie Delzeit** Hellmuth (Born: 27 FEB 1979 in Colby, Kansas; Living) *Divorced*

Emma Marie Kate Delzeit (Born: 19 FEB 2000 in Colby, Kansas; Living) *Raised by Brandon*

Kaitlyn Danae Hellmuth (Born: 22 MAY 2002 in Colby, Kansas: Living)

Blayke Kristopher Hellmuth (Born: 14 FEB 2003 in Colby, Kansas; Living)

Addie Madeline Hellmuth (Born: 5 FEB 2006 in Salina, Kansas; Living)

Tyler Christopher Hellmuth (Born: 25 JAN 1983 in Fort Morgan, Colorado; Living) *Fiancé of* **Alena Rae Canchola** (Born: 26 JUL 1984 in Corpus Christi, Texas; Living)

Payton Eileen Hellmuth (Born: 17 OCT 2005 in Corpus Christi, Texas; Living)

Donna Lee Ireland Lett (Born: 10 NOV 1938 in Steamboat Springs, Colorado; Died: 30 DEC 1994 in Sanford, North Carolina; Buried: Rocky Fork Christian Church Cemetery, Sanford, North Carolina) *Married 19 DEC 1959 to* **Hector Kimball Lett** (Born: 15 SEP 1935 in Knoxville, Tennessee; Died: 15 DEC 2017 in Pinellas, Florida; Buried Arlington National Cemetery, Washington, DC) *Divorced*

Laura Ann Harris Karrington **Ireland** (Born: 9 FEB 1958 in Fort Morgan, Colorado; Living)

Jeffery Alan Lett Sr. (Born: 12 SEP 1960 in Panama City, Florida; Living) *Married [date] to* **Brenda Louise Kinnaird** Lett (Born: 25 OCT 1963 [location]; Living) *Divorced and married [date] to* **Dinah (Dee) Sue Whitterer** Boryla Lett (Born: 17 FEB 1964 [location]; Living) *Divorced*

Jeffery Alan Lett Jr. (Born: 16 SEP 1988 in Sanford, North Carolina; Died: 22 OCT 1995 in Sanford, North Carolina; Buried: Rocky Fork Christian Church Cemetery, Sanford, North Carolina)

Genevieve Ireland Lett (Born: 17 JUL 1995 [location]; Living

Ruby Mabel Ireland Lawler (Born: 29 APR 1908 in DeKalb County, Illinois; Died: 4 MAY 1996 in Humble, Texas; Buried: Fairview Cemetery, Scottsbluff, Nebraska) *Married 26 JUN 1926 to* **Louis Edward Lawler** (Born: 10 AUG 1899, in Paxton, Nebraska; Died: 6 JUN 1980 in Scottsbluff, Nebraska; Buried: Fairview Cemetery, Scottsbluff, Nebraska) ☘-9-☘ ☘-10-☘

Mildred Maxine Lawler Forrest (Born: 9 JUL 1929 in Sutherland, Nebraska; Died: 7 AUG 2018 in Alamo Heights, Texas; Buried: Linn Grove Cemetery, Greeley, Colorado) *Married 28 JUL 1951 to* **Joseph Clough Forrest** (Born: 25 JAN 1922 in Mead, Nebraska; Died: 14 FEB 2015) *Divorced*

Anthony (Tony) Charles Forrest (Born: 27 MAY 1952 in Minneapolis, Minnesota; Living)

Patrick Lawler Forrest (Born: 14 JUN 1953 in Minneapolis, Minnesota; Living) *Married 4 NOV 1983 to* **Linda Louise Beach** Forrest (Born: 15 APR 1959 in Fruita, Colorado; Living)

Jarred Clayton (JC) Forrest (Born: 1 JUN 1985 in Grand Junction, Colorado; Living) *Married 7 JUL 2012 to* **Catriona Allison McCleery** Forrest (Born: 18 JUN 1983 in Edinburgh, Scotland; Living) *Divorced and married 8 JAN 2020 to* **Whitney Meyer** Forrest (Born: [date/location]; Living)

Angus Patrick Forrest (Born: 25 DEC 2015 in Sun City, Arizona; Living)

Caitlin Francine Forrest (Born: 16 DEC 1987 in Phoenix, Arizona; Living)

Francine Hope Forrest (Born: 28 MAY 1955 in Cuyahoga Falls, Ohio; Died: 6 NOV 1973 in Weld County, Colorado; Buried: Linn Grove Cemetery, Greeley, Colorado)

John Joseph Forrest (Born: 15 DEC 1957 in Elyria, Ohio; Living)

Michael Paul Forrest (Born: 30 NOV 1958 in Elyria, Ohio; Living) *Married 16 SEP 1998 (Civil) and 26 DEC 1998 (Church) to* **Margaret Gaybrielle Engel** Forrest (Born: 1 OCT 1970 in Fredericksburg, Texas; Living)

Nathan Everett Engel (Born: 27 JUN 1995 in Bexar County, San Antonio, Texas; Living) *Stepson*

Leigha Engel Forrest Engel (Born: 10 DEC 2001 in Grand Junction, Colorado; Living)

Stephen James Forrest (Born: 12 JAN 1960 in Greeley, Colorado; Living) *Married [date] to* **Sandra (Sandy) Lynn Otto** Forrest Oberlin (Born: 15 MAY 1961 [location]; Living) *Divorced*

Terence (Terry) Mark Forrest (Born: 16 SEP 1961 in Greeley, Colorado; Living)

Lawrence (Larry) Edward Lawler (Born: 28 JUL 1931 in Akron, Colorado, Nebraska; Died: 25 JUN 2018 in Lakewood, Colorado; Buried: Fort Logan National Cemetery, Fort Logan, Colorado) *Married 27 AUG 1955 to* **Thelma June Brekke** Lawler Auld (Born: [day] AUG 1934 [location]; Died: 1 MAY 2020 in Denver, Colorado; Buried: [location]) *Divorced and married 19 DEC 1970 to* **Peggy Ann Woodman** Murphy Lawler (Born: 25 OCT 1930 in Jamesville, Wisconsin; Living)

Peggy Lea Murphy (Born: 12 NOV 1949 [location]; Living) *Stepdaughter*

James __ Murphy (Born: 5 MAY 1950 in Denver, Colorado; Living) *Stepson*

Gerald Allen Murphy (Born: 4 NOV 1953 in Denver, Colorado; Living) *Stepson*

Patrick D. Murphy (Born: 22 MAY 1955 in Denver, Colorado; Living) *Stepson; Married [date] to* **Sherri __ __** Murphy (Born: [date/location]; Living)

__ __ Murphy (Born: [date/location]; Living)

Matthew __ Murphy (Born: [date/location]; Living)

Colleen __ Murphy Dickson (Born: 4 AUG 1957 in Denver, Colorado; Living) *Stepdaughter*

Stephen Scot Lawler (Born: 13 MAY 1963 in Denver, Colorado; Living) *Adopted*

Janette (Jan) Kae Lawler (Born: 10 JUN 1965 in Denver, Colorado; Living) *Partner with* **Christopher Joseph Cook** (Born: [day] FEB 1967 [location]; Living)

Joshua Adam Lawler (Born: [day/month] 1989 [location]; Living)

Frances Fae Lawler Robbins (Born: 8 NOV 1932 in Akron, Colorado; Living) *Married 26 JUN 1953 to* **Robert Richard Robbins** (Born: 11 MAR 1928 in Mitchell, Nebraska; Died: 18 FEB 2005 in Snellville, Georgia; Buried: __ Cemetery, Snellville, Georgia)

Lisa Ann Robbins Swails (Born: 28 DEC 1954 in Scottsbluff, Nebraska; Living) *Married [date] to* **Bradley Charles Swails** (Born: [day] SEP 1951 [location]; Died: 16 NOV 2004 in Walton, Georgia; Buried: Floral Hills Memory Gardens, Tucker, Georgia)

Casey Leigh Swails (Born: 22 AUG 1984 in Decatur, Georgia; Living)

Lauren Ashley Swails (Born: 12 JAN 1988 in Decatur, Georgia; Living)

Richard James Robbins (Born: 19 DEC 1955 in Scottsbluff, Nebraska; Died: 4 AUG 2008; Buried: __ Cemetery, Snellville, Georgia)

John (Jack) Lee Robbins (Born: 5 MAY 1960 in Fort Pierce, Florida; Living)

Gail Louise Robbins Thayer (Born: 5 APR 1966 in Fort Pierce, Florida; Living) *Married [date] to* **Rex Alan Thayer** (Born: 3 NOV 1960 [location]; Living)

Emily Jordan Thayer Bacon (Born: [day] JAN 1992 [location]; Living) *Married [date] to* **Bradley David Bacon** (Born: 23 FEB 1992 [location]; Living)

Luke __ Thayer (Born: [date/location]; Living)

John (Jack) Leroy Lawler (Born: 27 APR 1934 in Akron, Colorado; Living) *Married 4 MAY 1957 to* **Beverly Beatrice Schulte** Lawler (Born: 5 APR 1934 in Glen Elder, Kansas; Died: 2 APR 2019 in Fort Collins, CO; Burial: Ashes at [location]) *Divorced and married 20 JUN 1980 to* **Susan D. Sload** Perkins Lawler (Born: 3 JUN 1940 [location]; Living) *Divorced and married [date] to* **Kathryn Lee Lindahl** Lawler (Born: 12 JAN 1948 [location]; Living) *Divorced* ☘-11-☘ ☘-12-☘

Timothy Sean Lawler (Born: 29 JAN 1958 in Beaufort, South Carolina; Living) *Married [date] to* **Myoung Un (Malanie) Yi** Lawler Knight (Born: 3 JUL 1959 [location]; Living) *Divorced and married [date] to* **Loretta Ann Hoffman** Lawler (Born: 11 MAR 1958 in [city], Kentucky; Living)

Malanie __ Lawler (Born: 8 DEC 1987 [location]; Living) *Stepdaughter*

__ __ __ (Born: [date/location]; Living) *Stepdaughter*

__ __ __ (Born: [date/location]; Living) *Stepson*

| **Megan Lee Lawler** (Born: 8 DEC 1987 [location]; Living)

Christopher Mark Lawler (Born: 29 JAN 1958 in Beaufort, South Carolina; Living) *Married [date] to* **Lisa Elaine Talstad** Lawler (Born: 2 MAR 1962 [location]; Living)

Gregory James Lawler (Born: 25 JUL 1960 in Minneapolis, Minnesota; Living)

Ann Catherine Lawler Davis Perry (Born: 29 JUL 1963 in Denver, Colorado; Living) *Married [date] to* **Andrew James Davis** (Born: 20 FEB 1959 [location]; Living) *Divorced and married [date] to* **James John Perry** (Born: 8 NOV 1951 [location]; Living)

    | **Genelle Catherine Davis** Andrews (Born: 30 DEC 1988 [location]; Living)
    | **Rebecca Ann Davis** Carlson (Born: 11 JUN 1991 [location]; Living)
    | **Diana Maria Davis** (Born: 17 OCT 1994 [location]; Living)

Jane (Jan) Elizabeth Lawler Kochevar Preston (Born: 31 JUL 1965 in Arvada, Colorado; Living) *Married 30 SEP 1989 to* **Randall Eugene Kochevar** (Born: 2 AUG 1965 [location]; Living) *Divorced and married [date] to* **David Semler Preston** (Born: 16 NOV 1953 [location]; Living)

    | **Katrina Elise Kochevar** Brekke (Born: 8 NOV 1991 [location]; Living) *Married 16 JUN 2016 to* **Ian James Brekke** (Born: 14 MAR 1986 [location]; Living)

        | **Addison Leslie Brekke** (Born: 13 MAR 2020 [location]; Living)

    | **Joseph Nicholas Kochevar** (Born: 20 JUN 1994 [location]; Living) Married 15 FEB 2020 to **Toni Roxan Saylor** Kochevar (Born: 2 JUN 1994 [location]; Living)

    | **Thomas Anthony Kochevar** (Born: 20 JUN 1994 [location]; Living)

Dorothy LuAnn Lawler Werth Barton (Born: 26 DEC 1937 in Scottsbluff, Nebraska; Died: 14 APR 2018 in Boise, Idaho; Buried: Buried: Morris Hill Cemetery, Boise, Idaho) *Married 5 JUL 1958 to* **Jude Newman Werth** (Born: 28 JUL 1935 in Hays, Kansas; Died: 10 APR 1976 in Boise, Idaho; Buried: Morris Hill Cemetery, Boise, Idaho) *Widowed and married [day/month] 1986 to* **David M. Barton** (Born: 16 MAR 1931 in Rockford, Illinois; Died: 5 APR 2008 in Boise, Idaho; Buried: Morris Hill Cemetery, Boise, Idaho)

    | **Bradley Jude Werth** (Born: 19 MAY 1959 [location]; Living) *Married [date] to* **Maria K. Prochaska** Werth (Born: 9 FEB 1956 [location]; Living)

    | **Marsha Marie Werth** Clark (Born: 1 MAY 1960 [location]; Living) *Married [date] to* **Robert L. Clark** (Born: 10 OCT 1949 [location]; Living)

    | **Jason Marshall Clark** (Born: [date/location]; Living)

    | **Douglas Allen Werth** (Born: 9 NOV 1961 [location]; Living) *Married [date] to* **Ho Thi Thu Nga** *changed to* **Holly Thi Margolies** Werth (Born: 30 DEC 1967 in Nha Trang, Vietnam; Died: 3 MAY 2016 in Boise, Idaho; Buried: [location])

        | **Jude David Werth** (Born: [date/location]; Living)
        | **Trent Edward Werth** (Born: [date/location]; Living)

    | **Julie Anne Werth** Wipper (Born: 3 AUG 1963 [location]; Living) *Married [date] to* **David __ Wipper** (Born: [date/location]; Living)

        | **Audrey LuAnn Wipper** (Born: [date/location]; Living)

    | **David Michael Barton** (Born: 25 JAN 1955 [location]; Living) *Stepson; Married [date] to* **Deborah M. Daniels** Barton (Born: 1 JAN 1953 [location]; Living)

        | **Kelly Ann Barton** Iverson (Born: [day] FEB 1985 [location]; Living) *Married to / Partner with* **Christopher Donald Iverson** (Born: 21 MAR 1984 [location]; Living)

        | **Katherine Ellen Barton** (Born: 17 MAY 1988 [location]; Living)

Ann M. Barton Schonhardt (Born: 29 JUL 1958 [location]; Living) *Stepdaughter; Married [date] to* **Craig S. Schonhardt** (Born: [date/location]; Died: 6 JUN 2008; Buried: __ Cemetery [location])

Mary E. Barton Rose (Stepdaughter) (Born: 15 OCT 1961 Location; Living) *Married [date] to* **Christopher Charles Rose** (Born: 29 JAN 1961 [location]; Living)

> **Laura Anne Rose** (Born: [day] MAR 1993 [location]; Living)
> **Emily Christine Rose** (Born: [date/location]; Living)
> **Sarah Marie Rose** (Born: [date/location]; Living)

Patricia Rae Lawler Hewett Ham (Born: 19 FEB 1940 in Scottsbluff, Nebraska; Living) *Married 1 JUL 1959 to* **William Lester Hewitt** (Born: 1 JUL 1939 in Catawba, North Carolina; Living) *Divorced and married 27 JUN 1969 to* **Ray Junior Ham** (Born: 6 NOV 1929 in Benkelman, Nebraska; Died: 31 AUG 2018 in Dover, New Hampshire; Cremated)

> **Laura (Lori) Lynn** Hewitt **Ham** Mannle (Born: 31 JAN 1960 in Scottsbluff, Nebraska; Living) *Married 22 APR 1989 to* **Paul Matthew Mannle** (Born: 7 FEB 1957 in Greenwich, Connecticut; Living) *Divorced*
>
> > **Erin Elizabeth Mannle** (Born: 5 MAY 1990 in Stoneham, Massachusetts; Living)
> > **Alexandra Rose Mannle** (Born: 5 FEB 1996 in Portsmouth, New Hampshire; Living)
>
> **Michael (Mike) Lawrence Ham** (Born: 15 OCT 1951 in Stratton, Nebraska; Living) *Stepson; Married 6 MAY 1970 to* **Jane Marie Aragon** Ham (Born: 7 APR 1953 [location]; Living)
>
> > **Jaimee Rae Ham** Bean (Born: 30 SEP 1976 in Greeley, Colorado; Living) *Married 23 MAR 2001 to* **Marc Alan Bean** (Born: 19 NOV 1974 in London, Ohio; Living)
> >
> > > **Ashley Nicole Bean** (Born: 3 NOV 2007 in Aurora, Colorado; Living)
> > > **Hailey Michelle Bean** (Born: 3 NOV 2007 in Aurora, Colorado; Living)
> >
> > **Marc Alan Ham** (Born: 14 JUL 1979 in Greeley, Colorado; Living)
>
> **Randall (Randy) Scott Ham** (Born: 5 SEP 1952 in Benkleman, Nebraska; Died: 29 NOV 2016 in Greeley, Colorado; Buried: Sunset Memorial Gardens, Greeley, Colorado) *Stepson; Married [day] MAY 1980 to* **Elizabeth Anne Sandlian** Ham (Born: 12 DEC 1951 [location]; Living) *Divorced*
>
> **Jacqueline (Jacque) Louise Ham** Gilbert (Born: 23 APR 1955 in Benkleman, Nebraska; Living) *Stepdaughter; Married 19 DEC 1980 to* **Terry Lee Gilbert** (Born: 8 JUN 1956 in St. Louis, Illinois; Living)
>
> **Kristina (Kristi) Ann Ham** Trawick (Born: 30 AUG 1958 in Imperial, Nebraska; Living) *Stepdaughter; Married 20 FEB 1988 to* **Brian Keith Trawick** (Born: 14 NOV 1960 in Mobile, Alabama; Living)
>
> > **Samuel Alfred Trawick** (Born: 13 APR 1989 in Aurora, Colorado; Living) *Married 3 JUL 2010 to* **Tiffany Marie Pettis** Trawick (Born: 11 SEP 1988 in Glendale, Arizona; Living) *Divorced*
> >
> > > **Grayson Brian Trawick** (Born: 1 SEP 2015 in Corpus Christi, Texas; Living)
>
> **Anthony Allen Ham** (Born: 11 SEP 1963 in Greeley, Colorado; Living) *Stepson*

William Lynn Lawler (Born: 24 DEC 1941 in Scottsbluff, Nebraska; Living) *Married 12 JUN 1964 to* **Carol Mae Barlean** Lawler (Born: 15 JUL 1941 in Omaha, Nebraska; Living)

Wendy Lynn Lawler Sisler (Born: 6 SEP 1966 in Denver, Colorado; Living) *Married [date] to* **Thomas Shane Sisler** (Born: 21 APR 1970 [location]; Living) *Divorced*

> **Shane William Sisler** (Born: 16 FEB 2003 in The Woodlands, Texas; Living)
> **Shelby Lynn Sisler** (Born: 16 FEB 2003 in The Woodlands, Texas; Living)
> **Devin Thomas Sisler** (Born: 15 APR 2005 in Montrose, Colorado; Living)

Jeffrey William Lawler (Born: 22 AUG 1969 in Oklahoma City, Oklahoma; Living)

Michael David Lawler (Born: 22 OCT 1972 in Decatur, Illinois; Living) *Married [date] to* **Carrie Nicole Marshall** Norman Lawler (Born: 22 APR 1971 in Houston, Texas; Living)

> **Zachary Maxwell Norman** (Born: 3 AUG 1996 in Houston, Texas; Living)
> *Stepson*
> **Jonathan David Lawler** (Born: 9 MAY 2003 in Houston, Texas; Living)
> **Cole __ Lawler** (Born: 15 JUN 2005 in Houston, Texas; Living)
> **Jacob Jeffrey Lawler** (Born: 5 JUN 2008 in Houston, Texas; Living)

Clarence Joseph Ireland (Born: 16 MAY 1910 in St. Elmo, Illinois; Died: 15 AUG 1918 in Sedgwick, Colorado; Buried: Sedgwick Cemetery, Sedgwick, Colorado)

Gladys Jane Ireland (Born: 2 JUL 1912 in Sedgwick, Colorado; Died: 11 AUG 1918 in Sedgwick, Colorado; Buried: Sedgwick Cemetery, Sedgwick, Colorado)

Velma Rose Ireland Gebauer (Born: 16 JUL 1915 in Sedgwick, Colorado; Died: 23 SEP 2001 in Akron, Colorado; Buried: St. Joseph's Cemetery, Akron, Colorado) *Married 10 APR 1934 to* **Louis John Gebauer** (Born: 15 DEC 1907 in Akron, Colorado; Died: 15 SEP 1980 in Akron, Colorado; Buried: St. Joseph's Cemetery, Akron, Colorado)

David Louis Gebauer (Born: 3 NOV 1934 in Akron, Colorado; Living) *Married 10 DEC 1956 to* **Beverly Ann Daniels** Gebauer (Born: [date/location]; Living)

> **David Anthony (Tony) Gebauer** (Born: 10 AUG 1957 in Brush, Colorado; Living) *Married [date] to* **Deborah Louise Creasey** Gebauer (Born: 3 JUN 1960 [location]; Living)
>
> > **Darrell Allen Gebauer** (Born: 21 OCT 1984 [location]; Living)
> > **Dillion Hayes Gebauer** (Born: 1 JAN 1992 [location]; Living)
>
> **Douglas Kevin (Kevin) Gebauer** (Born: 21 NOV 1958; Died: 1 DEC 2014; Buried: St. Joseph Catholic Cemetery, Akron, Colorado) *Married 23 JUN 1979 to* **Vickie Sue Anderson** Gebauer (Born: 30 SEP 1959 [location]; Died: 7 OCT 1981 [location]; Buried Mountain View Cemetery, Longmont, Colorado) *Widowed and married 4 FEB 1986 to* **Cheryl Ann Foster** Sturch Gebauer (Born: 23 JUN 1959 [location]; Living) *Divorced*
>
> > **Christine Lynn Gebauer** Denniston (Born: 16 AUG 1979 [location]; Living) *Married [date] to* **Mark Wayne Denniston** (Born: 25 FEB 1975 [location]; Living)
> > **Jennifer Bree Gebauer** (Born: 11 MAR 1981 [location]; Living)
> > **Kevin Lee Sturch** (Born: 23 MAY 1980 [location]; Living) *Married [date] to* **Casey Diane Krause** Sturch (Born: 7 JAN 1983 [location]; Living) *Stepson*
> > **Kathryn Marie Gebauer** Stencel (Born: 4 DEC 1985 [location]; Living) *Married [date] to* **Tye Dale Stencel** (Born: 17 JUN 1983 [location]; Living)
> > **Kimberly Ann Gebauer** Smith (Born: 20 FEB 1989 [location]; Living) *Married [date] to* **Eric Lee Smith** (Born: 30 MAR 1985 [location]; Living)
>
> **Daniel (Danny) Jeffrey Gebauer** (Born: 14 SEP 1960 in Brush, Colorado; Living) *Married [date] to* **Samantha D. Foster** Gebauer (Born: 23 AUG 1969 in Akron, Colorado; Living)
>
> > **Christopher Louis Gebauer** (Born: 14 DEC 1989 [location]; Living)

Kayla Nicole Gebauer (Born: 3 OCT 1991 [location]; Living)

Dianna Renae Gebauer Hanson Arrington (Born: 18 NOV 1964 in Akron, Colorado; Living) *Married [date] to* **Kory Wade Hanson** (Born: 1 JAN 1963 [location]; Living) *Divorced and married [date] to* **Steven Legrande Arrington** (Born: 13 OCT 1962 [location]; Living) *Divorced*

> **Alexandrea Nichole Arrington** (Born: 1 JAN 1989 [location]; Living)
> **Olivia Renae Arrington** (Born: 1 FEB 1994 [location]; Living)

Charlotte Lorrainne Gebauer Kumor (Born: 21 FEB 1936 in Akron, Colorado; Living) *Married 30 JUN 1958 to* **Leon Joseph Kumor** (Born: 5 JUN 1935 in Imperial, Nebraska; Living)

Ronald Gary Kumor (Born: 27 NOV 1959 in Yuma, Colorado; Living) *Married 14 AUG 1981 to* **Joanne Rose Buss** Kumor (Born: 6 JAN 1960 in Ogallala, Nebraska; Living) ☘-13-☘

> **Laura Anne Kumor** Stack (Born: 7 JAN 1990 in Casper, Wyoming; Living) *Married 11 JUN 2016 to* **Michael Benjamin Stack** (Born: 14 MAR 1986 in Casper, Wyoming; Living)
> **Ripley Anne Darlene Stack** (Born: 6 JUN 2019 in Casper, Wyoming; Living)

Kammi Rae Kumor Shaw (Born: 13 FEB 1987 in Casper, Wyoming; Living) *Married 3 AUG 2013 to* **Albon G. Shaw** (Born: 20 OCT 1981 in Alliance, Nebraska; Living)

> **Jestine (Jesi) Marie Petley** (Born: 11 JUL 2005 in Casper, Wyoming; Living)
> **Elle Ashlyn Shaw** (Born: 12 DEC 2005 in Casper, Wyoming; Living)
> **Jayden Daniel Shaw** (Born: 10 AUG 2007 in Casper, Wyoming; Living)

Maureen Kaye Kumor Johnson (Born: 15 JUN 1961 in Grant, Nebraska; Living) *Married [day] MAY 1982 to* **Richard Charles Johnson** (Born: 3 DEC 1959 [location]; Living) *Divorced*

> **Devon Richard Johnson** (Born: 4 JUN 1989 in Laramie, Wyoming; Living)
> **Sven Dillon Johnson** (Born: 12 MAR 1993 in Laramie, Wyoming; Living)

Mary Lavonne Gebauer Sybrandt (Born: 14 SEP 1937 in Akron, Colorado; Died: 1 FEB 2015 in Steamboat Springs, Colorado; Buried: [location]) *Married 11 JUN 1960 to* **Van Jahns Sybrandt** (Born: 18 MAY 1937 in Brush, Colorado; Living)

Michael Lewis Sybrandt (Born: 2 DEC 1974) *Adopted*

Jeannette Lois Gebauer Walton (Born: 20 SEP 1940 in Akron, Colorado; Died: 2 APR 2018 in Greeley, Colorado; Buried: Akron Cemetery, Akron, Colorado) *Married 12 JUN 1958 to* **Richard (Dick) LeRoy Walton** (Born: 23 SEP 1938 in Otis, Colorado; Died: 15 OCT 1988 in Otis, Colorado; Buried: Akron Cemetery, Akron, Colorado)

Victoria Lynn Walton Manalabe (Born: 21 JUL 1960 in Brush, Colorado; Living) *Married 15 NOV 1986 to* **Mario V. Manalabe** (Born: 17 MAR 1960 in [city], The Philippines; Living)

> **Nia Marie Manalabe** Sharpe (Born: 15 JAN 1988 in [city], Japan; Living) *Married 6 JUN 2014 to* **Jared __ Sharpe** (Born: 27 JUN 1987 [location]; Living)
>> **Evan Grey Sharpe** (Born: 15 OCT 2016 in Fort Collins, Colorado; Living)
> **Amber Lynn Manalabe** (Born: 8 AUG 1989 in [city], Japan; Living)

Mary Lee Walton (Born: 13 JUN 1961 in Greeley, Colorado; Living)

Larry LeRoy Walton (Born: 21 SEP 1963 in Greeley, Colorado; Living) *Married [date] to* __ __ __ Walton (Born: [date/location]; Living) *Divorced and married [date] to* **Lisa Tracey Thomas** Walton (Born: 28 MAY 1966 [location]; Living) *Divorced and married [date] to* **Monica Yvette Reyes** Walton (Born: 12 FEB 1972 in Yuma, Arizona; Living)

Jacie Margeurite Walton (Born: 15 SEP 1993 in Colorado Springs, Colorado; Living) (Mother: Lisa Thomas)

John Delmar Walton (Born: 20 AUG 1996 in Mesa, Arizona; Living) (Mother: Monica Reyes)

Jacob Tzar Walton (Born: 23 FEB 1998 in Mesa, Arizona; Living) (Mother: Monica Reyes)

Jarrett Michael Walton (Born: 7 NOV 1999 in Mesa, Arizona; Living) (Mother: Monica Reyes)

Jake Harley Walton (Born: 11 FEB 2003 in Mesa Arizona; Living) (Mother: Monica Reyes)

Eric Jay Walton (Born: 30 JUN 1967 in Greeley, Colorado; Living)

Nora Violet Ireland Gebauer (Born: 23 MAY 1917 in Sedgwick, Colorado; Died: 27 MAY 1986 in Akron, Colorado; Buried: St. Joseph's Cemetery, Akron, Colorado) *Married 27 DEC 1934 to* **Joseph Florian Gebauer** (Born: 10 MAR 1904 in Akron, Colorado; Died: 13 JUN 1998 in Akron, Colorado; Buried: St. Joseph's Cemetery, Akron, Colorado) ☘-14-☘ ☘-15-☘

Joseph (Joey) Laverne Gebauer (Born: 23 JUN 1936 in Akron, Colorado; Died: 5 AUG 2005 in Golden, Colorado; Gravestone: St. Joseph Cemetery, Akron, Colorado) *Married 21 JUN 1954 to* **Carole Jean Jackson** Gebauer (Born: 10 OCT 1938 in Akron, Colorado; Living) *Divorced and married 31 JUL 1971 to* **Marilyn Joan (Dollie) Melvin** Neumann Gebauer (Born: 24 JAN 1940 in Pipestone, Minnesota; Living)

Christina (Christie) Marie Gebauer Brown Schienle (Born: 2 MAY 1955 in Brush, Colorado; Living) *Married 28 JUL 1973 to* **Michael Fred Brown** (Born: 28 NOV 1952 Fort Morgan, Colorado; Living) *Divorced and married 10 NOV 1984 to* **Eric (Rick) Karl Schienle** (Born: 3 MAR 1944 in Detroit, Michigan; Died: 12 SEP 2019 in Westminster, Colorado; Cremated with no gravestone)

Stacey Michelle Brown Janis (Born: 17 NOV 1974 in Denver, Colorado; Living) *Married 18 MAY 1996 to* **Clint Theodore Janis** (Born: 5 APR 1971 in Denver, Colorado; Living)

Chase Lane Janis (Born: 25 SEP 1996 in Denver, Colorado; Living)

Brandon John Janis (Born: 29 JAN 1999 in Denver, Colorado; Living)

Shaun Michael Brown (Born: 24 AUG 1977 in Denver, Colorado; Living) *Married 8 SEP 2001 to* **Leandra Jo Qualls** Brown (Born: 31 MAY 1979 in Denver, Colorado; Living) *Divorced*

Madison Olivia Brown (Born: 13 JUL 2004 in Westminster, Colorado; Living)

Damien Joseph Schienle (Born: 24 JAN 1986 in Westminster, Colorado; Living)

Sharron (Sherry) Kay Gebauer Stevens (Born: 4 AUG 1956 in Brush, Colorado; Living) *Married 28 SEP 1974 to* **Roy Lee Stevens** (Born: 18 NOV 1955 in Denver, Colorado; Died: 1 AUG 2009 in Las Vegas, Nevada; Buried: __ Cemetery, [city], Nevada) *Partner with* **Mark Douglas Krause** (Born: 10 NOV 1958 in Hayfield, Minnesota; Living)

Angie Lee Stevens (Born: 2 JAN 1975 in Denver, Colorado; Living) *Partner with* **Anthony __ Martinez** (Born: 19 JAN 1964 in Denver, Colorado; Living)

Jayce Holden Stevens (Born: 9 FEB 2003 in Denver, Colorado; Living)

Tristan Dean Joseph Bosworth (Born: 31 JUL 2005 in Denver, Colorado; Living)

Michael (Mike) Scott Gebauer (Born: 8 MAR 1960 in Akron, Colorado; Living) *7 JUN 1980 to* **Diane Dorothy Deimeyer** Gebauer (Born: 6 DEC 1960 in Denver, Colorado; Living) *Divorced and partner with* **Victoria Marie Anderson** (Born: 19 JUL 1955 in Denver, Colorado; Living)

> **Lucas Michael Gebauer** (Born: 26 JUL 1981 in Denver, Colorado; Living) *Married 28 JUL 2007 to* **Erisha Lane Sanchez** Gebauer (Born: 30 DEC 1984 [location]; Living) *Divorced and partner with* **Dannille Jaqueline Chapman** (Born: 7 JUN 1982 [location]; Living)
>
> **Brooke Lynn Gebauer** (Born: 16 APR 2006 in Denver, Colorado; Living)
> **Lucas Joseph Gebauer** (Born: 14 APR 2010 in Denver, Colorado; Living)
> **Taylor __ Chapman** (Born: 18 OCT 2006 [location]; Living)
> **Brynn __ Chapman** (Born: 8 SEP 2010 [location]; Living)
>
> **Mitchell (Mitch) Joe Gebauer** (Born: 31 MAY 1964 in Denver, Colorado; Living) Married 28 APR 1990 to **Susan (Susie) Ranee Whittington** Gebauer (Born: 30 OCT 1962 in Yuma, Colorado; Living)

Richard Eugene Gebauer (Born: 5 JUN 1938 in Akron, Colorado; Living) *Married 21 AUG 1965 to* **Linda Susan Monat** Gebauer (Born: 28 JAN 1944 in Moab, Utah; Living) ☘-16-☘

Agnes Marie Gebauer Friedly (Born: 30 JAN 1941 in Akron, Colorado; Living) *Married 24 AUG 1959 to* **Francis William Friedly** (Born: 4 JUN 1940 in Pawnee City, Nebraska; Died: 28 MAR 1984 in Akron, Colorado; Buried: Akron Cemetery, Akron, Colorado) ☘-17-☘ ☘-18-☘ ☘-19-☘

> **Victor William Friedly** (Born: 27 FEB 1960 in Denver, Colorado; Living) *Married 9 DEC 1983 to* **Joella Earleen Williams** Friedly (Born: 27 DEC 1958 in Sedan, Kansas; Living)
>
>> **Sylvia Dean Prince Ross** (Born: 30 DEC 1977 in Guymon, Oklahoma; Living) *Married 22 JUL 2005 to* Kenneth Allen Ross II (Born: 6 MAY 1975 in Texarkansas, Texas; Living)
>>
>>> **Jayce Anderson Tangler** (Born: 11 JUN 1997 in Sterling, Colorado; Living)
>>> **Kairi Deannalynne Ross** (Born: 1 SEP 2014 in Colorado Springs, Colorado; Living)
>>
>> **Kathryn Earleen Friedly** Travis (Born: 12 AUG 1981 in Garden City, Kansas; Living) *Adopted; Married 19 NOV 2001 to* **Christopher Lee Travis** (Born: 23 DEC 1980 in Sterling, Colorado; Living)
>>
>>> **Kaylie Dawn Travis** (Born: 4 SEP 2001 in Louisville, Colorado; Living)
>>> **Alysia Earleen Travis** (Born: 2 MAY 2004 in Fort Collins, Colorado; Living)
>>> **Savannah Jean Travis** (Born: 11 APR 2006 in Fort Collins, Colorado; Living)
>>
>> **Garrack William Friedly** (Born: 17 NOV 1985 in Akron, Colorado; Living) *Married 17 AUG 2003 to* **Maureen Linner Gard** Friedly (Born: 29 APR 1988 in Barrington, Illinois; Living)
>>
>>> **Arlette Spencer Friedly** (Born: 21 MAR 2014 in Bristol, Connecticut; Living)
>>> **Paxton William Friedly** (Born: 9 MAY 2018 in Houston, Texas; Living)
>>
>> **Bryce Roy Friedly** (Born: 20 SEP 1991 in Brush, Colorado; Living) *Married 20 AUG 2016 to* **Jessica Marie Crossland** Friedly (Born: 5 MAY 1992 in Wray, Colorado; Living) ☘-20-☘
>>
>>> **Remington Roy Friedly** (Born: 24 MAY 2017 in Wray, Colorado Living)
>>> **RayLee Jo Friedly** (Born: 19 MAY 2020 in Fort Morgan, Colorado; Living)

Vincent Lynn Friedly (Born: 7 APR 1961 in Brush, Colorado; Living) *Married 7 APR 1984 to* **Tina Dayl Duncan** Friedly (Born: 26 DEC 1963 in Akron, Colorado; Living)

> **Tianna Rae Friedly** Reid (Born: 19 APR 1982 in Akron, Colorado; Living) *Married 31 DEC 2011 to* **Justin Tyler Reid** (Born: 30 JUL 1982 in Akron, Colorado; Living)
>
>> **Maddox Jay Reid** (Born: 2 OCT 2012 in Denver, Colorado; Living)
>> **Ridge Tyler Reid** (Born: 26 JAN 2015 in Louisville, Colorado; Living)
>> **Carter Rae Reid** (Born: 25 AUG 2017 in Louisville, Colorado; Living)
>
> **Keisha Lynn Friedly** Hardy (Born: 30 JAN 1986 in Greeley, Colorado; Living) *Married 11 APR 2009 to* **Cody Dean Hardy** (Born: 15 FEB 1985 in Akron, Colorado; Living)
>
>> **Tignor Del Hardy** (Born: 29 MAR 2014 in Denver, Colorado; Living)
>
> **Chance Trey Friedly** (Born: 15 OCT 1991 in Greeley, Colorado; Living) *Married 17 SEP 2016 to* **Ashleigh Ranae Pautler** Friedly (Born: 4 MAR 1993 in Lexington, Kentucky; Living)
>
>> **Benton Lane Friedly** (Born: 8 AUG 2017 in Wray, Colorado; Living)

Verlin Joe Friedly (Born: 22 MAY 1962 in Brush, Colorado; Living) *Married 28 AUG 1982 to* **Stephanie Dee Daldegan** (Born: 10 JUN 1963 in Cheyenne Wells, Colorado; Living) *Divorced* ☘-21-☘ ☘-22-☘ ☘-23-☘

> **Dedric Paul Friedly** (Born: 10 JAN 1983 in Akron, Colorado; Living) *Married 4 APR 2012 to* **Jessica Margaret Eide** Friedly (Born: 28 JAN 1983 in Denver, Colorado; Living)
>
>> **Cayden Hudson Friedly** (Born: 14 JUL 2013 in Denver, Colorado; Living)
>> **Connor Joe Friedly** (Born: 3 MAR 2016 in Denver, Colorado)
>
> **Tonya Eliza Friedly** Gibson (Born: 8 OCT 1985 in Fort Collins, Colorado: Living) *Married 13 OCT 2018 to* **John Allen Gibson** (Born: 22 JAN 1982 in Sioux City, Iowa; Living)
>
> **JoDee Rae Friedly** Goracke (Born: 31 AUG 1988 in Fort Collins, Colorado; Living) *Married 18 SEP 2015 to* **Spencer Allen Goracke** (Born: 9 OCT 1986 in Fremont, Nebraska; Living)
>
>> **Rayne Marie Goracke** (Born: 12 MAY 2010 in Overland Park, Kansas; Living)
>> **Mahz Orin Goracke** (Born: 5 JAN 2017 in Omaha, Nebraska; Died: 18 JUL 2018 in Omaha, Nebraska; Buried in Resurrection Cemetery, Omaha, Nebraska) ☘-24-☘
>> **Asah Rae Goracke** (Born: 15 FEB 2019 in Omaha, Nebraska; Living)
>
> **Daisha Marie Friedly** Graves (Born: 4 APR 1992 in Winchester, Tennessee; Living) *Married 13 JUL 2012 to* **Justin Michael Graves** (Born: 20 DEC 1991 in San Antonio, Texas; Living)
>
>> **Norah Violet Graves** (Born: 16 NOV 2013 in Manhattan, Kansas; Living)
>> **Florence Ann Graves** (Born: 24 OCT 2016 in North Platte, Nebraska; Living)
>> **Theodore West Graves** (Born: 13 MAY 2020 in Hastings, Nebraska; Living)
>
> **Nina Francis Friedly** (Born: 19 MAR 1994 in Tullahoma, Tennessee; Living)

Vernita Marie Friedly Zubia (Born: 13 OCT 1963 in Brush, Colorado; Living) *Married 13 APR 1984 to* **Jose (Lalo) Liogardo Zubia** (Born: 21 AUG 1961 in [city], Mexico; Living)

Darian Francis Zubia (Born: 1 SEP 1984 in Akron, Colorado; Living) *Partner with* **Maty Matilde Salgado** (Born: [date/location]; Living)

> **Maya Flores Zubia Salgado** (Born: 18 JUN 2008 in Denver, Colorado; Living)

Dylan Ruben Zubia (Born: 24 JAN 1986 in Sterling, Colorado; Living)

Veronica Marie Friedly (Born: 7 OCT 1965 in Brush, Colorado; Died: 7 OCT 1965 in Brush, Colorado; Buried: Akron Cemetery, Akron, Colorado)

Vernon Ferdinand Friedly (Born: 1 MAR 1968 in Brush, Colorado; Died: 25 SEP 2020 in Clifton, Colorado; Buried: [location]) *Married 6 JUN 1992 to* **Amanda Rose Lockard** Friedly (Born: 6 MAR 1974 in Richland Center, Wisconsin; Living) *Divorced and married 19 AUG, 2000 to* **Janine Ellen Burke** Friedly (Born: 7 NOV 1966 in [city], Florida; Living) *Divorced and partner with* **Grace C. Chacon** (Born: 15 APR 1968 [location]; Living) ☘-25-☘

> **Alexis Symone Friedly** Schneider (Born: 6 NOV 1992 in Fort Collins Colorado; Living) *Married 11 JUN 2016 to* **Taylor Shane Schneider** (Born: 23 AUG 1992 in Sterling, Colorado; Living)
>
> > **Kortlynd Shayne Schneider** (Born: 22 JUL 2015 in Amarillo, Texas; Living)
> >
> > **Zailyn Renee Schneider** (Born: 6 OCT 2017 in Fort Collins, Colorado; Living)
>
> **Serena Marie Burke Friedly** (Born: 13 APR 2002 in Grand Junction, Colorado; Living)
>
> **Evangelina Grace (Ling) Chacon** (Born: 26 NOV 2002 [location]; Living) *Stepdaughter*

Valintina Sue Friedly Arroyo (Born: 23 APR 1972 in Brush, Colorado; Living) *Married 5 AUG 1995 to* **Shawn Isidro Arroyo** (Born: 20 AUG 1971 in Arlington, Texas; Living) ☘-26-☘

> **Aidan Isidro Arroyo** (Born: 15 FEB 1999 in Denver, Colorado; Living)
>
> **Cormac Emanuel Arroyo** (Born: 20 JUL 2001 in Denver, Colorado; Living)

Thomas Edward Gebauer (Born: 23 JUL 1943 in Akron, Colorado; Died: 30 DEC 2018 in Eldridge, Iowa; Buried: __ Cemetery, Akron, Colorado) *Married 12 AUG 1961 to* **Beverly Rose Snyder** Koppes Gebauer (Born: 26 SEP 1942 [location]; Living) *Divorced and married 12 MAY 1982 to* **Joanne Marie Conley** Gebauer (Born: 6 MAR 1952 in Guttenburg, Iowa; Living) *Divorced and married 14 FEB 2003 to* **Edith (Edie) Jo Ratliff** Gebauer (Born: 16 FEB 1951 in Denver, Colorado; Died: 4 SEP 2011 Rapid City, South Dakota; Buried: __ Cemetery, DeWitt, Iowa) ☘-27-☘

> **Tamela Rose Gebauer** Bryant (Born: 18 FEB 1962 in Brush, Colorado; Living) *Married 15 OCT 1994 to* **Jeffrey Lynn Bryant** (Born: 27 MAR 1961 [location]; Living)
>
> **Trina Kay Gebauer** Head Blair (Born: 23 JUL 1967 in Loredo, Texas; Living) *Married 29 JUL 1995 to* **Tom Eugene Head** (Born: 31 DEC 1960 [location]; Living) *Divorced and married 29 JAN 2002 to* **Anthony (Tony) Ray Blair** (Born: 6 SEP 1969 [location]; Living)
>
> > **Jordyn Nicole Head** (Born: 18 OCT 1996 [location]; Living)
> >
> > **Tyler Ray Blair** (Born: 16 OCT 2002 [location]; Living)
>
> **Tresha Ellen Gebauer** Ambrosy (Born: 8 NOV 1969 in Dubuque, Iowa; Living) *Married 10 JUN 1995 to* **Dale Ronald Ambrosy** (Born: 15 DEC 1964 [location]; Living)
>
> > **Karlee Ellen Ambrosy** (Born: 1 MAR 1997 [location]; Living)
> >
> > **Connor Joseph Ambrosy** (Born: 8 AUG 2000 [location]; Living)

Austin Lee Ambrosy (Born: 15 DEC 1986 [location]; Living) Married 12 OCT 2019 to **Justine Fleming Eller** Ambrosy (Born: [date/location]; Living) *Stepson*

> **Beckett __ Eller (**Born: 9 DEC 2012 [location]; Living) *Stepson*
> **Ruger __ Ambrosy** (Born: 8 MAR 2018 [location]; Living)

Jeffrey John Gebauer (Born: 2 JUL 1974 in Dubuque, Iowa; Living) *Married 1 AUG 2009 to* **Sarah Elizabeth Langley** Gebauer (Born: 26 APR 1980 in Austin, Texas; Living) *Adopted son of Joanne*

> **Liam Kevin Gebauer** (Born: 29 MAY 2011 in San Francisco, California; Living)
> **Roman John Gebauer** (Born: 19 SEP 2012 in San Diego, California; Living)
> **Fiona Elizabeth Gebauer** (Born: 16 JUN 2014 in Albuquerque, New Mexico; Living)
> **Eric Everest Gebauer** (Born: 29 JUL 2016 in Albuquerque, New Mexico; Living)

Jared Thomas Gebauer (Born: 22 MAY 1986 in Dubuque, Iowa; Living) *Married [date] to* **Rita __ Murray** Gebauer (Born: [date/location]; Living)

William John Gebauer (Born: 16 NOV 1945; Died: 28 JAN 1946 in Akron, Colorado; Buried St. Joseph Cemetery, Akron, Colorado)

Rosa (Rose) Irene Gebauer Allen Hazlett (Born: 16 JAN 1951 in Brush, Colorado; Died: 1 OCT 2020 in Akron, Colorado; Buried: St. Joseph Cemetery, Akron, Colorado) *Married 20 JUN 1969 to* **Gerald Lloyd Allen** (Born: [day] JUL 1949 [location]; Living) *Divorced and married 1 AUG 1978 to* **Steven Douglas Hazlett** (Born: 30 JUL 1949 [location]; Living) *Divorced*

> **Laina Ann Allen** Scheopner (Born: 2 DEC 1969 in Denver, Colorado; Living) *Married [date] to* **Kenneth (Ken) Dean Scheopner** (Born: 2 JAN 1958 [location]; Living) *Divorced*
>
> > **Levi Dean Scheopner** (Born: 2 MAY 1989 [location]; Living) *Married 14 AUG 2010 to* **Lindsey Nichole Miller** Scheopner (Born: 19 AUG 1991 [location]; Living)
> >
> > > **Trevor __ Scheopner** (Born: 15 JUN 2010 [location]; Living)
> > > **Josy __ Scheopner** (Born: 29 DEC 2013 [location]; Living)
> >
> > **Terrin Lee Scheopner** Smith (Born: 13 JAN 1992 [location]; Living) *Married 6 SEP 2014 to* **Shelby Dawn Smith** (Born: 3 APR 1990 [location]; Living)
> >
> > > **Emma __ Smith** (Born: 22 FEB 2013 [location]; Living)
> > > **Treycen __ Smith** (Born: 6 SEP 2014 [location]; Living)

William Brent Allen (Born: 14 JUL 1971 in Los Angeles, California; Living) *Partner with* **Brenda Gayle Christensen** Chapin (Born: 26 MAY 1972 [location]; Living) *Married [day/month] 2006 to* **Melissa Gay Olson** Allen (Born: 26 MAR 1968 [location]; Living)

> **Caleb Robert Christensen** (Born: 9 SEP 1993 [location]; Living)
> **Brooke __ Allen** (Born: 20 JAN 2005 [location]; Living)

Jason Todd Hazlett (Born: 9 OCT 1979 [location]; Living) *Married [date] to* **Ashley Nicole Lage** Hazlett (Born: 1 JUN 1985 [location]; Living)

> **Skyla Ammaris __** (Born: [date/location]; Living) *Stepdaughter*
> **Logan __ Hazlett** (Born: 29 APR 2008 [location]; Living)

Mandy Renee Hazlett Dreier (Born: 16 JUN 1981 in Colby, Kansas; Living) *16 JUL 2005 to* **Joshua (Josh) J. Dreier** (Born: 26 OCT 1974 in Hubbard, Iowa; Living)

> **Madison Jade Dreier** (Born: 20 DEC 2004 in Fort Morgan, Colorado; Living)

| Jacy Jo Dreier (Born: 19 MAR 2006 in Kearney, Nebraska; Living)

Patrick James Gebauer (Born: 27 DEC 1960 in Brush, Colorado; Living) *Married 30 JUN 1980 to* **Susan Inez Jones** Gebauer (Born: 21 DEC 1959 in Akron, Colorado; Living) *Divorced and partner with* **LuAn August** (Born: 2 JAN 1958 in Brush, Colorado; Living)

Jimmy Joseph Gebauer (Born: 31 MAR 1984 in Akron, Colorado; Living) *Partner with* **Kambree Meagan Collins** Drake (Born: 20 SEP 1987 [location]; Living) *Partner with* **Shannon Renea Davy** Sampson (Born: 20 NOV 1985 in Anchorage, Alaska; Died: 5 DEC 2013 in Greeley; Buried: Akron Cemetery, Akron, Colorado) *Divorced*

Reighlyn Reign Collins (Born: 17 MAR 2009 in Garden City, Kansas; Living)

Trey Alexander Gebauer (Born: 3 MAY 2012 in Greeley, Colorado; Living)

Morgan Elexis Gebauer (Born: 9 MAY 2013 in Greeley, Colorado; Living)

BreAnn Marie Gebauer Smith Hansen (Born: 8 JUN 1987 in Akron, Colorado; Living) *Married 12 JUN 2009 to* **Matthew Levi Smith** (Born: 1 JAN 1988 in Brush, Colorado; Living) *Divorced and married 7 APR 2014 to* **Joseph Kane Hansen** (Born: 10 APR 1974 in Yuma, Colorado; Living) ☘-28-☘

Tayte Levi Smith (Born: 8 JUL 2006 in Sterling, Colorado; Living)

Temperance Marie Smith (Born: 22 JUL 2009 in Sterling, Colorado; Living)

Faith Hansen (Born: 17 AUG 2014 in Sterling, Colorado; Died: 17 AUG 2014 in Sterling, Colorado)

Kenneth James Hansen (Born: 22 OCT 2015 in Sterling, Colorado; Living)

Doris Evelyn Ireland Ranch (Born: 27 DEC 1920 in Sedgwick, Colorado; Died: 3 DEC 2006, in Moab, Utah; Buried: Grand Valley Cemetery, Moab, Utah) *Married 1 MAR 1941 to* **Augustus Dafford Ranch** (Born: 27 MAR 1920 in Ogden, Utah; Died: 6 JUL 1983 in Moab, Utah; Buried: Grand Valley Cemetery, Moab, Utah)

Darrell Dafford Ranch (Born: 21 MAY 1942 in Steamboat Springs, Colorado; Died: 18 MAR 1999 in Sidney, Montana; Buried: Sidney Cemetery, Sidney, Montana) *Married 31 AUG 1963 to* **Loretta Anne Damm** Ranch (Born: 11 MAY 1944 in Poplar, Montana; Died: 11 JUL 2008 in Sidney, Montana; Buried: Sidney Cemetery, Sidney, Montana)

Kevin Eugene Ranch (Born: 17 FEB 1965 in Culbertson, Montana; Died: 20 JUL 1990 in Lewiston, Montana; Buried: Sidney Cemetery, Sidney, Montana)

Theresa Anne Ranch DeMary (Born: 10 APR 1967 in Culbertson, Montana; Living) *Married to/Partner with* **Max Morgan DeMary** (Born: [day] DEC 1967 [location]; Living)

Bradley DeMary (Born: [day] FEB 1985 [location]; Living)

David DeMary (Born: [day] JUN 1987 [location]; Living)

Brandy A. DeMary Sundheim (Born: 19 JUL 1989 [location]; Living) *Married [date] to* **Faron Wade Sundheim** (Born: 5 JUN 1973 [location]; Living)

Kristy Lynnet Ranch (Born: 17 FEB 1972 in Williston, North Dakota, Living)

Larry Augustus Ranch (Born: 14 AUG 1944 in Craig, Colorado; Living) *Married 16 AUG 1968 to* **Calleen E. Farrow** Ranch Cordero (Born: 1947 in Moab, Utah; Living) *Divorced and later married 15 NOV 1975 to* **Vera Loeffler** Ranch (Born: 22 MAR 1943 in Windsor, Colorado; Living) ☘-29-☘ ☘-30-☘ ☘-31-☘

Karen Lee Ranch (Born: 12 JUL 1969 in Moab, Utah; Living)

Tammy Lynn Ranch Gregg (Born: 27 APR 1976 in Greeley, Colorado; Living) *Married 15 JUN 2019 to* **Daniel Joseph Gregg** (Born: 5 DEC 1977 in Greeley, Colorado; Living)

Dusty Orrin Hert (Born: 28 SEP 1995 in Greeley, Colorado; Living)

Brandon Leo Hert (Born: 22 AUG 1999 in Greeley, Colorado; Living)
Jacob Daniel Gregg (Born: 27 SEP 1995 in Greeley, Colorado; Living)
Stepson
Aspen Rae Gregg (Born: 6 AUG 2000 in Greeley, Colorado; Living) *Partner with* **Christopher John Morris II** (Born: 28 MAY 1998 in Arlington, Washington; Living)
   Willow Rae Morris (Born: 1 OCT 2020 in Greeley, Colorado; Living)
Taryn Lee Ranch Schwartz Smithey Yost (Born: 27 APR 1976 in Greeley, Colorado; Living) *Married [date] to* **Jason Scott Schwartz** (Born: 24 SEP 1995 in Colorado Spring, Colorado; Died: 28 SEP 2001 in Penrose, Colorado; Buried: __ Cemetery, Canon City, Colorado) *Divorced and married to* **Andrew John Smithey** (Born: 30 APR 1975 [location]; Living) *Divorced and married 24 JUL 2015 to* **Joey Lee Yost** (Born: 23 AUG 1977 in Greeley, Colorado; Living)
☘-32-☘
   Jay Michael Schwartz (Born: 5 DEC 1992 in Greeley, Colorado; Living) *Partner with* **Christen Brianne Ransom** (Born: 18 AUG 1994 [location]; Living
      Elise Michelle Bledsoe (Born: 4 APR 2010 in Fort Collins, Colorado; Living)
   Ericka Suzanne Ranch [changed to] **Carla Leenig Walko** (Born: 24 JUL 1995 in Greeley, Colorado; Living) *Adopted but reunited with her birth mother in 2019*
   Justin Lynn Smithey (Born: 27 JAN 1999 in Greeley, Colorado; Living)
Troy Augustus Ranch (Born: 7 JUN 1980 in Denver, Colorado; Living) *Partner with* **Alexandra Lynn Waters** (Born: 11 DEC 1984 [location]; Living) *Partner with* **Donna Jean Micheaux** (Born: 3 MAR 1981 in Denver, Colorado; Living)
   Kayne Patrick Ranch (Born: 24 DEC 2002 in Denver, Colorado; Living)
   Jack Augustus Ranch (Born: 6 NOV 2005 in Greeley, Colorado; Living)
   Delores __ Micheaux (Born: [date/location]; Living)
Clifford Eugene Ranch (Born: 10 SEP 1947 in Craig, Colorado; Died: 2 DEC 2015 in Moab, Utah; Buried: Sunset Memorial Cemetery, Moab, Utah) *Married 16 SEP 1967 to* **Daphen Roean Bastian** Ranch (Born: 24 JAN 1949 in Salina, Utah; Living)
☘-33-☘ ☘-34-☘
   Jeffrey Augustus Ranch (Born: 9 OCT 1968 in Moab, Utah; Living) *Married 28 JUN 1997 to* **Lisa M. Maestas-Ranch** (Born: 21 MAY 1971 in Moriarty, New Mexico; Living)
      Robert Maestas (Born: 4 AUG 1988 in Moab, Utah; Living)
      Kayla Maestas Bienchetti (Born: 17 SEP 1991 in Moab, Utah; Living)
   Kimberly Ann Ranch (Born: 7 FEB 1972 in Moab, Utah; Living) *Partner with* **Robert Clyde Doyal** (Born: 18 SEP 1971 in Moab, Utah; Living) *Partner with* **William Kevin Duran** (Born: 17 DEC 1965 in Grand Junction, Colorado; Living) *Partner with* **Gregory Lee Nelson** (Born: 25 SEP 1962 in Crosby, Minnesota; Living)
      Machelle Kay Ranch (Born: 15 JUN 1995 in Monticello, Utah; Living) (Father: Robert Doyal)
      Nathanial Eugene Duran (Born: 3 JUL 2002 in Moab, Utah; Living)
      Samantha K. Nelson (Born: 2 JUN 1993 in Moab, Utah; Living) *Stepdaughter*
   Gary Newell Ranch (Born: 19 DEC 1978 in Moab, Utah; Living) *Married 9 OCT 2002 to* **Alicia Marie Glover** Ranch (Born: 25 SEP 1981 [location]; Living) *Divorced and married [date] to* **Shae Lynn Guerrero** (Born: 31 OCT 1990 [location]; Living)

Noah __ Ranch (Born: [date/location]; Living)
Emmalin __ Ranch (Born: [date/location]; Living)
Owen __ Ranch (Born: [date/location]; Living)
Dorothy Grace Ireland St. Louis Magill St. Louis (Born: 7 DEC 1922 in Sedgwick, Colorado; Died: 8 JUN 1998 in Grand Junction, Colorado; Buried: Reader Cemetery, Savery, Wyoming) *Married 9 NOV 1941 to* **George Edwin St. Louis** (Born: 26 JAN 1906 in Battle Creek, Colorado; Died: 1 JAN 1991 in Hattiesburg, Mississippi; Buried: Reader Cemetery, Savery, Wyoming) *Divorced and married 10 MAR 1978 to* **Nicholas Hugh Magill** (Born: 4 SEP 1920 in Steamboat Springs, Colorado; Died: 12 JUL 1989 in Las Vegas, Nevada; Buried Steamboat Springs Cemetery, Steamboat Springs, Colorado) *Divorced*

David George St. Louis (Born: 28 JUL 1943 in Hayden, Colorado; Living) *Married 4 DEC 1967 to* **Somchai Khamsayin** St. Louis (Born: 23 FEB 1939 in Ban Kwao, Mahasarakham, Thailand; Living)

Robert Pyboon St. Louis (Born: 7 DEC 1965 in Vientiane, Laos; Living) *Married 5 JUL 1986 to* **Nereida R. Padilla** St. Louis Collins (Born: 31 DEC 1962 in Bronx, New York; Living) *Divorced and married 18 SEP 1998 to* **Shannon Lee Pike** St. Louis (Born: 3 APR 1970 in Yukon, Oklahoma; Living) *Divorced and married to* **Karen Sue Smallwood** Garrett St. Louis (Born: 2 JUN 1959 in Jefferson City, Tennessee; Living)

Tai Francisco St. Louis (Born: 1 APR 1988 in Orlando, Florida; Living) *Partner with* **Ebony Bates** (Born: [day] JAN 1992; Living)

Mia Elizabeth St. Louis (Born: 6 JUN 2010 in Kissimmee, Florida; Living)
Navy St. Louis (Born: 20 OCT 2017 in Kissimmee, Florida; Living)

Jourdan Robert St. Louis (Born: 14 OCT 1990 in Jacksonville, Florida; Living) *Partner with* **Anne Ayala** (Born: [date/location]; Living) *Partner with* **Ivonne Guillen** (Born: [date/location]; Living)

Uree St. Louis (Born: 25 MAY 2010 in Kissimmee, Florida; Living) (Mother: Anne Ayala)
Avaleah Enid St. Louis (Born: 16 NOV 2012 in Kissimmee, Florida; Living) (Mother: Ivonne Guillen)

Kaeden Leland Lucas (Born: 23 JUN 2005 in Jacksonville, Florida; Living) *Step grandson; Full custody*

Benson Petsamone St. Louis (Born: 29 JUL 1968 in Vientiane, Laos; Living) *Married 29 AUG 1992 to* **Karol Leigh Scott** St. Louis (Born: 6 OCT 1968 in Hattiesburg, Mississippi; Living)

Griffin Scott St. Louis (Born: 23 APR 1995 in Tupelo, Mississippi; Living)
Spencer Morgan St. Louis (Born: 23 MAR 1998 in Hattiesburg, Mississippi; Living)

Lisa Surilak St. Louis Knight (Born: 13 JUL 1969 in Vientiane, Laos; Living) *Married 25 JUL 1992 to* **Joseph Odell Knight** (Born: 29 JUL 1969 in Philadelphia, Mississippi; Living)

Jeff David Knight (Born: 14 APR 1999 in Meridian, Mississippi; Living)

Kenneth Oliver St. Louis (Born: 9 NOV 1944 in Steamboat Springs, Colorado; Living) *Married 27 DEC 1970 to* **Karen Helen Waterman** St. Louis Teaman (Born: 13 MAR 1947 in Schenectady, New York; Living) *Divorced and married 26 FEB 1994 to* **Rae Jean V. Sielen** Farfsing Cousineau Sielen (Born: 30 DEC 1954 in Santa Monica, California; Living)

Melinda Joyce St. Louis (Born: 14 AUG 1975 in Plattsburgh, New York; Living) *Married 14 JUN 2002 to* **Pablo Javier Benavente Gonzalez** (Born: 14 FEB 1965 in Managua, Nicaragua; Living) *Divorced*

Lila Grace Benavente (Born: 2 OCT 2007 in Washington DC; Living)

Rita Grace St. Louis Maser St. Louis (Born: 11 FEB 1946 in Dixon, Wyoming; Living) *Married 2 JUL 1966 to* **Christopher Ottmar Maser** (Born: 13 OCT 1938 in Bronxville, New York; Living) *Divorced and married 17 JUN 1978 to* **Hugh Strane Richards III** (Born: 13 SEP 1945 in Danville, Pennsylvania; Living) *Divorced and married 23 DEC 2005 to* **John David Swan** (Born: 6 JUN 1945 in Murphy, North Carolina; Living)

> **Erik Maser Richards** (Born: 22 DEC 1971 in Coos Bay, Oregon; Living) *Married 2 JUN 2007 to* **Amy Barnes Stoyles** Richards (Born: 22 OCT 1973 in Syracuse, New York; Living)
>
> > **Evan McKinley Richards** (Born: 11 APR 2008 in Bradenton, Florida; Living)
> >
> > **Camden Taylor Richards** (Born: 9 MAR 2010 in Annapolis, Maryland; Living)
> >
> > **Scott Douglas Richards** (Born: 7 JUL 2011 in Las Cruces, New Mexico; Living)

Mary Lois Ireland (Born: 23 DEC 1927 in Sedgwick, Colorado; Died: 26 DEC 1927 in Sedgwick, Colorado; Buried: Sedgwick Cemetery, Sedgwick, Colorado)

☘-1-☘ *William and Jane Ireland's children as young adults: Bob, Fred, Lula, Dema, and Joe.*

☘-2-☘ *William and Jane Ireland and their older children. Back: Fred, Lula, Bob, Dema, and Joe; front: Jane and William.*

☘-3-☘ *William Ireland gravestone, St. Elmo, Illinois.*

☘-4-☘ *Joe and Fannie Galvin Ireland gravestone, Sedgwick, Colorado.*

☘-5-☘ *Hazel, Norma, Darlene, and Donna Ireland as children at Hahns Peak, 1939.*

☘-6-☘ *Hazel and Edwin at their wedding, 1952.*

☘-7-☘ *Hazel with children, Randy, Irwin, and Lyle, 1966.*

☘-8-☘ *Hazel and Edwin Jess family. Back: Irwin, Sue, Rhonda, and Randy; front: Hazel, Christi, Lyle, and Edwin, 1980.*

☘-9-☘ *The Lawler family in the 1970s. Back: Thelma Lawler, Larry Lawler with Steven Lawler, Ruby Lawler, Louis Lawler, Bill Lawler, Carol Lawler, Patricia Ham; front: Francine Forrest and Laura Ham Mannle.*

☘-10-☘ *The Lawler family with several spouses. Back: Larry Lawler, Jack Lawler, Ray Ham, Carol Lawler, Bill Lawler, Frances Robbins, David Barton, and Dorothy Barton; middle: Kathryn Lindahl and Patricia Ham; front: Peggy Lawler and Maxine Forrest.*

☘-11-☘ Left: *Ruby Lawler holding Jack Lawler's twin boys, Tim and Chris Lawler.*

☘-12-☘ Right: *Jack Lawler's children: Tim, Chris, Greg, Ann, and Jan.*

☘-13-☘ *Kumor family wedding photo, 2016. Back (adults): Leon Kumor, Charlotte Kumor, Mike Stack (groom), Laura Stack (bride), Ron Kumor, Joni Kumor, Kammi Shaw, and Albon Shaw; Front (children): Jayden Shaw, Elle Shaw, and Jesi Petley.*

☘-14-☘ *Joe and Violet Gebauer at their 50th wedding anniversary, 1984.*

☘-15-☘ *Violet and Joe Gebauer's offspring, 2018. Patrick Gebauer, Agnes Friedly, Richard Gebauer, and Rose Hazlett.*

☘-16-☘ *Nieces and nephews of Richard Gebauer at his 80th birthday party, 2018. Back: Jason Hazlett (1), Mitch Gebauer (3), Vernon Friedly (4), Vincent Friedly (4), Mike Gebauer (3), and Victor Friedly (4); front: Laina Scheopner (1), Breann Hansen (2), Verlin Friedly (4), Richard Gebauer, Christie Schienle (3), Sherry Stevens (3), Valintina Arroyo (4).*
Key: 1 – Rose's children; 2 – Patrick's children, 3 – Joey's children, and 4 – Agnes's children.

☘-17-☘ *Agnes and Francis Friedly, 1980.*

☘-18-☘ *The Friedly family, 1981. Back: Francis, Agnes, Vernita, Verlin, and Vincent; front: Vernon, Valintina, and Victor.*

☘-19-☘ *The Friedly family, 2018. Valintina, Victor, Vernon, Agnes, Verlin, and Vincent.*

♣-20-♣ Left: *Bryce and Jessica Friedly with their son Remington.* Right: *Remington with baby RayLee.*

♣-21-♣ *Members of Verlin Friedly's family, 2017.* Back three: *Nina Friedly, Norah Graves, and Verlin Friedly;* middle three: *Tonya Gibson, Daisha Graves, and JoDee Goracke;* front three: *Cayden Friedly, Dedric Friedly, and Rayne Goracke.*

♣-22-♣ *Tonya Gibson's wedding, 2018. Daisha Graves, Nina Friedly, Tonya Gibson (bride), JoDee Goracke, and Dedric Friedly.*

☘-23-☘ *Tonya Gibson's wedding, 2018.* Back left two: *Justin Graves, and Florence Graves;* back right three: *Spencer Goracke, Jess Friedly, and Dedric Friedly;* middle eight: *Nina Friedly, Daisha Graves, Stephanie Daldegan (Verlin's ex-wife), John Gibson (groom), Tonya Gibson (bride), Verlin Friedly, JoDee Goracke, and Agnes Friedly;* front four: *Cayden Friedly, Connor Friedly, Norah Graves, and Rayne Goracke.*

☘-24-☘ *Baby Mahz Goracke who lived until the age of 1 1/2 years.*

☘-25-☘ *The Vernon Friedly family, 2018.* Back: *Angie Chacon (Grace Chacon's daughter), Serena Friedly, Vernon Friedly holding Zailyn Schneider, Grace Chacon holding Kortlynd Schneider, and Taylor Schneider;* front: *Ayla Chacon (Angie Chacon's daughter), Evangelina Chacon, and Alexis Schneider.*

☘-26-☘ *The Valintina Arroyo family, 2018. Aiden, Valintina, Shawn, and Cormac.*

☘-27-☘ *Tom Gebauer with his son Jared, 1987.*

☘-28-☘ *BreAnn and Joseph Hansen's family, 2019. Joseph, Temperance, Kenneth, BreAnn, and Tayte.*

Appendix I: Generational Listing for Ireland Relatives / 481

☘-29-☘ Right: *Larry and Vera Ranch family, 1993. Vera, Troy, Tammy, Taryn, and Larry.*

☘-30-☘ Below: *Larry and Vera Ranch's family, 2006. Back: Taryn Yost, Joey Yost, Alexandra Waters (ex-partner of Troy), Troy Ranch holding Jack Ranch, Tammy Gregg, Donald Syring (ex-partner of Tammy), and Larry Ranch; middle: Jay Schwartz, Kayne Ranch, Brandon Hert, Dusty Hert, and Vera Ranch; front: Justin Smithey, and Aspen Gregg.*

☘-31-☘ *Members of Larry and Vera Ranch's family, 2018. Back: Troy Ranch, Brandon Hert, Danny Gregg, Jacob Gregg, and Kayne Ranch; middle: Aspen Gregg, Tammy Gregg, Jaiden Neito; front: Taryn Yost, Vera Ranch, Karen Ranch, Larry Ranch, and Delores Micheaux. (Jaiden Neito and Delores Micheaux are children of Troy Ranch's partner, Donna Micheaux.)*

☘-32-☘ *Taryn and Joey Yost at their wedding, 2015.*

☘-33-☘ *Clifford and Daphen Ranch family, 1993.*
Back: Clifford and Jeff; front: Kimberly, Daphen, and
Gary.

☘-34-☘ *The Clifford and Daphen Ranch family, 2006. Back: Nathaniel Duran holding William Duran,*
Jeffrey Ranch, Robert Maestas, Alicia Glover Ranch, Lisa Maestas Ranch, and Kayla Ranch Bianchetti;
middle: Clifford Ranch, Daphen Ranch, and Gary Ranch; front: Kimberly Ranch and Machelle Ranch.

Appendix I: Generational Listing for Ireland Relatives / 483

Index of Ireland Relatives: Generational Listing

Index of Ireland Relatives: Photographs

Appendix I: Generational Listing for Ireland Relatives / 491

Appendix J
Maps

Towns, Cities, and Routes Featured in This Book

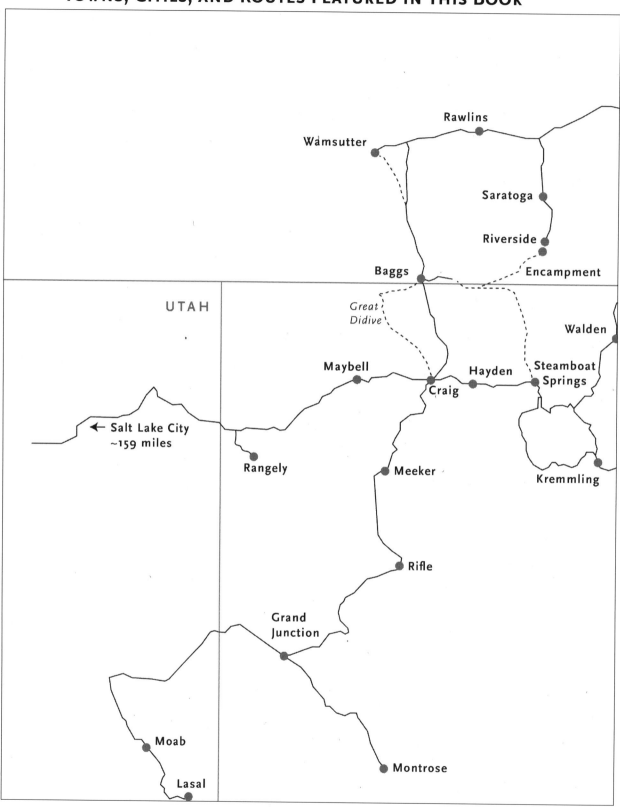

Rawlins

Wamsutter

Saratoga

Riverside

Baggs   Encampment

UTAH

Great   Walden
Didive

Maybell   Hayden   Steamboat
            Craig   Springs

← Salt Lake City
  ~159 miles

Rangely   Kremmling

            Meeker

                                  Rifle

        Grand
        Junction

Moab

                              Montrose

Lasal

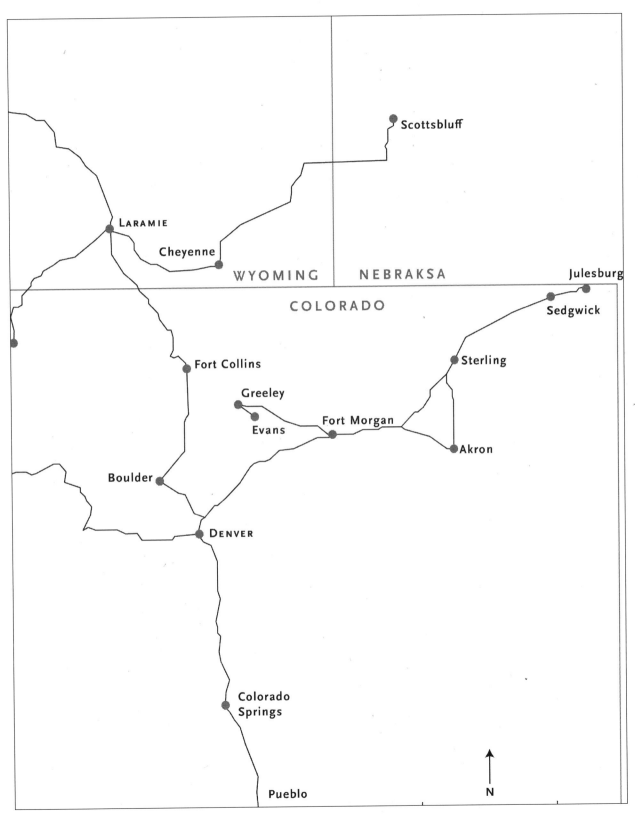

Scottsbluff

LARAMIE

Cheyenne

WYOMING   NEBRAKSA

COLORADO

Julesburg

Sedgwick

Fort Collins

Sterling

Greeley

Evans   Fort Morgan

Akron

Boulder

DENVER

Colorado
Springs

N

Pueblo

ROUTES TO TOWNS FROM THE ST. LOUIS RANCHES

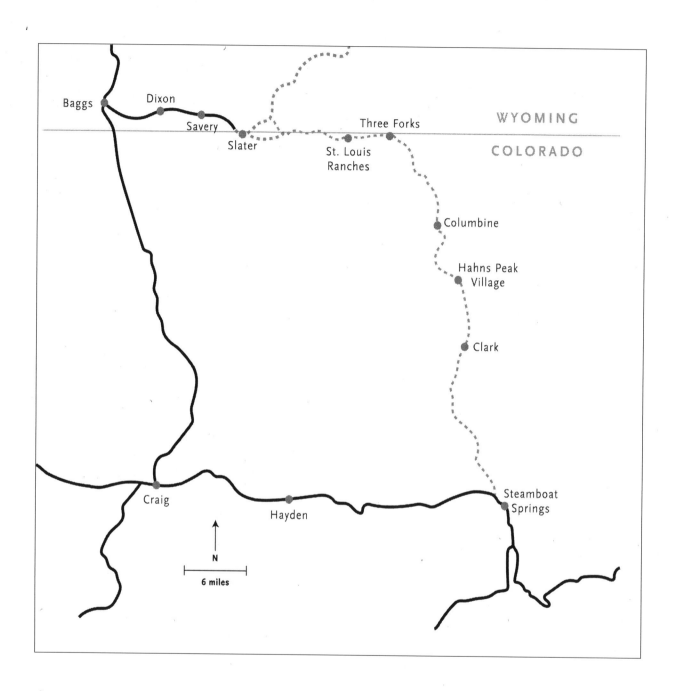

AERIAL VIEW IN 2010 OF LANDMARKS AND THE LOCATION OF OUR CHILDHOOD RANCH AND SCHOOL

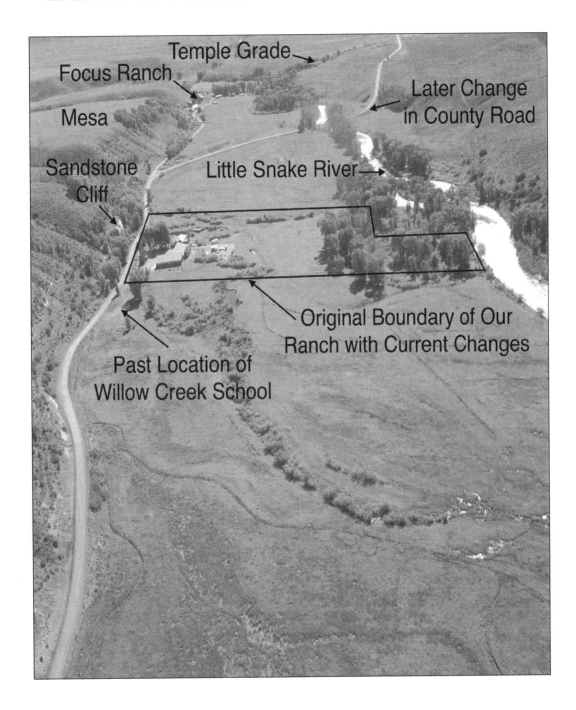

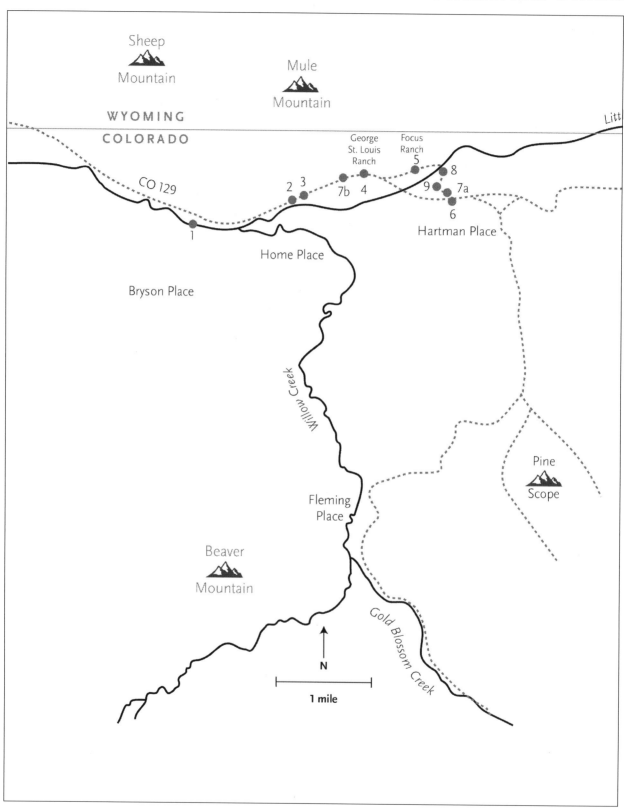

IN THE LITTLE SNAKE RIVER VALLEY

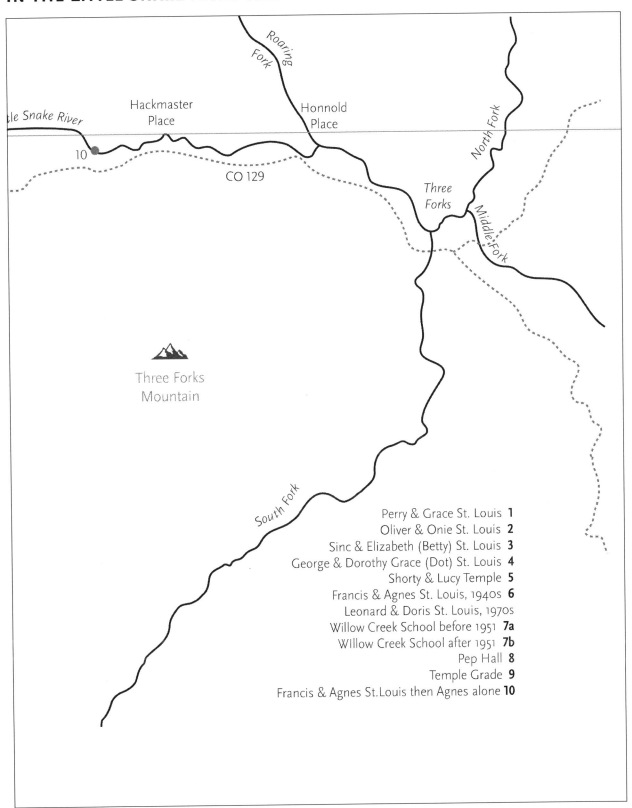

Roaring Fork

Hackmaster Place

Honnold Place

ttle Snake River

North Fork

10

CO 129

Three Forks

Middle Fork

Three Forks Mountain

South Fork

Perry & Grace St. Louis **1**
Oliver & Onie St. Louis **2**
Sinc & Elizabeth (Betty) St. Louis **3**
George & Dorothy Grace (Dot) St. Louis **4**
Shorty & Lucy Temple **5**
Francis & Agnes St. Louis, 1940s **6**
Leonard & Doris St. Louis, 1970s
Willow Creek School before 1951 **7a**
WIllow Creek School after 1951 **7b**
Pep Hall **8**
Temple Grade **9**
Francis & Agnes St.Louis then Agnes alone **10**

Index

Names

Index

Topics

Made in the USA
Columbia, SC
01 May 2022

59559198R00296